THE LAW
and
HIGHER EDUCATION:

A Casebook

Other books by John S. Brubacher

Modern Philosophies of Education
History of the Problems of Education
Higher Education in Transition (with Willis Rudy)
Bases for Policy in Higher Education

THE LAW
and
HIGHER EDUCATION:
A Casebook

John S. Brubacher

Volume I Students
Professors

Rutherford ● *Madison* ● *Teaneck*
FAIRLEIGH DICKINSON UNIVERSITY PRESS

© 1971 Associated University Presses, Inc.
Library of Congress Catalogue Card Number: 70-150238

Associated University Presses, Inc.
Cranbury, New Jersey 08512

ISBN: 0-8386-7897-1
Printed in the United States of America

*To the Center for the Study of Higher Education
at the University of Michigan*

Contents of Volume I

VOLUME I
pp. 1–332

VOLUME II
pp. 333–701

Table of Cases

Preface

Students have long been able to keep abreast of judicial decisions affecting higher education through the periodic digests which M. M. Chambers has written of the leading cases decided by the courts. More recently Thomas E. Blackwell has gone further and given us a treatise on the law of higher education. With the greatly increased attention the courts are paying to higher education in the past decade, it seems that what students now need is a casebook in the law of higher education where they can read not just summaries of cases but the published reports of the leading cases themselves. To put the matter another way, the courts have become such an important factor in shaping policies on the campus that it is high time we examine more in detail what it is they are saying to us.

In 1969 I published a first collection of leading cases on the law of higher education. In the summer of that year I had an opportunity at the University of Michigan to conduct a seminar based on my *Casebook in the Law of Higher Education*. The experience suggested a number of improvements in the book which I am now incorporating in this revised edition. First, I have withdrawn a number of cases which were found unsuitable for one reason or another. Second, I have reclassified a number of other cases and drastically rearranged the table of contents. Third, I have inserted a score of important new cases which have been adjudicated since the first edition.

Let me point out again, as in the previous edition, that this casebook is addressed, not to law students, but to students of higher education. Hence, the cases have been severely edited to point up substantive questions of higher education rather than technicalities of the law. For the most part, therefore, the categories in the table of contents are those of higher education rather than of the law. The main intent of the book is to make the reader more expert in higher education rather than expert in the law. If legal points arise in his subsequent career, a reading of these cases should not so much equip him to be his own lawyer as to alert him when to engage professional counsel.

THE LAW
and
HIGHER EDUCATION:

A Casebook

STUDENTS

1
Right to Higher Education

Esteb v. *Esteb*
138 Wash. 174 (244 P. 264)
March 25, 1926

ASKREN, J.

This is an action to modify a decree of divorce to provide for the support of a minor child. From an order modifying the decree, the husband has appealed. Since the hearing in this court the husband died and the executrix of his estate has been substituted as appellant.

The facts follow: In 1915, respondent secured a divorce from decedent. She was granted the custody of their two minor children, Esther and Carmelita, and provision was made for their support. Thereafter, under appropriated proceedings, the divorced wife was granted a certain amount of community property in settlement of the marriage relation. The older daughter, Esther, has since become of age. The younger, Carmelita, became 18 years of age in July, 1925. The decree originally provided for a certain sum per month for her support until she reached the age of 18 years, which was the legal age of majority at that time. In 1923, the Legislature, by chapter 72, Laws of 1923, placed the age of majority for females at 21 years. In January, 1925, the respondent brought this action to modify the decree and to require the decedent to contribute to the support of Carmelita the sum of $60 per month.

The record shows that the daughter Esther is employed as a stenographer earning approximately $110 per month; that she boards with her mother and pays $40 per month therefor. The mother has no financial means, and her health is such that she is unable to perform any labor other than ordinary household duties. The daughter Carmelita, in February, 1925, began to attend the College of Puget Sound, located in Tacoma, where she is majoring in English, with the intention of becoming a teacher thereof, and the record shows that she is especially adapted for this sort of work. She attempted to take a typewriting course, but was advised by her teacher that she was too nervous to follow that line. In her desire to secure an education quickly, she went to summer school 2 years, and was enabled to finish the regular 4-year course in 2½ years.

The record shows, also, her special aptitude for the class of work she is taking, it appearing that owing to her excellent grades in Latin she was permitted by the Foreign Language Department of the Lincoln high school to take Greek as a freshman, this being, according to the testimony of one witness, the only instance of its kind in the history of the school. While attending the College of Puget Sound she resides at the home of respondent.

Decedent, after his divorce, remarried twice, the first marriage lasting approximately 90 days, and the second taking place in February, 1923. He had living with him at the time of the trial his wife and two of her sons by a former marriage, one being 11 and the other about 18, both of whom are attending school, the older being in high school. Decedent was employed as a pilot conductor by the Chicago, Milwaukee & St. Paul Railway Company, in whose employ he had been almost continuously since 1900. Aside from severe nervous trouble which required him to be under restraint for a short period in 1912, and again in 1920, he had been continuously employed. Owing to his nervous condition, and to eye trouble, the position which he then occupied, which was described by one witness as a sort of "third conductor on the train," was the only available work that he was capable of performing. During the past 3 years his wages averaged something over $3,000 per year. He lived in his own home on a piece of rented ground near Cedar Falls, and in a portion of the Seattle watershed district. He was, at the time of the hearing, 52 years of age. He had on hand securities the amount of which he placed at between $9,000 and $11,000, and which draw interest at from 4 percent to 7 percent, averaging, according to his testimony, approximately 5½ percent.

The trial court, after hearing the evidence, concluded that Carmelita needed and required the education which she is receiving at the college, modified the previous decree, and placed the amount for her support at $60 per month until she became of age, 21 years. The court did not expressly provide that the money should be used to send her to college, but placed it upon the ground that it was necessary for her support. It is quite evident, however, from reading the court's oral decision, that it was intended and expected that this support money should be used for that purpose.

* * *

(2) The main and serious question in this case is this: Has the court the legal right to compel a divorced father to provide funds for

a college education for his minor child whose custody has been given to the mother?

(3) We have never been called upon to decide this precise question before. If the court has this legal right it must be upon the ground that the same is necessary, for the duty of a father to provide for his minor child when the custody be in another is restricted to necessaries.

From earliest times, the question of what is a necessary has frequently perplexed the courts. Under practically all the authorities, these things are necessary which include shelter, food, clothing, and medical attendance, together with an education. . . . What kind of food, clothing, shelter, etc. is necessary has usually been left to a jury to decide, taking into consideration the minor's position in life, station in society, and the fortune of the child or its parents.

As to the amount of education that should be considered necessary, courts have never laid down a hard and fast rule. The rule is stated in 14 R.C.L. p. 258, as follows:

> Some kind of education has been included from early times within the class of necessaries for which an infant may contract. The early cases, however, seem to have confined this to elementary or vocational education, and even in the latter cases a college, university or professional education has generally been excluded, though it has been judicially suggested that it might be allowed in a case where the infant's ability and prospects justify it.

Probably the earliest reported case in this country involving the question as to whether a college education is a necessity is *Middlebury College* v. *Chandler,* 16 Vt. 683 . . . where a suit was brought to recover from the father tuition and other bills which represented a charge for his minor son as a student of the college. This case appears to be authority and is referred to by nearly all text-writers upon the question. The court there refused to hold that a college education was a necessary, but the court's reasoning for its holding is very interesting:

> The practical meaning of the term [necessaries] has always been in some measure relative, having reference as well to what may be called the conventional necessities of others in the same walks of life with the infant as to his own pecuniary condition and other circumstances. Hence a good, common school education, at the least, is now fully recognized as one of the necessities for an infant. Without it he would lack an acquisition which would be common among his associates; he would suffer in his subsequent influence and usefulness in society; and would ever be liable to suffer in his transactions of business. Such an education is, moreover, essential to the intelligent discharge of civil, political, and religious duties.
> But it is obvious that the more extensive attainments in literature and science must be viewed in a light somewhat different. Though

they tend greatly to elevate and adorn personal character, are a source of much private enjoyment, and may justly be expected to prove of public utility, yet in reference to men in general they are far from being necessary in a legal sense. The mass of our citizens pass through life without them. I would not be understood as making any allusion to professional studies, or to the education and training which [are] requisite to the knowledge and practice of mechanic arts. These partake of the nature of apprenticeships, and stand on peculiar grounds of reason and policy. I speak only of the regular and full course of collegiate study, for such was the course upon which the defendant professedly entered. Now it does not appear that extraneous circumstances existed in the defendant's case, such as wealth or station in society, or that he exhibited peculiar indications of genius or talent, which would suggest the fitness and expediency of a college education for him, more than for the generality of youth in community.

It will be noted that this decision was in 1844. This appears to be the only reported case where the court has held that a college education is not a necessary, although . . . it was held that the incapacity imposed upon an infant extended to expenses incurred in acquiring a professional education, and especially to money loaned for that purpose. It was also held . . . where a boy 19 years of age desired to become a lawyer, that the father could not be required to pay such expenses. However, the decision in that case was based primarily upon the fact that the father and mother had not yet been divorced, but that suit was pending, and the court concluded that at such a stage of the case the order of the trial court was unwarranted.

There have arisen a great many cases involving the question of vocation training. Most of these cases have to do with courses in typewriting, stenography, or mechanical courses. It has been almost universally held that the question should be left to a jury to determine whether the commercial or vocational course was a necessary under all the circumstances shown by the evidence, including the situation of the minor and his parents.

The decision . . . involving the right to recover the cost of a commercial education in bookkeeping is interesting upon the point of what education is necessary. The court quoted approvingly . . .

It would be difficult to lay down any general rule upon this subject, and to say what would or would not be necessaries. It is a flexible, and not an absolute, term, having relation to the infant's condition in life, to the habits and pursuits of the place in which and the people among whom he lives, and to the changes in those habits and pursuits occurring in the progress of society.

The court then said:

It is clear from the foregoing statements of the law . . . that the word "necessaries" is a relative term, and is not limited to those things which are indispensable to the infant's personal support and comfort. Whether a college or a strictly professional education could be classed with necessaries under any circumstances, we are not called upon to decide. But that such an education and training as will fit one for the ordinary duties of life in the sphere in which he moves, and enable him to earn a respectable and honest living in his chosen vocation, should be so classed, we have no doubt.

The purpose of the education of minors is very well stated by Schouler in his work on *Domestic Relations,* at page 774:

The second duty of the parent is that of education; a duty which Blackstone pronounces to be far the greatest of all in importance. This importance is enhanced by the consideration that the usefulness of each new member of the human family to society depends chiefly upon his character, as developed by the training he receives in early life. Not the increase of population, but the increase of well-ordered, intelligent, and honorable population is to determine the strength of the state; and, as a civil writer observed, the parent who suffers his child to grow up like a mere beast, to lead a life useless to others and shameful to himself, has conferred a very questionable benefit upon bringing him into the world, and the education should be consistent with the station in life of the parties. Solon excused the children of Athens from maintaining their parents if they had neglected to train them up in some art or profession. So intimately is government concerned in the results of early training, that it interferes, and justly, too, both to aid the parent in giving his child a good education, and in compelling that education, where the parent himself, and not the child, is delinquent in improving the opportunities afforded.

(4) Applying the rule as stated by the courts and the text-writers, it will be seen that, the question of what sort of an education is necessary being a relative one, the court should determine this in a proper case from all the facts and circumstances. Nor should the court be restricted in the station of the minor in society, but should, in determining this fact, take into consideration the progress of society, and the attendant requirements upon the citizens of to-day. The rule in *Middlebury College* v. *Chandler,* supra, was clearly based upon conditions which existed at that time. An opportunity at that early date for a common school education was small, for a high school education less, and for a college education was almost impossible to the average family, and was generally considered as being only within the reach of the most affluent citizens. While there is no reported case, it is hardly to be doubted that the courts at that time would have even held that a high school education was not necessary, inasmuch as very few were

able to avail themselves of it. But conditions have changed greatly in almost a century that has elapsed since that time. Where the college graduate of that day was the exception, today such a person may almost be said to be the rule. The law in an attempt to keep up with the progress of society has gradually placed minimum standards for attendance upon public schools, and even provides punishment for those parents who fail to see that their children receive at least such minimum education. That it is the public policy of the state that a college education should be had, if possible, by all its citizens, is made manifest by the fact that the state of Washington maintains so many institutions of higher learning at public expense. It cannot be doubted that the minor who is unable to secure a college education is generally handicapped in pursuing most of the trades or professions of life, for most of those with whom he is required to compete will be possessed of that greater skill and ability which comes from such an education.

It seems to be contended that the minor in this case should be content with a commercial education, and it is argued that, since she is a graduate of the Lincoln high school, that fact demonstrates that she is able to earn her own living, and should no longer be a charge upon her father. But the record discloses that she has no aptitude for commercial work. It also appears that she completed her high school course in a little more than one-half the time usually taken, because of her genius for that class of work. It would seem, then, that she is not only unfitted for commercial life, but that she is exceptionally well-fitted for her chosen vocation.

If required, the necessity for this education can be grounded upon the authority of those cases involving vocational education. While there are many ways other than a college course to fit one for most of the vocations, there is no other suitable way to fit the minor for teaching English in the modern high school. But we think the court's order should be sustained upon the broader ground indicated herein.

(5) Appellant's counsel strenuously argued that it is the father's right to determine what education he will give his children, and that if he decides not to give them a college education, and to save his money for other purposes, the courts should not interfere. This rule is a salutary one, and should always be applied to a proper case. Whenever a father has the custody of a child, the law presumes that he will provide for the child's education in that vocation for which it is best fitted, and which will enable it to meet the conditions of modern life. But can the courts indulge that presumption where the custody of the child has been taken from the father? It seems to us that the mother, while she has the custody of the child, being in daily contact with her, and knowing her talents and abilities, should be the one to determine what education she should have. Parents, when deprived of the custody of their children, very often refuse to do for such children what natural

instinct would ordinarily prompt them to do. This is demonstrated in this case where the decedent refused to say upon the witness stand whether he would send Carmelita to college if she were living under his roof. In most cases the father, who is the one who holds the purse strings, and whose earning capacity is greater than that of the mother, is the one who is able to give the minor a proper education. To adopt the rule contended for by appellant would be to put the court, in providing for the custody of the child, in the dilemma of knowing that if the child is given to the mother the father would, in very many cases, refuse to give it an education greater than that required under the penalty of the law, and that the mother could not do so. The court would then be under the necessity of giving the child to the mother, who appeared to be the proper person to care for it, and leave the child without hope of an adequate education, or, to the father, who perhaps was an improper person, with the hope that it will receive its just opportunities.

Our conclusion is that, since the mother has the custody of this child, knows its character and ability, she is in position to determine what education it should have, what course should be pursued, and, this having received the approval of the court, we think it follows that the court's ruling should be upheld.

One other minor point remains to be considered. Many of the cases hold that a father will not be required to pay the expenses of keeping the child in a private or boarding school when the public institutions of the state are, in his opinion, as good, and where the expense of maintaining such child in such institutions will be less than in a private school. That point is really not involved in this case, for the reason that no contention is made that the minor could attend any of the state institutions at less expense than she could attend the College of Puget Sound while living in the home of her mother.

(6) The amount allowed, $60 per month, seems reasonable under all the circumstances. The minor child cannot attend college unless that amount is provided, and we think the financial situation of decedent demonstrated that the payments could be met without difficulty.

There being no reversible error in the record, the judgment is affirmed.

TOLMAN, C. J., and HOLCOMB, MAIN, and MACKINTOSH, JJ., concur.

PARKER, J. (dissenting).

I dissent from the view that a father is under legal obligation to furnish means for this child to acquire more than a high school edu-cation, situated as this father was prior to his decease; though I am ready to somewhat reluctantly yield to the amount of the award viewing the needs of the child apart from her claimed educational necessities.

2
Admission

People v. *Northwestern University*
396 Ill 233 (77 N.E. 2d 345)
Dec. 10, 1947

KILEY, Justice

This is a mandamus action seeking to compel defendants "to allow and to admit" the registration of Paysoff Tinkoff, Jr., as a freshman in the College of Liberal Arts of Northwestern University. Defendants' motion to dismiss was sustained and the suit dismissed. Plaintiffs appealed from the judgment of dismissal to the Supreme Court.

* * *

(2) The motion to dismiss admitted the facts well pleaded in the petition. The question is whether on those facts the trial court properly decided, as a matter of law, that the peition was substantially insufficient in that it failed to show a clear legal right to a writ of mandamus against the defendants.

Tinkoff, Jr. was born in November 1929; he was graduated and received a diploma from Senn High School, Chicago, in February 1945. The previous September he applied formally for admission to Northwestern University's College of Liberal Arts, and took and passed the requisite entrance examination. He was denied admission on the ground that, being fourteen years of age, he was too young for enrollment. At the time the certificate of his thirty-six high school credits and a letter from his father had not reached the University. Thirty-six credits met the entrance requirement of the University.

Following denial by the University, Tinkoff, Jr. filed a mandamus action in the Superior Court, seeking to compel his admission. The proceeding was dismissed "with the understanding" that he would be permitted to register at the September term of 1945. Meanwhile, during the school year of 1944–1945, he was enrolled in the University evening Commerce course, where he completed fourteen hours of work.

10

In June of 1945 he was denied admission to the Commerce School summer course at the Evanston Campus. In September of 1945 he was again denied admission to the College of Liberal Arts. He was denied admission in these instances because he had filed the previous mandamus action in the Superior Court.

The grounds of the motion to dismiss were that no showing was made of a right in Tinkoff, Jr. to admission and no duty on the part of the University to admit him, and that the petition sought to join a mandamus action with an equitable action.

Plaintiff contends that the University is a private corporation affected with a public interest; that its charter was granted for the great public purpose of education of youth, and because of that purpose its property is exempted from taxation; that there was an implied condition and understanding in the grant that the University would perform its functions for the "common good of the public at large, and not for the benefit of a favored few"; and that Tinkoff, Jr. had the right of admission since he met the entrance requirements.

The charter of the University was granted January 4, 1851. It was amended in 1855, 1861 and 1867. The amendments are not important to this case. The charter provides that the trustees shall have power "to make and alter from time to time such by-laws as they may deem necessary for the government of said institution, its officers and servants; provided such by-laws are not inconsistent with the constitution and laws of this State and of the United States." It further provides that they shall have power to confer "on such persons as may be considered worthy" degrees such as are usually conferred by similar institutions. It provides that the University's property should be held for educational purposes and not for the private benefit of trustees or contributors to the endowment. Power of visitation was lodged by the grant in appointees of the Methodist Episcopal Church.

There is no provision in the charter with respect to admissions. Section 8 authorizes appointment of a board to examine applicants for diplomas. Section 9 provides for legal proceedings to forfeit the charter for any act contrary to the grant. Finally there is a provision that the charter should be construed liberally "in all courts" to aid the attainment of the purposes of the University.

(3–7) The University is a private charitable corporation . . . and its charter is a contract. . . . The Dartmouth College case is authority for the following principles: That education is an object of national concern and a proper subject of legislation; that the grant of a charter by a State to a private educational institution is given in consideration of the benefits the public shall receive through the education of the youth; that the charter is a contract whose obligations cannot be impaired by law; and that the legislature has only such power over the chartered institution as was reserved in the contract. There was no power reserved by the legislature of Illinois with respect to the admission of students at Northwestern University.

(8, 9) To say that the University thought a private corporation is affected with a public interest is to beg the question. Those corporations are affected with a public interest which are amenable to State supervision. . . . We cannot say that a private educational institution is in a business essentially public in its nature, rendering the corporation so engaged subject to public control, as a telegraph and telephone company.

* * *

(12, 13) Under its charter the University had the power to adopt whatever rules were necessary in its judgment to the proper attainment of the University's purpose. Its bulletin for the College of Liberal Arts for the years 1943–1945 regulating admissions expressly stated it was not possible to admit all who met the specific entrance requirements. For the years 1945–1946 the bulletin in addition stated that the University reserved the right to reject any application for any reason it considers adequate. Are we to say that it should have admitted Tinkoff, Jr., though the University considered its reason for rejecting him adequate? He had no right to be admitted. His admission rested in the discretion of the University. The allegation that he was denied admission contrary to an "understanding" added nothing to the force of the petition even if the allegation were properly made. The only compulsion arising out of the University's charter with respect to admissions is that "no particular religious faith shall be required of those who become students." There is no point before us based on breach of this command.

(14–17) Cases involving legislative control of State universities and schools are not helpful. The State through the legislature has no power to take from or interfere with the power of the trustees of the University to make such rules as are necessary to conduct the University's business. *Dartmouth College* v. *Woodward,* 4 Wheat. 518, 17 U.S. 518, 4 L.Ed. 629. The State through its courts has not the power. There is no provision in the University charter that the rules enacted should be reasonable. The charter provides that they shall not be repugnant to the constitution of Illinois or of the United States. It is our view that the bulletins were within the University's power to promulgate; that the University was not required to give a reason for denying Tinkoff, Jr. admission; and that it could refuse for any reason it considered adequate. Plaintiff says he was excluded because he was under fourteen years of age and because he instituted litigation against the University. He says these are arbitrary denials. The minimum age provision for admission to the University of Illinois is fifteen years. . . . The University may have considered the commencement of the suit an adequate reason for denying Tinkoff, Jr. admission.

(18, 19) Courts have refused to coerce private educational institutions in the exercise of lawful discretion. . . . Plaintiffs have cited numerous cases to support their contention that regulations for admission to educational institutions must be reasonable. These cases involve public schools and are, accordingly, not pertinent. The public schools belong to the public. Private schools do not. Students stand in different position as to each class of schools.

* * *

Judgment is accordingly affirmed.

Kirstein v. *University of Virginia*
309 Fed. Supp. 184
February 9, 1970

CRAVEN, Circuit Judge

* * *

Until recently the University of Virginia at Charlottesville was substantially an all-male institution. It is difficult to evaluate the quality of education. Without attempting to do so, we think it fair to say from the evidence that the most prestigious institution of higher education in Virginia is the University of Virginia at Charlottesville, despite the apparent high quality of education offered at other Virginia institutions. The University of Virginia at Charlottesville is by far the largest educational institution, and its diversity of instruction is not paralleled in Virginia.

At the first hearing of this case we indicated our reluctance to interfere with the internal operation of any Virginia college or university, and particularly that of the University of Virginia at Charlottesville. We expended our best efforts to encourage the litigants to agree upon a consent judgment that might satisfactorily implement the Board of Visitors' contemplated changes in structure and nature of the University of Virginia at Charlottesville. We were impressed with the so-called Woody Commission report and its strong recommendation that sex barriers to admission to any Virginia institution of higher education be removed. In the context of long-established separation by sex in institutions of learning, we were most favorably impressed with the willingness of the authorities controlling Virginia higher education to innovate and favorably entertain the relatively new idea that there must be no discrimination by sex in offering educational opportunity.

Since the Richmond hearing, there has been submitted to the court the University Board of Visitors' resolution of October 3, 1969, which adopts a plan for the admission of women on an equal basis with men to the University of Virginia at Charlottesville. In order to smoothly adjust the dislocations to be caused by increased numbers of women on a campus that has been substantially all-male, the plan provides for a three-stage change in admission policies: (1) 450 women will be admitted in September, 1970; (2) an additional 550 women will be admitted in September, 1971; and (3) women will be admitted on precisely the same basis as men beginning in September, 1972, with no limitation thereafter on the number of women admitted.

Plaintiffs have filed objections to the plan, but it is quite significant that their objections do not relate to the merits or even to the speed of the plan with respect to the University of Virginia at Charlottesville. Instead, plaintiffs insist that there is no assurance that the plan will ever be permanently effectuated because final authority rests with the Legislature of Virginia and because the plan may be undone by future boards of visitors. Plaintiffs' other ground of objection is that the plan does not solve the question of sex discrimination at other institutions of higher education and is limited to the University of Virginia at Charlottesville.

(1) The pattern of separation by sex of educational institutions is a long established one in America and a system widely and generally accepted until the last decade. Despite this history, it seems clear to us that the Commonwealth of Virginia may not now deny to women, on the basis of sex, educational opportunities at the Charlottesville campus that are not afforded in other institutions operated by the state.* Unquestionably the facilities at Charlottesville do offer courses of instruction that are not available elsewhere. Furthermore, as we have noted, there exists at Charlottesville a "prestige" factor that is not available at other Virginia educational institutions. These paricular individual plaintiffs are not in a position, without regard to the type of instruction sought, to go elsewhere without harm to themselves and disruption of their lives. Two of the plaintiffs are married to graduate students who must remain at the University of Virginia at Charlottesville. A pattern of continued sex restriction would present these plaintiffs with the dilemma of choosing between the marriage relationship and further education. We think the state may not constitutionally impose upon a qualified young woman applicant the necessity of making such a choice.

(2) The plain effect of the Equal Protection Clause of the Fourteenth Amendment is "to prohibit prejudicial disparities before the law. This means prejudicial disparities for all citizens—including women." . . . We hold, and this is all we hold, that on the facts of this case these particular plaintiffs have been, until the entry of the order of the district

---

* We need not decide on the facts of this case whether the now discountenanced principle of "separate but equal" may have lingering validity in another area—for the facilities elsewhere are not equal with respect to these plaintiffs.

judge,** denied their constitutional right to an education equal with that offered men at Charlottesville and that such discrimination on the basis of sex violates the Equal Protection Clause of the Fourteenth Amendment.

(3) We are urged to go further and to hold that Virginia may not operate any educational institution separated according to the sexes. We decline to do so. Obvious problems beyond our capacity to decide on this record readily occur. One of Virginia's educational institutions is military in character. Are women to be admitted on an equal basis, and, if so, are they to wear uniforms and be taught to bear arms? . . . Some of Virginia's educational institutions have thus far been attended only by persons of the female sex. We think that these plaintiffs lack standing to challenge discrimination in such institutions. They are not harmed by the operation of an all-female institution that they do not wish to attend. Whether women attending such an institution are harmed by the absence of male students is, on this record, hypothetical. This and similar questions can better be determined in a case involving male applicants who sincerely wish to enter an all-female school, or female students at the school who believe it should be coeducational, and the governing authorities of the school, who may present the opposing viewpoint. We note, of course, that one of the parties plaintiff is the National Student Association. Although a proper party, we think that even this association cannot sharpen for us the questions that arise with respect to whether or not there may, under any circumstances, be continued operation of schools separated according to sex.

(4) The Board of Visitors of the University of Virginia at Charlottesville has made easy for us the proper disposition of this case. Within the limited constitutional duty which we have adjudged, it is beyond argument that the plan to implement the right of women applicants to attend the University of Virginia at Charlottesville is constitutionally adequate. Substantial numbers of women are to be admitted next fall and an even greater number the year following, with no limitation whatsoever thereafter. Any change in the method of operation of an institution as large as the University of Virginia at Charlottesville is bound to take some time. "It is not uncommon for courts, when declaring constitutional rights not previously recognized and declared, to delay for a reasonable time, in consideration of practical problems incident to the implementation of those rights, the actual exercise of the newly declared right." . . . This time schedule seems to us far more than deliberate and, indeed, reflects a genuine intent and purpose on the part of the authorities to make the University of Virginia at Charlottesville coeducational as soon as is reasonably feasible. The plan

---

** By preliminary order on September 8, 1969, United States District Judge Robert R. Merhige, Jr. ordered the University at Charlottesville to consider without regard to sex plaintiffs' application for admission.

as a whole is in keeping with the trend toward coeducation now apparent among many colleges and universities that once admitted only one sex, but now admit both. We approve the plan as proposed by the Board of Visitors.

＊　＊　＊

For the reasons stated, plaintiff's suit will be ordered dismissed as moot, provided, however, that upon motion, and for good cause shown within one year of date of dismissal, the action may be reinstated.

Dismissed.

Dehaan v. *Brandeis University*
150 F. Supp. 626
April 12, 1957

SWEENEY, Chief Judge

I have before me now the defendant's motion to dismiss the complaint for "failure to state a claim upon which relief can be granted." . . . The plaintiff instituted this action praying that the defendant, Brandeis University, be enjoined from withholding a scholarship award and from refusal to permit the plaintiff to renew his registration at the school, or in the alternative, for money damages. . . . The plaintiff's motion for a preliminary injunction was denied at the hearing on the ground that its allowance at this time would be a futile gesture, for the school year was more than half completed.

The plaintiff, a student at the defendant's Graduate School of Arts and Sciences, applied for and was awarded a fellowship in the amount of $700 and a scholarship to cover tuition for the academic year 1956–1957. The plaintiff's reply to the offer of award was a lengthy protest at its inadequacy, and he accused the defendant of bad faith with respect to promises allegedly made at the time of admission to the school. By a subsequent letter, dated April 21, 1956, the plaintiff accepted the award offered "under protest and pending reply to my petition . . ." and included a proviso that he reserved "the right to accept employment elsewhere." The defendant on April 23 withdrew the award previously offered and by a letter dated June 22, 1956, the plaintiff was informed that there "cannot be renewed registration by you for further work at the University. This recommendation of the Graduate Committee was unanimous and has been approved by the Administration."

The issue to be decided now is whether the university had a right to dismiss the plaintiff summarily or whether it must grant him a hearing before any decision on his status is made.

(1) As a preliminary matter I reject the plaintiff's suggestion that the court refuse to consider the incriminating letter of April 14, 1956 which is the apparent cause of the plaintiff's difficulties with the University. This letter was conspicuously missing from the appendix to the complaint and was properly introduced by the defendant as a part of its motion at the hearing. . . .

(2) Brandeis University, a privately endowed institution, by regulation which is set forth in its General Catalog, "reserves the right to sever the connection of any student with the university for appropriate reason." The problem of what constitutes an appropriate reason must clearly be left to those authorities charged with the duty of maintaining the standards and discipline of the school. . . . The court is in a poor position indeed to substitute its judgment for that of the university, particularly in this case, which involves a graduate student enrolled in a very small department where the major part of instruction is given on an individual and personal basis.

(3) The plaintiff insists, however, that the college overstepped the bounds of its discretion in dismissing him without giving him the opportunity to be heard. While it might be a better policy to hold a hearing whenever any disciplinary action is contemplated by the university, I hold as a matter of law that the defendant is not required to do so. Dismissal without a hearing under a regulation no more sweeping than the one in issue here was upheld by the Pennsylvania Supreme Court in *Barker* v. *Trustees of Bryn Mawr College*, 278 Pa. 121, 122 A. 220, 221, where the court said: ". . . in view of the regulation, on which the relator obtained entrance to the college, providing that the latter 'reserves the right to exclude at any time students whose conduct . . . it regards as undesirable,' defendant is not required to prefer charges and hold a trial thereof, before dismissing a student regarded by it as undesirable." . . .

Massachusetts statutes and decisions have strictly limited the hearing requirement to public schools. . . . Furthermore, even in cases involving dismissal from public schools, no hearing is necessary where the exclusion was for reasons other than misconduct. . . . It follows that private colleges be given at least the same freedom of choice of students. The plaintiff's qualifications as a scholar and prospective teacher can be judged only by his professors, who must have complete autonomy [as to] their decision concerning the qualities of his work and his good character.

Accordingly, the motion to dismiss is allowed.

Woods v. *Simpson*
146 Md. 547 (126 A. 882)
Dec. 4, 1924

BOND, C. J.

(1) This appeal is from an order granting the petition of a student of the University of Maryland for the writ of mandamus to compel the officers and regents of the University to permit her to continue her course. She had been refused admittance to the third year of work after she had finished the first two years. The case was heard before the court below without a jury. . . .

It appears from the testimony taken that the petitioner was a young woman not readily submissive to rules and regulations, and that during her two years at the University she was to a considerable extent in conflict with the authorities who had her in charge. And at the conclusion of her second scholastic year, in June, 1923, when her father applied for a reservation of a room for her for the third year, the president of the institution replied that experience with the daughter had not been satisfactory, and that it was considered for her best interest, as well as that of the students and the University, that she should not live in a dormitory. The letter concluded:

"I think it is only fair to say to you in this connection that an investigation in progress may reveal facts which may lead us to ask you to arrange for your daughter's transfer to some other institution. She is apparently not in sympathy with the management of the institution, or with the majority of the students, in their system of student government. I am calling this to your attention now, so that you may have time to decide where she is to go, in case we decide not to re-enter her here."

A letter of a week later, replying to a second effort of the father to secure a dormitory room, advised him definitely that a room would not be available for the daughter, and that, if she was readmitted, it would be as a day student.

The investigation referred to in the letter quoted was an effort to trace the source of a report, professing to have been furnished by girl students to a Washington newspaper, and there published, that men officials of the University were making objectionable suggestions to girl students, and otherwise exhibiting a wrong moral attitude toward them. Instances were described in the report. It depicted a dangerous condition, and was a serious attack on the institution, obviously demanding an investigation and correction of the condition, if it existed. It is conceded by both sides in this litigation that the report was false, but investigation was none the less necessary at the time. A students' mass meeting passed a resolution of confidence in the administration, denying the report, and all voted in favor of the resolution, except the petitioner and one other. All the girl students were asked if they knew anything of the charges, and when the petitioner was asked by the dean of women, she turned and left, without answering. Sometime in July the petitioner was invited to a conference by the president, and told by him that he had reason to believe that she signed some of the charges given to the newspaper, and was asked whether or not she had done so. The president said he wanted an answer to aid him, and that unless she answered she would not be registered for the following term. She then asked him if the charges did not appear in the newspaper, and the president said he was not asking the newspaper, he was asking her. She replied that she could not answer that question. Again in September, 1923, she saw the president, and was told by him that unless she complied with his demands made in July she would not be registered. She was thereupon transferred to George Washington University, and brought this proceeding in Baltimore.

(2) The maintenance of discipline, the upkeep of the necessary tone and standards of behavior in a body of students in a college, is, of course, a task committed to its faculty and officers, not to the courts. It is a task which demands special experience, and is often one of much delicacy, especially in dealing with girl students; and the officers must, of necessity, be left untrammeled in handling the problems which arise, as their judgment and discretion may dictate, looking to the ends to be accomplished. Only in extraordinary situations can a court of law ever be called upon to step in between students and the officers in charge of them. When it is made clear that an action with respect to a student has been, not an honest exercise of discretion, looking to the proper ends, but beyond the limits of that discretion, or arising from some motive extraneous to the purposes committed to that discretion, the courts may be called upon for relief. In such case, the officials have, as it is sometimes stated, acted arbitrarily, or abused their discretion; and the courts may be required to remedy that. In *Manger* v. *Board of Examiners*, 90 Md. 659, 671, 45 A. 891, 894, Chief Judge McSherry said:

> The exercise of a discretion, though erroneously, if not corruptly exercised, cannot be reviewed in a petition for a mandamus; but an officer clothed with a power . . . may be compelled by mandamus to exercise that power, though his honest discretion in the exercise of it cannot be controlled.

And this is the general rule applied to controversies over matters of discipline and order in educational institutions. . . .

Any other rule would be subversive of all discipline in the schools, and of the educational interests of the state. To hold that dissatisfied students in the colleges and schools of this state can review the discretion of faculties, in cases where the facts justify the exercise of discretion, would be most unwise.

(3, 4) In the case now before us, the petitioner, and to some extent the court below in its opinion, have viewed the refusal to let the petitioner continue her course as a penalty attached to the one isolated act of her declining to answer as to her authorship of the damaging aspersions on the life at the University. And it is suggested that any fault on her part in her previous difficulties had been condoned. But we have not been able to take this view. The relation of university officials and their students is one in which condonation or waiver has no place. There is nothing in that relation, as there often is in marriage or in business, which requires that single incidents justifying breaches either be at once made the basis of breach or be forever after disregarded. On the contrary, college officials are required to act upon their ultimate judgment of the student, derived from experience, the longer the better; and the greater the number of incidents covered the better. We do not mean to pass judgment on the sufficiency of this student's declining to answer the question of the president and the dean as a separate ground for refusing her admittance to her third year; it would not be necessary to do so, even if it were within our province, for we conclude from the testimony that during the student's previous two years also she had given the officials some reason to consider the effect of her actions and her attitude on the University and its proper upkeep, and that, on the whole, experience with her did fairly raise a question whether she could be continued in this student body without results which ought to be avoided; and the decision of that question was within the discretion of the officials, and is, in our opinion, not to be interfered with by the courts. The petition for the writ of mandamus should therefore have been dismissed.

(5) The record in this case, containing, as it does, a verbatim report of all that took place at the trial, including all colloquies and remarks, and a reproduction of all exhibits at length, constitutes such a violation of the fifth rule of the Court of Appeals that we have concluded that the appellants should pay one-third of the cost of it.

Judgment reversed and petition dismissed, with cost to the appellant, except as to one-third of the cost of the record.

Williams v. *Wheeler*
138 P. 937
Dec. 31, 1913

RICHARDS, J.

This is an appeal from a judgment of the superior court of the county of Alameda, denying the application of the appellants for a writ of mandate.

The facts are briefly as follows: The plaintiff, Alan Frank Williams, a young man of the age of 18 years, applied to be enrolled as a student at the University of California. The rules of the board of regents of the university require that every person in attendance as a student, or applying for enrollment as such in the university, shall produce evidence satisfactory to the authorities thereof that he has been successfully vaccinated within seven years prior to such attendance or application, or else be vaccinated. The plaintiff had not been successfully vaccinated within such period, and refused to be vaccinated, but presented to the authorities in charge of the university a statement in writing, signed by his parents, stating that such parents were conscientiously opposed to the practice of vaccination, and would not consent to the vaccination of said plaintiff. The authorities of the university still refusing him admission as a student therein, the plaintiff, by his guardian ad litem, applied to the superior court for a writ of mandate to compel such admission. The application was heard upon stipulated facts, and was denied, whereupon plaintiff prosecutes this appeal.

It is the contention of the appellant that, having met the requirements of the general law as set forth in the Statutes of 1911, prescribing the conditions with respect to vaccination to be complied with for admission as a student to the educational institutions of the state, he is entitled to enrollment in the university. The Act of 1911 (Stats. 1911, p. 295) provides that within five days after any child or person shall be received, enrolled, entered, or employed in any school, college, university, academy or other educational institution within the state of California, such child or person shall file with those in authority over such institution: (a) A certificate showing that such child or person has been successfully vaccinated within seven years prior to the date thereof; or (b) a statement in writing signed by his or her parent, or guardian if such child or person be a minor, or by himself in other cases, stating that such parent or guardian or person is conscientiously opposed to the practice of vaccination, and will not consent to the vaccination of such child or person; or (c) a certificate of a duly licensed and practicing physician, stating that the physical condition of such child or person is, at the time, such that vaccination would seriously endanger the life or health of such child or person. The act further provides that any child or person failing, neglecting, or refusing to file either the certificate showing successful vaccination within the prescribed period, or the statement or certificate required to work an exemption of the child from the requirement of vaccination, shall be excluded from admission to the institution until he or she complies with the law.

The appellant, having presented to the authorities in charge of the university a statement of his parents in proper form, to the effect that they were conscientiously opposed to the practice of vaccination and would not consent to his vaccination, insists that he thereby, being otherwise qualified, became entitled to admission to the university, and is now entitled to a writ of mandate to compel his enrollment as a student therein.

The respondents oppose this contention of the appellant upon several grounds: (1) That the board of regents of the University of California have been invested by the Constitution and statutes governing its foundation and control with full power over the matter of the admission of students to the university, and with exclusive authority to make and enforce rules for its government, and to prescribe the terms upon which students may exercise the right to enter or be enrolled therein, and that the power and authority with which the regents are thus invested is independent of legislative action, and is not subject to legislative control; that in the exercise of this power and authority the board of regents have adopted a rule that no person shall be admitted or enrolled as a student in the university unless he shall either produce satisfactory evidence that he has been successfully vaccinated within the period of seven years next preceding his application for admission or else that he be vaccinated; (2) that the act of 1911, insofar as it attempts to interfere with the power and authority with which the regents of the university are thus invested, or with the rule which they have adopted, is inoperative as to them, for the reason that it is not in that respect a health regulation; and (3) that the act of 1911, in that it undertakes to exempt those persons who are conscientiously opposed to vaccination from the other requirements of the act, is not a general law, and hence is unconstitutional and void. We shall consider these several contentions in the order of their presentation.

The University of California looks for its foundation as a state institution to the act of the Legislature of March 23, 1868, entitled "An act to create and organize the University of California." Stats. 1867–68, p. 248. By the provisions of this act the university was established and declared to be under the charge and control of a board of directors, to be known and styled the "Regents of the University of California"; and to this body was entrusted the general government and superintendence of the institution, with the power to prescribe rules for its government and to fix the qualifications for the admission of students thereto. The act also provided that: "Any resident of California, of the age of 14 years or upwards, of approved moral character, shall have the right to enter himself in the university as a student at large . . . on such terms as the board of regents may prescribe." The act of 1868 was subjected to one unimportant amendment in 1871–72, and the general subject and terms of the act were carried into the Political Code adopted in 1872, where they remain without material change, as to the matters involved in this inquiry, to the present time. Pol. Code, §§ 1385 to 1477. By the Constitution of 1879 the University of California was raised to the dignity of a constitutional department or function of the state government, by the provisions of section 9 of article 9 thereof, which read as follows: "Sec. 9. The University of California shall constitute a public trust, and its organization and government shall be perpetually continued in the form and character prescribed by the organic act creating the same passed March 23rd, 1868 (and the several acts amendatory thereof), subject only to such legislative control as may be necessary to ensure compliance with the terms of its endowments and the proper investment and security of its funds."

(1) Whether or not the framers of the Constitution intended by the terms of the above section that the organic act of 1868, and the substance of that act as embraced in the Political Code adopted in 1872, and in being when the Constitution was framed, were to be so far read into the Constitution itself as to place the university thereafter, in respect to the details of its internal government, beyond all future legislative interference or control, it is not necessary at this time to determine; but it would seem to be very plain that it was the intention of the framers of the Constitution to invest the board of regents with a larger degree of independence and discretion in respect to these matters than is usually held to exist in such inferior boards and commissions as are solely the subjects of legislative creation and control. This would seem to be a necessary conclusion from the fact of the elevation of the university to the place and dignity of a constitutional department of the body politic, and from the express terms of the Constitution itself, to the effect that its organization and government should be perpetually continued in the form and character prescribed by the act of its foundation, and that in those respects it should not be subject to legislative control. The investment of the authorities of the university with this amplitude of power and discretion in the management of its affairs must be held to include the power to make reasonable rules and regulations relating to the health of its students, and especially to make and enforce such reasonable regulations as would tend to prevent the introduction and spread of contagious disorders among the student body. In the making of such rules and regulations they might doubtless adopt whatever preventive means had met the approval of medical science and experience. The practice of vaccination as a means of preventing the infection and spread of smallpox has had the approval of both science and experience for more than a century in the old world and in the older states of our Republic, and has been an approved method of inoculation for more than 60 years in the state of California, as will appear from our legislation on the subject dating as far back at 1852. In the absence of any express legislative action looking to the adoption of a general law requiring vaccination as a

condition of admission to a public educational institution, we think it undeniable that the board of regents had the right to make and enforce a reasonable rule upon that subject.

That the foregoing rule which the board of regents did adopt, and are still seeking to enforce, is a reasonable rule would seem to have been determined by the Supreme Court and the appellate courts of this state with respect to a similar rule enacted by the state Legislature in 1889. . . . In the leading case of *Abeel* v. *Clark*, supra, the language of the Supreme Court is enlightening and instructive upon the point under present consideration. The court says: "The act referred to is designed to prevent the dissemination of what, notwithstanding all that medical science has done to reduce its severity, still remains a highly contagious and much dreaded disease. While vaccination may not be the best and safest preventive possible, experience and observation—the test of value of such discoveries dating from the year 1786, when Jenner disclosed it to the world—have proved it the best method known to medical science to lessen the liability to infection with the disease. This being so, it seems highly proper that the spread of smallpox through public schools should be prevented and lessened by vaccination, thus affording protection both to the scholars and to the community."

In the light of this long-held attitude of the law toward the practice of vaccination as a preventive of smallpox, we are of the opinion that the board of regents of the University of California had power to adopt and enforce the rule requiring vaccination as a prerequisite to the admission of a student to the university, in the absence of legislation lawfully limiting the exercise of that power.

(2) This brings us to the question as to what, if any, power remains with the Legislature to pass laws controlling the matter of the admission of students to the University of California, or limiting the operation of a rule of the regents of the university with respect to the terms of admission of students thereto, in the light of the foregoing provision of the Constitution that as to such matters the authorities in charge of the university shall not be subject to legislative control. It is undoubtedly true, as conceded by the respondents, that there are certain subjects affecting the general welfare over which the Legislature has been wisely invested with ultimate control. These subjects are those embraced within the general police powers of the state, and among them is the subject of the general health. It is admitted that over this subject the state Legislature has the ultimate control, and that in the exercise of that control it has power to pass general laws, in the nature of health regulations, upon the subject of vaccination, prescribing the extent to which persons seeking entrance as students in educational institutions within the state must submit to its requirements as a condition of their admission; and it is also conceded by the respondents that insofar as such an act of the Legislature comes within the definition of a general

law, and as such also comes within the general police powers of the state as a health regulation, the rules and regulations of the board of regents of the university must give way before it.

The appellant herein contends that the act of the Legislature of 1911 relating to vaccination is such a law. The respondents contend that the act of 1911, insofar as it provides for the general vaccination of those seeking admission as students in educational institutions, is a re-enactment of the rule of the university, and hence that the appellant is not aided by it; but that insofar as it undertakes to provide that those persons seeking admission to educational institutions who aver them-selves to be conscientiously opposed to vaccination need not comply with the provisions of the act requiring vaccination, it is not a health regulation; and hence that the authorities in charge of the university are not subject to its control. The respondents further contend that the act of 1911, in that it contains the aforesaid exemption, is not a general law, and is therefore unconstitutional and void.

As has been heretofore seen, the state of California stands committed to the policy of requiring vaccination as the best preventive means known to medical science for lessening the liability to infection with a dreaded and dangerous disease. The act of 1889 (St. 1889, p. 32) upon that subject was entitled "An act to encourage and provide for a general vaccination in the state of California," and the act of 1911, which replaces the former act, is also entitled "An act to encourage and provide for a general vaccination for all public and private schools of California," etc. If, as the titles of these two acts indicate, it is the policy of the state of California to encourage and provide for a general vaccination as the most effective method known to medical science for preventing the spread of an infectious and dangerous disease and as such is a reasonable and proper health regulation, how can a pro-vision of the law be also held to be a health regulation which exempts from vaccination all those who are conscientiously opposed to that means of prevention? Vaccination is a surgical operation and medical treatment addressed to the physical system of the individual patient and effectuating his inoculation from the contagious disease of smallpox, without regard, so far as medical science teaches, to the mental attitude of the patient toward the law requiring submission to it, and more certainly regardless of what the mental attitude of his parents or guardians may be. It would rather seem to be the very opposite of a health regulation for a law, whose title declares its purpose to be "To encourage and provide for a general vaccination," to have embraced within it a proviso exempting from such vaccination those whose mental attitude is that of opposition to the avowed object of the law. To take an extreme illustration: Suppose that a law requiring the quarantine of persons actually afflicted with smallpox should contain a proviso exempting from its operation those who should declare themselves conscientiously opposed to being quarantined. Would such an exemption be valid as a health regulation? Clearly not. The object and effect of such an exemption in such case, as in this, would be to defeat the very intent of the law itself by an exception not founded upon considerations of health, destroying that generality within the sphere of its operation which would be essential to its effectiveness as a health regulation.

(3) In our opinion, therefore, the provision of the act of 1911, which seeks to exempt those persons who are conscientiously opposed to the practice of vaccination from the operation of the law, otherwise general in its terms, requiring vaccination of persons seeking admission to educational institutions, is not in the nature of a health regulation, and that being so, it is not such a proviso as would come within the general police powers with which the Legislature is invested, and hence that it cannot be availed of by those seeking enrollment in the University of California to nullify and avoid the operation and effect of the existing rule of the authorities of the university upon the subject of vaccination.

These views make it unnecessary in this case to decide whether the act of 1911, considered in its entirety and with reference to its effect upon other educational institutions which do not stand in the same relation to it or to the state as the University of California, and which are not before the court, is or is not a general law.

The judgment is affirmed.

We concur: LENNON, P.J.; KERRIGAN, J.

Bryan v. *Regents of University of California*
188 Cal. 559 (205 P. 1071)
California. March 31, 1922

WILBUR, J.

The petitioner seeks a writ of mandate to compel the respondent to admit her to the University of California. The respondent is willing to admit her as a student providing she will pay the fee fixed by the respondent for nonresidents, amounting to $75 a semester. This refusal of the respondent is in accordance with section 1394½ of the Political Code and rules of the state board of regents adopted in accordance therewith. This section, adopted in 1921, reads as follows:

An admission fee and rate of tuition fixed by the board of regents must be required of each nonresident student. The board of regents shall cause to be computed the actual cost to the university of maintaining one student in each of the respective courses of the several colleges for the period of one year. Each nonresident student shall be required to pay as the rate of tuition the sum provided for by the above computation for the particular course such student is following: Provided, that the maximum sum to be remitted in whole or in part in the case of graduate students in other than professional colleges and schools. A nonresident student as used in in this section shall mean any person who has not for more than one year immediately preceding his entrance into the university been a bona fide resident of the state of California. Stats. 1921, p. 541.

It is contended that this legislation and the rule of the board of regents adopted in pursuance thereof violates article 1, sections 11 and 21 of the Constitution of the state of California. These sections prohibit the granting of privileges or immunities to any citizen or class of citizens "which upon the same terms shall not be granted to all citizens." It is pointed out that all persons residing within the state of California, except the children of transient aliens and of alien public ministers and consuls, are citizens (Pol. Code, § 51) and that, therefore, the petitioner is a citizen within the meaning of article 1, section 21, of the state Constitution. It is conceded that the Legislature has power to enact laws classifying citizens, where the classification is not unreasonable and arbitrary, and that legislation with reference to such classification is constitutional, but it is contended that there is no reasonable basis for extending the rights of the university to all other citizens and denying such privileges to citizens who have not resided within the state for one year. It must be conceded that it is permissible to classify citizens who have resided within the state one year for certain purposes, notably, that of voting. Section 50 of the Political Code provides:

The people, as a political body, consist: (1) Of citizens who are electors; (2) of citizens not electors.

The Constitution itself makes this classification, Article 2, § 1. Now, one reason for denying a citizen of the state the right to vote in the state until he has been a resident of the state one year is that his residence for one year within the state is evidence of his bona fide intent to remain in the state permanently, and for the same reason the requirement that the voter shall reside 90 days in the county and 30 days in the election precinct in which he seeks to vote, is also considered necessary. Only such persons are eligible to become public officers. Pol. Code, § 58.

There seems to be no good reason for holding that the Legislature may not make a similar classification in fixing the privilege for attendance upon the state university. It would be impossible for the state university to provide educational opportunities for all the citizens of the state. These facilities are necessarily limited. It is stated by the respondent that the number of scholars at the university have increased from 1,783 in 1900 to 10,599 in 1920. The expenditures for the next current biennial period are estimated at $9,000,000, almost equal to the entire annual expenditures of the United States government during the first years of its existence ($10,000,000). This expenditure is a heavy burden upon the taxpayers of the state. Taxes are payable annually, and the requirement that a student shall maintain a residence in the state of California during one taxation period as an evidence of the *bona fides* of his intention to remain a permanent resident of the state and not temporarily reside within the state for the mere purpose of securing the advantages of the university, cannot be held to be an unreasonable exercise of discretion by the Legislature or by the respondent. It follows that the exclusion of the petitioner does not violate her constitutional rights.

Petition denied.

We concur: SHAW, C. J.; SHURTLEFF, J.; LAWLOR, J.; LENNON, J.

Connell et al. v. *Gray*
33 Okl. 591 (127 P. 417)
Oct. 8, 1912

WILLIAMS, J.

. . . the plaintiff states that on the 2d day of September, 1912, she being a citizen of Oklahoma, and of the age of 16 years, and having applied for instruction as a student in said institution, did then and there comply with all the lawful rules and regulations prescribed by the board of regents and the faculty of said institution, and did present her certificate of qualifications entitling her to admission as such student to the committee on entrance of such college, and the said committee on entrance of said college did then and there examine the same and in all things approve the same, and by its chairman did duly certify her as entitled to admission as a student in said college; . . . that, notwithstanding that this plaintiff had complied with all the lawful rules and regulations relating or pertaining to the admission of citizens of the state of Oklahoma as students entitled to be admitted to instruction therein, the said defendants, unlawfully conspiring and acting together for the purpose of depriving plaintiff of her property, did unlawfully, illegally, willfully, without authority of law, and in violation of law, demand of the plaintiff that she pay over to and deposit with the said president and said registrar, or some other person acting in collusion with them, the sum of $5 in good and lawful money of the United States, worth and of the value of $5, as a condition precedent to enrolling her as a student thereof and admitting her to instruction therein.

Plaintiff further states that said defendants further demand the payment of other and further fees from the plaintiff and others in like situation with her as conditions of admission to instruction in said institution, to wit, a deposit of $6, with which the defendants shall purchase for her a certain dress and equipment for use by her in the gymnasium of said institution, and a like fee of all other students for like dress and equipment for such use; also from all male students a deposit of $17 for the purchase of a suit or uniform for use in the military department of the said college while receiving instruction in said department, such gymnasium and military instruction being compulsory under the rules and regulations of such college; also a fee of $2 per term for the use of a typewriting machine by students in the commercial department, and $2 per term for the use of a piano in the music department from each student about to take instruction, said pianos and said typewriting machines being the property of said college and a part of its equipment, and being owned by it as fully and to the same extent as it owns its grounds, campus, and other buildings, all such fees in the various classes and departments being demanded and required from students applying for instruction in said college, and being exacted by defendants before said defendants will register, accept, admit, or certify any such student as entitled to admission to instruction therein.

Defendants, answering, admit:

That the said Ruth Gray, on September 2, 1912, applied to the defendants for admission into the said Oklahoma Agricultural and Mechanical College, and that admission into the college was denied said Ruth Gray for and on account of her failure and refusal to pay the term fees of $5 to be charged all students, of which $2.50 is not returnable, and the balance to become a trust fund, which may be returned at the end of the term, unless absorbed by charges for breakage and repairs made against the individuals and the student body, as provided by the orders, rules, and regulations promulgated by the faculty of said college, and duly approved by the state board of agriculture of the state of Oklahoma, the board of regents of said college. The said defendants, in demanding such term fee of $5, acted under and by virtue of the following proceedings of the faculty, of April 11, 1912, which was confirmed by the college committee of the board of regents on August 14, 1912, which proceedings were in words and figures as follows: "Moved that a fee of $5.00 per term be charged all students, of which $2.50 shall not be returnable, the balance to be a trust fund, which may be returned at the end of the term, unless absorbed by charges for breakage and repairs made against individuals and the student body. This to take the place of all fees, with the exception of music and typewriting fees, and that the change be published in the catalog." Further answering, defendants state that the said term fee of $5 is in no sense a tuition, and will not be used for that purpose. The funds arising from the collection of this fee will be expended for the purchase of supplies and materials consumed by students and for services rendered and for the support of student organizations necessary to the highest efficiency of the college, viz., the Y.M.C.A., the Y.W.C.A., student literary societies the students' college paper, the athletic association for women, the athletic association for men, and similar student enterprises. That the fund arising from the collection of such fee will be wholly insufficient to meet all the expenses incident to the enterprises named.

On application, a temporary injunction was granted the plaintiff (defendant in error) against the defendants (plaintiffs in error), which is, in part, as follows:

. . . It is considered and ordered by the court that the defendants herein, J. H. Connell, president of the Oklahoma Agricultural and Mechanical College of the state of Oklahoma, and J. E. Hasselle, registrar thereof, be and the same are hereby enjoined and restrained until the further order of the court herein from demanding, requiring or compelling the payment of any money or sum of money to them or into their hands or into the hands of any one else by the plaintiff as a condition for her admission to instruction as a student in the said Agricultural and Mechanical College of the state of Oklahoma; that they be, and they are hereby, enjoined and restrained from demanding, requiring, and compelling the payment of any money or sums of money to them, or into their hands, or into the hands of any one else, by any person being a citizen of the state of Oklahoma and entitled to admission to instruction under the rules and regulations prescribed by the board of regents of said college, other than prescribing the payment of money as a condition for admission. It is further ordered by the court that the said defendants may, and they are hereby expressly permitted to, require from students taking military drill or gymnasium instruction in said institution proper uniforms and clothing as prescribed by the board of regents and faculty, and necessary and proper for use in said instruction, and may accept from persons taking any such instruction deposits of money for the furnishing of such uniforms and equipment for such purpose, and may require deposits from students taking instruction in any department of the college, wherein breakage to equipment and supplies may occur, or other damages that are liable to be made, the same to be held as a trust fund, and to be repaid to the student depositing the same in case the student shall not cause sufficient damage or breakage to absorb the amount thereof, and in case he shall cause such damage or breakage same shall be prorated and the balance returned to him.

This proceeding in error is prosecuted to reverse this order. The Oklahoma Agricultural and Mechanical College was organized or provided for by the first Legislative Assembly of the territory of Oklahoma. . . . Nothing in said acts of Congress, or the act creating said institution, requires said college to be maintained free of tuition, and that students be admitted therein for instruction free from all fees and charges, unless it be section 25 of said act . . . which provides: "Males and females shall be admitted to all the privileges of the institution hereby established, and all citizens of the territory of Oklahoma between the ages of twelve and thirty years shall be admitted to instruction therein, if they apply as students therefor." In Kansas the statute provides: "Admission into the university shall be free to all the inhabitants of this state, but a sufficient fee shall be required from nonresident applicants, to be fixed by the board of regents, and no person shall be debarred on account of age, race or sex."

In *State of Kansas ex rel. Attorney General* v. *Board of Regents of the University of Kansas et al.,* 55 Kan. 389, 40 Pac. 656 . . . it was held that the board of regents had no power to collect a fee of $5, or any other fee, for the use of library, or exclude students from the use of the library for the nonpayment of such fee, and that the assumption by the board of the power to collect such fees and to exclude students from the library for the nonpayment thereof was an unwarranted assumption of corporate powers, from the exercise of which they will be ousted by that court in a suit brought in the name of the state by the Attorney General. In the opinion it is said:

It is contended that the board of regents may yet collect a reasonable fee for the wear and tear of the books; that the word "free" must be taken with qualifications; that in the nature of things there must be rules and regulations; that each and every student cannot be permitted to occupy the chancellor's seat at his desk, or any other place in the university he may choose at his own sweet will, but that the regents and the chancellor have a right to make proper regulations; and that the fee imposed is no more than is reasonable to preserve and protect the library. We fully agree with so much of the claim of the learned counsel as asserts the right of the regents and the chancellor to make all necessary and proper rules and regulations for the orderly management of the school, the preservation of discipline therein, and the protection of its property, but that it may require the payment of money as a condition precedent to the use of the property of the state is another and a different claim, with which we do not agree. If the regents may collect $5 for the use of the library, why may they not collect also for the use of the rooms of the building and of its furniture? Why may they not impose fees for walking in the campus, or for the payment for instructors? All these things have cost money. There are expenses incurred by the state on behalf of the students in connection with every department of the school. If they may collect for one thing, it is not apparent why they may not collect for another. It is suggested that supplies are furnished in the laboratories for the use of students, which are destroyed; that vessels and implements may be broken; and that the students should certainly be required to pay for these things. No question of that kind, however, is now presented. . . . The library is provided for permanent use. Each volume, with proper care, may be used by a great number of students and for a long term of years. The library as a whole is subjected to wear and tear, but only in the same manner as furniture and other properties furnished by the state. The buildings, furniture, library, and apparatus, as well as the services of the faculty, are furnished and paid for by the state. These, we hold, under the provisions of the statute quoted, are free to all residents of the state who are entitled to admission into the university. The regents have no power to raise a fund, to be managed and disposed of at their discretion, by charging fees for the use of the library, or under any other claim for any other purpose, unless expressly authorized to do so by law.

* * *

The board of regents have the implied power to do everything necessary and convenient, where it is not prohibited, either express or implied, by law, to accomplish the objects for which the institution was founded. To do this the property, grounds, buildings, halls, and apparatus, furniture, etc., must be reasonably preserved against negligent destruction. To require a reasonable deposit by each student as a condition precedent to entrance, to cover any such breakage or damage thereto, to be refunded at the close of the term or session in the event no breakage or damage is done by such student, appears to be necessary and reasonably within the implied powers of said board. The fee of $2.50 for such purpose is not unreasonable.

It is conceded by counsel for all parties in this proceeding that the board has authority to prescribe the kind of uniform and require same to be worn by the students. Such being the case, it is within the power of said board to require the students, at the time of entrance, to provide themselves with such uniform, or make a reasonable deposit to cover the cost of same.

As to the Young Men's and the Young Women's Christian Associations, it is not permissible for said board to make it compulsory upon any student in said institution to contribute to the maintenance of the same. Section 5, art. 2, of the Constitution of this state provides: "No public money or property shall ever be appropriated, applied, donated, or used, directly or indirectly, for the use, benefit, or support of any sect, church, denomination, or system of religion, or for the use, benefit, or support of any priest, preacher, minister, or other religious teacher or dignitary, or sectarian institution as such."

*   *   *

But the question here for determination is as to whether the board of regents of the Agricultural and Mechanical College have authority to levy a fee on every proposed student as a condition precedent to entrance therein, to be used for the maintenance of the Young Men's and the Young Women's Christian Associations. Said section 5 of article 2 is self-executing, and requires no act of the Legislature to become operative, but by itself controls all legislation upon the subject of appropriating money or other property for such purposes. . . . Obviously it would not be permissible for said board to use any funds appropriated by the state for the purpose of maintaining these associations, teaching and promulgating a system of religion. If the Legislature is powerless to appropriate a fund for the purpose of maintaining such associations, or to authorize said board to use said funds for such purposes, it follows that it is not within its power to authorize said board to require a fee to be paid by the student as a condition precedent to entrance, to be used by said board for said purposes. . . .

It is not only within the power of said board to provide for athletics to be taught but also for an athletic association of the students in said institution. It is also within the power of said board to provide for a college magazine. But to say that it was reasonably within the implied powers of said board, as a condition precedent to entrance, to require a deposit to be made for the maintenance of said athletic association and magazine would be equivalent to saying that it was within the power of said board to require a deposit by each student for the payment of all books and appliances necessary. . . .

The order, as modified, to conform to this opinion, will be affirmed. All the justices concur.

3

Race

Missouri ex. rel. Gaines v. *Canada*
305 U.S. 337
Nov. 9, 1938
Mr. CHIEF JUSTICE HUGHES delivered the opinion of the Court.

Petitioner Lloyd Gaines, a Negro, was refused admission to the School of Law at the State University of Missouri. Asserting that this refusal constituted a denial by the State of the equal protection of the laws in violation of the Fourteenth Amendment of the Federal Constitution, petitioner brought this action for mandamus to compel the curators of the University to admit him. . . .

Petitioner is a citizen of Missouri. In August, 1935, he was graduated with the degree of Bachelor of Arts at the Lincoln University, an institution maintained by the State of Missouri for the higher education of negroes. That University has no law school. Upon the filing of his application for admission to the law school of the University of Missouri, the registrar advised him to communicate with the president of Lincoln University and the latter directed petitioner's attention to § 9622 of the Revised Statutes of Missouri (1929), providing as follows:

"Sec. 9622. May arrange for attendance at university of any adjacent state—Tuition fees.—Pending the full development of the Lincoln university, the board of curators shall have the authority to arrange for the attendance of negro residents of the state of Missouri at the university of any adjacent state to take any course or to study any subjects provided for at the state university of Missouri, and which are not taught at the Lincoln university and to pay the reasonable tuition fees for such attendance; *provided* that whenever the board of curators deem it advisable they shall have the power to open any necessary school or department. . . .

Petitioner was advised to apply to the State Superintendent of Schools

34

for aid under that statute. It was admitted on the trial that petitioner's "work and credits at the Lincoln University would qualify him for admission to the School of Law of the University of Missouri if he were found otherwise eligible." He was refused admission upon the ground that it was "contrary to the constitution, laws and public policy of the State to admit a negro as a student in the University of Missouri." It appears that there are schools of law in connection with the state universities of four adjacent States, Kansas, Nebraska, Iowa and Illinois, where nonresident negroes are admitted.

The clear and definite conclusions of the state court in construing the pertinent state legislation narrow the issue. The action of the curators, who are representatives of the State in the management of the state university . . . must be regarded as state action. The state constitution provides that separate free public schools shall be established for the education of children of African descent . . . and by statute separate high school facilities are supplied for colored students equal to those provided for white students. . . . While there is no express constitutional provision requiring that the white and Negro races be separated for the purpose of higher education, the state court on a comprehensive review of the state statutes held that it was intended to separate the white and Negro races for that purpose also. Referring in particular to Lincoln University, the court deemed it to be clear "that the Legislature intended to bring the Lincoln University up to the standard of the University of Missouri, and give to the whites and Negroes an equal opportunity for higher education—the whites at the University of Missouri, and the Negroes at Lincoln University." Further, the court concluded that the provisions of § 9622 (above quoted) to the effect that Negro residents "may attend the university of any adjacent State with their tuition paid, pending the full development of Lincoln University," made it evident "that the Legislature did not intend that Negroes and whites should attend the same university in this State." In that view it necessarily followed that the curators of the University of Missouri acted in accordance with the policy of the State in denying petitioner admission to its School of Law upon the sole ground of his race.

In answering petitioner's contention that this discrimination constituted a denial of his constitutional right, the state court has fully recognized the obligation of the State to provide Negroes with advantages for higher education substantially equal to the advantages afforded to white students. The State has sought to fulfill that obligation by furnishing equal facilities in separate schools, a method the validity of which has been sustained by our decisions. . . . Respondents' counsel have appropriately emphasized the special solicitude of the State for the higher education of Negroes as shown in the establishment of Lincoln University, a state institution well conducted on a plane with the University of Missouri so far as the offered courses are concerned. It is said that Missouri is a pioneer in that field and is the only State in the Union which has established a separate university for Negroes on the same basis as the state university for white students. But, commendable as is that action, the fact remains that instruction in law for Negroes is not now afforded by the State, either at Lincoln University or elsewhere within the State, and that the State excludes Negroes from the advantages of the law school it has established at the University of Missouri.

It is manifest that this discrimination, if not relieved by the provisions we shall presently discuss, would constitute a denial of equal protection. That was the conclusion of the Court of Appeals of Maryland in circumstances substantially similar in that aspect. *University of Maryland* v. *Murry*, 169 Md. 478; 182 A. 590. It there appeared that the State of Maryland had "undertaken the function of education in the law" but had "omitted students of one race from the only adequate provision made for it, and omitted them solely because of their color"; that if those students were to be offered "equal treatment in the performance of the function, they must, at present, be admitted to the one school provided." *Id.,* p. 489. A provision for scholarships to enable Negroes to attend colleges outside the State, mainly for the purpose of professional studies, was found to be inadequate (*Id.,* pp. 485, 486) and the question, "whether with aid in any amount it is sufficient to send the Negroes outside the State for legal education," the Court of Appeals found it unnecessary to discuss. Accordingly, a writ of mandamus to admit the applicant was issued to the officers and regents of the University of Maryland as the agents of the State entrusted with the conduct of that institution.

The Supreme Court of Missouri in the instant case has distinguished the decision in Maryland upon the grounds (1) that in Missouri, but not in Maryland, there is "a legislative declaration of a purpose to establish a law school for Negroes at Lincoln University whenever necessary or practical"; and (2) that, "pending the establishment of such a school, adequate provision has been made for the legal education of Negro students in recognized schools outside of this State." . . .

As to the first ground, it appears that the policy of establishing a law school at Lincoln University has not yet ripened into an actual establishment, and it cannot be said that a mere declaration of purpose, still unfulfilled, is enough. The provision for legal education at Lincoln is at present entirely lacking. Respondents' counsel urge that if, on the date when petitioner applied for admission to the University of Missouri, he had instead applied to the curators of Lincoln University it would have been their duty to establish a law school; that this "agency of the State," to which he should have applied, was "specifically charged with the mandatory duty to furnish him what he seeks." We do not read the opinion of the Supreme Court as construing the state statute to impose such a "mandatory duty" as the argument seems to assert. The state court quoted the language of § 9618, R.S. Mo. 1929, set forth in the margin, making it the mandatory duty of the board of curators to establish a law school in Lincoln University "whenever necessary and practicable in their opinion." This qualification of their duty, explicitly stated in the statute, manifestly leaves it to the judgment of the curators to decide when it will be necessary and practicable to establish a law school, and the state court so construed the statute. Emphasizing the discretion of the curators, the court said:

> The statute was enacted in 1921. Since its enactment no Negro, not even appellant, has applied to Lincoln University for a law education. This fact demonstrates the wisdom of the legislature in leaving it to the judgment of the board of curators to determine when it would be necessary or practicable to establish a law school for Negroes at Lincoln University. Pending that time adequate provision is made for the legal education of Negroes in the university of some adjacent State as heretofore pointed out. . . .

The state court has not held that it would have been the duty of the curators to establish a law school at Lincoln University for the petitioner on his application. Their duty, as the court defined it, would have been either to supply a law school at Lincoln University as provided in § 9618 or to furnish him the opportunity to obtain his legal training in another State as provided in § 9622. Thus the law left the curators free to adopt the latter course. The state court has not ruled or intimated that their failure or refusal to establish a law school for a very few students, still less for one student, would have been an abuse of the discretion with which the curators were entrusted. And, apparently, it was because of that discretion, and of the postponement which its exercise in accordance with the terms of the statute would entail until necessity and practicability appeared, that the state court considered and upheld as adequate the provision for the legal education of Negroes, who were citizens of Missouri, in the universities of adjacent States. We may put on one side respondent's contention that there were funds available at Lincoln University for the creation of a law department and the suggestions with respect to the number of instructors who would be needed for that purpose and the cost of supplying them. The president of Lincoln University did not advert to the existence or prospective use of funds for that purpose when he advised petitioner to apply to the State Superintendent of Schools for aid under § 9622. At best, the evidence to which argument as to available funds is addressed admits of conflicting inferences, and the decision of the state court did not hinge on any such matter. In the light of its ruling we must regard the question whether the provision for the legal education in other

States of Negroes resident in Missouri is sufficient to satisfy the constitutional requirement of equal protection, as the pivot upon which this case turns.

The state court stresses the advantages that are afforded by the law schools of the adjacent States—Kansas, Nebraska, Iowa and Illinois—which admit nonresident Negroes. The court considered that these were schools of high standing where one desiring to practice law in Missouri can get "as sound, comprehensive, valuable legal education" as in the University of Missouri; that the system of education in the former is the same as that in the latter and is designed to give the students a basis for the practice of law in any State where the Anglo-American system of law obtains; that the law school of the University of Missouri does not specialize in Missouri law and that the course of study and the casebooks used in the five schools are substantially identical. Petitioner insists that for one intending to practice in Missouri there are special advantages in attending a law school there, both in relation to the opportunities for the particular study of Missouri law and for the observation of the local courts, and also in view of the prestige of the Missouri law school among the citizens of the State, his prospective clients. Proceeding with its examination of relative advantages, the state court found that the difference in distances to be traveled afforded no substantial ground of complaint and that there was an adequate appropriation to meet the full tuition fees which petitioner would have to pay.

We think that these matters are beside the point. The basic consideration is not as to what sort of opportunities other States provide, or whether they are as good as those in Missouri, but as to what opportunities Missouri itself furnishes to white students and denies to Negroes solely upon the ground of color. The admissibility of laws separating the races in the enjoyment of privileges afforded by the State rests wholly upon the equality of the privileges which the laws give to the separated groups within the State. The question here is not of a duty of the State to supply legal training, or of the quality of the training which it does supply, but of its duty when it provides such training to furnish it to the residents of the State upon the basis of an equality of right. By the operation of the laws of Missouri a privilege has been created for white law students which is denied to Negroes by reason of their race. The white resident is afforded legal education within the State; the Negro resident having the same qualifications is refused it there and must go outside the State to obtain it. That is a denial of the equality of legal right to the enjoyment of the privilege which the State has set up, and the provision for the payment of tuition fees in another State does not remove the discrimination.

The equal protection of the laws is "a pledge of the protection of equal laws." . . . Manifestly, the obligation of the state to give the protection of equal laws can be performed only where its laws operate, that is, within its own jurisdiction. It is there that the equality of legal right must be maintained. That obligation is imposed by the Constitution upon the States severally as governmental entities, each responsible for its own laws establishing the rights and duties of persons within its borders. It is an obligation the burden of which cannot be cast by one State upon another, and no State can be excused from performance by what another State may do or fail to do. That separate responsibility of each State within its own sphere is of the essence of statehood maintained under our dual system. It seems to be implicit in respondents' argument that if other States did not provide courses for legal education, it would nevertheless be the constitutional duty of Missouri when it supplied such courses for white students to make equivalent provision for Negroes. But that plain duty would exist because it rested upon the State independently of the action of other States. We find it impossible to conclude that what otherwise would be an unconstitutional discrimination, with respect to the legal right to the enjoyment of opportunities within the State, can be justified by requiring resort to opportunities elsewhere. That resort may mitigate the inconvenience of the discrimination but cannot serve to validate it.

* * *

Here, petitioner's right was a personal one. It was as an individual that he was entitled to the equal protection of the laws, and the State was bound to furnish him within its borders facilities for legal education substantially equal to those which the State there afforded for persons of the white race, whether or not other Negroes sought the same opportunity.

It is urged, however, that the provision for tuition outside the State is a temporary one, that it is intended to operate merely pending the establishment of a law department for Negroes at Lincoln University. While in that sense the discrimination may be termed temporary, it may nevertheless continue for an indefinite period by reason of the discretion given to the curators of Lincoln University and the alternative of arranging for tuition in other States, as permitted by the state law as construed by the state court, so long as the curators find it unnecessary and impracticable to provide facilities for the legal instruction of Negroes within the State. In that view, we cannot regard the discrimination as excused by what is called its temporary character.

We do not find that decision of the state court turns on any procedural question. The action was for mandamus, but it does not appear that the remedy would have been deemed inappropriate if the asserted federal right had been sustained. . . . In the instant case, the state court did note that petitioner had not applied to the management of Lincoln University for legal training. But, as we have said, the state court did not rule that it would have been the duty of the curators to grant such an application but on the contrary took the view, as we understand it, that the curators were entitled under the state law to refuse such an application and in its stead to provide for petitioner's tuition in an adjacent State. That conclusion presented the federal question as to the constitutional adequacy of such a provision while equal opportunity for legal training within the State was not furnished and this federal question the state court entertained and passed upon. We must conclude that in so doing the court denied the federal right which petitioner set up and the question as to the correctness of that decision is before us. We are of the opinion that the ruling was error, and that petitioner was entitled to be admitted to the law school of the State University in the absence of other and proper provision for his legal training within the State.

The judgment of the Supreme Court of Missouri is reversed and the cause is remanded for further proceedings not inconsistent with this opinion.

Reversed.

*   *   *

4
Dismissal (Private Institutions)

Edde v. *Columbia University*
168 N.Y.S.2d 643
Dec. 2, 1957

GOLD, Justice

This is an application by the petitioner for an order directing Columbia University to reinstate him "as a certified candidate for the degree of Doctor of Philosophy at Columbia University in the City of New York and to have him finally examined for that degree on the basis of his dissertation as it now stands." Petitioner seeks, in the alternative, an order transferring the proceeding to the Appellate Division for disposition.

For the purposes of this opinion it will be assumed that, in a proper case, a proceeding of this nature may be maintained against a private university, such as Columbia is alleged in the petition to be. Even on this assumption, the application must be denied.

(1, 2) It was within the discretion of the University's proper authorities to reject petitioner's doctoral dissertation. There is ample evidence to support the refusal of the dissertation, and it is not established that the rejection was arbitrary, capricious or unreasonable. The court may not substitute its own opinion as to the merits of a doctoral dissertation for that of the faculty members whom the University has selected to make a determination as to the quality of the dissertation. . . .

(3) Although the committee's rejection of the petitioner's dissertation was originally not final, in that it allowed petitioner an opportunity to revise his dissertation and continue his candidacy on that condition, petitioner refused to accept this condition. The rejection of the dissertation thus became final. In the circumstances, the University authorities did not abuse their discretion in terminating petitioner's candidacy for the degree of Doctor of Philosophy. The University was under no

legal compulsion or requirement to continue the candidacy of a person whose dissertation had been disapproved and who refused to revise it for further consideration.

* * *

Motion denied.

Carr v. St. John's University, New York
231 N.Y.S.2d 410
Memorandum by the Court
July 2, 1962

* * *

Subdivision (1) of section 313 of the Education Law provides that it "is a fundamental American right for members of various religious faiths to establish and maintain educational institutions exclusively or primarily for students of their own religious faith or to effectuate the religious principles in furtherance of which they are maintained."

The University is operated and conducted by a Roman Catholic order of priests. Although admission to study in the University is open to qualified applicants irrespective of religious faith, over 94% of the students attending the University are of the Roman Catholic faith. The University's general objective, as stated in its bulletins, is the offering of "such opportunities to achieve traditionally classical and professional education as will enable men and women to develop in learning and culture according to the philosophical and theological principles and traditions of the Roman Catholic Church."

The University's bulletins from 1957 to and including 1961–1962 included a regulation as follows:

Regulation on Discipline
In conformity with the ideals of Christian education and conduct, the University reserves the right to dismiss a student at any time on whatever grounds the University judges advisable. Each student by his admission to the University recognizes this right.

The continuance of any student on the roster of the University, the receipt of academic credit, graduation, the granting of a degree or a certificate, rest solely within the powers of the University.

In September 1957, the petitioner Howard Glenn Carr matriculated at the University for the degree of Bachelor of Science; he completed all the courses required for said degree in January 1962; and he paid all tuition fees and charges requested by the University. He was scheduled to receive his degree at the June 1962 commencement. The other two petitioners matriculated at the University in September, 1958.

On March 13, 1962, the petitioners Carr were civilly married in the presence of two witnesses: the petitioner Catto and another student. The four students involved are members of the Roman Catholic faith. According to the Canon Law of the Roman Catholic Church, Catholic parties to a marriage must conform to the requirements of a Catholic marriage, that is, they must be married before a Catholic priest and two witnesses. In the eyes of the Catholic Church, a civil marriage in the United States of members of the Catholic faith is invalid, and the act of each person who participates in such a ceremony, whether as a party to the marriage or as a witness, is seriously sinful.

On or about April 6, 1962, petitioner Catto made it known publicly at the University that petitioners Carr had been civilly married and that she (Catto) and the fourth student had been the witnesses.

The four students were given full opportunity to justify and explain their actions. They admitted that they were familiar with the regulation on discipline, and they gave no satisfactory explanation either for their failure to live up to their obligations as Catholic students at a Catholic University or for their failure to seek the advice and counsel of a priest. On April 12, 1962, petitioner Catto and the other witness were orally informed of the determination of the Executive Committee of the University's Board of Trustees that the four students should be dismissed. On the same day the petitioners Carr were married by a priest in the presence of the aforesaid witnesses to the civil marriage. On April 18, 1962, formal notices were sent to the four students, notifying them of their dismissal. Petitioners thereupon instituted this proceeding.

(1) When a student is duly admitted by a private university, secular or religious, there is an implied contract between the student and the university that, if he complies with the terms prescribed by the university, he will obtain the degree which he sought. The university cannot take the student's money, allow him to remain and waste his time in whole or in part (because the student might regard it as a waste of time if he does not obtain the degree), and then arbitrarily expel him or arbitrarily refuse, when he has completed the required courses, to confer on him that which it promised, namely, the degree. . . .

[O]bviously, and of necessity, there is implied in such contract a term or condition that the student will not be guilty of such misconduct as would be subversive to the discipline of the college or school, or as would show him to be morally unfit to be continued as a member thereof. The power of suspension or expulsion of students is an attribute of government of educational institutions (*Goldstein* v. *New York University* . . . 78 N.Y.S. p. 740). "Misconduct" perhaps refers more particularly to demeanor within the walls of the institution or in connection with the ordinary activities of student life. . . . But the implied stipulation of good conduct, variable in its meaning and incapable of precise definition as that term must always be, is not . . . to receive the restricted construction that the student's conduct may be the subject of control only in so far as it relates to his actions in his capacity and status of student. . . .

The regulation on discipline provides that "In conformity with the ideals of Christian education and conduct, the University reserves the right to dismiss a student at any time on whatever grounds the University judges advisable." To the Catholic students and authorities at the University, "Christian education and conduct" meant and means "Catholic education and conduct." The petitioners do not claim that they understood it to mean anything else, nor do they claim that they did not understand what they were doing or the consequences of their act in the eyes of their Church.

(2, 3) When a university, in expelling a student, acts within its jurisdiction, not arbitrarily but in the exercise of an honest discretion based on facts within its knowledge that justify the exercise of discretion, a court may not review the exercise of its discretion. . . . Here, the discretion exercised by the University was of that character.

Under the circumstances, the court may not review the University's exercise of its discretion in dismissing petitioners as students.

KLEINFELD, BRENNAN and HOPKINS, JJ., concur.

BELDOCK, P.J., and HILL, J., dissent and vote to affirm the order, with the following memorandum:

In our opinion, under the facts in this case, there was no basis for the University's exercise of discretion to dismiss these petitioners. The University is a public institution, chartered by the State, open to persons of all religious faiths, and engaged in providing secular learning leading to a general academic degree. Such a University may not enforce against a student an ecclesiastical law, the breach of which is not immoral according to the standards of society in general, or which it does not enforce equally against all students at the University, whether Catholic or non-Catholic.

Samson v. *Trustees of Columbia University*
167 N.Y.S. 202 (101 Misc. 146)
September, 1917

MULLAN, J.

The plaintiff brings this action to procure a decree requiring Columbia University to allow him to continue in that institution as a student, and he makes this motion for the relief he seeks pendente lite. At some time prior to September 26, 1916, the date not being stated in the papers, the plaintiff, while a student at the College of the City of New York, was suspended by the faculty thereof for creating a disturbance at a general meeting of the students of that college, on the occasion of an address by Gen. Leonard Wood on the subject of preparedness. Just what he did does not appear. He later applied to the defendant university for admission as a student, and he was so admitted on September 26, 1916, entering the upper division of the sophomore class. In February, 1917, he was graduated from the sophomore class into a junior class, and at the close of the academic year of 1916–1917 he was a member of the junior class, having successfully completed his studies in the lower division of that class. After the conclusion of that academic year, and on June 14, 1917, the defendant, through its acting dean, notified plaintiff that he would not be permitted to receive any further instruction at Columbia University. The reasons assigned by the defendant for its refusal to allow the plaintiff to continue as one of its students are: That on June 11, 1917, the plaintiff made an address at an "Emma Goldman" meeting, held in the Royal Lyceum, No. 10 West 114th street, in which he said: "We have no love for the Kaiser; but, as much as we hate the German Kaiser, we hate still more the American Kaiser." That he also said on that occasion that there had been draft riots in the Civil War, but that there would be a draft revolution during the war of 1917, and that the following report of the meeting was published in the New York Times on June 12, 1917:

> At 8 o'clock Samson arose to open the meeting. . . . In his opening harangue he devoted much of his time to the Workmen's and Soldiers' Council of Russia. He announced that he was about to organize such a council to run things in the United States. . . . He said the time had come when "we are going to refuse to stand up and shoot down our brothers." The war, he declared with great solemnity, is a "dollar war," and he reached his climax by prophesying a draft riot which would be more than a riot. "It's going to be a draft revolution," he said. He is also quoted as saying: "As much as we hate the German Kaiser, we hate still more the American Kaiser."

And a similar report of that meeting was published in the New York World of June 12, 1917. The plaintiff, in his replying affidavit, alleges that the newspaper account of his speech was a garbled version; but it is significant that he makes no denial that the published account correctly represented the substance and spirit of his address, and that he does not state what it was he did say on the occasion in question.

The defendant urges three grounds for the defeat of the plaintiff's motion: First, that as the plaintiff has completed his studies for the academic year for which he had been admitted, his contract with the University had expired; second, that plaintiff was admitted only on probation, and upon the express understanding that he "should not engage in any activities or take part in any movement which would involve the University in undesirable notoriety"; and, third, that the refusal of the University to allow the plaintiff to continue as a member of its student body was a proper exercise of the discretion and disciplinary power necessarily vested in an institution of learning, and actually conferred by its charter upon the defendant, and controlled by by-laws of its making. . . .

Considering these grounds in the order stated, I incline to the view that while, in a strict sense, a student contracts with an institution of learning for only a given part of a course, usually measured by the period of an academic year, the circumstances frequently permit of the implication that the institution had obligated itself—subject, of course, to changes of plan, curriculum and the like—to permit a student in good standing to continue the particular course for which he has entered, upon payment of the necessary fees and compliance with other reasonable requirements. At least, it would seem that a strong argument may be made for such a rule of construction. But as I think the relief the plaintiff here seeks must be denied upon another ground I shall not pursue further the inquiry upon this head, but shall resolve the doubt in the plaintiff's favor for the purpose of this motion.

Coming to the defendant's second ground of opposition, it is to be noted that the statement of the University's secretary upon the subject contains nothing more than the bare allegation that the plaintiff was admitted on probation, as hereinbefore mentioned, without any supporting or evidentiary facts, and that the plaintiff flatly denies that there was any agreement or stipulation whatsoever upon the subject of his future conduct. If I considered a determination of that question of fact necessary to the decision here, I should ask for further affidavits; but I have concluded to decide the motion upon the third ground, namely, that dealing with the disciplinary powers of the defendant over its student body.

Assuming, then, that the plaintiff is correct in his assertion that a contractual relationship subsisted between him and the University after the close of the past academic year, I think it is plain that it was one of the implied terms of the agreement that the plaintiff would comport himself in such manner as not to destroy or interfere with the discipline, good order and fair name of the University, which had admitted him as one of the students. . . .

Obviously and of necessity there is implied in such contract a term or condition that the student will not be guilty of such misconduct as would be subversive of the discipline of the college or school, or as would show him to be morally unfit to be continued as a member thereof. The power of suspension or expulsion of students is an attribute of government of educational institutions.

The question for determination here is, therefore: Has the plaintiff been guilty of such misconduct as to disentitle him to be continued, or has he shown himself to be morally unfit to be continued, as a member of the student body of the defendant? "Misconduct," perhaps, refers more particularly to demeanor within the walls of the institution or in connection with the ordinary activities of student life, and of improper practices by the plaintiff in that regard there is no claim made here. But the implied stipulation of good conduct, variable in its meaning and incapable of precise definition as that term must always be, is not, I think, to receive the restricted construction that the student's conduct may be the subject of control only in so far as it relates to his actions in his capacity and status of student. The term "morally unfit," as used by Mr. Justice Patterson, must be given the broader meaning and should be construed as comprising any conduct that may interfere with or injure the University, or lessen its proper control over its student body, or impair its influence for good upon its students and the community.

Viewing the matter in that light, I think it will be conceded that the duty of an institution of learning is not met by the mere imparting of what commonly goes under the name of knowledge. By the common consent of civilized mankind through the ages, not the least important of the functions of a school or college has been to instill and sink deep in the minds of its students the love of truth and the love of country. Is such conduct as that of the plaintiff calculated to make it more difficult for the defendant University to inculcate patriotism in those of its student members—if there be such unfortunates—who are without it? Does language of the sort used by the plaintiff at public meetings— for I assume that he is in substance correctly quoted—make him a real or potential menace to the morale of the defendant's student body and a blot on the good name of the famous and honored University whose degree he seeks? There may be two answers to those questions, but I see only one.

We are a tolerant people, not easily stirred, prone to an easygoing indulgence to those who are opposed to the very essentials and vitals of our organized social life; but there must of necessity be a limit somewhere to the forbearance that can with safety be extended to the forces of destruction that hide behind the dishonestly assumed mask of the constitutional right of free speech. To attempt to state in general terms the difference between an honest and a dishonest exercise of the wholesome right of free speech that our Constitution so completely and properly protects would be as vain as it would be unprofitable here. In some cases, in many cases perhaps, reasonable men would differ. But in some cases reasonable men could not differ, and I think we are dealing with such a case here. To counsel resistance to the draft ordained by lawful authority in accordance with our form of government is as culpable as it is cowardly; and one who does so is doing the work of the enemy without—thus far, at least—incurring the risks and braving the dangers that are the accepted lot of an enemy who is recognized as such because he has the courage openly to avow his true allegiance. Whether the plaintiff's conduct comes within the accepted definitions of sedition or treason, I have not concerned myself to inquire. It suffices me that he and his kind are attempting to make unsuccessful a war that this our country has declared and is waging. That it should be made impossible for such a person to remain at liberty to make common cause with our enemy is the view of many, but that consideration is beyond the scope of this inquiry. What I have to do with is the question of whether the plaintiff's continuance at Columbia University, with the inevitably close contact in which that would place him with impressionable young men of his own age who might thus be inoculated by him with the poison of his disloyalty, is likely to constitute a menace to the University. I think it would, and that the defendant was well within its rights in refusing further to extend to him its privileges and opportunities.

Motion denied, with $10 costs.

John B. Stetson University v. Hunt
88 Fla. 510 (102 So. 637)
Jan. 21, 1925

TERRELL, J.

Helen Hunt sued John B. Stetson University, a corporation, and Lincoln Hulley, its president, in an action of tort. The declaration among other things alleged that she (Helen Hunt) was "maliciously, wantonly, and without cause in bad faith expelled" from said University, and that such expulsion was confirmed, ratified, and approved by its board of trustees.

The case was tried in Orlando on the 16th of May, 1922, all pleas except the general issue having been stricken or withdrawn. The trial resulted in a verdict and judgment against both defendants in favor of the plaintiff in the sum of $25,000. Motion for a new trial was denied, and writ of error was taken to this court.

(1, 2) Defendants below contend that the plaintiff was suspended rather than expelled from the University. The catalog current at the time defined expulsion as "a final separation from the University," while it avers that "suspension separates the student temporarily from the University." These definitions are in harmony with Webster, who defines expulsion as ejecting, banishing or cutting off from the privileges of an institution or society permanently, and suspension as temporarily cutting off or debarring one from the privileges of an institution.

For the purpose of disposing of this case it is not material whether Miss Hunt was suspended or expelled, but to clarify the situation we have examined all the evidence on this point carefully, and it shows that she was suspended rather than expelled.

(3) Was the suspension of Miss Hunt malicious? Malice in law as defined by the authorities is that condition of the mind which shows a heart regardless of social duty and fatally bent on mischief, the existence of which is inferred from acts committed or words spoken. Malice is also defined as the intentional doing of a wrongful act toward another without legal justification or excuse, or, in other words, the willful violation of a known right.

The Supreme Court of the United States . . . approved the famous definition of malice by Bayley, J. . . . whose remarks have become a classic in the law and are as follows:

> Malice, in common acceptation, means ill will against a person, but in its legal sense it means a wrongful act, done intentionally, without just cause or excuse. If I give a perfect stranger a blow likely to produce death, I do it of malice, because I do it intentionally and without just cause or excuse. If I maim cattle, without knowing whose they are, if I poison a fishery, without knowing the owner, I do it of malice, because it is a wrongful act, and done intentionally. If I am arraigned of felony, and wilfully stand mute, I am said to do it of malice, because it is intentional and without just cause or excuse. And if I traduce a man, whether I know him or not and whether I intend to do him an injury or not, I apprehend the law considers it as done of malice, because it is wrongful and intentional. It equally works an injury, whether I meant to produce an injury or not.

In the light of the law as thus defined, how stand the charges against the defendants Dr. Hulley and John B. Stetson University? The evidence shows that Helen Hunt had been a student at the University for almost two years; that for some time immediately preceding her suspension, which took place April 6, 1907, numerous disorders took place in the girls' dormitory where Miss Hunt resided, some of which were described as hazing the normals, ringing cow bells and parading in the halls of the dormitory at forbidden hours, cutting the lights, and such other events as were subversive of the discipline and rules of the University. Some of the witnesses spoke of these disorders as bordering on insurrection.

Consequent to such infractions of the rules Miss Hunt and several other students were summoned before Dr. Hulley, and, on being briefly interrogated, Miss Hunt was commanded to go home that day, Miss

Keeling was commanded to move from the dormitory and secure quarters down town, and Miss Webster was told that she would be dealt with later. Miss Tiffany and Mr. Wilder had been previously suspended, and Mr. Clayburg had been expelled. All these students were subsequently reinstated in the University except Miss Hunt, who entered another reputable college in about two or three weeks, though she and her parents within such time were advised by Dr. Hulley that she would be expected to return to the University.

John B. Stetson University . . . is a private institution of learning, and the act of incorporation fully empowers the trustees "to make rules for the general management of the affairs of the institution and for the regulation of the conduct of the students." They are further empowered to "make, adopt and from time to time alter any such constitution, rules, regulations and by-laws as their convenience may require, and are not inconsistent with the constitution and laws of the United States or of this state." These powers within their scope give the trustees of John B. Stetson large discretion, though they are not unlike charter and corporate rights under which such institutions are generally conducted.

(4) Having in mind such powers the courts have universally applied the rule that a private institution of learning may prescribe requirements for admission and rules for the conduct of its students, and all who enter such institutions as students impliedly agree to conform to the rules of government. The only limit on this rule is as to institutions supported in whole or in part by appropriations from the public treasury. As to such institutions the rule is viewed more critically and is generally subject to legislative regulation. . . .

(5) As to mental training, moral and physical discipline, and welfare of the pupils, college authorities stand in loco parentis and in their discretion may make any regulation for their government which a parent could make for the same purpose, and so long as such regulations to not violate divine or human law, courts have no more authority to interfere than they have to control the domestic discipline of a father in his family. . . .

Pursuant to the provisions of law as above quoted, the trustees of John B. Stetson University among others adopted the following regulations which were in effect at the time of Miss Hunt's suspension:

> Offensive habits that interfere with the comforts of others, or that retard the pupil's work, etc., are prohibited.
> The government and discipline of the University are administered by the president. The University does not outline in detail either its requirements or its prohibitions. Students are met on a plane of mutual regard and helpfulness and honor. The ideals of the University are those of modern civilization in its best sense. The conventions and proprieties of refined society obtain here. A student may

forfeit his connection with the University without any overt act if he is not in accord with its standards.

(6) We think the trustees were fully authorized to adopt these regulations, that they are reasonable, and that it is well settled that unless such regulations or rules are unauthorized, against common right or palpably unreasonable, the courts will not annul or revise them. Neither will the courts afford relief in case of the enforcement thereof, unless those whose duty it is to enforce them act arbitrarily and for fraudulent purposes. . . .

(7) The relation between a student and an institution of learning privately conducted, and which receives no aid from the public treasury, is solely contractual in character, and there is an implied condition that the student knows and will conform to the rules and regulations of the institution, and for breach of which he may be suspended or expelled. . . .

(8, 9) Under the law it was competent for the trustees of John B. Stetson University to vest in the president authority to enforce discipline, and when acting in this capacity . . . :

He stands for the time being in loco parentis to his pupils, and because of that relation he must necessarily exercise authority over them in many things concerning which the board may have remained silent. In the school, as in the family, there exists on the part of the pupils the obligations of obedience to lawful commands, subordination, civil deportment, respect for the rights of other pupils, and fidelity to duty. These obligations are inherent in any proper school system, and constitute, so to speak, the common law of the school. Every pupil is presumed to know this law, and is subject to it, whether it has or has not been reenacted by the district board in the form of written rules and regulations. Indeed, it would seem impossible to frame rules which would cover all cases of insubordination and all acts of vicious tendency which the teacher is liable to encounter daily and hourly.

* * *

(10) It is proper to state in this connection that a mere mistake of judgment on the part of a school officer in governing his school, either as to his duties under the law or as to facts submitted to him, does not make him liable, but it must be shown that he acted in the manner complained of wantonly, willfully or maliciously. Any other rule would work a hardship to honest men, who with the best of motives endeavor to perform the duties imposed on them. *Fertich* v. *Michener*, supra, and the cases there cited.

It would very materially impair the discipline and usefulness of an institution of learning and would lead to vexatious litigation to hold that whenever a teacher sends a child home, as a punishment for insubordinate conduct, the child or the parent may treat it as an expulsion and sue the teacher or other governing authority. . . .

(11) Where the rules and regulations of a private institution of learning receiving no aid from the public treasury, in effect provide that a student may forfeit his connection with the institution without any overt act if he is not in accord with its standards, it is not incumbent on the institution to prefer charges and prove them at trial before dismissing permanently or temporarily a student regarded by it as undesirable. The acceptance and enjoyment of the benefits afforded by such institution is necessarily conditioned upon that degree of good conduct on the part of each which is indispensable to the comfort and progress of others. . . .

It was further, in effect, held in the last-cited case that every pupil, when called upon by the superintendent or by the board, should, as a matter of duty and loyalty to what is essential for the common welfare, freely state anything within his knowledge not self-incriminating, that will assist in bringing the offender to justice and thereby tend to the repression of all offenses. This is necessarily sound for, barring parental control, the power of school authorities over pupils extends to all acts detrimental to the best interests of the school, whether committed during school hours or intermission. To hold otherwise would tend to paralyze discipline in every department of our school system.

Counsel on behalf of Miss Hunt contend that at the time of her suspension she was a mere child of 15 or 16 years of age; that she was a stranger without friends in De Land; that she was forced out of the dormitory by Dr. Hulley; that he did not previously advise her parents of her suspension; that he made no inquiry as to her financial condition; that no provision was made to take care of her till she could notify her parents; and no opportunity was given her to rebut the charges against her.

The record in this case shows that Miss Hunt was suspended by Dr. Tulley between 8:30 and 9 A.M., April 6, 1907; that in all matters pertaining to such suspension Dr. Hulley was firm and positive, but was in no wise actuated by malice; that she could have gone home about noon of that date, but that she stayed at a private boarding house in De Land that night where other pupils were boarding, and went home with her father the following day; that she and her family had friends in De Land whom she was at liberty to go to for counsel and assistance at any time, and that within two or three weeks she entered and continued her studies in another reputable college, though she was advised by Dr. Hulley in the meantime that she would be expected to return to John B. Stetson University.

(12) In an action of this kind where malice is the gist of the offense, every presumption must be indulged in favor of the school authorities to the extent that they acted in good faith, for the best interests of the

school and the pupil as they saw it, and no recovery can be had for error of judgment, but may be had for error grounded on malice. . . .

We have examined all the evidence carefully, and find nothing in the acts committed, words spoken or any other facts and circumstances connected with Miss Hunt's suspension that imputes malice as here defined on the part of either Dr. Hulley or Stetson University.

We have given due consideration to citations by defendants in error, supporting the contention that she should have been awarded a hearing before being sent away from the University, but these are all dealing with cases from jurisdictions where statutes, by-laws or regulations are in effect requiring such hearings, but such is not the case here.

For reasons announced in this opinion, the judgment below is accordingly reversed.

TAYLOR, C.J., and ELLIS, J., concur.
WEST, J., concurs in the conclusion.
WHITFIELD, J., dissents in part.
BROWNE, J., disqualified.

Grossner v. *Trustees of Columbia University*
287 Fed. Supp. 535
July 9, 1968
FRANKEL, District Judge

In this lawsuit, which grows out of grave troubles recently experienced at Columbia University, nine assorted plaintiffs—five students, the pastor of a church near the University, a chapter president of the Congress of Racial Equality, an alumnus, and a lecturer in the College and Graduate Faculties—assert for "themselves and all persons similarly situated" various "causes of action" and demands for injunctive relief. They have moved for an injuction *pendente lite*. The application for such extraordinary relief is without merit, and will be denied. A cross-motion for summary judgment will be held in abeyance.

I

The plaintiffs complain broadly that they and members of their "classes" have for some time been protesting against the "policy-making structure of the University," the President's "unlimited and undefined" disciplinary powers, the planned construction of a University gymnasium in a public recreational area, and the University's involvement in the "Institute for Defense Analysis (*sic*) . . . , a consortium of twelve American universities conduction (*sic*) research for the Department of

Defense." Before April 23, 1968, it is alleged, plaintiffs attempted to communicate such protests "to the appropriate officials of the University without any serious consideration or response thereto being given." Complaint, par. 14. Moreover, they charge, on September 25, 1967, defendant Kirk, the University President, "issued an edict prohibiting further protest demonstrations within the buildings of the University, no matter how peaceful or nonviolent." *Ibid.* On April 23, plaintiffs and others assembled and went to the offices of the President in Low Memorial Library. When they learned that the President was refusing to meet with them, they proceeded to the site of the disputed gymnasium, but they were soon dispersed by the police. The plaintiffs then "returned to the campus to begin a peaceful demonstration in Hamilton Hall to protest the refusals of the University to give reasonable consideration to the structural and policy changes hereinabove referred to." *Id.,* par. 15. "In addition to the said demonstration in Hamilton Hall, from April 23 to April 30, 1968, plaintiffs, in their attempt to bring about a discussion and negotiations of the said structural and policy changes with the appropriate University officials, assembled" in three other University buildings and in "the offices of the defendant KIRK, where they remained until their arrest on the latter date. . . ." *Id.,* par. 16.

In other words, as the complaint goes on to say, the plaintiffs and others for whom they purport to speak occupied by "sit-ins" four of the school's buildings and the President's office uninterruptedly for a week until they were forcibly removed. *Ibid.*

Notwithstanding that their occupation of the buildings was "peaceful and orderly," plaintiffs charge, defendant President called in the police, who, at about two A.M. on April 30, 1968, "without any provocation by plaintiffs and members of their classes, . . . utilizing excessive and unnecessary force and in a brutal and inhuman manner physically assaulted and beat plaintiffs and the members of their classes and arrested more than 700 thereof." Then, it is asserted "upon information and belief," various charges of criminal trespass, resisting arrest, disorderly conduct, loitering, inciting to riot, and possession of weapons and dangerous instruments and appliances were filed against those so arrested.

The complaint goes on to allege that defendant University officials have brought or are threatening disciplinary proceedings arising from the foregoing events under University statutes which are vague, devoid of standards, offensive to principles of due process, and contrary to the protections of the First and Fourteenth Amendments. The threats of discipline "and/or arrest" are allegedly "being made . . . in bad faith without any hope of ultimate success and with the basic purpose and effect of intimidating and harassing . . . and punishing (plaintiffs) for, and deterring them from," exercising their First Amendment rights.

In order to avoid the "chilling effect" of such action by defendants, plaintiffs' first "cause of action" is to enjoin the University disciplinary proceedings and declare void a general statute of the University announcing its disciplinary powers.

In their second "cause of action" plaintiffs charge that the 700-odd people arrested on the morning of April 30 committed no illegal acts; that they are facing criminal charges only because they "resisted an unprecedented invasion of their University . . . and an uncontrolled exercise of violence" by the police; that the criminal charges against them are designed only to "chill" First Amendment freedoms; and that the pending prosecutions should be enjoined.

A third "cause of action" adds that defendant Hogan is both District Attorney of New York County, in charge of the pending prosecutions, and a Trustee of the University. These dual roles, plaintiffs allege, will deny them equal protection and due process if the criminal proceedings are not enjoined.

In their fourth "cause of action," plaintiffs reiterate the charges of police brutality on the morning of April 30; predict that such official violence "may" recur as a response to further acts of peaceful protest; and ask that the police be enjoined from perpetrating further assaults of a similar nature.

A fifth "cause of action" says the campus was "taken over" by the police upon the invitation of defendant Kirk; that this was "in violation of the fundamental integrity of the University community and without regard for appropriate institutions of self-government, including the faculty and student body" . . .; that plaintiffs, "in seeking to protect the integrity of the institutions of the University from invasion by the police, are invoking not only the ancient and historic regard for the integrity of the academic community but as well their rights" of free speech and due process . . .; and that defendant Kirk should be enjoined or he "may again resort to a violation of the integrity of the academic community by surrendering control of the University to the police."

The sixth and final "cause of action" charges that the University structure, "essentially unchanged since 1754, affords no participatory power in the faculty or student body in the determination of policies and programs of the University." . . . Plaintiffs say this structure violates unspecified "constitutional rights of faculty and students as well as the rights of members of the community affected by the actions of the University, in that it provides for a self-perpetuating body" of irresponsible trustees, "all in violation of the fundamental tenets of a democratic society as outlined in the Constitution of the United States." The court is asked to order a restructuring of the University under a "program to be submitted to this Court for its approval."

II

* * *

From the several affidavits on both sides, the undisputed facts and the unresolved disputes become sufficiently apparent for present purposes. It is clear that some hundreds of students and others conducted round-the-clock sit-ins occupying University buildings and the President's office for the week or so beginning April 23, and that they left on April 30 only because they were forcibly removed. At the outset of this "peaceful" protest, the Acting Dean of Columbia College was held captive in his office in Hamilton Hall for some 24 hours. During the occupancy of President Kirk's office, his files were rifled, documents were removed, and copies were made of correspondence, memoranda, diaries and other records. Since that time, copies of such records have been widely circulated on the campus and to public communications media.

It is undisputed, despite some equivocal legalisms for plaintiffs, that those participating in the sit-ins denied access to the buildings to faculty members, students and University personnel, among others.* Through the week of sit-ins, faculty members and others sought to persuade the occupants to leave peaceably. When these negotiations failed, the police moved in on the night of April 29–30 to force the departures and make the arrests which are central in the plaintiffs' complaint. Plaintiff Morris Grossner was among those arrested on that night.

As part of his efforts to cope with the disturbances in the University community, defendant Kirk proceeded shortly after April 30 to appoint a Joint Committee on Disciplinary Affairs, comprised of faculty members, students and administrators. On May 9, 1968, this Committee recommended disciplinary measures and general procedures "predicated

---

* The reply affiant, plaintiff Rothschild, "from his own personal observation of the events of April 23–30, 1968, and on the basis of interviews with persons involved, denies that access was at any time denied to other students, members of the faculty, or administrators, *except insofar as those persons threatened, upon entry into the buildings, to illegally and forcefully expel the protesters from the buildings, and disrupt and destroy their non-violent sit-in, activity which is protected under the First and Fourteenth Amendments to the Constitution.*" Affidavit, p. 3 (emphasis added).

This sort of "denial" scarcely furthers plaintiffs' theory that they are entitled to thwart the University's efforts to find out what happened and impose discipline upon students who may (or may not) have done the things Rothschild disputes in quasi-legal terms. Even more patently inapposite is his denial that the protesters made capitulation to their demands a condition for voluntarily ending the sit-ins. Rather, he says, "it was the intransigence of the defendants, and their refusal to meet with the representatives of the protesting students or even to negotiate with them in good faith through members of the faculty or other intermediaries, which caused the continuation and intensification of the protests on the part of the students." *Ibid.* What emerges is the undisputed fact that the "protesters" stayed in the buildings and refused to get out unless the University officials did things which may or may not have been good things to do, but were not in any event legally required as conditions to terminating the seizures.

on the assumption that trespass charges will be dropped." In this initial expression of its views, the Committee observed that the "demonstrations" beginning April 23 had "involved a number of unprecedented offenses against the University community"; that buildings had been entered and occupied illegally; that students, faculty and others had been excluded from their classrooms and offices; that University and personal property had been damaged; and that acts of such kinds, if committed by a single person or group "in an ordinary atmosphere," would deserve "maximum punishment." However, the Committee said, the atmosphere had not been "ordinary"; many of the demonstrators had "acted out of deep commitment, not personal animus, convinced that the University was not responsive to legitimate demands"; and there was a possible measure of shared responsibility to be assessed by a recently created fact-finding body. Recognizing that there might be mitigating factors, the Committee nevertheless concluded:

> It is clear, in any case, that no apportionment of responsibility can justify these violations of established rules, whether explicit regulations of the University or the unwritten rules of behavior that govern any community. The actions of the demonstrators were wholly out of proportion to their declared grievances.

Finding that the demonstrators shared "a common responsibility for (the) . . . chief consequences" of the demonstrations, the Committee recommended that there be "a uniform discipline . . . for the act of participation as such"—namely "disciplinary probation through June 30, 1969." Elaborating on this proposal, the Committee observed that such probation should serve mainly as "a clear warning to the offender" of "more severe penalties" for future infractions, but should not entail loss of "financial aid, or comparable hardship," or denial "of the right to participate in political activities in the University."

While proposing such limited and uniform punishment "for the act of participation as such," the Committee went on to say that "the University should investigate every charge of malicious action such as willful injury to persons, theft, deliberate damage to property, or invasion of private papers, and should bring appropriate charges against the individual offenders."

In broad outline, the Committee described as follows the procedural framework for implementing its substantive judgments:

> In the light of these initial conclusions, the Dean of each School or Faculty should determine which students in that School or Faculty were involved in the demonstrations and, following discussions with those students, should impose the discipline recommended above. *A student who fails to appear before the Dean should be suspended.*

If the student believes that the penalty imposed upon him by the Dean is excessive in view of that recommendation, he may appeal directly to the Joint Committee on Disciplinary Affairs.

If a student denies the Dean's charge of participation, the Dean should invoke procedures of the kind outlined hereafter. If the Dean concludes that more serious penalties are appropriate, because the student was already on probation or because he charges the student with offenses additional to participation in the demonstrations, the Dean should proceed against the student in this same formal manner. (emphasis added.)

The Committee went on then to prescribe detailed procedures—notice by the dean in writing; the convening of disciplinary tribunals, each to be comprised of two faculty members, two students, and an administrator selected by the dean (from persons not normally concerned with discipline) ; and the right of students before the tribunals "to be advised by counsel . . . and to present evidence" ("but counsel should not participate in the proceedings") . Further, the Committee said, students should not be required to give evidence against themselves; a transcript should be made; the proceedings should be public unless the tribunal "rules that the spectators are disrupting the proceedings"; students should be presumed to be innocent "until their guilt has been clearly proven in the proceeding"; and conduct must be judged only by "public or University statutes, rules, or regulations" to be "clearly identified" as the grounds of the alleged violations. The Joint Committee went on to prescribe a right of appeal, and undertook to serve as an appellate tribunal. Provision was made for further review by the President, with the stipulation that he was not to increase any penalty "sustained or imposed by the Joint Committee."

After defendant President and the Trustees had responded to its pronouncements of May 9, the Joint Committee issued a further statement on May 13. It recalled its earlier premise that the trespass charges would be dropped; noted that this was not being done; observed, however, that it was "now prepared to exercise its appellate jurisdiction"; and suggested that the Deans "begin to implement its recommendations concerning intramural discipline, but that application of all penalties be held in abeyance, pending action in the courts." Further, it said:

> The Joint Committee will entertain an appeal from a penalty applied before the final disposition of trespass charges against a student, even if that penalty is otherwise consistent with the Joint Committee's recommendations.

Appellate and other procedures were prescribed in fuller detail. And, finally, the Committee concluded with this reminder:

> A student who fails to appear before the Dean is liable to immediate

suspension, even though a trespass charge is still pending against him.

Acting along the lines formulated by the Joint Committee, the deans of the several schools proceeded within a few days to send letters to students charged with participation in the demonstrations of April 23–30. In each case, the student addressee was invited as the first step to appear for a meeting with the dean no later than a specified date. A warning was given that failure to make such an appearance would result in suspension. The initial meeting with the dean was to serve in essence as the "pleading" stage of the proceeding. The student summoned was given three choices: to admit the charge, deny it, or say nothing. An admission of the participation charged would lead to the disciplinary probation recommended by the Joint Committee. If the student denied the charge or stood mute, his case would be referred for hearing before a five-member tribunal of the type the Joint Committee had recommended.

The plaintiff Grossner and three other students (Rudd, Freudenberg, and Hyman, who are described as "plaintiffs" in plaintiffs' papers, but are not named as such and have nowhere said they want to be plaintiffs) received letters of the foregoing type from their Dean, Alexander Platt. These letters, mailed on May 16, 1968, informed the addressees that they were to meet with the Dean not later than May 21, or face suspension.

On the following night, May 17, Rudd led a group of demonstrators conducting a sit-in at a University-owned apartment building on West 114th Street. The group was ordered to leave, but refused to do so. The police were called; the demonstrators were ousted; and Rudd was arrested and charged with criminal trespass. It is this arrest and criminal charge on May 17, after the Dean's notice relating to events of April 23–30, which are said by plaintiffs to be a crucial constitutional obstacle to the University's taking even the initial step of its disciplinary procedure. As to the students Freudenberg and Hyman, while the Attorney's affidavit says that they (like Rudd) "have criminal charges pending against them" on Columbia's complaint, no date is given for such charges or for the events to which they relate.

In any event, the four named students made clear that they would not—and they did not—comply with Dean Platt's notice of a meeting with him. Instead, they declared through counsel that the Dean was acting illegally, and proceeded to occupy a University building again in another sit-in. On May 20, counsel for these students sent a telegram to Dean Platt reading in pertinent part as follows:

> The undersigned are attorneys for John Doe, in the criminal case brought upon complaint of Columbia University. John Doe has informed us that Columbia University has started disciplinary proceedings against him arising out of the same general set of facts and

has threatened that failure to appear before you on May —, 1968, will result in suspension.

Appearance before you as a representative of the same University that has brought the criminal charges against him would: 1) make a nullity of John Doe's constitutional rights and protections; 2) make Columbia University prosecutor in one instance and judge in another; 3) be contrary to common practice of staying administrative hearings pending disposition of criminal charges, and 4) be contrary to recognized concepts of fair play and justice.

In addition, while you refer to the Joint Committee's recommendation, at no time have you informed our client that the trespass charge against him will be dropped, which you know is the assumption upon which the Committee's recommendations are based.

For those reasons and at this time John Doe declines to testify before you at the time set forth in your letter.

At five P.M. on the following day, May 21, the last day for the appearances called for by the Dean's letters, the attorneys who had sent the quoted telegram met in person with the Dean and repeated orally what the telegram had said. Dean Platt stated that the students were required to appear in person; that the appearance of lawyers *instead* of them was not acceptable; and that failure to appear, as the letters warned, would lead to suspension. Plaintiff Grossner and the others persevered in their refusals and were suspended for this.

In the meantime, while counsel were explaining on May 21 to Dean Platt why the procedures formulated by the Joint Committee could be blocked and ignored in their inception, the four named students and others were demonstrating on the campus, publicizing their activity in handbills as a "Discipline the Deans Rally." This activity began outdoors. Then Rudd and others proceeded once more to Hamilton Hall to conduct another sit-in. Demands and requests that they depart voluntarily were unavailing. In the night of May 21–22, the police were called again, the occupants were ousted, and arrests were made of 75 University students, a few former students, some Barnard and Teachers College students, and 38 outsiders unaffiliated with the University.

When the night was over, it was found that a professor's irreplaceable research papers, representing years of work, had been removed from his Hamilton Hall office and burned in a nearby room.*

---

* Plaintiff Rothschild finds it appropriate to assert in his affidavit "on information and belief that it was not persons supporting or sympathizing with the student protests who were responsible for the destruction of the papers of Professor Ranum, or for the fires or other acts of vandalism on the night of May 21–22, 1968, an allegation also denied publicly by various members of the Strike Coordinating Committee." Similarly, his affidavit goes on to say: "It is a matter of public record that numerous undercover agents, *agents provocateurs,* and various other persons opposed to the actions of the student protestors have nevertheless participated in the protests for the purpose of embarrassing and undermining them; the arrest of Rudd, a member of a class of plaintiffs, for instance, was effectuated by an undercover agent posing as a student striker."

The parties go on to describe other acts of violence and destruction, with disputes about the details and the blame, but it seems unnecessary for present purposes to pursue further the sorrowful accounts. Enough has been recounted to give the setting in which plaintiffs now move for a preliminary injunction, the sweep of which is best described in their own terms. The prayer of the motion is:

1. For a preliminary injunction enjoining and restraining the defendants from taking any disciplinary action and from instituting disciplinary proceedings, including but not limited to expulsion, probation, and the making of any notation in any school records of the names or other identifying symbols of plaintiffs and members of their classes pursuant to Section 352 of Chapter XXXV of the Statutes of Columbia University, or pursuant to any other University rule, regulation, or procedure, or pursuant to the recommendations of the Joint Committee on Disciplinary Affairs, against plaintiffs and members of their classes, for their alleged activities on the Columbia Campus set forth in plaintiffs' complaint, on the grounds that such disciplinary action and/or hearings constitute a violation of plaintiffs' First, Fifth and Fourteenth Amendment rights under the United States Constitution;

2. For a preliminary mandatory injunction ordering and requiring defendants to immediately revoke the suspension of and to reinstate Morris Grossner, Mark Rudd, Nicholas Freudenberg and Edward Hyman as students in good standing at Columbia University;

Such injunctions to run until such time that all criminal cases now pending in the Courts of the State of New York against plaintiffs and members of their classes are disposed or (*sic*) or until further order of this court. . . .

III

(1–4) Our highest Court has made clear in the labors of a long generation that the First Amendment's mandate protecting free expression "must be taken as a command of the broadest scope that explicit language, read in the context of a liberty-loving society, will allow." . . . The Court has insisted steadily on the "principle that debate on public issues should be uninhibited, robust, and wide-open. . . ." It has also made clear, however, the gross error of believing that every kind of conduct (however nonverbal and physically destructive or obstructive) must be treated simply as protected "speech" because those engaged in it intend to express some view or position. . . . Similarly, the Court has rejected the notion that "everyone with opinions or beliefs to express may do so at any time and at any place." . . . Without such inescapably necessary limits, the First Amendment would be a self-destroying license for "peaceful" "expression" by the seizure of streets, buildings and offices by mobs, large or small, driven by motives (and toward objectives) that different viewers might deem "good or bad." . . . It is such a license plaintiffs claim when they state the basic premise of their lawsuit as follows:

> Plaintiffs maintain, consistent with the American tradition of democratic and legal confrontation, that the nonviolent occupation of five buildings of Columbia University for less than one week in the circumstances of this case is fully protected by the First Amendment guarantees of the right to petition government for the redress of grievances, . . . to assemble and to speak. Plaintiffs maintain that the nonviolent occupation of the buildings was absolutely necessary to breathe life into the First Amendment principle that government institutions should reflect the will of the people and that this interest must prevail under any balancing test against the inconvenience to defendant Columbia University in having five of its buildings occupied by students for approximately one week.

Embellishing such untenable propositions, plaintiffs (or, more fairly, the sixteen attorneys who sign their brief) proceed to argue that the rhetoric and the tactics of the American Revolution are the guides by which judges are to construe the First Amendment. The "rule of law," they explain, must not be overrated: "Had the Americans agreed that the rule of law, however despotic, must always prevail; had the Americans felt that dropping the tea in the harbor was going too far; had the Americans not focused on fundamental principles, this country might still be a colony today." The message, insofar as it is intelligible, possibly means that a tea party today, if nothing else could achieve repeal of a hated tax, would be protected by the First Amendment. Or possibly it means something else. Whatever it is meant to mean, and whatever virtues somebody might think such ideas might have in other forums, arguments like this are at best useless (at worst deeply pernicious) nonsense in courts of law. See Fortas, Concerning Dissent and Civil Disobedience 34 (1968); and see *id.* at 15, 18, 30, 46–47, 62–63.

It is surely non-sense of the most literal kind to argue that a court of law should subordinate the "rule of law" in favor of more "fundamental principles" of revolutionary action designed forcibly to oust governments, courts and all. But this self-contradictory sort of theory— all decked out in the forms of law with thick papers, strings of precedent, and the rest—is ultimately at the heart of plaintiffs' case. And so it is not surprising that plaintiffs' efforts to implement the theory have led them to champion a series of propositions of unsound constitutional law.

Specifically, the pending motion for a preliminary injunction is doomed, *first,* because it fails the threshold test of showing jurisdiction in this court to enjoin the University's disciplinary proceedings, and, *second,* because even if there were jurisdiction, there would be no basis on the merits for awarding such relief.

* * *

(5) As it affects all or most of the claims in the complaint, and all of the temporary injunctive relief sought on the pending motion, the question is whether the disputed actions or proceedings by Columbia University or its officials should be deemed to be "state action" in the pertinent sense. Plaintiffs recognize, of course, that the University is no part of state "government" in any general or formal sense. They urge, however, that it "is so impressed with a public interest as to render it amenable to the reach of the Fourteenth Amendment and therefore to the protection afforded by that Amendment to the rights guaranteed in the First and Fifth Amendments." And they rely upon the now settled, but not always simply applied, principle that "private" conduct, normally outside the Fourteenth Amendment, may be controlled by that Amendment when "to some significant extent the State in any of its manifestations has been found to have become involved. . . ."

To show state "involvement," plaintiffs point out that a large percentage of the University's income comes from public funds—some $49,500,000 in 1966 out of a total of $117,500,000 and, in 1967, about $59,700,000 of a total of $134,300,000. The government monies, plaintiffs add, reflect in considerable measure the performance of research for, and the rendition of other forms of assistance to, the Federal Government, including agencies like Central Intelligence, Defense, and the Space Administration. There are, plaintiffs say, other forms of governmental "benefits" and "assistance" to the University, and they specify in this connection a lease by New York City of public land for construction of the controversial gymnasium. Finally, apart from specific research projects and similar activities, plaintiffs would have the court hold that the University is in the very nature of its functioning "so impregnated with a governmental character as to become subject to the constitutional limitations upon state action."

* * *

(6) A more fundamental point against plaintiffs is that receipt of money from the State is not, without a good deal more, enough to make the recipient an agency or instrumentality of the Government. Otherwise, all kinds of contractors and enterprises, increasingly dependent upon government business for much larger proportions of income than those here in question, would find themselves charged with "state action" in the performance of all kinds of functions we still consider and treat as essentially "private" for all presently relevant purposes. . . .

2. The serious inquiry is not into the source of the "private" person's or organization's income, but into either or both of two subjects (which are not necessarily separate and distinct from each other) :

(a) How far are the State and the formally "private" agency truly independent of each other, or, what amounts to the same thing, how far has the State so "insinuated itself into a position of interdependence . . . that it must be recognized as a joint participant in the challenged activity?" . . .

(b) To what extent, if at all, is the University engaged in "state action" because, as plaintiffs argue, it "fulfills a public function of educating persons?"

On both of these questions, which are considered by the court to point toward the genuinely material area, plaintiffs' thesis fails.

(7) a. There is nothing, even in the somewhat baroque rhetoric of plaintiffs' affidavits and memoranda, to suggest any substantial or relevant degree of interconnection between the State and the University. There is a good deal of talk about the University's large and (it is more than implied) sinister work for the military, diplomatic, and intelligence agencies of the Federal Government. But, as has been noted already, that is no basis for the claim of state action upon which plaintiffs must proceed.

(8) What is still more striking is the total absence of any indication that the State (or any government) is involved as a participant in the University disciplinary proceedings to which the motion for a preliminary injunction is directed.

* * *

(9) b. Plaintiffs' remaining thought—that Columbia performs a "public function" in "educating persons" which may be "likened to a 'company town' or a party primary system"—is, briefly, without any basis. It is not sounder for Columbia than it would be for Notre Dame or Yeshiva. Of course, plaintiffs are corrected in a trivial way when they say education is "impressed with a public interest." Many things are. And it may even be that action in some context or other by such a University as Columbia would be subject to limitations like those confining the State. But nothing supports the thesis that university (or private elementary) "education" as such is "state action." . . .

While considerations of legal logic have made jurisdiction the first subject for discussion, the weakness of plaintiffs' case is still clearer in its substantive aspects. Thus, even if there were (or is) jurisdiction, the motion for a temporary injunction would have to be denied.

1. As has been noted, the core theory of the suit is that plaintiffs (or those they purport to represent) had a "right" under the First Amendment to occupy the University buildings, including the President's office, and "nonviolently" to imprison a Dean "to dramatize to the University their views and positions concerning fundamental problems affecting their society." From this they reason that anything which would inhibit or "chill" this enterprise offends the Constitution. As has also been noted, this supposed axiom is wrong. . . .

(10) Mistaken in their first premise, plaintiffs also fail in their effort to show that the disciplinary proceedings against them are groundless. . . .

(11) 2. Another point argued at length, and totally devoid of substance, is that failure to enjoin the disciplinary proceedings will somehow infringe the privilege against self-incrimination. In the name of the privilege, plaintiffs claim that any student called for a meeting by a Dean concerning the events of April 23–30 (and warned that unexcused failure to turn up will result in suspension) has the right to thumb his note at the Dean. To enforce this right, it is argued, the federal court should forbid the suspension of any student and bar any further disciplinary proceedings until the pending criminal charges are finally adjudicated in the state courts. Plaintiffs tender a whole series of errors to support this line of argument.

The basic error appeared at the outset (and has been pressed throughout) when plaintiffs' attorneys sent telegrams to the various Deans explaining that it was unconstitutional to require anybody to appear and "testify." It is not disputed (though plaintiffs choose to ignore) that neither the appearance before the Dean nor any other step in the prescribed procedures was an occasion for compelled testimony (or for any adverse inference from silence). The case is clearest with respect to the meeting with the Dean. The student was not expected on this occasion to do more than appear and signify whether further steps in the disciplinary procedures would be required. He could stand mute or plead not guilty, in which case reference to the hearing tribunal was the next step. Or he could admit the charge (a step not unknown even in criminal courts), ending the proceeding at that stage. Nothing in the Fifth or any other Amendment supports plaintiffs' contention that they (and every other student sent a notice) had a right to nullify the disciplinary procedures simply by announcing that they would not appear even to "plead" to the charges.

Perhaps the clearest fallacy in the argument concerning the privilege against self-incrimination is the idea, as it is expressed in the prayer for injunctive relief, that this privilege could somehow justify a blanket order "restraining the defendants from taking any disciplinary proceedings" against any of hundreds of individual students in the unknown circumstances of their varying cases. This thought is said to rest upon the ground that the disciplinary charges and the pending criminal prosecutions rest "on the same set of facts." Though this is said in an affidavit of counsel, it not only remains to be demonstrated separately in the hundreds of cases; it is also shown to be probably inaccurate in one of the four specific cases presented with comparative concreteness in the motion papers.

The case in question, mentioned earlier, is the odd one of the student Rudd. His notice from the Dean, concerned with the period April 23–30, was sent on May 16. He was arrested and charged for seemingly separate activities on May 17. It is at least not certain in advance that the charges by the school relate to "the same set of facts" as do those by the State. It may be, of course, that if Rudd's University proceeding had gone to a hearing, valid claims of privilege might have arisen; testimony relating to April 23–30 might conceivably have supplied "a link in the chain of evidence" . . . affecting events of May 17. Or, since the Joint Committee had concluded that the student "should not be required to give evidence against himself," no question might ever have been presented if Rudd had decided simply to remain silent. But all this must be speculative. The inevitability of such speculation is alone sufficient to show plaintiffs' error in supporting that they may block the disciplinary proceedings in advance and across the board because some students in some specific cases might at some future point have a valid privilege of silence. The error is only made more vivid by the citation of cases which sustained particular claims of privilege in response to particular questions put to witnesses who had appeared, not refused to appear.

* * *

(14) 4. Plaintiffs devote many pages to a misconceived argument that the students facing school disciplinary charges are being deprived of substantial due process because Chapter XXXV, §352, of the University's Statutes is vague and overbroad. This general provision, of ancient vintage, provides:

> The continuance of each student upon the rolls of the University, the receipt by him of academic credits, his graduation, and the conferring of any degree or the granting of any certificate, shall be subject to the disciplinary powers of the University which shall be free to cancel his registration at any time on any grounds it deems advisable.

The quoted statute is, indeed, sweeping in its terms. But the several gross flaws in plaintiffs' argument include the sufficient answer that the students are not being "prosecuted" under this general provision.

* * *

(15,16) (a) Viewed generally, in advance of any specific problems that might arise in specific cases, the prescribed procedures, sufficiently sketched above, seem entirely fair and amply protective of student rights. They are not required, obviously, to duplicate the criminal trial process. Bearing in mind that the process which is "due" may vary with the nature of the subject and the occasion . . . the court perceives no valid basis whatever for the abstract criticisms plaintiffs tender.

(17) (b) The vice of abstractness is itself a separate ground for dismissing the arguments concerning procedural due process. Plaintiffs chose not to appear even at the step preceding the hearing process, but

they now find a variety of objectionable things in that untried process. There was no occasion to test, and no opportunity to cure in concrete terms, the flaws they claim to discern. So, for example, had plaintiffs presented in an actual case their assertion that the hearing rules unduly circumscribed the participation of counsel, the hearing tribunal might have obviated the problem by construing differently, or choosing to relax, the specific item of alleged restriction. What the court may not and will not countenance is the proposition that procedures plaintiffs decided unilaterally to nullify—procedures obviously designed in an earnest effort to assure fundamental fairness—must be condemned out of hand as basically and inevitably deficient.

*　*　*

As to plaintiffs' motion for a preliminary injunction, it is, for reasons stated above, in all respects denied. So ordered.

5
Dismissal (Public Institutions)

Miller v. *Dailey*
136 Cal. 212 (68 P. 1029)
April 4, 1902

CHIPMAN, C.

A writ of mandate was asked by plaintiff to compel defendants to admit him to the state normal school at San Jose, and to permit him to enjoy the privileges thereof as a student. The writ was granted, and defendants appeal from the judgment.

The action is brought against defendant Dailey, as president, and all the teachers, constituting the faculty of said normal school. Among other defenses, defendants set forth in their answer, as authority for their action, a resolution passed on September 21, 1899, by the local board of trustees of said school, which is as follows: "Resolved, that the faculty of this state normal school is hereby directed to drop any student who, by reason of poor scholarship, bad character, or evident unfitness for teaching, is disqualified to become a teacher." The court found that plaintiff entered the school in 1895, and was duly readmitted February 25, 1899, as alleged, with all the rights and privileges common to students therein; that he conformed to all the rules and regulations adopted for the government of the school, and continued to be such student until September 4, 1900 . . . that plaintiff was not permitted to complete the course of practice teaching as prescribed by the rules of the school; that said board of trustees had no authority to pass the resolution set forth in the answer, and "the said resolution is unreasonable, oppressive, and deprives the said Miller of his legal rights to attend said school in an arbitrary manner."

* * *

4. It is urged that the resolution set out in the findings and in the answer is a reasonable and valid regulation, and that the board had the

power to make it, and that plaintiff was rightfully dropped from the rolls under the resolution. Section 1489 gives the local board power "to prescribe rules for their government and the government of the school." The statute gives to the joint board the power to prescribe a uniform series of textbooks "for use in the grades and classes for which they are adopted"; to prescribe a uniform course of study and time and standard for graduation; to prescribe also a uniform standard of admission for students; and also to pass "general regulations that may be applied to all the state normal schools, thus affecting their well-being." Section 1492. No claim is made by appellants that plaintiff was denied the privilege of attendance because he had violated or come short of any regulation of the joint board. The local board can make no written or oral rules under the powers given to the joint board. They can make only such regulations as may reasonably be said to be "rules for their government and the government of the school" not inconsistent with the specific powers given the joint board. The studies to be pursued, the standard of admission, the time and standard for graduation, are all matters the regulation of which is devolved on the joint board. The local board cannot set up an arbitrary standard of its own, either as to the standard of admission, the studies to be pursued, or the time or standard for graduation, for these powers are conferred on the joint board. The purpose of the law is to secure uniformity in all the schools, so far as possible, in these matters, and to prevent different standards of proficiency in the different schools. The entire evidence in the case is not before us, but from what we have it appears that plaintiff had "passed" and had "a record in everything except practice teaching." As to this branch of studies the evidence is that "the regular course in practice teaching is twenty weeks—five months"; that "a good many students who fail in the subject take it more than once, and sometimes more than twice." One of the teachers testified that "five weeks is the usual time for us to judge whether a teacher is failing or not. We pass judgment at the end of five weeks, and final judgment at the end of ten weeks (one-half the time allowed to this branch of studies). If the work isn't successfully done, for the children's sake we take the class away from the teacher, and sometimes we give the student another class." The court found that plaintiff had made no failures in the subject of practice teaching, and that it is not true that he will never attain such degree of proficiency in the subject as will warrant the faculty in refusing to recommend him as worthy to receive a diploma; and it was further found that he was not permitted to complete the course of practice teaching prescribed by the regulations of the school. It is manifest that the teachers cut plaintiff off from the privileges of the school under the authority given them by the resolution passed by the local board on the assumption that they could, by their arbitrary will, decide him to be "disqualified to become a teacher," and dismiss him from the school, even though he had passed in all branches except practice teaching, and had never failed in his examinations in the subject of practice teaching although he had not completed the time given to it. In this, we think, the teachers exceeded their power, and deprived plaintiff of a right given him by the statute. What has been said is not to be understood as holding that the board could be compelled to grant plaintiff a diploma in the face of the teachers' reports showing lack of proficiency or other facts from which it would be evident that he was unfit to become a teacher. The question of plaintiff's right now or hereafter to a diploma is in no sense involved. He asks only to be permitted to enjoy the right given him by the law to pursue his studies in the school, and this much, we think, may be secured to him by the writ. We do not think it within the power of the teachers to anticipate the result of the final examination, and exclude a student from the privileges of the school at any time they may elect to do so, simply because in their judgment he will never make a successful teacher.

Woody v. *Burns*
Fla., 188 So.2d 56
June 21, 1966

RAWLS, Chief Judge

Oscar Woody, Jr. has appealed from an order of the circuit court quashing an alternative writ of mandamus by which the appellant was seeking an order requiring the University of Florida to admit him to the College of Architecture and Fine Arts.

Woody was admitted to the University of Florida as a junior, but on January 3, 1963, he was prevented from reregistering when he voluntarily disclosed that during the preceding trimester he had not taken the Art 207 course as he had been instructed to do by his department head and student advisor, Professor Grissom, who had refused to accept a Pensacola Junior College course as a substitute for the required Art 207. For this offense Woody was charged with altering a "basic record of the university; that is, the course assignment card, without prior permission of Professor Grissom." The charge was heard by the Faculty Discipline Committee. Woody was present and testified that at his request the card was altered by Professor Ward, the faculty member who was authorized to make course changes during registration. On January 14, 1963, the Committee by split decision with the chairman casting the deciding vote found that "Mr. Woody was not proven guilty of physically altering the Course Assignment Card . . . [but was] guilty of conduct unbecoming a University of Florida student in that he did knowingly cause a university record to be altered against the stated wishes of his Department Head." The Committee recommended to Dr. J. Wayne Reitz, President of the University of Florida, that Woody be placed on disciplinary probation for the remainder of his undergraduate career, which recommendation was approved.

The Faculty Discipline Committee's decision was not appealed, but two days after rendition of same Woody petitioned to register late. This petition was acted upon and denied by the faculty committee of the College of Architecture and Fine Arts without granting notice and hearing to Oscar Woody. Woody remained out of school for the remainder of the trimester, but applied for enrollment at the commencement of the next succeeding trimester. This application was summarily denied by the University officials without notice or hearing. The matter was eventually brought before Dr. Reitz, who informed Woody's attorney that the faculty committee took the position that Woody's failure to take Art 207 constituted a defiance of the college requirements and resulted in his disqualifying himself from further attendance in the college due to failure to maintain a satisfactory academic record. In affirming the committee's decision Dr. Reitz noted that the committee's action was influenced by the report of both departments that his conduct and behavior had created a disturbing influence in classes and his defiance of regulations and lack of cooperation had been demonstrated in situations prior to the incident relating to failure to register for Art 207. Thus, the faculty committee for the College of Architecture and Fine Arts, when considering Woody's petition to register late, went beyond the question presented and expelled him permanently from that college. It made that decision without notice and hearing, and based same upon incidents which are not matters of record and upon which the student had never been given an opportunity to be heard.

In due course the matter was appealed to the Board of Regents. The hearing held by the Board was attended by Woody and his counsel who presented evidence showing that Woody had maintained a "B" average at the University. The Board further heard the argument of Dr. Reitz to the effect that the faculty of the College of Architecture & Fine Arts "did not wish Mr. Woody to continue as a student in that college" and that according to accepted university administration principles the faculty has the right to admit or exclude any student from its program because in awarding degrees it places its stamp of approval and recommendation on the individual. The Board affirmed the decision of the President to deny Woody further enrollment in the College of Architecture and Fine Arts *without prejudice to apply for enrollment in the other colleges of the University.* This decision was subsequently affirmed by the State Board of Education, and Oscar

Woody, Jr. filed his alternative writ of mandamus seeking to compel his admission for the following trimester. The alternative writ was quashed by the trial judge and this appeal followed.

The only point posed by this appeal is, Has ample administrative due process of law been afforded a student excluded from a state-supported institution of higher learning, when such exclusion results from an ex parte order of university officials issued as a result of a hearing held without an opportunity being afforded the student to defend himself against charges of misconduct?

At the outset we note that the decision of the faculty committee of the College of Architecture and Fine Arts is tantamount to expulsion. It was based solely upon misconduct and not upon failure to maintain the required academic standard. The decision for exclusion was made without notice and hearing to Appellant, was based upon matters concerning which he had never had an opportunity to be heard, and in spite of these deficiencies it was approved by the President of the University, the Board of Regents, and the State Board of Education.

(1–3) It has been held that constitutional due process requires notice and opportunity for hearing before a student at a tax-supported college or university can be expelled for misconduct. This court is compelled to follow these decisions, the basis of which is that a charge of misconduct, as opposed to failure to meet the scholastic standards of the college, depends upon a collection of the facts which are easily colored by the point of view of the witness. The minimum criteria of due process governing disciplinary bodies of tax-supported institutions are set forth in *Due v. Florida A. & M. University.** Briefly they include: 1. Notice containing a statement of the specific charges and grounds which if proven would justify expulsion under duly established regulations, 2. A hearing which gives the disciplinary body opportunity to hear both sides in considerable detail and allows the student to produce his own defense either by oral testimony or written affidavits of witnesses, 3. The action to be taken only by an authorized duly established disciplinary body organized and operated by well-defined procedures, and 4. The results and findings of the hearing to be presented in a report open to the student's inspection. Not one of these four elements is present here. This court adopts the views set forth in *Due,* supra, and reiterates that a full-dress judicial hearing is not required. However the principles of fair play require that before a student may be denied the right to continue his studies at a state-supported university due to misconduct he shall be advised of all the charges against him and be given an opportunity to refute same. When these requirements are met, the judgment of a duly constituted disciplinary committee functioning in a normal manner by well-defined procedures will not be lightly

---

* *Due* v. *Florida A. & M. University.* [233 F.Supp. 396]

disturbed although it is not required to operate by a system of rigid procedure.

(4) Unlike the Due case, the action here is invalid on its face not only because Appellant was never confronted with the charges against him and was not given an opportunity to present has case before the committee that excluded him, but also because the faculty committee, instead of bringing open charges of misconduct in the usual manner before the disciplinary committee, circumvented that duly authorized committee and arrogated unto itself the authority of imposing its own penalty for Appellant's misconduct. In this respect the 1962–1963 University of Florida catalog charges each college with the responsibility of enforcing only its *academic standards,* in the following words:

> Any college of the University may enforce additional *academic* standards and each student is responsible to his college for observing the regulations relating to such additional standards [emphasis supplied].

(5–7) Those charged with the administration of the state's institutions of higher learning are vested with broad discretion in determining the scholastic and moral standards students must meet to obtain admission to the various colleges of the university system. They likewise must determine the standard of behavior necessary to maintain discipline and general good conduct of the members of the student body as is essential to preserve high public regard for the graduates and alumni of our state-supported universities and to properly utilize the facilities and services which the universities are intended to provide. However here the essence of the decision ordering exclusion is that Appellant's conduct and behavior were of a standard which would not preclude his attendance at the University of Florida, but was such as would exclude his attendance in the College of Architecture and Fine Arts solely because the faculty of that college "did not wish Mr. Woody to continue as a student." There was no determination that Appellant's conduct did not meet the behavior standard required of University of Florida students as set by those who are authorized to exercise their discretion in determining what shall be considered unacceptable conduct warranting expulsion. Appellant's conduct relative to his failure to register in the appropriate courses was determined by the duly constituted Discipline Committee by a split vote to warrant only probation.

The University of Florida is not the private property of those employed by the citizens of this state to perform the responsibility of providing a program of higher education primarily for the students of this state. This record presents an incongruous situation wherein the University of Florida says this student's conduct is not acceptable to the faculty members of one college but that the same conduct does not make him ineligible for acceptance by other colleges of the university complex. We are not aware of the delegation by the legislature or the State Board of Education or the Board of Regents to the faculty members of any college of the higher education system of this state to arbitrarily or capriciously decide whom they desire to teach, and should such delegation be attempted it would amount to creating a hierarchy contrary to all of the fundamental concepts of a democratic society. This is not to say that those charged with the responsibility of operating our universities are not responsible for establishing basic standards of conduct and enforcing same on the campuses of our state-supported colleges and universities. On the contrary, it is their duty to take affirmative action to exclude from the student body those individuals not conforming to the established standards. However, the manner of enforcement must be by a duly authorized body in accordance with procedures which permit the student an opportunity to vindicate himself, if he can and so desires.

*   *   *

The judgment appealed is reversed. . . .

Hammond v. South Carolina State College
272 Fed. Supp. 947
Aug. 31, 1967
HEMPHILL, District Judge

Plaintiffs Hammond, Stroman and Bryant, Jr. seek protection of their individual and collective constitutional rights. On February 23, 1967, while enrolled as students in South Carolina State College in Orangeburg they "assembled themselves with numerous other students . . . upon the campus of said college . . . and expressed themselves . . . concerning certain practices then in existence at said college." On February 24, 1967, each received a communication from the Dean of Students which read:

> You are directed to meet the Faculty Discipline Committee in my office, Room 207, Mechanical Building, at 2:15 P.M. today, February 24, 1967, to answer charges that you were in violation of College regulations, specifically #1, under 4, page 49 of the Student Handbook which reads . . . The student body or any part of the student body is not to celebrate, parade, or demonstrate on the campus at any time without the approval of the Office of the President. The Board of Trustees meeting in March of 1960 went on record as disapproving of demonstrations which involve violation of laws or of

College regulations, or which disrupt the normal College routine.

Thereafter, as directed, they severally met with the Faculty Discipline Committee. After the meetings each plaintiff was advised:

Reference is made to the Discipline Committee hearing held in my office this afternoon on a report brought through the Office of the Dean of Students that you violated Rule 1, under 4, page 49 of the College Handbook by participating in a demonstration on campus without approval.

The Committee feels that it gave you ample opportunity to refute the charge, but your refusal to do so left it no alternative but to take action.

The Committee has instructed me to inform you that its decision is that you be indefinitely suspended from the College effective February 24, 1967, until August 1, 1970. On or after that date (August 1, 1970) you may reapply for admission, but readmission shall depend upon unanimous approval of the Discipline Committee in full session assembled.

In accordance with the suspension you are to remain away from the campus until the end of the suspension period.

A requested rehearing with the Faculty Discipline Committee was held on March 2, 1967, and they were advised that the suspension was to remain in effect but that each could apply for readmittance in August, 1967. Suit was commenced March 10, 1967. On March 15, 1967, plaintiffs filed Petition for a Temporary Restraining Order, and the same day this court ordered their readmittance pendente lite and ruled defendant to show cause why the suspensions should not be enjoined. . . .

(1) Defendant initially challenges the jurisdiction of this court. The issue is not seriously pressed. Plaintiffs complain that defendant has deprived them of their rights under the First Amendment to the Constitution of the United States, and have done so by virtue of the authority or color of office enjoyed by the administrators and faculty of defendant. Defendant is a state institution and its administrative personnel are vested with state authority. . . .

The facts whilch are not in dispute are essentially as follows.

On February 23, 1967, these three plaintiffs in the company of approximately three hundred others gathered together on the campus of the school to express their feelings regarding some of the school's practices.

This, they claim, they did in an orderly and peaceful fashion. The school, however, maintains that the plaintiffs were leaders of the demonstration and that it was noisy and disorderly.

The plaintiffs were unquestionably aware of the rule against unauthorized demonstrations. However, on February 21, 1967, the President of the institution had delivered a written report publicly assuring the students that no rule deprived them of the constitutional rights of free speech and of peaceable assembly.

According to their testimony to the Faculty Discipline Committee on that day, they received the notice only a matter of several hours prior to the meeting.

At the Discipline Committee hearing each of them objected to the notice given and refused to answer questions on the grounds that they desired the assistance of counsel. One felt that he might incriminate himself. They demanded to be confronted with their accusers and to be allowed to cross-examine them.

The Faculty Discipline Committee was not disposed to postpone the hearing to allow time for counsel nor was it disposed to allow confrontation and cross-examination of the witnesses. The plaintiffs, however, did establish that they were participants in an assembly and that in exercising the right to do so they would deny having violated Rule 1.

The same date all of the plaintiffs were notified as to their suspensions as set forth above.

The school's Board of Trustees had in March of 1960 passed the following resolution in the avowed interest of protecting the "students of this institution from violence and to preserve public peace and order."

Be It Resolved that hereafter any student at South Carolina State College who shall engage in any public demonstrations without prior approval of the College administration shall be summarily expelled.

The controversy here revolves around the school rules of deportment and discipline. Their obvious purpose is to protect the authority and administrative responsibility which is imposed on the officers of the institution. Unless the officials have authority to keep order, they have no power to guarantee education. If they cannot preserve order by rule and regulation, and insist on obedience to those rules, they will be helpless in the face of the mob, powerless to command or rebuke the fanatic, the irritant, the malingerer, the rabble rouser. To be sure, this is a tax-supported institution, but this does not give license to chaos, or the hope to create chaos. The majority of the taxpayers who established, through representative government, the institution, and all the taxpayers who support this institution, have a vested interest in a peaceful campus, an academic climate of order and culture. The power of the president to oversee, to rule, is an integral part of the mechanism for providing and promoting education at State College. Be that as it may, colleges, like all other institutions, are subject to the Constitution. Academic progress and academic freedom demand their share of Constitutional protection. Here we find a clash between the Rules of the school and the First Amendment to the Constitution of the United States.

(2, 3) The First Amendment does not speak equivocally. It prohibits any law "abridging the freedom of speech, or of the press. It must be taken as a command of the broadest scope that explicit language, read in the context of a liberty-loving society, will allow." . . . These rights of the First Amendment, including the right to peaceably assemble, are not to be restricted except upon the showing of a clear and present danger, of riot, disorder, or immediate threat to public safety, peace, or order. . . . "Only the gravest abuses, endangering paramount interests, give occasion for permissible limitation." . . . Conduct which involves activities such as picketing and marching, however, is a departure from the exercise of the rights in pristine form and it does not receive the same degree of freedom. . . . It has been argued to me that Rule 1 of the Student Handbook as it is written is a previous restraint upon these rights and as such it is unlawful and must be struck down as being "incompatible with the guaranties of the first amendment." . . . I am persuaded that Rule 1 is on its face a prior restraint on the right to freedom to speech and the right to assemble. The rule does not purport to prohibit assemblies which have qualities that are unacceptable to responsible standards of conduct: it prohibits "parades, celebrations, and demonstrations" without prior approval without any regard to limiting its proscription to assemblies involving misconduct or disruption of government activities or nonpeaceable gatherings. On this ground I do not feel that it is necessary to make a finding as to the nature of the demonstration. It was alleged by the defendant that the students were suspended not under Rule 1 but under Rule 4, presumably a rule covering misconduct. It may well be that the conduct of these students would have warranted disciplinary action under some disciplinary rule such as Rule 4* but in point of fact they were not suspended under Rule 4. They were charged under Rule 1, they were given hearings under Rule 1, and they were suspended under Rule 1.

In no way is it my intention to rule that school officials may not make disciplinary rules and enforce them. Most certainly they may. I am constrained to rule, however, that the rule under which these students were suspended was incompatible with the constitutional guaranties and is invalid.

The defendant has argued that it, no less than a private citizen, has

---

* For instance, rule 13 provides: Students are expected to conduct themselves as ladies and gentlemen at all times. Boisterousness, profanity, insubordination, unkempt appearances, and any other undesirable quality will not be tolerated and is not expected of students at the College.

the right to control the use of its property, and that . . . no one has the right to demonstrate at any time at any place he may choose. The campus, under this argument, being dedicated to scholarship and learning would be likened to a hospital or the jail entrance . . . and prohibiting demonstrations would, similarly, not infringe any constitutional rights. In principle the argument is unassailable; however, it does not apply to this case. The rule broadly brings the entire campus of a state college within its ambit . . . that assembling at the site of government for peaceful expression of grievances constituted exercise of First Amendment rights in their pristine form. I am not persuaded that the campus of a state college is not similarly available for the same purposes for its students.

Therefore . . . I find that the suspension of the students was unlawful and cannot be given effect. This, of course, does not mean that the school may not institute proper disciplinary proceedings against the students for lack of [proper] deportment and violations of other appropriate disciplinary regulations.

I therefore order that the defendants be permanently enjoined from enforcing the decisions of the Faculty Discipline Committee which dismissed these plaintiffs for breach of Rule 1 of Part 4 of the Student Handbook.

And it is so ordered.

Reichenberg v. *Nelson*
310 Fed. Supp. 248
1970

VAN PELT, District Judge

Robert E. Reichenberg, Jr. brought this action on January 21, 1970, to prevent the defendant, Dr. Edwin Nelson, who is President of Chadron State College, from denying him registration at the College for the second semester. He claims he was denied registration on January 20th because his hair and moustache failed to meet the requirements of the College dress code. . . .

A hearing was had upon an application for a restraining order, at which time arrangements were made for plaintiff to attend classes awaiting a hearing on the merits. The parties agreed to an early hearing, which the court set for February 9, 1970. Following the two-day hearing, at which evidence was offered by both parties, the court announced its findings and ordered that plaintiff and two other students be permitted to register. This memorandum will constitute the findings of fact and conclusions of law of the court.

Plaintiff, age 24, is a citizen of the State of Nebraska. He is a veteran of the United States Armed Forces. He entered Chadron State College under the provisions of the G.I. Bill in September 1969, and completed the first semester satisfactorily. His grades were slightly above average.

On September 18, 1969, a dress code for students at Chadron State College was adopted. This code included a provision reading:

> MALE STUDENTS must be clean shaven (*neat* mustaches and side burns excepted) and must not wear long hair. [emphasis in original]

During the week of January 9 to 16 of 1970, a clarification of the code was adopted. The changes here relevant provide:

> Male students will wear their hair short enough that eyebrows, ears, and collars are in full view. Sideburns will be no lower than the ear lobe, and mustaches will be trimmed even with the mouth. ALL MEN REGISTERING FOR SECOND SEMESTER CLASSES WILL BE EXPECTED TO MEET THE ABOVE STANDARDS.

It should be noted that it is not entirely clear where this clarification originated. There are groups within the campus structure which act in the area of student affairs. These groups include the Student Senate, Faculty Senate, and the Campus Affairs Committee. It would appear from the evidence that the January clarification was recommended by the Campus Affairs Committee and later approved by Dr. Nelson.

The procedural genesis of the regulation is not determinative of this case. It is clear from the evidence that the above-noted committees act solely in an advisory capacity. Dr. Nelson, as President of the College, has the ultimate authority, and he may accept, reject, or modify a code such as we have here. All appeals from enforcement of the code are subject to final administrative review by him.

Plaintiff, as above noted, was a student in good standing at Chadron the first semester of the 1969–70 academic year. No disciplinary action was taken against him and he was not cited for any violation of the dress code as it then existed. Plaintiff had a moustache and sideburns at the time he enrolled at the College. Photographs introduced into evidence indicate that the moustache plaintiff is presently wearing is substantially similar to his moustache when he enrolled in September. His sideburns were shorter at that time. . . . A photograph of Reichenberg which appeared in the college newspaper of January 9, 1970, shows his appearance to be substantially the same at that time as when he appeared at the trial.

In preparing to register for the second semester, plaintiff anticipated trouble in registering in that his sideburns did extend below the ear lobe and his moustache extended below the corners of his mouth. Plaintiff, with three others, met with Dr. Nelson on Sunday, January 18, 1970, and requested him not to refuse registration to those who did not comply with the so-called clarification. Registration was to take place on January 19 and 20. They also requested that Dr. Nelson address an assembly of students on the subject. Dr. Nelson refused both requests.

On January 20th plaintiff presented himself for registration for the second semester and was turned away by Donald Duncan, the Director of Housing for the College, who told him he could not register until he trimmed his moustache and hair. Plaintiff then filed this suit.

(1, 2) The statute relied on by plaintiff provides:

Every person who, under color of any statute, ordinance, regulation, custom, or usage, of any State or Territory, subjects, or causes to be subjected, any citizen of the United States or other person within the jurisdiction thereof, to the deprivation of any rights, privileges, or immunities secured by the Constitution and laws, shall be liable to the party injured in an action at law, suit in equity, or other proper proceeding for redress.

This statute, of course, provides the basis for a substantive claim for an individual so injured.

* * *

(5, 6) This leads to consideration of the merits of the case. Courts are reluctant to interfere with the relationship existing between student and administrator within the school system unless conflicts arise which "directly and sharply implicate basic constitutional values." . . . However, it is also clear that students do not leave fundamental rights on the school doorstep as they enter. . . . Therefore, when the state, acting through its public schools, abridges or limits a right guaranteed to the individual by the Constitution, it bears a substantial burden of justification. . . .

This is not the first court to consider a case brought by a student who has been refused admission to a public school because hair was too long. In fact, numerous courts have ruled in this area. . . .

(7) The state of the law as it exists today is fairly summarized by Judge Kerner of the Seventh Circuit in Breen v. Kahl, supra.

The right to wear one's hair at any length or in any desired manner is an ingredient of personal freedom protected by the United States Constitution. [citations omitted] Whether this is right is designated as within the "penumbras" of the first amendment freedom of speech . . . or as encompassed within the ninth amendment as "additional fundamental rights . . . which exist alongside those fundamental rights specifically mentioned in the first eight amendments" . . . it clearly exists and is applicable to the states through the due process clause of the fourteenth amendment.

To limit or curtail this or any other fundamental right, the state has a "substantial burden of justification."

At the close of the plaintiff's testimony, defendant moved for summary judgment, claiming that Reichenberg had failed to establish that he had been excluded from registration at Chadron State College. The motion was overruled and this position is here reaffirmed. Plaintiffs Reichenberg, Streep and Hume were each refused admission to the college. Such refusal was solely by reason of their noncompliance with the January 9 clarification of the dress code.

Before proceeding to the question of justification of the regulation, it is necessary to comment briefly on one issue raised by the defendant in this case. Defendant argues that attendance at Chadron State College is not a right but a privilege, and that if attendance is not a right, then refusal on the part of the College to admit a student does not violate any federally protected right and the student cannot maintain a suit such as this.

(7) The court finds this argument to be without merit. We are concerned here with the right of a student to wear his hair as he desires. Even assuming attendance at Chadron State College is a privilege, the College cannot refuse entrance to one in all other respects qualified because he chooses to exercise his constitutional rights. . . .

Thus we turn to the question as framed by Judge Hanson in *Sims* v. *Colfax Community School District,* supra:

> School hair rules are reasonable thus constitutional only if the school can objectively show that such a rule does in fact prevent some disruption or interference of the school system.

In the court's comments from the bench at the conclusion of the trial, it was noted that the burden is upon the state officials to show the reasonableness of the hair regulation. It was pointed out that this burden, as heretofore mentioned, is substantial.

The evidence is conclusive, and the court finds, that there has been no disruption of classes at Chadron State College by virtue of individuals with long hair being in attendance. Dr. Nelson testified that a moustache or long hair, limited perhaps to moustaches and hair of the length worn by the three here involved, presents no health or safety danger. It must be pointed out, as the court did orally, that this is not the usual long-hair case. The hair is not shoulder length. No claim was made that the eyebrows, ears or collars were not in full view.

The testimony that was offered in justification of the hair length regulation may be fairly summarized as follows:

1. Students whose appearances conform to the regulation perform better in school, both in strictly academic work and in extra-curricular activity, than those whose appearances do not conform.
2. Presently Chadron graduates are highly sought after as teachers in the state. If students are allowed to attend the College wearing hair or moustaches in violation of the regulations, this will reflect adversely upon the College and thus on future graduates.
3. There are difficulties in placing students with hair and moustaches in violation of the regulation in student teaching positions as area high schools are reluctant to accept them.
4. Students conforming to the regulation will have an easier time finding a job upon graduation than those who do not conform.

The first contention, that people with long hair and moustaches do not perform as well as those with short hair, was supported by the testimony of Dr. Bruce Bartels, a Chadron College official. No empirical data or studies were introduced to this effect. It is, rather, the opinion of Dr. Bartels. Without being critical of Dr. Bartels, we note that he has been associated with Chadron College for a period of eight years, during which time a dress code was in effect. Thus, he has had little opportunity to observe the comparative performance of conforming versus nonconforming students. He could not refer to any studies supporting his conclusion. When questioned concerning the particular dress clarification in question, he was unable to state that a moustache such as the plaintiff's, which extended below the corner of the mouth, would be more detrimental to the performance of academic work than a moustache which was even with the corner of the mouth. This claim is not supported. Chadron is the only one of the four similar state colleges in Nebraska which has such a rule. The court has observed and been connected with college education in Nebraska for many years and cannot conclude that Chadron stands above Peru, Kearney or Wayne.

Turning to the defendant's second contention, which must be classified as highly speculative, the court concludes that even if true this does not supply the necessary justification for the rule. To accept this justification is to accept the theory that the exercise of constitutional rights adhering to the individual is governed by the prejudices and biases of others. . . .

The last two contentions of the defendant similarly fail to provide the requisite justification. There is no evidence that Chadron State College has been unable to place a male student in a student teaching position by virtue of his hair or moustache. Nor has any evidence been offered that it is more difficult to place such individuals in jobs upon graduation. It should be noted that if this is the case, it would place the impetus to conform on the student. Assuming that student teaching is a required course for graduation and if, after a good faith attempt on the part of the school to place an individual in student teaching, they have failed by virtue of hair length, the student at that time must decide whether to trim the hair to the desired length or fail to meet the requirements for graduation. While colleges are concerned with the placement of their graduates after graduation, and rightly so, it is again the prerogative of the student to decide where he will work and under what conditions.

(9, 10) The court cannot say, based upon the foregoing, that the Chadron State College officials have met the burden imposed upon them by the law of showing justification for the January 9 clarification, or that, as applied to the three before the court, the rule is reasonable.

It is ordered that the plaintiffs in this case, Robert E. Reichenberg, John S. Streep and Donald Hume be allowed to register at Chadron State College.

It is further ordered that costs in this case be taxed to the defendant, with the exception of attorneys' fees which, for the reasons heretofore stated by the court at the February 9 hearing, are to be borne by the respective parties.

Knight v. *State Board of Education*
200 Fed. Supp. 174
Dec. 16, 1961
WILLIAM E. MILLER, Chief Judge

In this action the plaintiffs, thirteen Negro students of Tennessee A & I State University, challenge upon constitutional grounds their suspension from the University at the end of the 1960–1961 school year. They contend that the action taken by the University through its discipline committee violated the plaintiffs' rights under the equal protection and due process clauses of the Fourteenth Amendment, in that such action was arbitrary, discriminatory, and without either notice to the plaintiffs on the charges against them or opportunity to be heard.

* * *

Pertinent and material facts in the controversy are as follows: Tennessee Agricultural and Industrial State University, located at Nashville, was organized as a college or university for Negroes but presently is operated on an integrated basis. Its President, its operating and teaching personnel, and most of its students are members of the Negro race. It is one of the six tax-supported institutions of higher learning in the State under the general management, supervision and control of the State Board of Education. Prior to April 8, 1960, the State Board had not prescribed written or definite rules or regulations for disciplining students at the institutions under its control. Matters of discipline were largely left to each institution, although there is some evidence to indicate that there was a tacit rule or general understanding on the part of the Board that each institution would have the right to dismiss a student summarily for personal misconduct or upon being convicted of a criminal offense involving personal misconduct. Whether or not there was such an unwritten rule, it is clear from the record that it did not receive uniform interpretation by the authorities in control of the various colleges and universities under the jurisdiction of the Board, some schools acting on the assumption that the power to discipline students could be exercised without notice or any kind of hearing and other schools taking the contrary view. This was the posture on April 8, 1960, when the Tennessee Commissioner of Education, in his capacity as Chairman of the State Board of Education, addressed a letter to each of the institutions of higher learning under the Board's jurisdiction formulating a rule governing the disciplining of students for misconduct, which was later ratified and approved by the entire Board. The letter of April 8, 1960, reads as follows:

> The necessity for maintaining the integrity and honor of the student body at each of the State colleges and universities under the jurisdiction of the State Board of Education has long been recognized. The misconduct of any student enrolled in an institution of higher learning reflects dishonor and discredit upon the institution in which he is enrolled and upon higher education in general.
>
> It is for this reason, therefore, that as Chairman of the State Board of Education and acting on behalf of the Board, I am instructing you to dismiss promptly any student enrolled in the institution of which you are president who shall, in the future, be arrested and convicted on charges involving personal misconduct.
>
> This policy is to be placed into effect immediately.

The regulation so prescribed was construed by the President of Tennessee A & I as requiring prompt and mandatory suspension or dismissal of any student convicted of a criminal offense involving personal misconduct, regardless of whether such conviction may have been appealed to a higher court. This was also the construction placed upon the regulation by the authorities of other schools and by the Chairman of the State Board. The letter of April 8, 1960, was written at the time of the lunch-counter demonstrations in the City of Nashville, in which some of the plaintiffs and other Tennessee A & I students participated, protesting the prevailing practice in restaurants and at lunch counters in that city denying service to members of the Negro race. As a result of such demonstrations, many students of Tennessee A & I were arrested and convicted for alleged disorderly conduct, but the proof shows that no disciplinary action was taken by the University against any of the student participants under the regulation of April 8, 1960.

In May and June, 1961, the plaintiffs, after completion of their school work for the year, in different groups and at different times, traveled by interstate bus to Jackson, Mississippi, where they entered the waiting rooms of the Greyhound and Trailways Bus Terminals. When they refused to leave the bus terminals in response to an order from a local police officer, they were arrested, charged with disorderly conduct in violation of a Mississippi statute defining that offense, and later convicted in a Magistrate's Court. Each plaintiff received a fine of $200.00 and a 60-day suspended jail sentence. Each plaintiff spent approximately 30 days in jail pending efforts to post an appeal bond. They were finally successful in perfecting appeals of their convictions to a higher court in Mississippi, which appeals are still pending. On June 1, 1961, a day or so after most of the convictions, but on the same day as one of the convictions and even before one of them, the discipline committee of Tennessee A & I University suspended the plaintiffs from the University after an ex parte hearing, without notice to the plaintiffs, and at a time when they were still in jail in Mississippi pending attempts to post bonds for appeals. On the same date, the committee addressed to the plaintiffs at their local residences in Nashville a letter setting forth the action of the committee as follows:

> In view of the fact that you have been arrested and convicted for violating a Mississippi law and are now in litigation to prove or disprove the validity of that arrest and conviction, and in light of the policy of the State Board of Education that provides for the dismissal of a student from a college or university under its jurisdiction when such student is arrested and convicted of charges involving misconduct, you have been placed on probation and will be denied the privilege of continuing your education at the Tennessee A & I State University. If it is later indicated that you have not violated this policy of the State Board of Education, your case may be reconsidered.
>
> *   *   *

If the regulation of April 8, 1960, means that a student convicted of any criminal offense regardless of its nature and seriousness should be automatically dismissed, and if the regulation so construed should be deemed a reasonable one, then there would be merit in the defendants' argument that the discipline committee was vested with no discretion and that its sole function was to determine whether or not the plaintiffs had actually been convicted of a criminal violation. Since it is admitted that the plaintiffs were so convicted in Mississippi, notice to the plaintiffs and an opportunity to be heard before disciplinary action was taken would have served no useful purpose. But is this the correct construction of the regulation? The Court is satisfied that it is not.

In the first place, the unreasonableness of such a construction argues strongly against it. There are countless convictions for violations of the criminal law which do not necessarily reflect seriously upon the person so convicted. For example, it is inconceivable that the State Board intended in promulgating the regulation of April 8 that a minor traffic violation, such as overtime parking or running a traffic light, would subject a student to summary dismissal without any discretion whatever being vested in the schools involved. Examples of similar technical infractions could be multiplied indefinitely, and the Court cannot escape the conclusion that the State Board of Education had in mind a different meaning when the rule of April 8 was adopted. This leads to the question: What is the true meaning of the regulation?

(4) In determining this question, it would appear that the answer is supplied by the letter of April 8 when construed in its entirety. By the express language of the second paragraph, each institution under the jurisdiction of the Board was directed to dismiss promptly, not any student convicted of a criminal charge, but any student convicted on charges "involving personal misconduct." It thus appears that it is not enough for a school to determine the fact of conviction alone but it must go further and find that the charge on which the conviction is based is one which does in fact involve personal misconduct on the part of the student. It must be conceded that the term "personal misconduct" is, generally speaking, a very broad one and, if without definition for a special purpose, could embrace any type of behavior in conflict with the criminal law or even with general practice and custom. However, the term as used in the letter of April 8, 1960, is not without definition or limitation. The term "personal misconduct" as used in the second paragraph must be interpreted in the light of the first paragraph of the same letter wherein the purpose in promulgating the regulation is stated as follows: "The misconduct of any student enrolled in an institution of higher learning reflects dishonor and discredit upon the institution in which he is enrolled and upon higher education in general." In this view the intent of the regulation was not that the schools should summarily dismiss students upon convictions of criminal offenses but only those students convicted of offenses accompanied by personal misconduct of a kind which reflected dishonor and discredit upon the institution. Such a construction not only meets the test of reasonableness, as it appears to the Court, but it is required by the language of the letter itself.

(5) By accepting such interpretation of the letter of April 8, the Court does not mean to imply that an institution under the jurisdiction of the State Board would necessarily be required in all cases to serve notice upon the student concerned and afford him an opportunity to

be heard with respect to his actual conduct. There may be cases where the fact of conviction alone would necessarily import personal misconduct reflecting dishonor and discredit upon the institution, such as convictions for murder, rape, house-breaking and larceny, and numerous other examples which might be mentioned. But where the fact of conviction alone is not clearly indicative of personal misconduct in the sense used in the April 8 regulation, the Court is of the opinion that the due process clause of the Fourteenth Amendment, as construed by the Supreme Court, requires in the case of a state college or university notice to the student and an opportunity to be heard before the penalty of dismissal is inflicted. Otherwise, the school authorities are not in position to exercise their discretion and judgment in a fair and reasonable manner, either from the standpoint of the school or of the student. This is most certainly true as to the technical violations which the Court has already mentioned, and the Court is convinced that it is true in the present case.

(6) In this connection, it is noteworthy that the discipline committee wrote the letter of June 1, 1961, suspending the plaintiffs from school on the basis of hearsay information which they had received that the plaintiffs had been convicted in Mississippi for breach of the peace. Presumably the committee also knew that the plaintiffs had traveled to Mississippi by interstate bus in connection with the freedom rides, but when the severe penalty of suspension was imposed upon the plaintiffs, the committee did not know and had no way of knowing what the plaintiffs had actually done and what their conduct actually was in bringing about their supposed convictions upon such a general and uncertain charge as a breach of the peace. The committee did not know and had no way of knowing whether the specific conduct of each plaintiff was of such character that it reflected dishonor or discredit upon Tennessee A & I State University as required by the regulation of April 8. In brief, the committee was not in possession of sufficient facts to enable it to exercise a fair or intelligent judgment. The necessity for a hearing in such a case is strongly emphasized by what actually occurred. As it turned out, the plaintiffs were not in fact convicted in Mississippi for a breach of the peace, as the committee had supposed, but were convicted under a Mississippi Statute, Section 2087.5 of the Mississippi Code of 1942, which defines the offense of "disorderly conduct" as follows:

Whoever with intent to provoke a breach of the peace, or under circumstances such that a breach of the peace may be occasioned thereby: (1) crowds or congregates with others in or upon . . . (naming certain public places) and who fails or refuses to disperse and move on, or disperse or move on, when ordered so to do by any law enforcement officer of any municipality, or county, in which such act or acts are committed . . . *shall be guilty of disorderly conduct* [emphasis added].

Under the general terms of this statute the plaintiffs were convicted on a charge that "with intent to provoke a breach of the peace" they congregated with others in or around a bus terminal in Jackson, Mississippi, and failed or refused to disperse and move on when ordered to do so by a law enforcement officer. The committee, in fact, did not even have before it the exact terms of this charge against the plaintiffs at the time they took disciplinary action. But even if the charge itself had been before the committee it would have conveyed very little information as to what the plaintiffs had actually done and at best would have left a serious doubt as to whether the plaintiffs had been guilty of such misconduct as would reflect dishonor or discredit upon the University. It is entirely conceivable under the vague and indefinite terms of the Mississippi Statute and the equally vague charge upon which the plaintiffs were convicted that they were guilty at most of a technical violation which the committee, if apprised of the true facts, could have decided did not call for the penalty of dismissal.

Defendants' argument that the discipline committee should not be required to go behind the convictions of a court of competent jurisdiction fails to meet the real issue. In investigating the facts attending the commission of the offense, the committee would not go behind the convictions for the purpose of determining whether they were valid or whether the students were guilty or not guilty of the offense charged, but for the purpose of determining whether the convictions, conceding their existence and validity, were for offenses actually involving the type of conduct which is aimed at by the regulation of April 8, 1960. The purpose of the investigation would be for the University to decide for itself whether there had been in fact a violation of its own disciplinary regulation.

* * *

Nothing in this opinion should be construed or taken as indicating any view on the part of the Court upon the merits of any issues to be presented to the discipline committee of the University or any view as to whether the regulation of April 8, 1960, was or was not violated by the plaintiffs or any of them.

Norton v. Discipline Committee
419 Fed. 2nd. 105
Nov. 29, 1969

WEICK, Circuit Judge

Appellants, students of East Tennessee State University, were suspended by the University's Discipline Committee after a hearing on charges of distributing on the campus "material of a false, seditious and inflammatory nature." This material was calculated to cause a disturbance and disruption of school activities and to bring about ridicule of and contempt for the school authorities. The students perfected an administrative appeal to the President of the University, who upheld the decision of the Discipline Committee.

The students then instituted the present action in the District Court under the civil rights statutes for a mandatory injuncion to compel their reinstatement, claiming that their constitutional rights had been denied them. The District Judge, who had previous experience in cases of this type, granted them an evidentiary hearing. Each of the appellants, the Chairman of the Discipline Committee, and the President of the University testified. A stipulation was admitted in evidence containing the alleged inflammatory literature and an admission that each of the appellants distributed one or both pieces of it. Transcripts of the hearings conducted by the Discipline Committee were received in evidence. The District Judge at the conclusion of the hearing rendered an oral opinion and adopted findings of fact and conclusion of law, in which he denied the injunction. This appeal followed.

Two pieces of the alleged inflammatory literature were distributed, one on May 28, 1968, and the second on May 30, 1968, the latter being only one day before the beginning of final examinations. The Discipline Committee took immediate action and sent three-day notice of a hearing to be held on the charges to all of the students who had distributed the literature except two students who received only one day's notices. Copies of the offensive literature are appended hereto.

The District Judge was of the view that the inflammatory nature and disruptive characteristics of the literature appeared on its face. He made the following finding of fact:

XIV

That the Discipline Committee could properly have found that these documents were abrasive, abrupt and rude in character and that they were calculated to arouse resentment both on the part of the administration and on the part of the students of East Tennessee State University.

XV

That at least one document is susceptible of the interpretation that the writer of the article is encouraging demonstrations similar to those which had occurred on other campuses throughout the country; and the article can be reasonably and logically construed to mean that the writer of the article was calling upon the students of East Tennessee State University to engage in the same kind of conduct and activity which had occurred at Columbia University and elsewhere.

This finding would appear to be supported by the following excerpt from the first sheet:

> And how has the ETSU student body reacted: Have they precipitated a revolution like French students? No. Have they brought about an entirely new and liberal administration like Polish students? No. Have they been the forerunners of a new democratic spirit like Czech students? No. Have they seized buildings and raised havoc until they got what they were entitled to like other American students? No. What then have the ETSU students done? They have sat upon their rears and let the administration crap upon their heads, that's what.
>
> That's right folks, in case you'd not noticed, ETSU students are in the vast majority apathetic—they open their mouths only to yawn, life (sic) their arms only to stretch, and like L'il Abner's Smoos, exist only to serve those who would take advantage of them.
>
> Well, Smoos, what have you to look forward to next year? Maybe the administration will buy some Dean's turnip patch for ninety grand. Maybe all the girls will be required to wear chastity belts (the keys to be kept on reserve at the library—check 'em out for an hour at a time). Maybe social hours will be made applicable to males as well as females. Maybe— Maybe— Maybe—
>
> Maybe students will get some sense and learn that this should cease and that the only way to see that it does is to stand up and fight. Maybe students will learn that the Supreme Court has declared that young people do not sacrifice their citizenship and all rights and privileges therewith by enrolling in a university. Maybe students will learn that no matter what the despots who run this school say, students have the constitutional right to protest, demonstrate, and demand their rights; that women students may not constitutionally be campussed; that students may damned well wear what they want and say what they please. And maybe, just maybe, they will discover that there are student leaders, organizers to rally around so as to assault the bastions of administrative tyranny. Maybe students will learn that at least. And remember that when the time comes to fight for what you are justly entitled to, that if you refuse to come along then you have no justification whatsoever for ever complaining again. When you are called to protest and you sit back on your butt, then baby, that means that whatever the administration does is O.K. with you. When we move against them, remember, like the man says, "Put up or shut up."*

The students were urged to "stand up and fight" and to "assault the bastions of administrative tyranny." This was an open exhortation to the students to engage in disorderly and destructive activities.

---

* The language, referring to their fellow students, "Have they seized buildings and raised havoc until they got what they were entitled to like other American students," was obviously intended to call their attention to campus disturbances around the country, and would include such universities as Columbia, Berkeley, Harvard, Cornell, Ohio State and Kent State.

The University administration was referred to with an obscenity and called "despots." This vicious attack on the administration was calculated to subject it to ridicule and contempt, and to damage the reputation of the University.

The reference to "chastity belts" for girls is a crude, vulgar remark offensive to women students and beyond the dignity of most college students to make.

Reliance was made on the Supreme Court for declaration of the constitutional rights of the students to "damned well wear what they want and say what they please." In our opinion such reliance is misplaced. The students have no constitutional right to misbehave on the college campus.

In the second piece, which impliedly approved the first piece, the school administration was referred to as a "problem child"; and stated that it is a crime for their students to shelter by their silence that "problem child," and that the students should now reprimand "our misguided child" and educate him. "We must now educate the educators" and "teach them the lesson of reality . . . although they may be shocked by it."

Ordinarily students go to college to acquire an education, but these students apparently want to educate the teachers.

It would indeed be difficult to maintain discipline on the campus of an institution of higher learning if conduct of this type were tolerated. We would doubt that parents would send their college-age children to such an institution if they knew the philosophy as contained in the literature was taught or sanctioned there. We cannot imagine that a student could have confidence in the teachers in a university such as the literature portrays.

Appellants contend that distribution of the two handouts was privileged under the First Amendment to the Constitution as an expression of free speech unaccompanied by acts of violence. They rely principally on *Tinker* v. *Des Moines Independent Community School Dist.,* 393 U.S. 503, 89 S.Ct. 733, 21 L. Ed.2d 731 (1969), and cases cited therein. *Tinker* involved a few high school children who did nothing except wear black arm bands for a few days to publicize their objections to hostilities in Vietnam. These children did not urge a riot, nor were they disrespectful to their teachers.

Mr. Justice Fortas, who wrote the opinion in *Tinker,* was careful to mention: "As we have discussed, the record does not demonstrate any facts which might reasonably have led school authorities to forecast substantial disruption of or material interference with school activities, and no disturbances or disorders on the school premises in fact occurred."

In the present case, Dean Davis and President Culp did forecast disturbances and they acted quickly to prevent threatened disorders by making the charges against inciters and holding the hearings.

After distribution of the first piece in the present case, twenty-five students went to the office of Dean Thomas and wanted to get rid of this group of agitators.

(2) It is not required that the college authorities delay action against the inciters until after the riot has started and buildings have been taken over and damaged. The college authorities had the right to nip such action in the bud and prevent it in its inception. This is authorized even in criminal cases.

As well stated by Chief Justice Vinson: "Obviously, the words cannot mean that before the Government may act, it must wait until the *putsch* is about to be executed, the plans have been laid and the signal is awaited. If Government is aware that a group aiming at its overthrow is attempting to indoctrinate its members and to commit them to a course whereby they will strike when the leaders feel circumstances permit, action by the Government is required."

Finally, it should be emphasized that appellants were not expelled from the University, but were merely suspended. The difference between expulsion and suspension was explained by Dr. Davis as follows:

> I continue to hear reference to the matter of expel or expulsion. We at no time even mentioned the word expel or expulsion.
>
> The plan of suspension is a restraint from enrollment which gives those of us who are concerned with the administration affairs time to reflect and to study what has happened. It also gives the student time to reflect and to study, and to appear before the committee then so that the committee and the student can, if possible, come to an agreement about future attendance.
>
> There is a difference in the meaning of suspension and expulsion.

. . . The District Judge at the close of the hearing suggested that the University give hearings on applications for reinstatements. The record does not reveal that any such applications were made. The students are apparently insistent that they had the right to do what they did and they are going to stand by it.

In our judgment there is no basis for federal interference with the disciplinary procedures of the State University in this case.

(4) We agree with the District Court that the charges that the literature was false and inflammatory were sufficiently definite.

(5, 6) It was not necessary to have a specific regulation providing for disciplinary action for the circulation of false and inflammatory literature. The University had inherent authority to maintain order and to discipline students. We do not believe that there is a good analogy between student discipline and criminal procedure.

Affirmed.

* * *

Buttny v. *Smiley*
281 Fed. Supp. 280
Feb. 14, 1968

ARRAJ, Chief Judge

Plaintiffs are students or former students at the University of Colorado who have been subjected to disciplinary action by the University. Their complaint and motion for a preliminary injunction allege violations of rights guaranteed to them by the First and Fourteenth Amendments to the United States Constitution. They have exhausted their available administrative remedies. . . .

This case arises out of disciplinary action taken by the University against plaintiffs after an October 25, 1967, protest demonstration at the University Placement Service on campus. Individually and collectively (as a group) the plaintiffs have admitted taking part in the protest activity which involved physically blocking and prohibiting entrance to the Placement Service by standing in the doorways to the offices. As a result of this activity students with scheduled interviews, students who desired to schedule interviews, personnel of the Placement Service, University officials and persons recruiting for various concerns were denied access to the offices of this department of the University. The plaintiffs were specifically protesting the recruiter from the Central Intelligence Agency of the United States.

Because of these activities plaintiffs were individually charged with the following:

1. Depriving students of the right of access to the Placement Bureau by physically blocking and prohibiting entrance to the Placement office.
2. Depriving University officials the right of access to the Placement Bureau by physically blocking and prohibiting entrance to Placement offices.
3. Prohibiting Placement office personnel from properly maintaining the University's Placement Service.
4. Depriving recruiters, who were scheduled under current University policies, their right to properly interview students for job placement.
5. Refusing to cease and desist from physically blocking entrance to said offices when requested to do so by University officials.

A full and open hearing was held before the University Discipline Committee. The hearing was conducted in conformity with the procedures set out in a document entitled "University of Colorado Discipline Procedures and Structure," approved by the Board of Regents of the

University April 28, 1960. The decision of the University Discipline Committee (U.D.C.) was appealed to the Appellate Subcommittee of the Administrative Council and the decision of that body was further appealed to the Board of Regents. As a result of the hearing and appeals, nine of the plaintiffs have been suspended from the University with the right to apply for readmission after the 1968 spring semester, nine were suspended and immediately readmitted under probationary status for the remainder of their enrollment, and four were placed on indefinite probation. At each level, the decisions were unanimous.

In their complaint and motion plaintiffs assert that the defendants violated their constitutional right to due process of law in the following particulars:

1. The defendants accepted jurisdiction of the matter based on rules that did not exist.

2. The rules which the plaintiffs allegedly violated are vague and uncertain in that they (a) fail to provide sufficient notice to the plaintiffs of the proscribed conduct, and (b) they fail to provide sufficient standards to guide the University disciplinary bodies in determining if a violation has occurred.

3. The rules are over-broad and sweeping, so that they prohibit conduct protected by the First Amendment to the United States Constitution by their chilling effect upon the exercise of the guaranteed right of free speech.

4. The defendants agreed to hear the case of the plaintiffs together, then to act on each case individually in determining culpability and punishment, but they violated their own rule by acting on the plaintiffs as a group.

Plaintiffs further allege that their constitutional right to equal protection of the law was encroached upon by defendants in the following manner: (1) The U.D.C. imposed upon the plaintiffs differential punishment, discriminatory because there was no evidence to substantiate any differential treatment, and (2) the punishment is arbitrary and unrelated to the evidence.

Additionally, plaintiff Brian McQuerrey complains that he was further denied due process and equal protection within the meaning of the Fourteenth Amendment because the punishment imposed upon him (suspension) was founded on evidence of prior disciplinary action, which prior action was constitutionally infirm. In the fall of 1962 McQuerrey, then a freshman, pleaded guilty to a charge of "interference" in a Boulder court. At that time he was not advised of his federal constitutional rights to remain silent and to have the advice of counsel. As a result of this conviction he was called before an Assistant Dean of Men and was given a "University warning," which is a form of punishment; if there is an accumulation of these warnings more severe action is taken, possibly probation or suspension. In effect, McQuerrey is making a collateral attack on the original conviction; if the conviction is void, so also is the disciplinary action taken by the University. In October 1963 McQuerrey appeared before the University Discipline Committee on a charge of gambling in the residence halls. At that hearing he was not advised of his rights to counsel and to appeal. He was then placed on probation. The two prior proceedings against Mr. McQuerrey were considered by the U.D.C. in setting his punishment in the present action.

We are asked to permanently enjoin defendants from interfering with the pursuit by plaintiffs of their studies and to readmit the suspended plaintiffs. They also ask that defendants be ordered to strike from their files any reference to the disciplinary action and its results.

(1) Plaintiffs' claim that defendants based jurisdiction on rules that did not exist belies the record. They were advised, in writing, that the University was relying on the following rules:

> Students have equivalent responsibility with the faculty for study and learning. They should be judged on the merits of their performance without reference to their political, social, or religious views. The University of Colorado expects its students to obey national, state and local laws; to respect the rights and privileges of other people; and to conduct themselves in such manner that reflects credit upon the University. (From University of Colorado Discipline Procedures and Structure, approved by the Board of Regents April 28, 1960.)
> HAZING. Hazing in all forms is prohibited in this University. Students who thus interfere with the personal liberty of a fellow student are rendered liable to immediate discipline. This rule is extended to cover class conflicts, injury to property on the campus or elsewhere and interference in any manner with the public or private rights of citizens. (From Article XIV, Section 2, of the Laws of the Regents, compiled January 1, 1964.)

Both of these rules were promulgated by the Board of Regents, a body created by the State Constitution to govern the University.

*   *   *

2, 3) These rules are not so vague or uncertain as to require us to declare them invalid. Although they are not in a form of specific prohibitions, such as "Thou shalt not physically prevent other students from using University facilities," nevertheless they do set standards for acceptable conduct which are readily determinable and should be easily understood. As noted by the Administrative Council in its decision, "The University is not required to provide a negative type of behavioral code typical of criminal laws"; we fully agree with that finding.

*   *   *

The United States Supreme Court has frequently enunciated the test for determining whether a statute is unconstitutionally vague.

> a statute which either forbids or requires the doing of an act in terms so vague that men of common intelligence must necessarily guess at its meaning and differ as to its application violates the first essential of due process of law.

Assuming that the rules under which the plaintiffs were charged are required to meet this test, we do not believe that the "Hazing" rule, Laws of the Regents, which was the rule upon which the Administrative Council based their decision, is so vague that students of common intelligence must necessarily guess at its meaning. The record clearly reflects that each of the plaintiffs knew he was violating recognized standards of conduct and each expected to be punished in some manner. In some instances the plaintiffs admitted their awareness of the rules.

(4–7) We are not convinced that because there may be borderline cases the University officials must be denied the goals and protections they seek. Where there is doubt as to the nature of a student's activity we cannot assume that the disciplinary bodies will not accord them full protection. Regulations and rules which are necessary in maintaining order and discipline are always considered reasonable. . . . We are persuaded that the "Hazing" rule is not on its face a prior restraint on the right to freedom of speech and the right to assemble. The language is clear; it authorizes discipline for "any interference with the public or private rights of citizens." Since the "Hazing" rule is not constitutionally vague, it is not necessary for us to make a specific finding regarding the other rules involved. Certainly their language is broad; however, we are unable to find any cases, nor were any called to our attention, which have held university regulations such as these to be invalid because they are so vague as to deny due process of law. In fact the recent cases have not denied the validity and reasonableness of some very broad disciplinary regulations. In addition, it cannot be denied that university authorities have an inherent general power to maintain order on campus and to exclude those who are detrimental to its wellbeing. . . .

* * *

(8–10) The right of the University administration to invoke its disciplinary powers in this instance need not be entirely bottomed on any published rule or regulation. As previously noted, it is an inherent power that the school administration authorities have to maintain order on its campus, and to afford students, school officials, employees and invited guests freedom of movement on the campus and the right of ingress and egress to the school's physical facilities. We agree with the students that the doctrine of "In Loco Parentis" is no longer tenable in a university community; and we believe that there is a trend to reject the authority of university officials to regulate "off-campus" activity of students. However, that is not to say that conduct disruptive of good order on the campus should not properly lead to disciplinary action.

(11–12) We do not subscribe to the notion that a citizen surrenders his civil rights upon enrollment as a student in a university. . . . As a corollary to this, enrollment does not give him a right to immunity or special consideration, and certainly it does not give him the right to violate the constitutional rights of others.

Here plaintiffs freely admitted and openly boasted that their accused activity was "civil disobedience." They expected and wanted to be arrested by the civil authorities, and they wanted to be tried in civil court as a means of pointing up their intense opposition to the C.I.A. And all of this took place "on campus."

Their conduct in this Court's opinion was much more than is fairly understood to be embraced within the term "political activity." Plaintiffs engaged in overt physical acts which effectively interfered with one of the normal activities of the University, namely interviewing students for employment.

(13) Plaintiffs contended that the action of the University officials had a "chilling" effect on the First Amendment right of freedom of speech. What they said on the occasion in question is not the basis for the disciplinary proceedings; it is what they did. We hold that the First Amendment guarantee of freedom of speech, as it is related to plaintiffs' activities here, does not give them the right to prevent lawful access to campus facilities. We have been unable to find any case that holds that active, aggressive physical action may properly be characterized by the courts as free speech.

(15) Plaintiffs cannot complain that they were tried as a group. The evidence clearly shows that they were acting as a group with a common purpose; they were partners in the transaction and they acted in concert, one segment of the group deployed at one door and the other segment deployed at another door. They locked hands or arms to prevent others from gaining access to the rooms. One of the documents filed with the University Discipline Committee and signed by all plaintiffs contained this statement: "We acted as a group and we request to be tried as a group." Additionally, they called themselves "The Ad Hoc Committee Against the C.I.A." and signed some documents as members of such Committee.

(16) Plaintiffs' claim that they were denied equal protection of the laws is not supported by the record. There were three distinct types of punishment imposed: (1) Suspension with permission to reapply after the end of the 1968 spring semester; (2) Suspension with immediate reinstatement and probation; and (3) Probation. With the ex-

ception of plaintiff Brian McQuerrey, the punishment meted out to the respective plaintiffs was in direct relation to the student's class year at the University and his maturity. The group receiving the most severe punishment were graduate students, some of whom were receiving financial aid as research or teaching assistants. Those receiving the least punishment were the first-semester students. We think it just and proper that the graduate students should be held more strictly accountable and responsible for their individual acts. Certainly we do not believe that the classification of the plaintiffs in this manner is unreasonable. . . .

(17) Mr. McQuerrey was in a different situation. He was not a graduate student and the basis for his being given the same punishment as those students was his involvement in two prior disciplinary actions. The first one resulted after he had been arrested by the Boulder city police, pleaded guilty, and was assessed a fine. At that time he was not advised of his constitutional right to remain silent and his right to counsel. He then asserts that the disciplinary action at the University based on his guilty plea cannot be used against him. He attempts to make a collateral attack on the original plea of guilty; certainly in the present proceeding we cannot determine that the conviction in the city court was constitutionally infirm. . . .

(18) The second offense that was used as a basis for the disciplinary action against McQuerrey was a previous admission by him that he had been involved in gambling in a dormitory on campus. He now complains that he had not been informed of his federal constitutional rights, and although he was placed on probation by the University authorities, he claims that he left school and did not know that such punishment had been imposed. The record before us does not support his position; it shows conclusively that he did know that he had been placed on probation and he made no effort to appeal from that status. We know of no legal authority that requires university officials to advise a student involved in disciplinary proceedings of his right to remain silent and to be provided with counsel.

(19) Once the facts have been found by the disciplinary body and the guilt has been established, punishment is then a matter of judgment and discretion within the recognized limits. Our only inquiry here relating to the punishment imposed is: "Is the punishment meted out within accepted limits, and, if it is, did the authorities act arbitrarily or capriciously?"

(20) We are to consider the constitutional validity of the action taken by the University authorities. We have heretofore discussed the legality of the rules and regulations involved, and we have found them to be constitutionally sound and acceptable. We have found that the equal protection clause of the Fourteenth Amendment was not violated,

and now we deal with the important question of whether or not the plaintiffs were afforded procedural due process by the University authorities. Our unequivocal answer is, they were.

* * *

(23, 24) In the record before us, there are communications from several University faculty members; the communications suggest that the punishment imposed on plaintiffs is unduly harsh. This may very well be so. It is a matter of opinion and judgment. We find that the punishment meted out to the respective plaintiffs was neither arbitrary nor capricious. It was within recognized and accepted limits. It was not in bad faith and was not an abuse of discretion. Plaintiffs' constitutional rights were not invaded, violated or denied. Even if we were disposed to do so, we are without authority to modify the punishment in any way. We cannot determine the wisdom of what has been done in this case by the University administration.

For the foregoing reasons, it is

Ordered that the motion for preliminary and permanent injunction be and hereby is denied. It is further

Ordered that the complaint and cause of action be and hereby is dismissed.

Soglin et al. v. *Kaufmann et al.*
295 Fed. Supp. 978
Dec. 13, 1968

DOYLE, J.

* * *

Plaintiffs are alleged to be ten students at the Madison campus of the University of Wisconsin, and an unincorporated association known as Students for a Democratic Society (Madison chapter). They undertake to sue on behalf of others similarly situated, as well as for themselves. Several of the defendants are alleged to be officials of the University of Wisconsin, having duties with respect to discipline.

* * *

On or about November 1, 1967, certain of the plaintiffs, and others, received a copy of a document described as "Amended Charges" and signed by the chairman of the Administrative Division. The amended charges were that the named students:

I. Intentionally, denied to others their right to interview for jobs with the Dow Chemical Corporation and to carry out that purpose. . . .

* * *

II. Intentionally incited and counselled others to deny to others their right to interview for jobs with the Dow Chemical Corporation and to carry out that purpose did intentionally incite and counsel others. . . .

* * *

III. Intentionally refused repeated requests to move and to unblock the hall and doorways of the first floor of the Commerce Building for the purpose of denying to others their right to interview for jobs with the Dow Chemical Corporation . . .

* * *

All of the foregoing constituting:
1. Misconduct, as well as
2. A violation of Chapter 11.02, and 11.15 of the *University Policies on Use of Facilities and Outside Speakers.**

The complaint alleges that the defendants, or some of them, have in fact expelled two of the plaintiffs and "another member of plaintiffs' classes . . . by application of the doctrine of 'misconduct,' and are threatening suspension, expulsion or other denial of matriculation . . . to other members of plaintiffs' classes for alleged violation of the doctrine of 'misconduct' and by reason of the application of the doctrine of 'misconduct.' "

So far as the present action is concerned, then, the defendants assert authority to discipline students: (1) for "misconduct"; and (2) for violations of Chapter 11.02 of the Laws and Regulations of the University, which provides:

Scope of Student Freedom. Students have the right, accorded to all

---

* Chapter 11.15 of the Laws and Regulations of the University of Wisconsin provides:

Those who attend a speech or program sponsored by student organizations, University departments, or other authorized groups, have the duty not to obstruct it, and the University has the obligation to protect the right to listen or participate.

Counsel for the defendants have stipulated in this action that Chapter 11.15 is inapplicable to the circumstances of this case and that it is not relied upon as support for disciplinary action with respect to the events of October 18.

Also, on or about November 1, 1967, in the course of proceedings in this court, defendants filed a brief in which it was stated that "the plaintiffs have been charged with misconduct under Section 36.12, Wisconsin Statutes"; in oral argument counsel for the defendants asserted the disciplinary proceedings were grounded in part upon an alleged violation of Sec. 36.12, Wis. Stats. Sec. 36.12 provides, in part:

the regents shall have the power . . . to confer upon the faculty by by-laws the power to suspend or expel students for misconduct or other cause prescribed in such by-laws.

Counsel for the defendants have since stipulated that Sec. 36.12 is enabling legislation, that the section itself expresses no command or prohibition capable of being violated, and that no alleged violation of its terms is relied upon as support for disciplinary action with respect to the events of October 18.

persons by the Constitution, to freedom of speech, peaceable assembly, petition and association. Students and student organizations may examine and discuss all questions of interest to them, and express opinions publicly as well as privately. They may support causes by lawful means which do not disrupt the operations of the University, or organizations accorded the use of University facilities.*

Plaintiffs contend that the term "misconduct,' as a standard for disciplinary action by the University, violates the First and Fourteenth Amendments to the Constitution of the United States because of its vagueness and overbreadth. Plaintiffs also contend that Chapter 11.02 as written violates the First and Fourteenth Amendments because of its vagueness and overbreadth. Pursuant to pretrial order, defendants have filed a partial answer to these two contentions, each of which has been denied. With respect to these two contentions, the relief sought is a declaratory judgment and injunctive relief consistent with the declaration. This opinion and the order entered pursuant to it reach only these two contentions and the relief sought with respect to them.

* * *

"MISCONDUCT" AS A STANDARD

The amended charges of November 1, 1967, set forth in full above, allege rather specific behavior on the part of the named students and conclude with the following:

All of the foregoing constituting:
1. Misconduct, as well as
2. A violation of Chapter 11.02 . . .

If the term "misconduct," without more, may serve as a standard for disciplinary action, it is not essential to the defendants' position that Chapter 11.02 be vindicated as a prohibitory regulation. For reasons which will be explained herein, I turn initially to the broader contention of the defendants: that the term "misconduct" may serve as a standard for disciplinary action, and that no more specific or definite substantive rules are required as a prerequisite for disciplinary action.

With respect to the imposition of criminal sanctions in the non-

---

* In response to an application by plaintiffs at the commencement of this action, I restrained the defendants from imposing any sanction by reason of alleged violations of Chapter 11.02 based on the events of October 18, and from conducting hearings or other similar steps in proceedings theretofore commenced for violations of Chapter 11.02. I declined to restrain the defendants from conducting disciplinary proceedings or from imposing sanctions based upon the term "misconduct" as a standard for discipline, as distinguished from Chapter 11.02. Defendants continue to assert their authority to discipline students for violations of Chapter 11.02.

university society,* such a regime would grossly violate the Constitution of the United States.

> [A] statute which either forbids or requires the doing of an act in terms so vague that men of common intelligence must necessarily guess at its meaning and differ as to its application, violates the first essential of due process of law.

A federal, state, or local statute, ordinance, regulation, order or rule, subjecting one to imprisonment or fine or other serious sanction for "misconduct" would surely fall as unconstitutionally vague. Moreover, it would not be necessary that a challenger await the outcome of an attempted application of so vague a rule to him in a specific judicial or administrative proceeding, and then dispute the validity of the rule only as applied. He could challenge the prospective application of a vague rule and obtain a judicial declaration of its invalidity and injunctive relief against attempts to enforce it. . . .

Defendants here contend that, given the opportunity, they can prove that with respect to the events of October 18, those students who were subsequently subjected to disciplinary action had received prior warnings from certain university administrators that they would be punished if they performed the acts which they are alleged to have proceeded nevertheless to perform. It is not contended that defendants could prove that those administrators who issued the warnings were themselves . . . empowered to promulgate generally applicable rules of conduct for university students. Nor could it be contended that the term "misconduct" itself prescribes intelligible standards or criteria by which these administrators might exercise discretion to issue a specific warning or order in a specific case. In the nonuniversity society, in the absence of a reasonably clear rule or standard or criterion promulgated by those duly enmpowered to promulgate them, one may not be puished for violating the order of an administrator, such as a policeman. . . .

Moreover, the vagueness doctrine is not to be conceived as being limited solely to the concept of fair notice as an element of substantive due process. The vagueness doctrine embodies a First Amendment concept as well:

> The objectionable quality of vagueness and overbreadth does not depend upon absence of fair notice to a criminally accused or upon unchanneled delegation of legislative powers, but upon the danger of tolerating, in the area of First Amendment freedoms, the existence

---

* "Nonuniversity society," as used herein, is a shorthand expression not intended to be wholly precise. Colleges, secondary schools, primary schools, the military, or penal institutions, for example, may or may not be comparable to universities for certain constitutional purposes. Some implications of these comparisons will be referred to hereinafter.

of a penal statute susceptible of sweeping and improper application. . . .

* * *

Defendants do not appear to dispute that with respect to the criminal law in nonuniversity society the doctrines of vagueness and overbreadth, and the availability of these doctrines in prospective attacks upon criminal regulations, are substantially as stated above. Rather, it appears that their contention may be summarized as follows:

Whether the power is conceived to be inherent or statutory (Sec. 36.12, Wis. Stats.), those charged with the governance of the university are empowered to discipline students for misconduct. (This proposition is conceded by the plaintiffs; conceded or not, I conclude that it is correct.)

In exercising this power to discipline for misconduct, the university is not bound to promulgate any rules defining misconduct. The function of fair notice can be effectuated by means other than the promulgation of rules of general application. For example, university administrators can inform particular students in advance of a particular occasion that if the students behave in a particular manner, they will be punished. Notice of this latter type is constitutionally sufficient with respect to university disciplinary matters, although the vagueness doctrine might render it invalid in certain nonuniversity situations.

With respect to First Amendment guarantees as implemented both by the vagueness and "overbreadth" tests, it is sufficient that disciplinary action be reasonably related to the maintenance of that order and decorum necessary to performance of the university's function. This determination is to be made by the courts by balancing the governmental interest in the university's program against the individual student's interest in his freedom. This "balancing" test is sharply to be distinguished from the tests of vagueness and overbreadth ("facial invalidity"). Moreover, the balancing test is not to be judicially applied prospectively, but case by case, after the disciplinary proceeding has been completed.

The reason for sparing disciplinary proceedings from the tests of vagueness and overbreadth, and particularly from prospective application of these tests, lies in the uniqueness of the university as an institution and in the university's historically demonstrated attachment to freedom.

Historically, universities and colleges and schools, both public and private, have enjoyed wide latitude in student discipline. Various "models" of the relationship between the university and its students have been employed by the courts for the purpose of determining the legal attributes of the relationship: parent-child (*in loco parentis*);

owner-tenant; parties to a contract.* Van Alstyne, "The Student as University Resident," 45 *Denver L.J.* 582–598 (1968). Whatever the model or combination of models employed, the dominant pattern has been judicial nonintervention in the discipline of students by faculty, administrators, school boards, trustees, or regents.

In recent years, however, courts have been increasingly disposed to intervene in school disciplinary situations involving major sanctions. This has been most marked when intervention has appeared necessary to assure that procedural due process is observed: for example, specification of charges, notice of hearing, and hearing. . . . But judicial intervention in school disciplinary cases in more recent years has not been confined to matters of procedural due process. The validity of substantive school rules has been the subject of judicial scrutiny. *Burnside* v. *Byars*, 363 F.2d 744 (C.A. 5th, 1966) (high school regulation prohibiting students from wearing "freedom buttons" held invalid); *Hammond* v. *South Carolina State College*, 272 F. Supp. 947 (D.S.C., 1967) (rule prohibiting "parades, celebrations, and demonstrations" without prior approval of college authorities, held invalid); *Dickey* v. *Alabama State Board of Education*, 273 F. Supp. 613 (M.D. Ala., N.D. 1967) (rule that no editorial in school paper could criticize governor or legislature, held invalid). See *Buttny* v. *Smiley*, 281 F. Supp. 280 (D. Colo., 1968) (upholding a regent rule against a vagueness contention).

* * *

Indeed, in numerous contexts, the Supreme Court has assigned a special importance to First Amendment guarantees in the educational setting.

> Judicial interposition in the operation of the public school system of the Nation raises problems requiring care and restraint. Our courts, however, have not failed to apply the First Amendment's mandate in our educational system where essential to safeguard the fundamental values of freedom of speech and inquiry and of belief. By and large, public education in our Nation is committed to the control of state and local authorities. Courts do not and cannot intervene in the resolution of conflicts which arise in the daily operation of school systems and which do not directly and sharply implicate basic constitutional values.

Underlying these developments in the relationship of academic institutions to the courts has been a profound shift in the nature of American schools and colleges and universities, and in the relationships between younger and older people. These changes seldom have been articulated in judicial decisions but they are increasingly reflected there. The facts of life have long since undermined the concepts, such as *in*

---

* The trustee-beneficiary model has been suggested. Goldman, "The University and the Liberty of its Students—A Fiduciary Theory", 54 Ky. L.J. 643 (1966).

loco parentis, which have been invoked historically for conferring upon university authorities virtually limitless disciplinary discretion.

* * *

I take notice that in the present day, expulsion from an institution or higher learning, or suspension for a period of time substantial enough to prevent one from obtaining academic credit for a particular term, may well be, and often is in fact, a more severe sanction than a monetary fine or a relatively brief confinement imposed by a court in a criminal proceeding.

The world is much with the modern state university. Some find this regrettable, mourning the passing of what is said to have been the old order. I do not share this view. But whether the developments are pleasing is irrelevant to the present issue. What is relevant is that the University of Wisconsin at Madison may continue to encompass functions and situations such as those which characterized a small liberal arts college of the early 20th century (of which some no doubt exist today), but that it encompasses many more functions and situations which bear little or no resemblance to the "models" which appear to have underlain, and continue in some cases to underlie, judicial response to cases involving college or university discipline. What is relevant is that in today's world university disciplinary proceedings are likely to involve many forms of misconduct other than fraternity hazing or plagiarism, and that the sanctions imposed may involve consequences for a particular student more grave than those involved in some criminal court proceedings.

The question here concerns the relationship, in today's world, between the university board, faculty, and administrators as the governors, and students as the governed. Although there is considerable ferment in the universities about this very relationship, I see no constitutional bar to an arrangement by which the state vests in a board of regents and the faculty the power to govern a university and to discipline its students; nor do I see any constitutional bar to a prompt and severe disciplinary response to violence and rioting and other constitutionally unprotected conduct. The more precise question concerns the manner in which this power to govern and to discipline is exercised. It concerns whether the manner of its exercise is wholly immune to the application of the standards of vagueness and overbreadth. Even more precisely, it concerns whether the courts may—and if they may, whether they should—measure the sufficiency of university rules and regulations against these constitutional standards.

* * *

The present . . . distinction between state universities at which attendance is optional, and public elementary and secondary schools at which attendance is compulsory, is difficult to evaluate. It has not been expressly overruled. . . . It seems unnecessary here to invade the thicket of conceptual difficulties involved in the "rights-privileges" distinction and the doctrine of unconstitutional conditions. . . . It should be sufficient to observe that many courts have now concluded that whether the opportunity to attend a state institution of higher learning is viewed as a right or as a privilege, it may not be conditioned on the student's acceptance of a regime in which procedural due process is abdicated . . . or in which substantive rules flatly restricting free expression are enforced. . . . Thus, it cannot presently be contended that in order to enjoy the "privilege" of higher education, one may be obliged to consent that he may be expelled without specification of charges, notice, or hearing, or to consent to remain silent on the political and social issues of his time. "A state cannot force a college student to forfeit his constitutionally protected right of freedom of expression as a condition to his attending a state-supported institution." . . .

Finally, then, the issue is reached whether admission to the University of Wisconsin as a student, and continued enrollment there, may be made to depend upon consent to a regime in which due process may be denied by vague prohibitory standards, or freedom of expression may be threatened or denied by vague and overly broad prohibitory standards. For the reasons I have discussed the answer must be no, unless there is some compelling reason why the university should escape this particular constitutional stricture, some reason why it should be wholly free to refrain from promulgating reasonably definite and narrow rules of conduct. In *Esteban* v. *Central Missouri State College,* 290 F. Supp. 622 . . . it was said:

> Judicial notice is taken that outstanding educational authorities in the field of higher education believe, on the basis of experience, that detailed codes of prohibited student conduct are provocative and should not be employed in higher education. See Brady and Snoxell, *Student Personnel Work in Higher Education,* p. 378 (Houghton-Mifflin, Boston, 1961). For this reason, general affirmative statements of what is expected of a student may be preferable in higher education. Such affirmative statements should, of course, be reasonably construed and applied in individual cases.

I cannot agree that university students should be deprived of these significant constitutional protections on so slender a showing. The American Association of University Professors has declared:

> Disciplinary proceedings should be instituted only for violation of standards of conduct defined in advance and published through such means as a student handbook or a generally available body of university regulations. Offenses should be as clearly defined as possible and such vague phrases as "undesirable conduct" or "conduct injurious to the best interests of the institution" should be avoided. Conceptions of misconduct particular to the institution need a clear

and explicit definition. Statement of The Academic Freedom of Students, 51 A.A.U.P. Bull., 447, 449 (1965).

See Van Alstyne, "Student Academic Freedom and the Rule-Making Powers of Public Universities: Some Constitutional Considerations," 2 *Law in Transition Quarterly* 1, 2–6 (1965), and Van Alstyne, "The Student as University Resident," 45 *Denver L.J.* 582, 592–593, nn. 23, 24 (Special 1968). The subject is discussed extensively in a "Symposium: Student Rights and Campus Rules," 54 *Calif. L. Rev.* (March, 1966), and specifically therein in Linde, "Campus Law: Berkeley Viewed from Eugene," 54 *Calif. L. Rev.* 40, in which the efforts to develop a student conduct code at the University of Oregon are discussed in detail. I am not persuaded that the impossibility or inadvisability of the task must be accepted so readily when important Fourteenth Amendment and First Amendment guarantees are at stake.

For the reasons stated, and upon the basis of the entire record herein, I conclude that the constitutional doctrines of vagueness and overbreadth are applicable, in some measure, to the standard or standards to be applied by the university in disciplining its students, and that a regime in which the term "misconduct" serves as the sole standard violates the due process clause of the Fourteenth Amendment by reason of its vagueness, or, in the alternative, violates the First Amendment as embodied in the Fourteenth by reason of its vagueness and overbreadth.

I have said that these doctrines are applicable "in some measure." It is neither necessary nor wise presently to decide whether they are applicable to disciplinary proceedings in which the range of possible sanctions is mild, such as the denial of social privileges or a minor loss of academic credits or perhaps expulsion from a specific course or perhaps a brief suspension. Nor is it necessary or wise presently to decide whether the standards of vagueness and overbreadth are to be applied as stringently to university regulations of conduct as to criminal statutes in nonuniversity life. Nor is it necessary or wise presently to decide whether these standards are to be applied with equal stringency in every phase of the life of the university; in nonuniversity society, it appears that they are not applied with equal stringency to economic regulations, regulations of speech or assembly, public employment, penal institutions, court room decorum, the military establishment, and other situations; it may be that within the university community the standards may permissibly apply differently to the teacher's control of the classroom, demonstrations, dormitory life, picketing, parking regulations, and decorum in disciplinary hearings.

The judgment here declared is that a standard of "misconduct," without more, may not serve as the sole foundation for the imposition of the sanction of expulsion or the sanction of suspension for any significant time, throughout the entire range of student life in the university.

CHAPTER 11.02, LAWS AND REGULATIONS
OF THE UNIVERSITY OF WISCONSIN

I turn, then, from the defendants' contention that the term "misconduct" alone is sufficient to support the imposition of serious disciplinary sanctions for the behavior which allegedly occurred on the campus on October 18. I turn to the only university rule or regulation, then in existence, which defendants continue to assert as a basis for such disciplinary sanctions. This is Chapter 11.02 of the Laws and Regulations of the Madison campus of the University of Wisconsin, which provides:

Scope of Student Freedom. Students have the right, accorded to all persons by the Constitution, to freedom of speech, peaceable assembly, petition and association. Students and student organizations may examine and discuss all questions of interest to them, and express opinions publicly as well as privately. They may support causes by lawful means which do not disrupt the operations of the University, or organizations accorded the use of University facilities.

The language of Chapter 11.02 does not lend itself readily to the construction that it is a prohibitory regulation. When it appeared in this action, nevertheless, that the defendants viewed it as a prohibition and that they intended to persist in disciplinary proceedings for alleged violations of the prohibition, I considered myself, as the district judge, constrained to view it as an "order made by an administrative board or commission acting under State statutes," 28 U.S.E. § 2281. Viewed as an "order," I considered it of statewise import. Since an injunction against its enforcement was being sought upon the ground that it violates the Constitution of the United States, I considered that the issue required the convening of a three-judge court. The Chief Judge of the Circuit disagreed. In an order entered herein declining to convene a three-judge court, the Chief Judge commented in part as follows with respect to Chapter 11.02:

It is not a regulation, but merely a statement of the rights of students. It contains no proscriptions or sanctions. Nor is it compulsory. . . . [W]e are not concerned here with a statute or University regulation requiring a student to perform an act, i.e., enroll in a compulsory military training course of instruction, or precluding the admission or enrollment of a student because of race. We are reviewing a so-called regulation which is merely a broad declaration of rights extended to students of the University of Wisconsin, whose support of causes is limited to the use of "peaceful means which do not disrupt the operations of the University, or organizations accorded the use of university facilities."

The disposition of the challenge to Chapter 11.02 was left to the single district judge.

The resulting situation is anomalous. Under the view reflected in the comments of the Chief Judge of the Circuit, Chapter 11.02 is not available to the defendants as a basis for disciplinary action. However, it is alleged (obviously not frivolously, as appears from the exhibits attached to the complaint and from exhibits received at a hearing on an application for temporary restraints) that the defendants do in fact assert that Chapter 11.02 is a prohibitory regulation which may serve as a basis for disciplinary action; counsel for the defendants represent that defendants intend so to employ and apply Chapter 11.02. Under the circumstances, I will construe Chapter 11.02 as if it forbids students to "support causes by means which disrupt the operations of the university, or organizations accorded the use of university facilities."*

Obviously it is not a simple matter to draft a regulation which deals with means by which "causes" are supported or opposed, and which undertakes to prohibit those means unprotected by the First Amendment without impairing those which are so protected, and which also avoids the vice of vagueness. I appreciate that those who drafted and approved Chapter 11.02 may reasonably have supposed it sufficient to use a general phrase, such as "lawful means which do not disrupt the operations of the university," and allow its narrower meanings and scope "to be hammered out case by case. . . ." But in the view I have taken, expressed in the preceding section of this opinion, such vagueness or overbreadth, or both, are impermissible in the First Amendment area when the potential of serious disciplinary sanctions exists. When the standards of vagueness and overbreadth are applied to Chapter 11.02, however mildly, I am obliged to find it invalid. Neither the element of intention, nor that of proximity of cause and effect, nor that of substantiality, for example, is dealt with by its language. Nor does it contain even the most general description of the kinds of conduct which might be considered disruptive of the operations of the university, or does it undertake to draw any distinctions whatever as among the various categories of university "operations."

I conclude that Chapter 11.02 is unconstitutionally vague.

---

* Conceivably, viewed as a prohibition, Chapter 11.02 could be construed only to forbid students to "support caused by *unlawful* means which disrupt the operations of the university, or organizations accorded the use of university facilities." However, the actual language is: "They may support causes by lawful means which [means] do not disrupt. . . ." The most reasonable construction is that it was intended to view with disfavor those who support causes by lawful means which do disrupt. Thus I conclude that, viewed as a prohibition, Chapter 11.02 forbids students to support causes by otherwise lawful means if these means disrupt the operations of the university. However, even if it were construed as prohibiting only "unlawful" means which disrupt, my conclusion concerning the vagueness or overbreadth would be unchanged.

* * *

A "possible application" of Chapter 11.02 in a practical, realistic, factual context is its application to the organizing of a midday campus mass meeting, otherwise lawful, as a "means" of demonstrating "support" for the "cause" of peace or civil rights. If a substantial number of students are attracted to the mass meeting and absent themselves from classes scheduled at that hour, the "operations of the university" may well be "disrupted."

Another "possible application" of Chapter 11.02 to a practical and realistic factual context is its application to an otherwise lawful campus meeting of a group to support a cause which is so offensive to others that the latter are moved to physical attack upon those in attendance. The meeting may well be a means which disrupts the operations of the university.

I conclude that Chapter 11.02 violates the First Amendment, as embodied in the Fourteenth, and that its prohibitory scope is overly broad.

The judgment is to declare that Chapter 11.02 is unconstitutional and invalid by reason of its vagueness and overbreadth.

PRAYER FOR INJUNCTIVE RELIEF

I have declared herein that Chapter 11.02 is unconstitutional and invalid. I had previously temporarily enjoined its enforcement. I conclude now that its enforcement should be permanently enjoined.

I have also declared herein that a standard of "misconduct," without more, may not serve as the sole foundation for the imposition of the sanction of expulsion, or the sanction of suspension for any significant time, throughout the entire range of student life in the university. I had not previously temporarily enjoined its use and, as the complaint alleges, it apparently has in fact been used since October 18, 1967, is the basis for the imposition of the sanction of expulsion. For reasons which I am about to explain, I conclude that I should not presently prospectively enjoin the use of "misconduct" as a standard for the imposition of disciplinary sanctions by the university and that, for the present, the use of this standard for the imposition of disciplinary sanctions by the university should be permitted to await judicial review, case by case, following the imposition of the sanction.

* * *

Logic would seem to require that the declaration of invalidity with respect to the standard of "misconduct" be accompanied by injunctive relief. As I have said above . . . this prospective, anticipatory, wholesale method of attack upon vague and overly broad prohibitions has been vindicated by the Supreme Court. The principal reason for permitting this method of attack—as distinguished from retrospective, case by case, review of the validity of prohibitions, as actually applied—is said to be that the mere presence or existence of such prohibitions in the area of First Amendment freedoms may have a "chilling effect" upon the exercise of these freedoms . . . which are accorded an exalted and prime position in the constellation of constitutional values.

Whatever the apparent dictates of logic, the same considerations which prompted me to withhold the temporary injunctive relief sought with respect to the "misconduct" standard prompt me now to withhold permanent injunctive relief with respect to this standard.

To hold, as I have held herein, that the university may not escape the necessity to formulate reasonably definite and narrow regulations, at least in some areas of student life and at least with respect to the imposition of serious sanctions, will itself require a considerable readjustment within the university. To take a second step—that is, to confront the university with a sudden application of the tests of vagueness and of overbreadth in a prospective, anticipatory, and wholesale manner—is to impose too radical a transitional strain upon the institution. It is not a matter of record in this action whether the university has anticipated the judicial declarations contained herein. But even assuming that it has done so to a degree, it is unreasonable to suppose that there has been sufficient opportunity for it to review the framework of its laws and regulations in the light of these judicial declarations.

* * *

But historically the regulation of conduct within the university has been the handiwork of lawmakers who have had little reason to suppose that it would be subjected to constitutional scrutiny, at least in substantive terms. Not only to subject it to such scrutiny, as I have held it must be, but simultaneously to recognize special rules of standing to challengers and to enjoin enforcement of vague or overly broad regulations, is too strong medicine. Its effects cannot immediately be perceived. Whether the resulting holes in the complex of the university's regulations of conduct would be few and minor and readily filled, or numerous and major and difficult to fill, cannot be evaluated by this court on this record. A reasonable time must be permitted for the university to review its situation. Even so, it will be necessary to compress into a very short interval a process which has required many years in nonuniversity society. For the present, to grant injunctive relief and to leave the university defenseless, so far as its regulation of conduct is concerned, would be to permit, and possibly to encourage, a situation in which many values, including the exercise of First Amendment freedoms themselves, might be impaired.

I have concluded that injunctive relief with respect to the application of the standard of "misconduct," without more, should be denied in this action, and that the plaintiffs and the members of their classes should be left to seek judicial review of the validity of this standard retrospectively, case by case, as it has actually been applied.

In the future and after a reasonable time, depending of course upon intervening rulings by superior courts, this court will be prepared to afford injunctive relief to parties who may seek it, consistently with the judicial declarations contained herein.

Accordingly, it is hereby ordered and adjudged:

1. that a standard of "misconduct," without more, may not constitutionally serve as the sole foundation for the imposition, by the University of Wisconsin at Madison, of the sanction of expulsion, or the sanction of suspension for any significant time, throughout the entire range of student life in the university;

2. that Chapter 11.02 of the Laws and Regulations of the University of Wisconsin at Madison is unconstitutional and invalid because it violates the Fourteenth Amendment to the Constitution of the United States by reason of its vagueness and overbreadth; and

3. that the defendants, and each of them, and their agents, assistants, employees and successors are hereby permanently enjoined from further use, operation or enforcement of Chapter 11.02 of the Laws and Regulations of the University of Wisconsin at Madison.

Entered this 13th day of December, 1968,

> By the Court:
> James E. Doyle
> District Judge

Esteban v. *Central Missouri State College*
415 Fed. 2nd. 1077
April 28, 1969

BLACKMUN, Circuit Judge

Alfredo Esteban and Steve Craig Roberds, students at Central Missouri State College, a tax-supported institution at Warrensburg, Missouri, were suspended on March 31, 1967, for two semesters but with the right thereafter to apply for readmission. The two, by their next friends, instituted the present action for declaratory and injunctive relief. The named defendants are the College, its President, and its Board of Regents. The plaintiffs allege primarily, First, Fifth, and Fourteenth Amendment violations. Judge Hunter, with a detailed memorandum, denied them relief and dismissed their complaint.

* * *

The disciplinary action against the plaintiffs arose out of events which took place on or adjacent to the college campus on the nights of March 29 and 30, 1967. At that time Esteban was on scholastic probation and Roberds was on disciplinary probation. Esteban also had been on disciplinary probation over a knifing incident with a fellow student, but his disciplinary probation had expired a short time before.

Both sides in their appellate briefs specifically adopt findings of fact made by Judge Hunter with respect to these March 1967 events. Accordingly, we set forth certain of those findings here:

> ... These demonstrations took place at the intersection of the public street adjacent to the school campus and State Highway 13 and overflowed onto the sidewalks and campus. On the evening of March 29, some 350 students were present in the mass and on March 30, there were some 600 students included. As a partial result of these two mass demonstrations there was in excess of $600 damages and destruction of college property, including broken school building windows and destroyed shrubbery; eggs were thrown; the Dean of Men, Dr. Chalquist, was hanged in effigy, his "dummy" torn up and set on fire; traffic was halted and blocked, cars were rocked, and their occupants ordered out into the street. The college president directed a number of his personnel, including Dr. Meverden, to go to the scene to restore order.

> ESTEBAN EVENT:
> ... The evening of March 29, 1967, around 11:30 P.M., he left his dormitory about the time the "disturbance" had subsided. Some of the students were proceeding along the street from the mass demonstration to their dormitories. Esteban proceeded down the sidewalk to within about 100 feet of the intersection of the scene of the mass demonstration and stayed there awhile. Dr. Meverden, a faculty member, who was seeking to disperse students standing outside their dorms, approached Esteban and asked him to go inside the dormitory. Instead of complying, Esteban asked why, and on again being requested to go in, again asked why.
> He told Dr. Meverden that he was not in violation of any state, county, or federal law and that he had a right to be out there. Dr. Meverden asked for his student identification card which by college regulation he was required to have in his possession at all times. Esteban said ("in rough words" according to one witness) he did not have it. Nor did he give his name. Dr. Meverden again requested him to go in the dormitory and get off the street. Esteban argued with Dr. Meverden and questioned his authority, saying there were no rules limiting the time men could stay outside the dorms. Shortly, and with the encouragement of other students present, he went into the dormitory. Dr. Meverden also went in and asked Gerald Haddock, the resident assistant of Esteban's dormitory, who Esteban was. Haddock was overheard by Esteban telling Dr. Meverden Esteban's name. Esteban, as Dr. Meverden was leaving, called Haddock a prick and a bastard and told him he "would not be around very long." According to Esteban's roommate, Esteban then angrily picked up a waste can and emptied the contents on the floor at the feet of Haddock.

* * *

The college regulations in effect at the time, and to the extent pertinent, provided:

> The conduct of the individual student is an important indication of character and future usefulness in life. It is therefore important that each student maintain the highest standards of integrity, honesty and morality. All students are expected to conform to ordinary and accepted social customs and to conduct themselves at all times and in all places in a manner befitting a student of Central Missouri State College.
>
> All students that enroll at C. M. S. C. assume an obligation to abide by the rules and regulations of the college as well as all local, state and federal laws.
>
> When a breach of regulations involves a mixed group, ALL MEMBERS ARE HELD EQUALLY RESPONSIBLE.
>
> Conduct unbefitting a student which reflects adversely upon himself or the institution will result in disciplinary action.
>
> Mass Gatherings—Participation in mass gatherings which might be considered as unruly or unlawful will subject a student to possible immediate dismissal from the College. Only a few students intentionally get involved in mob misconduct, but many so-called "spectators" get drawn into a fracas and by their very presence contribute to the dimensions of the problems. It should be understood that the College considers no student to be immune from due process of law enforcement when he is in violation as an individual or as a member of a crowd.

* * *

(7) So it is here. Judge Hunter's findings have been quoted above. We have found them sufficiently supported by the record. They, too, concern an aggressive and violent demonstration and something quite apart from "peaceful, nondisruptive expression." They, too, focus upon "destructive interference with the rights of others." They disclose actual or potentially disruptive conduct, aggressive action, disorder and disturbance, and acts of violence and participation therein by these plaintiffs. Their conduct, therefore, was not protected by the First and Fourteenth Amendments.

3. The regulations. These are additionally attacked for vagueness and overbreadth and hence on substantive due process grounds. Some of the loyalty oath cases are cited and it is said that the regulations' word "unlawful" is only a legal conclusion and that their references to "unruly" and "spectators" and "which might be considered" are likened to city ordinances which have been struck down when they lack sufficiency of definition. It is then argued that "young people should be told clearly what is right and what is wrong, as well as the consequences of their acts." . . . Finally, it is said that the regulations impinge and have a chilling effect upon First and Fourteenth Amendment rights.

The answers to all this, we think, are several. First, the college's regulations, per se, do not appear to us to constitute the fulcrum of the plaintiffs' discomfiture. The charges against Esteban and Roberds did not even refer to the regulations. Roberds was disciplined because he had participated in the demonstrations in the face of specific warning delivered by personal interview with the dean. This was defiance of proper college authority. Esteban was disciplined because of his refusal to comply with an appropriate request by Doctor Meverden and because of his childish behavior and obscenity toward college officials. This, too, was defiance of proper college authority. There was no confusion or unawareness in either case. The exercise of common sense was all that was required. Each plaintiff knew the situation very well, knew what he was doing, and knew the consequences. Each, we might note, had had prior disciplinary experience. Their respective protestations of young and injured innocence have a hollow ring.

Secondly, we agree with Judge Hunter that it is not sound to draw an analogy between student discipline and criminal procedure, that the standard of conduct which a college seeks to impose must be one relevant to "a lawful mission, process or function of the educational institution," and that,

> . . . Certainly the regulation concerning mass demonstrations, reasonably interpreted, and as interpreted and applied by the college in the instant case to a participant in student mass demonstrations involving unlawful conduct such as the illegal blocking of a public highway and street, and the destruction of school property, is relevant to a lawful mission of the educational institution. 290 F.Supp. at 629. (footnote omitted)

(8) Thirdly, we do not find the regulation at all difficult to understand and we are positive that the college student, who is appropriately expected to possess some minimum intelligence, would not find it difficult. It asks for the adherence to standards of conduct which befit a student and it warns of the danger of mass involvement. We must assume Esteban and Roberds can read and that they possess some power of comprehension. Their difficulty was that they chose not to read or not to comprehend.

Fourthly, we see little basically or constitutionally wrong with flexibility and reasonable breadth, rather than meticulous specificity, in college regulations relating to conduct. Certainly these regulations are not to be compared with the criminal statute. They are codes of general conduct which those qualified and experienced in the field have characterized not as punishment but as part of the educational process itself and as preferably to be expressed in general rather than in specific terms. . . .

(9, 10) We agree with those courts which have held that a school has inherent authority to maintain order and to discipline students. We further agree that a school has latitude and discretion in its formulation of rules and regulations and of general standards of conduct. . . .

We regard as quite distinguishable cases such as *Hammond* v. *South Carolina State College*, 272 F.Supp. 947 (D.S.C. 1967), and *Dickey* v. *Alabama State Bd. of Educ.*, supra, where the focus was on an attempted restraint of peaceful assembly or speech. Our attention has been called to the fact that Judge Doyle, in his recent opinion in *Soglin* v. *Kauffman*, 295 F.Supp. 978, 990–991 (W.D. Wis. 1968), expresses disagreement with the observations of Judge Hunter on this aspect of the case. To the extent that, in this area, Judge Doyle is in disagreement with Judge Hunter, we must respectfully disagree with Judge Doyle.

* * *

These plaintiffs are no longer children. While they may have been minors, they were beyond the age of 18. Their days of accomplishing ends and status by force are at an end. It was time they assumed at least the outward appearance of adulthood and of manhood. The mass denial of rights of others is irresponsible and childish. So is the defiance of proper college administrative authority ("I have the right to be here"; "I refuse to identify myself"; gutter abuse of an official; the dumping of a trash can at a resident's feet; "I plan on turning this school into a Berkeley if . . ."; and being a part of the proscribed college peace-disturbing and property-destroying demonstration). One might expect this from the spoiled child of tender years. One rightly does not expect it from the college student who has had two decades of life and who, in theory, is close to being "grown up."

(11–14) Let there be no misunderstanding as to our precise holding. We do not hold that any college regulation, however loosely framed, is necessarily valid. We do not hold that a school has the authority to require a student to discard any constitutional right when he matriculates. We do hold that a college has the inherent power to promulgate rules and regulations; that it has the inherent power properly to discipline; that it has power appropriately to protect itself and its property; that it may expect that its students adhere to generally accepted standards of conduct; that, as to these, flexibility and elbow room are to be preferred over specificity; that procedural due process must be afforded (as Judge Hunter by his first opinion here specifically required) by way of adequate notice, definite charge, and a hearing with opportunity to present one's own side of the case and with all necessary protective measures; that school regulations are not to be measured by the standards which prevail for the criminal law and for the criminal procedure; and that the courts should interfere only where there is a clear case of constitutional infringement.

After all, the test, we feel, is that of reasonableness. . . .

Affirmed.

6
Dismissal Procedure

People v. *Board of Trustees of University of Illinois*
10 Ill. App. 2d 207 (134 N.E.2d 635)
May 7, 1956
NIEMEYER, Judge

Relator (hereinafter called plaintiff), a student in the medical school of the University of Illinois in Chicago from October 1, 1949, to and including May 1953, appeals from an order striking her amended complaint and dismissing her action for mandamus to compel the defendant, The Board of Trustees of the University of Illinois, to vacate an order of expulsion of plaintiff entered July 22, 1954, by the Committee on Policy and Discipline of the Chicago Professional Colleges of the University of Illinois; to reinstate plaintiff as an active student in good standing on the rolls of the medical school and to permit her to take all necessary examinations to determine her right to advance to classes to which she would have been entitled had the order of expulsion not been entered. Plaintiff's appeal to the Supreme Court was transferred to this court.

Plaintiff's action is based on the want of a formal charge and a formal hearing at which she would be confronted with the accusing witnesses and given an opportunity to cross-examine them. Defendant attacks the sufficiency of the amended complaint and the power of the court in a mandamus proceeding to vacate the existing order of expulsion and award the further relief asked by plaintiff. As to the merits, defendant contends that in the procedure adopted and the action taken, plaintiff was not deprived of any legal right.

The material facts alleged will be stated briefly. In May 1953 plaintiff was suspended and prohibited from further continuing her course at the university. She was not informed as to the cause of her suspension until on or about June 15, 1954, when she appeared with her attorney before the Committee on Policy and Discipline and was advised by the counsel for the university that she had been suspended for planning, intending and attempting to turn in an examination paper in an examination in physical diagnosis as her examination paper, which in fact had been written by a Doctor Wong; that prior thereto, in examinations in a class in obstetrics and a class in pharmacology, she had turned in or caused to be turned in examination papers as her own which in fact had also been written by Doctor Wong. No witnesses were produced at the meeting to support the charges and no other evidence was heard than the testimony of plaintiff, not under oath, denying the charges. The committee on July 15, 1954, "After having given careful and thorough consideration to all the evidence before it pertaining to the charges of cheating, or attempting to cheat, in examinations in pharmacology, obstetrics, and physical diagnosis against Miss Patricia Bluett (plaintiff), including her own testimony," as stated in the certificate of the secretary of the committee sent to plaintiff, unanimously found her guilty with respect to each of the charges and changed her status as a student under suspension to that of one expelled and dismissed from the College of Medicine, and recommended to the Dean of the college that she be accorded failing grades in her courses of pharmacology, obstetrics and physical diagnosis. Plaintiff petitioned the committee to reconsider its action, but the committee, after hearing the attorney for plaintiff, reaffirmed its previous decision expelling plaintiff from the university and thereafter failed, refused and neglected to reinstate plaintiff, although she continually made demands upon the committee for reinstatement.

Plaintiff denies her guilt of the charges of cheating or attempting to cheat in examinations, and further alleges that the charges were not sworn to and the only knowledge plaintiff had concerning them was the oral statement of the attorney for the university, hereinbefore mentioned, and that "the Committee in the presence of this Relator heard no evidence of any nature, either sworn or not sworn, which would tend in any manner to substantiate in any degree the charges as related by the attorney for the university," and that the committee "denied her an opportunity of facing her accusers and denied her the rights of cross-examining anyone who made any charge against her."

Plaintiff concedes the right of the committee to expel a student for cheating or attempting to cheat in examinations, and that the court should not attempt to control the exercise of that power unless it is substantially abused. . . . No authorities are cited in plaintiff's original brief to support her contention of a right to sworn charges and an open hearing in which she is confronted with witnesses and given the right of cross-examination.

* * *

As above pointed out, the president of the university has no authority to compel the attendance of witnesses at a hearing or to compel them to testify if they were present. To hold that the power of suspension could only be exercised after a hearing had been held, such as is indicated in the cases last referred to, would be to hold that the power was practically ineffective, except where witnesses voluntarily attended and testified.

* * *

The order appealed from is affirmed.
FRIEND, P.J., and BURKE, J., concur.

Anthony v. *Syracuse University*
231 N.Y.S. 435
Nov. 14, 1928

SEARS, J.

The defendant is an educational corporation incorporated under a special act of the Legislature of the state of New York (Laws 1887, c. 414), and conducts various departments for the higher education of men and women at Syracuse, N.Y. It is exempt from taxation. It is subject to visitation by the board of regents.

The plaintiff, from September 15, 1923, to October 6, 1926, was a student in the Department of Domestic Science or Home Economics of the defendant. This department is not shown to receive any financial aid from the state. On the day last mentioned she was dismissed from the defendant's institution by the officers without the assignment of any adequate cause for such action. She was simply advised that the authorities of the defendant had heard rumors about her; that they had talked with several girls "in the house"—that is, in the house of the Greek letter society of which she was a member—and found she had done nothing lately, but that they had learned that she had caused a lot of trouble in the house; and that they did not think her "a typical Syracuse girl."

In September, 1923, when the plaintiff was first received as a student at the University, she signed a registration card, which contained these words:

I agree in honor to comply with the regulations and requirements of Syracuse University and to co-operate with the University authorities and my fellow students in maintaining high standards of conduct and scholarship and in promoting the general welfare of the University. It is understood that I accept registration as a student in Syracuse

University subject to the rule as to continuance therein found on page 47 of the University Catalogue.

The regulation referred to in the registration card as to continuance at the University, printed on page 47 of the University Catalogue, was as follows:

> Attendance at the University is a privilege and not a right. In order to safeguard its scholarship and its moral atmosphere, the University reserves the right to request the withdrawal of any student whose presence is deemed detrimental. Specific charges may or may not accompany a request for withdrawal.

In September 1924 and again in September 1925 she signed similar registration cards. The regulation quoted above was slightly amended before the 1924 registration card was signed, and as printed in the catalogue, and referred to in the registration cards of 1924 and 1925, it was as follows:

> Attendance at the University is a privilege and not a right. In order to safeguard those ideals of scholarship and that moral atmosphere which are in the very purpose of its founding and maintenance, the University reserves the right and the student concedes to the University the right to require the withdrawal of any student at any time for any reason deemed sufficient to it, and no reason for requiring such withdrawal need be given.

The plaintiff does not allege in the complaint that her dismissal was malicious, but simply that it was arbitrary and unjust and founds her action upon a contract which she claims to have existed between herself and the University for her continued attendance. In substance she seeks a specific performance of this contract. The defendant, on the other hand, relies on what it claims to be one of the terms of the contract, namely, that the plaintiff's continuance as a student at the University was strictly at the pleasure of that institution. No question is raised by the defendant as to the form of the action, or the right of the plaintiff to the judgment she obtained, if she is entitled to any judgment whatever.

(1) Under ordinary circumstances and conditions a person matriculating at a university establishes a contractual relationship under which, upon compliance with all reasonable regulations as to scholastic standing, attendance, deportment, payment of tuition, and otherwise, he is entitled to pursue his selected course to completion, and receive the degree or certificate awarded for the successful completion of such course. . . . The defendant, for the purpose of this litigation, concedes

such to be the law. It rests its case upon the claim that an express contract between the parties takes this case out of the general rule stated, and that, under such express contract, a right to dismiss the plaintiff at any time for any cause whatever was granted to the defendant.

(2–6) The regulation in force in 1923, assented to by plaintiff's signature to the registration card, did, doubtless, as claimed by the defendant, modify the ordinary rule, and this regulation continued to be a part of the contract between the parties throughout the term of the plaintiff's attendance at the University, except as it was modified in 1924. By signing the later registration cards, the plaintiff assented to the modification. Plaintiff argues that the regulation is not binding upon her, first, because at no time did she read the catalogue or have actual knowledge of the regulation printed in it; and, second, because the regulation is contrary to public policy. It is also suggested that it is not binding on her because she was an infant at the time all registration cards were signed. In my judgment none of these arguments is sound.

* * *

The fact that the plaintiff had no actual knowledge of the existence of this rule would not alter the situation, assuming that the rule of constructive knowledge be under the circumstances applicable.

* * *

Second, the argument on public policy is based upon the theory that consent to such a regulation as was here printed in the catalogue amounts to a permission given the University authorities to do an act which would necessarily injure the reputation of the student. Such injury to reputation, however, if it occurred, would be merely incidental. As both parties argue, the relation between plaintiff and defendant was wholly contractual. It was voluntary in its inception on both sides. A student is not required to enter the University, and may in fact, after entry, withdraw without reason at any time. The University need not accept as a student one desiring to become such. It may, therefore, limit the effect of such acceptance by express agreement, and thus retain the position of contractual freedom in which it stood before the student's course was entered upon. I can discover no reason why a student may not agree to grant to the institution an optional right to terminate the relations between them. The contract between an institution and a student does not differ in this respect from contracts of employment. . . .

(7) Third, infancy is not material. The plaintiff relies upon a contract made when she was an infant. She cannot recover, except upon the contract. The only contract existing between the plaintiff and defendant embodied the regulation permitting the defendant to terminate

the contractual relationship. If she repudiates her contract because of her infancy, she then becomes a stranger to the University. She cannot repudiate part and not repudiate all.

(8, 9) The construction of the regulation may be material. The regulation, in my judgment, does not reserve to the defendant an absolute right to dismiss the plaintiff for any cause whatever. Its right to dismiss is limited, for the regulation must be read as a whole. The University may only dismiss a student for reasons falling within two classes, one in connection with safeguarding the University's ideals of scholarship, and the other in connection with safeguarding the University's moral atmosphere. When dismissing a student, no reason for dismissing need be given. The University must, however, have a reason, and that reason must fall within one of the two classes mentioned above. Of course, the University authorities have wide discretion in determining what situation does and what does not fall within the classes mentioned, and the courts would be slow indeed in disturbing any decision of the University authorities in this respect.

(10) When the plaintiff comes into court and alleges a breach of contract, the burden rests upon her to establish such breach. She must show that her dismissal was not for a reason within the terms of the regulation. The record here is meager on this subject. While no adequate reason was assigned by the University authorities for the dismissal, I find nothing in the record on which to base a finding that no such reason existed. She offered no testimony, either as to her character and relation with her college associates, or as to her scholarship and attention to her academic duties. The evidence discloses no reason for her dismissal not falling within the terms of the regulation. It follows, therefore, that the action fails. The judgment should be reversed on the law and the facts, with costs, and judgment granted to the defendant, dismissing the complaint, with costs. Certain findings of fact and conclusions of law disapproved and reversed, and new findings of fact made.

Judgment reversed on the law and facts, with costs, and complaint dismissed, with costs. Certain findings of fact and conclusions of law disapproved and reversed, and new findings and conclusions made. All concur; TAYLOR, J., in result, on the ground that the special contract gave defendant an absolute and unlimited right to remove plaintiff from the University at any time, the recitals in the contract being merely a statement of the motives prompting defendant to reserve its right to dismiss at its option.

Dixon v. *Alabama State Board of Education*
294 F.2d 150
United States Court of Appeals
Fifth Circuit
Aug. 4, 1961

RIVES, Circuit Judge

The question presented by the pleadings and evidence,* and decisive of this appeal, is whether due process requires notice and some opportunity for hearing before students at a tax-supported college are expelled for misconduct. We answer that question in the affirmative.

The misconduct for which the students were expelled has never been definitely specified. Defendant Trenholm, the President of the College, testified that he did not know why the plaintiffs and three additional students were expelled and twenty other students were placed on probation. The notice of expulsion** which Dr. Trenholm mailed to each of

---

* The complaint alleges that "Defendant Trenholm on March 4, 1960, notified plaintiffs of their expulsion effective March 5, 1960, without any notice, hearing, or appeal," and further avers:

Expulsion from Alabama State College came without warning, notice of charges, opportunity to appear before defendants or at any other hearing, opportunity to offer testimony in defense, cross-examination of accusers, appeal, or other opportunity to defend plaintiffs' right not to be arbitrarily expelled from defendant College. Defendants' expulsion order, issued by the defendants functioning under the statutes, laws and regulations of the State of Alabama, thereby deprived plaintiffs of rights protected by the due process clause of the Fourteenth Amendment to the United States Constitution.

To this averment the defendants respond:
. . . that the facts set forth in plaintiffs' complaint show no violation of the due process clause of the Fourteenth Amendment to the Constitution of the United States; that plaintiffs have no constitutional right to attend Alabama State College; that the facts stated by plaintiffs in their complaint show that this Court is without jurisdiction for no arbitrary action is alleged except as conclusions unsupported by the facts alleged; that the defendants determined in good faith and within their authority as the governing authorities of Alabama State College that the expulsions of the plaintiffs were for the best interests of the college and based upon undisputed conduct of plaintiffs while students at said college.

As will appear later in this opinion, the issue thus squarely presented by the pleadings was fully developed in the evidence.

** Letter from Alabama State College, Montgomery, Alabama, dated March 4, 1960, signed by H. Councill Trenholm, President:

Dear Sir:
This communication is the official notification of your expulsion from Alabama State College as of the end of the 1960 Winter Quarter.

As reported through the various news media, The State Board of Education considered this problem of Alabama State College at its meeting on this past Wednesday afternoon. You were one of the students involved in this expulsion-directive by the State Board of Education. I was directed to proceed accordingly.

On Friday of last week, I had made the recommendation that any subsequently-confirmed action would not be effective until the close of the 1960 Winter

the plaintiffs assigned no specific ground for expulsion, but referred in general terms to "this problem of Alabama State College."

The acts of the students considered by the State Board of Education before it ordered their expulsion are described in the opinion of the district court reported in 186 F.Supp. 945, 947, from which we quote in the margin.*

Quarter so that each student could thus have the opportunity to take this quarter's examinations and to qualify for as much OH-Pt credit as possible for the 1960 Winter Quarter.

The State Board of Education, which is made responsible for the supervision of the six higher institutions at Montgomery, Normal, Florence, Jacksonville, Livingston, and Troy (each of the other three institutions at Tuscaloosa, Auburn, and Montevallo having separate boards) includes the following in its regulations (as carried in page 32 of The 1958–59 Registration-Announcement of Alabama State College) :

"a. For willful disobedience to the rules and regulations established for the conduct of the schools.

"b. For willful and continued neglect of studies and continued failure to maintain the standards of efficiency required by the rules and regulations.

"c. For Conduct Prejudicial to the School and for Conduct Unbecoming a Student or Future Teacher in Schools of Alabama, for Insubordination and Insurrection, or for Inciting Other Pupils to Like Conduct.

"d. For any conduct involving moral turpitude."

In the notice received by each of the students, paragraph "c," just quoted, was capitalized.

---

* On the 25th day of February, 1960, the six plaintiffs in this case were students in good standing at the Alabama State College for Negroes in Montgomery, Alabama. . . . On this date, approximately twenty-nine Negro students, including these six plaintiffs, according to a prearranged plan, entered as a group a publicly owned lunch grill located in the basement of the county courthouse in Montgomery, Alabama, and asked to be served. Service was refused; the lunchroom was closed; the Negroes refused to leave; police authorities were summoned; and the Negroes were ordered outside where they remained in the corridor of the courthouse for approximately one hour. On the same date, John Patterson, as Governor of the State of Alabama and as chairman of the State Board of Education, conferred with Dr. Trenholm, a Negro Educator and president of the Alabama State College, concerning this activity on the part of some of the students. Dr. Trenholm was advised by the Governor that the incident should be investigated, and that if he were in the president's position he could consider expulsion and/or other appropriate disciplinary action. On February 26, 1960, several hundred Negro students from the Alabama State College, including several if not all of these plaintiffs, staged a mass attendance at a trial being held in the Montgomery County Courthouse, involving the perjury prosecution of a fellow student. After the trial these students filed two by two from the courthouse and marched through the city approximately two miles back to the college. On February 27, 1960, several hundred Negro students from this school, including several if not all of the plaintiffs in this case, staged mass demonstrations in Montgomery and Tuskegee, Alabama. On this same date, Dr. Trenholm advised all of the student body that these demonstrations and meetings were disrupting the orderly conduct of the business at the college and were affecting the work of other students, as well as work of the participating students. Dr. Trenholm personally warned plaintiffs Bernard Lee, Joseph Peterson and Elroy Embry to cease these disruptive demonstrations immediately, and advised the members of the student body at the Alabama State College to behave themselves and return to their classes. . . .

On or about March 1, 1960, approximately six hundred students of the Alabama State College engaged in hymn singing and speech making on the steps of the

As shown by the findings of the district court, just quoted in footnote, the only demonstration which the evidence showed that *all* of the expelled students took part in was that in the lunch grill located in the basement of the Montgomery County Courthouse. The other demonstrations were found to be attended "by several if not all of the plaintiffs." We have carefully read and studied the record, and agree with the district court that the evidence does not affirmatively show that *all* of the plaintiffs were present at any but the one demonstration.

Only one member of the State Board of Education assigned the demonstration attended by all of the plaintiffs as the sole basis for his vote to expel them.

* * *

Superintendent of Education Stewart testified that he voted for expulsion because the students had broken rules and regulations pertaining to all of the State institutions. . . .

The testimony of other members of the Board assigned somewhat varying and differing grounds and reasons for their votes to expel the plaintiffs.

The district court found the general nature of the proceedings before the State Board of Education, the action of the Board, and the official notice of expulsion given to the students as follows:

Investigations into this conduct were made by Dr. Trenholm, as president of the Alabama State College, the Director of Public Safety for the State of Alabama under directions of the Governor, and by the investigative staff of the Attorney General for the State of Alabama.

On or about March 2, 1960, the State Board of Education met and received reports from the Governor of the State of Alabama, which reports embodied the investigations that had been made and which reports identified these six plaintiffs, together with several others, as the "ring leaders" for the group of students that had been participating in the above-recited activities. During this meeting, Dr. Trenholm, in his capacity as president of the college, reported to the assembled members of the State Board of Education that the action of these students in demonstrating on the college campus and in certain downtown areas was having a disruptive influence on the work of the other students at the college and upon the orderly operation of the college in general. Dr. Trenholm further reported to the Board that, in his opinion, he as president of the college could not control future disruptions and demonstrations. There were twenty-nine of the Negro students identified as the core of the organization that was responsible for these demonstrations. This group of twenty-nine included these six plaintiffs. After hearing these reports and recommendations and upon the recommendation of the Governor as chair-

---

State Capitol. Plaintiff Bernard Lee addressed students at this demonstration, and the demonstration was attended by several if not all of the plaintiffs. Plaintiff Bernard Lee at this time called on the students to strike and boycott the college if any students were expelled because of these demonstrations.

man of the Board, the Board voted unanimously, expelling nine plaintiffs, and placing twenty students on probation. This action was taken by Dr. Trenholm as president of the college, acting pursuant to the instructions of the State Board of Education. Each of these plaintiffs, together with the other students expelled, was officially notified of his expulsion on March 4th or 5th, 1960.* No formal charges were placed against these students and no hearing was granted any of them prior to their expulsion.

* * *

The evidence clearly shows that the question for decision does not concern the sufficiency of the notice or the adequacy of the hearing, but is whether the students had a right to any notice or hearing whatever before being expelled. The district court wrote at some length on that question, as appears from its opinion. *Dixon* v. *Alabama State Board of Education,* supra, 186 F.Supp. at pages 950–952. After careful study and consideration, we find ourselves unable to agree with the conclusion of the district court that no notice or opportunity for any kind of hearing was required before these students were expelled.

It is true, as the district court said, that "there is no statute or rule that requires formal charges and/or a hearing," but the evidence is

---

* The plaintiff Dixon testified:

Q. Now on that day—from February 25 until the date that you received your letter of expulsion, which you have already identified, will you tell the Court whether any person at the College gave you any official notice that your conduct was unbecoming as a student of Alabama State College? A. No.

Q. Did the president or any other person at the College arrange for any type of hearing where you had an opportunity to present your side prior to the time you were expelled? A. No.

Q. Your answer was no? A. No.

The testimony of Governor Patterson, Chairman of the State Board of Education, was in accord:

Q. Did the State Board of Education, prior to the time it expelled the plaintiffs, give them an opportunity to appear either before the College or before the Board in order to present their sides of this pic—of this incident? A. No, other than receiving the report from Dr. Trenholm about it.

Q. Did the Board direct Dr. Trenholm to give the students formal notice of why they were expelled? A. No, the Board—the Board passed a resolution instructing Dr. Trenholm to expel the students and put twenty on probation, and Dr. Trenholm carried that out.

State Superintendent of Education Stewart testified:

Q. Were these students given any type of hearing, or were formal charges filed against them before they were expelled? A. They were—Dr. Trenholm expelled the students; they weren't given any hearing.

Q. No hearing? A. I don't think they would be given a hearing in any of our schools in this State; if they couldn't behave themselves, I think they should go home.

Q. Do you—were they warned at all prior to expulsion? A. Not as I know of; I can't answer that question. Dr. Trenholm was in the meeting, and that afternoon after the Board meeting, he was given the—the decision, and he was the one who took action.

Q. When the State Board of Education expels a student, is there any possibility of appeal or any opportunity for him to present his side of the story? A. I never have heard of it.

without dispute that the usual practice at Alabama State College had been to give a hearing and opportunity to offer defenses before expelling a student. Defendant Trenholm, the College President, testified:

> Q. The essence of the question was, Will you relate to the Court the usual steps that are taken when a student's conduct has developed to the point where it is necessary for the administration to punish him for that conduct?
> A. We normally would have conference with the student and notify him that he was being asked to withdraw, and we would indicate why he was being asked to withdraw. That would be applicable to academic reasons, academic deficiency, as well as to any conduct difficulty.
> Q. And at this hearing ordinarily that you would set, then the student would have a right to offer whatever defense he may have to the charges that have been brought against him?
> A. Yes.

Whenever a governmental body acts so as to injure an individual, the Constitution requires that the act be consonant with due process of law. The minimum procedural requirements necessary to satisfy due process depend upon the circumstances and the interests of the parties involved. As stated by Mr. Justice Frankfurter . . .:

> Whether the *ex parte* procedure to which the petitioners were subjected duly observed "the rudiments of fair play," . . . cannot . . . be tested by mere generalities or sentiments abstractly appealing. The precise nature of the interest that has been adversely affected, the manner in which this was done, the reasons for doing it, the available alternatives to the procedure that was followed, the protection implicit in the office of the functionary whose conduct is challenged, the balance of hurt complained of and good accomplished—these are some of the considerations that must enter into the judicial judgment.

* * *

It is not enough to say, as did the district court in the present case, "The right to attend a public college or university is not in and of itself a constitutional right." . . . One may not have a constitutional right to go to Bagdad, but the Government may not prohibit one from going there unless by means consonant with due process of law. As in that case, so here, it is necessary to consider "the nature both of the private interest which has been impaired and the governmental power which has been exercised."

The appellees urge upon us that under a provision of the Board of Education's regulations the appellants waived any right to notice and a hearing before being expelled for misconduct.

Attendance at any college is on the basis of a mutual decision of the student's parents and of the college. Attendance at a particular college is voluntary and is different from attendance at a public school where the pupil may be required to attend a particular school which is located in the neighborhood or district in which the pupil's family may live. Just as a student may choose to withdraw from a particular college at any time for any personally determined reason, the college may also at any time decline to continue to accept responsibility for the supervision and service to any student with whom the relationship becomes unpleasant and difficult.

We do not read this provision to clearly indicate an intent on the part of the student to waive notice and a hearing before expulsion. If, however, we should so assume, it nonetheless remains true that the State cannot condition the granting of even a privilege upon the renunciation of the constitutional right to procedural due process. . . . Only private associations have the right to obtain a waiver of notice and hearing before depriving a member of a valuable right. And even here, the right to notice and a hearing is so fundamental to the conduct of our society that the waiver must be clear and explicit. . . .

The precise nature of the private interest involved in this case is the right to remain at a public institution of higher learning in which the plaintiffs were students in good standing. It requires no argument to demonstrate that education is vital and, indeed, basic to civilized society. Without sufficient education the plaintiffs would not be able to earn an adequate livelihood, to enjoy life to the fullest, or to fulfill as completely as possible the duties and responsibilities of good citizens.

There was no offer to prove that other colleges are open to the plaintiffs. If so, the plaintiffs would nonetheless be injured by the interruption of their course of studies in mid-term. It is most unlikely that a public college would accept a student expelled from another public college of the same state. Indeed, expulsion may well prejudice the student in completing his education at any other institution. Surely no one can question that the right to remain at the college in which the plaintiffs were students in good standing is an interest of extremely great value.

Turning then to the nature of the governmental power to expel the plaintiffs, it must be conceded, as was held by the district court, that the power is not unlimited and cannot be arbitrarily exercised. Admittedly, there must be some reasonable and constitutional ground for expulsion or the courts would have a duty to require reinstatement. The possibility of arbitrary action is not excluded by the existence of reasonable regulations. There may be arbitrary application of the rule to the facts of a particular case. Indeed, that result is well nigh inevitable when the Board heard only one side of the issue. In the disciplining of college students there are no considerations of immediate danger to the public, or of peril to the national security, which should prevent the Board from exercising at least the fundamental principles of fairness by giving the accused students notice of the charges and an opportunity to be heard in their own defense. Indeed, the example set by the Board in failing so to do, if not corrected by the courts, can well break the spirits of the expelled students and of others familiar with the injustice, and do inestimable harm to their education.

The district court, however, felt that it was governed by precedent, and stated that, "the courts have consistently upheld the validity of regulations that have the effect of reserving to the college the right to dismiss students at any time for any reason without divulging its reason other than its being for the general benefit of the institution." [186 F.Supp. 951.] With deference, we must hold that the district court has simply misinterpreted the precedents.

The language above quoted from the district court is based upon language found in . . . Anthony v. Syracuse University . . . 231 N.Y.S. 435, reversing 130 Misc.2d 249, 223 N.Y.S. 796, 797. . . . This case, how-ever, concerns a private university and follows the well-settled rule that the relations between a student and a private university are a matter of contract. The Anthony case held that the plaintiffs had specifically waived their rights to notice and hearing. See also Barker v. Bryn Mawr, 1923, 278 Pa. 121, 122 A. 220. The precedents for public colleges are collected in a recent annotation cited by the district court. 58 A.L.R.2d 903–920. We have read all of the cases cited to the point, and we agree with what the annotator himself says: "The cases involv-ing suspension or expulsion of a student from a public college or uni-versity all involve the question whether the hearing given to the student was adequate. In every instance the sufficiency of the hearing was upheld." . . . None held that no hearing whatsoever was required. Two cases not found in the annotation have held that some form of hearing is required. In Commonwealth ex rel. Hill v. McCauley, 1886, 3 Pa.Co.Ct.R. 77, the court went so far as to say that an informal presenta-tion of the charges was insufficient and that a state-supported college must grant a student a full hearing on the charges before expulsion for misconduct.

* * *

It was not a case denying any hearing whatsoever but one passing upon the adequacy of the hearing, which provoked from Professor Warren A. Seavey of Harvard the eloquent comment:

> At this time when many are worried about dismissal from public service, when only because of the overriding need to protect the public safety is the identity of informers kept secret, when we proudly contrast the full hearings before our courts with those in the be-nighted countries which have no due process protection, when many of our courts are so careful in the protection of those charged with crimes that they will not permit the use of evidence illegally obtained, our sense of justice should be outraged by denial to students of the

normal safeguards. It is shocking that the officials of a state education institution, which can function properly only if our freedoms are preserved, should not understand the elementary principles of fair play. It is equally shocking to find that a court supports them in denying to a student the protection given to a pickpocket. *Dismissal of Students: "Due Process,"* Warren A. Seavey, 70 Harvard Law Review 1406, 1407. We are confident that precedent as well as a most fundamental constitutional principle support our holding that due process requires notice and some opportunity for hearing before a student at a tax-supported college is expelled for misconduct.

For the guidance of the parties in the event of further proceedings, we state our views on the nature of the notice and hearing required by due process prior to expulsion from a state college or university. They should, we think, comply with the following standards. The notice should contain a statement of the specific charges and grounds which, if proven, would justify expulsion under the regulations of the Board of Education. The nature of the hearing should vary, depending upon the circumstances of the particular case. The case before us requires something more than an informal interview with an administrative authority of the college. By its nature, a charge of misconduct, as opposed to a failure to meet the scholastic standards of the college, depends upon a collection of the facts concerning the charged misconduct, easily colored by the point of view of the witnesses. In such circumstances, a hearing which gives the Board or the administrative authorities of the college an opportunity to hear both sides in considerable detail is best suited to protect the rights of all involved. This is not to imply that a full-dress judicial hearing, with the right to cross-examine witnesses, is required. Such a hearing, with the attending publicity and disturbance of college activities, might be detrimental to the college's educational atmosphere and impractical to carry out. Nevertheless, the rudiments of an adversary proceeding may be preserved without encroaching upon the interests of the college. In the instant case, the student should be given the names of the witnesses against him and an oral or written report of the facts to which each witness testifies. He should also be given the opportunity to present to the Board, or at least to an administrative official of the college, his own defense against the charges and to produce either oral testimony or written affidavits of witnesses in his behalf. If the hearing is not before the Board directly, the results and findings of the hearing should be presented in a report open to the student's inspection. If these rudimentary elements of fair play are followed in a case of misconduct of this particular type, we feel that the requirements of due process of law will have been fulfilled.

The judgment of the district court is reversed and the cause is remanded for further proceedings consistent with this opinion.

Reversed and remanded.

CAMERON, Circuit Judge (dissenting)

The opinion of the district court in this case* is so lucid, literate and moderate that I cannot forgo expressing surprise that my brethren of the majority can find fault with it. In this dissent I shall try to avoid repeating what the lower court has so well said and to confine myself to an effort to refute the holdings of the majority where they do attack and reject the lower court's opinion.

A good place to start is the quotation made by the majority . . . of one's right to "go to Bagdad." I would add to the language quoted by the majority from that case the sentences which follow it:

> It is the petitioner's claim that due process in this case required that Rachel Brawner be advised of the specific grounds for her exclusion and be accorded a hearing at which she might refute them. We are satisfied, however, that under the circumstances of this case such a procedure was not constitutionally required.
> The Fifth Amendment does not require a trial-type hearing in every conceivable case of government impairment of private interests. "The very nature of due process negates any concept of inflexible procedures universally applicable to every imaginable situation. . . . 'Due process,' unlike some legal rules, is not a technical conception with a fixed content unrelated to time, place and circumstances." It is "compounded of history, reason, and the past course of decisions. . . ."
> As these and other cases make clear, consideration of what procedure due process may require under any given set of circumstances must begin with a determination of the *precise nature of the government function involved as well as of the private interest that has been affected by governmental action.* Where it has been possible to characterize that private interest (perhaps in oversimplification) as a mere privilege subject to the Executive's plenary power, it has traditionally been held that notice and hearing are not constitutionally required. . . . [emphasis added].

The failure of the majority to follow the reasoning . . . supra, results, in my opinion, from a basic failure to understand the nature and mission of schools. The problem presented is *sui generis.*

Everyone who has dealt with schools knows that it is necessary to make many rules governing the conduct of those who attend them, which do not reach the concept of criminality but which are designed to regulate the relationship between school management and the student based upon practical and ethical considerations which the courts know very little about and with which they are not equipped to deal. To extend the injunctive power of federal courts to the problems of day-to-day dealings between school authority and student discipline

---

* 1960, 186 F. Supp. 945.

and morale is to add to the now crushing responsibilities of federal functionaries, the necessity of qualifying as a Gargantuan aggregation of wet nurses or baby sitters. I do not believe that a balanced consideration of the problem with which we are dealing contemplates any such extreme attitude. Indeed, I think that the majority has had to adopt the minority view of the courts in order to reach the determination it has here announced.

Nor do I find of favorable (to the majority) significance the introductory sentence quoted by it from the annotation in 58 A.L.R. at page 909. The quoted statement implies, rather, that there is no case where a student at a public college or university has taken the position that he was entitled to a hearing before being expelled. More in point, it seems to me, is the addition to the text . . .:

> Where the conduct of a student is such that his continued presence in the school will be disastrous to its proper discipline and to the morals of the other pupils, his expulsion is justifiable. Only where it is clear that such an action with respect to a student has not been an honest exercise of discretion, or has arisen from some motive extraneous to the purposes committee to that discretion, may the courts be called upon for relief.
>
> There is a conflict of authority as to whether notice of the charges and hearing are required before suspensions or expulsion of a student. Assuming that a student is entitled to a hearing prior to his expulsion from an institution of learning, the authorities are not in agreement as to what kind of hearing must be given to him. A few cases hold that he is entitled to a formal hearing clothed with all the attributes of a judicial hearing. However, the weight of authority is to the effect that no formal hearing is required.

The general rule covering the subtitle "Government and Discipline" in the general treatise on Colleges and Universities is thus stated . . .:

> Broadly speaking, the right of a student to attend a public or private college or university is subject to the condition that he comply with its scholastic and disciplinary requirements, and the proper college authorities may in the exercise of a broad discretion formulate and enforce reasonable rules and regulations in both respects. The courts will not interfere in the absence of an abuse of such discretion.

All of these expressions of the general rule seem to me to justify and require our adherence to that rule under the facts of this case. The majority opinion sets out many of them, but I think its statement should be supplemented and set forth in chronological order.

* * *

Powe, et al. v. *Miles*
407 Fed. 2d 73
Dec. 23, 1968

FRIENDLY, Circuit Judge
* * *

II

In recent years students at Alfred, like those at many other universities, have engaged in protests and demonstrations, sparked in particular by opposition to the war in Vietnam and commitment to improving relations between black and white citizens. Fully recognizing the propriety of such action the University issued a Policy on Demonstrations effective January 1, 1968, which is reproduced as an Appendix to this opinion.

The events giving rise to this suit took place on May 11, 1968. We summarize them as follows:

Alfred has for years sponsored an annual Parents Day, on which the parents of students are invited to visit the campus and attend various gatherings. Since the founding of an Army ROTC unit on campus in 1952, a military review has been scheduled as one of the Parents Day activities. Held on the university's football field, the review allows the parents to see the cadet corps in marching maneuvers and serves as the occasion for the presentation of awards to cadets who have excelled in the military science program. During the week prior to the 1968 Parents Day on Saturday, May 11, several Alfred students, members of the SDS chapter on campus, met to discuss the possibility of staging a demonstration during the ceremonies. They considered the event an appropriate occasion for demonstration because there had recently been controversy over the requirement that each male student at Alfred participate in the ROTC program during his freshman and sophomore years and the assembly of parents would furnish a large audience to witness the expression of views. The students did not confer with the Dean of Students about their plan to demonstrate or give his office the 48-hour prior notice required by the Policy on Demonstrations. There was testimony that two of the students attempted unsuccessfully to meet with President Miles during that week, but apparently the President was informed only that this related to "the matter of compulsory ROTC on the campus" and not that it concerned a planned demonstration. By Thursday evening these students had agreed among themselves that they would demonstrate at the military review on Saturday. When they met Saturday morning, they were joined by several other students and one faculty member, their number totaling sixteen.

Just before the ROTC ceremony was scheduled to begin on Saturday morning, several hundred parents and school officials had assembled in the grandstand at the football field. Four or five feet in front of the grandstand, straddling the 50-yard line, a reviewing stand had been erected in which military and other officials were to sit and review the cadets' march. To one side of this stand was a small table bearing trophies and awards to be presented to honored cadets. On the field itself red flags marked out the line of march that would be taken by the 500 cadets participating in the program.

After the stands had filled, the "adjutant's call" was sounded and the band began to march onto the field. The sixteen demonstrators entered from the end, walking single-file down the sideline four feet in front of the reviewing stand between the stand and the cadets then assembling on the field. Carrying signs that advocated scholarships for black students, the teaching of Negro history, an end to compulsory ROTC, and peace in Vietnam, the demonstrators marched once or twice down the sideline and then came to rest directly before the stands, facing the audience and holding their signs for maximum visibility. Shouts were exchanged between the demonstrators and the spectators; the plaintiffs testified that their presence was greeted with boos and hisses from parts of the grandstand and clapping from other parts. At no time, however, did the onlookers indicate an intention to interfere physically with the demonstration. About five minutes after the demonstrators entered the field, when the Dean of Students concluded that they intended to remain indefinitely where they were, he announced by microphone from the press box at the top of the grandstand that their actions were in violation of the demonstration guidelines and requested them to "conform" by "removing" themselves from the field. Eight of the student demonstrators obeyed this announcement by moving past the end of the grandstand, where they sat on the sidelines with their signs for the remainder of the event; seven students and the faculty member stayed where they were. The Dean repeated his request four times, twice to the students and twice to the faculty member. He then declared those disobeying his order to be "provisionally suspended" from the university, and informed them that they could pick up the charges against them at his office that afternoon and that a hearing would be held the following morning. The eight persisting demonstrators remained in their places, seating themselves for a few moments but rising again at the playing of the Star Spangled Banner that began the presentation of awards. A second faculty member joined them, and they remained standing before the reviewing stand for the duration of the ROTC parade, about 45 minutes, holding their signs at chest level and occasionally raising them above their heads. The demonstrators were thus a direct obstacle to the vision of those in the reviewing stand and in the lower tiers of the grandstand.

* * *

The hearing for the seven students before the faculty-student review board was adjourned to May 20 at their request; when it resumed, they were represented by counsel. The board recommended to President Miles that the students "be separated forthwith from the University." The President modified this by suspending them for the remainder of the semester and for the first semester of 1968–1969, with leave to apply for readmission in January 1969. He made arrangements to allow them to take final examinations off campus and receive credit for the courses then being taken.

III

The seven students thus suspended brought this action late in August 1968, in the District Court for the Western District of New York. Four are students at the Liberal Arts College, three at the New York State College of Ceramics. Alleging violation of the Civil Rights Act . . . they invoked the court's jurisdiction . . . and sought temporary and final injunctions compelling Alfred to reinstate them for the fall semester and preventing it from imposing penalties on students for exercising their right of free speech, a judgment declaring the Policy on Demonstrations to be void, and damages. The action was tried by Judge Curtin as on final hearing . . . with commendable despatch. He concluded, in a thoroughly reasoned opinion, that plaintiffs had failed to show action "under color of any State law, statute, ordinance, regulation, custom or usage" . . . and dismissed the complaint for want of federal jurisdiction. We expedited the appeal.

* * *

VI

* * *

We need not deal at length with plaintiffs' argument that guideline (8) of the Policy on Demonstrations, which requires 48 hours advance notice, is an invalid prior restraint on the right of expression. The provision does not seem objectionable as applied to a demonstration, such as this one, that had been planned well in advance; such notice affords a desirable opportunity for the administration and the demonstrators to work out detailed methods for the conduct of the protest in a manner compatible with the legitimate interests of all. . . . The guideline requires only that notice be given, not that approval be obtained. Contrast *Hammond* v. *South Carolina State College*, 272 F. Supp. 947 (1967), where a regulation required that demonstrators obtain prior approval from the college president and furnished no standards to limit his discretion in denying approval. . . . We are not required to decide whether the First Amendment rights of the CC students would have been violated if the University sought to enforce this provision under circumstances where advance notice was not feasible, as, for example, in the case of the spontaneous demonstrations following the lamentable assassination of Dr. King. The University had made clear it would not insist on advance notice under such circumstances; indeed the Dean of Students testified that, on the basis of an earlier discussion between President Miles and some of the plaintiffs, he regarded the 48-hour provision as a dead letter entirely. Accordingly, students had disregarded the provision on several occasions prior to the present demonstration, and the suspensions in this case were not bottomed on a failure to furnish notice to the administration.

The thrust of plaintiffs' argument is rather that while the guidelines may be reasonable in their substantive requirements, the vesting in the Dean of Students of what plaintiffs consider an unreviewable authority to construe them constitutes an unreasonable prior restraint. . . . Plaintiffs here argue that a similarly invalid prior restraint was imposed by the Dean's determination that their conduct was violating the guidelines and his announcement that continuation of the conduct would subject them to suspension. We do not, however, read the Policy on Demonstrations as placing unbridled authority for application in the Dean of Students. The Policy states that if the demonstrators "view the request as unreasonable, they may appeal later to the President for a ruling." While the document could be better drafted in this regard, as we are told is being done, we understand it to mean that, in addition to the appeal to the review board, which is limited to the issue of violation of the Dean's order, there may also be an appeal to the President on the ground that the Dean's request was unreasonable. Further, it was made plain to plaintiffs' counsel at the hearing before the review board that the University recognizes a right to appeal to the President for review of any matter involving dismissal or separation of a student. The record does not disclose whether plaintiffs took their opportunity to present their case to President Miles; but it is clear from his modification of the recommendation of the board that he considered the circumstances of the demonstration in imposing his sanction.

We thus need not consider whether the procedure would be unreasonable in the absence of this channel for subsequent review. The Policy as it stands is an appropriate response to the legitimate need for effective regulation of on-campus conduct. The vesting in the Dean of Students of authority for on-the-spot application of the guidelines permits prompt and decisive action that would be impossible from a committee that would engage in long debate. His warning that he considers a demonstration to be violating the guidelines provides an opportunity for the demonstrators to correct their conduct and avoid incurring any penalty; and his construction of the guidelines is open to reappraisal by the

President at a later time when excitement has waned. Finally we see nothing unreasonable in what the Dean of Students did here. Assuming as we do that the campus outside the CC buildings was sufficiently "public" that Alfred could not deny the CC students some opportunity to demonstrate, the protesters here had been given ample chance to make their point. The demonstration was violating guideline (6) and was threatening to violate guideline (5) as well. The fact that the demonstration was much less violent than other unhappy incidents of the recent past does not mean it had not passed the limits that Alfred was required to tolerate; the ROTC cadets and the parents had rights too. While the plaintiffs construe the Dean's remark, "Please conform to the guidelines by removing yourselves from the field," as a command to stop the demonstration altogether, we think it meant just what it said; the students were free to withdraw from the field and continue to display their signs, as many did. They were free also to resume their marching elsewhere after the ROTC exercises were completed. Even with respect to a public park "the principles of the First Amendment are not to be treated as a promise that everyone with opinions or beliefs to express may gather around him at any public place and at any time a group for discussion or instruction" . . . London does not make all of Hyde Park available for speechifying. What applies to a public park would be true *a fortiori* of the grounds of a state university, see *Zanders* v. *Louisiana State Board of Education,* 281 F. Supp. 747 (W. D. La. 1968) ; *Barker* v. *Hardway,* 283 F. Supp. 228 (S. D. W. Va. 1968) , and *a multo fortiori* of the campus of a private one even though the Dean was acting as the State's representative vis-a-vis the CC students.

The judgment is modified so that the dismissal of the complaint with respect to the CC students is on the merits rather than for lack of federal jurisdiction. As so modified it is affirmed. In view of the novelty and importance of the issue, we shall relieve the plaintiffs of costs.

————

APPENDIX A

ALFRED UNIVERSITY
POLICY ON DEMONSTRATIONS
Effective January 1, 1968

The University cherishes the right of individual students or student groups to dissent and to demonstrate, provided such demonstrations do not disrupt normal campus activities, or infringe on the rights of others. In fact, the University is proud that some students care enough about world issues that they feel compelled in conscience publicly to proclaim their views.

On the other hand, the University cannot condone student or faculty groups which, under the banner of free speech, proceed to violate the freedom of speech, choice, assembly, or movement of other individuals or groups. In short, responsible dissent carries with it a sensitivity for the civil rights of others, and a recognition that other students have a right to dissent from the dissenters.

Accordingly, the University will in any given instance take whatever steps it deems necessary to (1) protect the right of any group to demonstrate and publicly proclaim any lawful view, however unpopular; (2) protect the freedom of speech, assembly, and movement of any group which is the object of demonstrations.

Greene v. *Howard University*
271 Fed. Supp. 609
Aug. 28, 1967
HOLTZOFF, District Judge

The primary question presented in these consolidated cases is whether the relations between a University and its students, and between a University and its faculty, are subject to judicial control; specifically, whether the termination by a University of the status of a student, or of a member of the faculty, is subject in whole or in part to judicial review.

The defendant in these cases is Howard University, an institution of higher learning located in Washington, D.C. The plaintiffs may be divided into two classes. Some of them are students, whose status was terminated by the University as of the close of the academic year ending June 30, 1967. Others are members of the faculty, who held temporary appointments for a specific period only, and whose appointments the University declined to renew. This action is brought to require the University to restore the plaintiffs to their former status. The matter is before the Court at this time on motions for a preliminary injunction to reinstate the plaintiffs pending the trial of this action.

In view of the disposition of the issues about to be made by this Court, it would be superfluous to review in detail the incidents that led to the action taken by the University against the plaintiffs. Suffice it to say that it arose out of a series of disorders that took place on the campus of Howard University. In one instance, the head of the Selective Service System of the United States had been invited to make a speech at the University. A group of students created such a disturbance as made it impossible for him to address the audience. At another time the University authorities were about to conduct a hearing on charges of misconduct against a student. A group composed of some students and of some members of the faculty created such a commotion and uproar as to render it impracticable for the hearing to proceed. Threatening utterances were heard on the campus. Several fires took place. The University authorities concluded, after a careful and thorough investigation, that the student plaintiffs, as well as those plaintiffs who were members of the faculty, actively participated in creating these chaotic conditions and disorder. Accordingly, in an effort to bar a continuation and repetition of such disruptive incidents, the University, in June 1967, sent a formal letter to each of the student plaintiffs, notifying him that he would not be permitted to return to the institution for the next academic year. The other plaintiffs were instructors, or junior professors, who had only temporary appointments without any permanent tenure. If such appointments were not renewed, their connection with the faculty would be automatically terminated at the expiration of the academic year. The University, again in June 1967, sent a letter to each of this group of plaintiffs formally notifying him that his appointment, which was about to expire on June 30, 1967, would not be renewed.

As the questions of law relating to the two types of plaintiffs are somewhat different, we shall deal with each category separately. We shall first consider the student plaintiffs. Their complaint is predicated on the contention that they were not accorded their alleged Constitutional right to receive notices of charges and a hearing, but were dismissed from the University by *ex parte* decisions. The relief that they seek is to require the University to vacate its action and to give them notices of charges and a hearing.

(1, 2) This contention is based on a misconception of the scope of the Bill of Rights. The procedural safeguards and the privileges accorded by the Constitution of the United States are confined solely to judicial and quasi-judicial proceedings, either in the courts or before administrative agencies. They are directed solely against Governmental action.* They do not extend to any other relation in life, such as that of parent and child, teacher and pupil, or employer and employee. These relations are of a private character. While some of them, such as that of employer and employee, may be circumscribed by contract or by statute, they are not controlled by the Constitution. For example, until the enactment of the Civil Service laws, the Federal Government had the right to discharge any of its employees at will. In fact, it may do so even now in respect to those persons who are exempt from the

* See in this connection *Parsons College* v. *North Central Ass'n of Colleges and Secondary Schools* (N.D.Ill. July 26, 1967) 271 F. Supp. 65.

various limitations of the Civil Service statutes.* To take another example, arbitrary discharge of employees of private concerns may be limited by statute or by agreements between the employers and labor unions, but Constitutional restrictions are not applicable.

Counsel for the plaintiffs rely principally on the decision of the Court of Appeals for the Fifth Circuit in *Dixon* v. *Alabama State Board of Education,* 294 F.2d 150, which held by a vote of 2 to 1, that a State College had no authority to expel a student without first giving him notice and some opportunity for a hearing. The Court referred to the State college as "a governmental body." Counsel for the student plaintiffs in the case at bar argued that there are sufficient contacts and a strong enough connection between Howard University and the Federal Government to render the principle of the *Dixon* case applicable. Decisions of Courts of Appeals of other circuits must be regarded with respect and may be persuasive, but they are not necessarily controlling. For the reasons about to be stated, it is not necessary, however, to determine whether the principle evolved by the *Dixon* case should constitute the law in the District of Columbia.

Unlike the college involved in the *Dixon* case, Howard University is not a governmental body. It is a private corporation created by an Act of Congress. True, a large percentage of its expenses are paid by annual appropriations made by Congress. As a condition of receiving such money, the Secretary of Health, Education and Welfare is given authority to visit and inspect Howard University and to control and supervise the expenditures of those funds which have been appropriated by Congress, 20 U.S.C. § 122. In addition, the President and Directors of Howard University are required to file an annual report with the Secretary. No Government officer, however, is a member of the Board of Trustees of the Institution, nor is any control over the institution vested in the Federal Government.

The status of Howard University is not open for determination by this Court, for it has already been held by the Court of Appeals for this Circuit that the University is a private corporation and is not a public institution. . . . It is clear, therefore, that the principle which counsel for the plaintiffs seek to invoke, namely, that a Government college or university may not expel its students without notice of charges and an opportunity to be heard, is not applicable to Howard University, for it is not a public institution nor does it partake of any governmental character.

---

* When President Andrew Jackson took office, he summarily caused the discharge of numerous Government employees in order to appoint his own followers to the positions so vacated, on the theory, as expressed by one of his contemporaries, that "To the victor belong the spoils." While this action may have been a bar sinister on his escutcheon, it did not constitute a violation of any Constitutional or statutory rights, because there were none. It was not until many years later that Civil Service laws were enacted to protect the tenure of certain Government employees.

It would be a dangerous doctrine to permit the Government to interpose any degree of control over an institution of higher learning merely because it extends financial assistance to it. There are numerous colleges in this country whose establishment was made financially possible by grants of land by the Federal Government. It is inconceivable that for this reason every "land grant college," as such institutions are generally denominated, should to some degree be subject to the control of the Federal Government, or that the Federal courts should be empowered to interfere with the administration of discipline, or the appointment of members of the faculty in such schools. In recent years, numerous universities, colleges and technical schools have received Governmental aid of various kinds by being granted funds to carry on scientific research projects. Surely it should not be held that any institution by entering into a contract with the United States for the conduct of some project of this sort and receiving funds for that purpose, has placed its head in a noose and subjected itself to some degree of control by the Federal Government. Such a result would be intolerable, for it would tend to hinder and control the progress of higher learning and scientific research. Higher education can flourish only in an atmosphere of freedom, untrammeled by Governmental influence in any degree. The courts may not interject themselves into the midst of matters of school discipline. Such discipline cannot be administered successfully in the same manner as governs the trial of a criminal case or a hearing before an administrative agency.

Students entering Howard University are formally advised by the University authorities that attendance at the institution is not a right but a privilege. In that important respect, among many others, Howard University differs from some State colleges. It is further indicated that this privilege may be withdrawn by the authorities if in their own judgment a student who has been accepted for admission does not conform to standards of conduct that the University exacts from its student body. Nowhere is it stated directly or by implication that a student would be accorded a hearing before his connection with the University could be terminated.

* * *

(4) The conclusion necessarily follows that the student plaintiffs had no constitutional, statutory, or contractual right to a notice of charges and a hearing before they could be expelled or their connection with the University could be otherwise severed. It was entirely within the discretion of the University authorities to grant or withhold a hearing. Consequently, the student plaintiffs are not entitled to any relief requiring the University to reinstate them until they have received a notice of charges and a hearing.

The issues relating to those plaintiffs who were members of the faculty are somewhat different. The faculty plaintiffs were instructors or junior professors, who had no permanent appointments or indefinite tenure. Each of them held an appointment for a temporary period. Appointments of this type are frequently renewed, but by the same token, the renewal could be denied. In this instance the appointments of the faculty plaintiffs were not renewed as of the end of the academic year ending June 30, 1967. They were so notified prior to the expiration date. In following this course the University was entirely within its legal rights.

(5) It is claimed in behalf of plaintiffs in this category, however, that under what are asserted to be regulations of the University, they were entitled to notice prior to specified dates that their appointments would not be renewed, and that failure to give such notice required the University to renew the appointments. This contention is lacking in merit.

The Faculty Handbook of Howard University, which embodies regulations affecting members of the faculty and which is available to all of them, contains the following significant provision in regard to a renewal of term appointments in Section V, paragraph B, p. 19:

> The University shall be under no obligation to renew term appointments and therefore holders of academic positions under term appointments should have neither presumption of permanence nor expectancy of automatic reappointment.

Counsel for the faculty plaintiffs relies on Section IX of the same Handbook, page 22, which reads as follows:

> Notice of Non-reappointment and Reappointment: It will be the practice of the University, *without contractual obligation to do so,* to give written notice at the following times to officers of instruction whose services are no longer required: A) Deans will give notice each year to those whose terms expire and whom they do not propose to recommend for reappointment, not later than December 15 of that year; B) The Board of Trustees will give notice to those teachers whose terms expire and whose services are no longer required, directly following its meeting in January of each year [emphasis supplied].

It is contended by counsel that Section IX constitutes an obligation to give notice of an intention not to renew a term appointment not later than a specified date, and in case of failure to give such a notice, the appointment must be deemed renewed. To construe Section IX in this manner would do violence to its very language. That regulation provides that it will be the practice of the University *without contractual obligation to do so,* to give written notice prior to specified dates. Section IX and Section V must be read together. Instructors and professors holding term appointments are expressly warned that there is no obligation to renew term appointments and holders of such positions should have neither presumption of permanence nor expectancy of automatic reappointment. While Section IX sets forth a practice of giving advance notice of intention not to reappoint, it is expressly provided that there is no contractual obligation to do so. It is entirely conceivable that a situation may arise subsequently to the specified date that would lead the University not to renew a term appointment. Such were the circumstances in this instance.

The conclusion is inescapable that the faculty plaintiffs were not entitled to a renewal of their appointments as a matter of law, and that the University had a legal right not to reappoint them. Complete discretion in the matter is vested in the University authorities.

(6) Even if there were a contractual obligation of some type, that circumstance would not entitle these plaintiffs to equitable relief. At most it might give rise to an action for damages. A contract to hire a teacher may not be enforced by specific performance. It is not within those few categories of agreements that are enforceable in equity. It would be intolerable for the courts to interject themselves and to require an educational institution to hire or to maintain on its staff a professor or instructor whom it deemed undesirable and did not wish to employ. For the courts to impose such a requirement would be an interference with the operation of institutions of higher learning contrary to established principles of law and to the best traditions of education.

The intellectual history of Western Europe and the United States is marked by the establishment and gradual growth of universities that are self-governing, in the selection of their faculties, in prescribing their curriculum, and in administering discipline of their student bodies. This history demonstrates that centers of higher learning can best develop and flourish in an atmosphere of liberty and independence, where they are free from governmental influence in any respect as to any aspect of their activities. A glace at this history is convincing. Universities in Italy, such as Bologna;* universities in France, such as Paris;** and Universities of Oxford and Cambridge in England,*** all of which originated in the Middle Ages, were from their very inception and always have remained independent bodies, unfettered by any intrusion on the part of any governmental agency, or of the courts. In this country, with the early establishment of Harvard, William and Mary, Yale, Princeton and King's College (later Columbia), this tradition was continued and has prevailed. Such institutions have been free of governmental control. One attempt to the contrary was defeated by the decision of the Supreme Court in the *Dartmouth College* case,**** in which the college was eloquently and forcibly represented

---

* Rashdall, *The Universities of Europe in The Middle Ages,* Vol. I, pp. 151 et seq., 176 et seq.
** *Id.* pp. 298–320, 398–432.
*** *Id.* Vol. III, pp. 55 et seq., 279–292.
**** *Trustees of Dartmouth College* v. *Woodward,* 4 Wheat. 518, 4 L.Ed. 629.

by Daniel Webster as counsel. Fortunately, even State universities in this country, which came later, particularly the larger institutions, have been left singularly free of governmental control or interference.

It would be a sad blow to institutions of higher learning and to the development of independent thought and culture if the courts were to step in and control and direct the administration of discipline and the selection of members of the faculty in universities and colleges. An entering wedge seemingly innocuous at first blush, may lead step-by-step to a serious external domination of universities and colleges and a consequent damper and hindrance to their intellectual development and growth.

In the light of the foregoing considerations, the motions for a preliminary injunction are denied.

This opinion will constitute findings of fact and conclusions of law.

Steier v. *New York State Education Commissioner*
161 F. Supp. 549
April 24, 1958
RAYFIELD, District Judge

The facts, so far as they are beyond substantial dispute, are, briefly stated, as follows: In March 1955 the plaintiff, who entered Brooklyn College as a student in 1952, was suspended for the remainder of the semester by the Dean of Students for breaches of discipline. Following a period of probation he was reinstated in September 1955, on condition, however, that he discontinue certain practices and activities, which, in part, had resulted in his suspension.

On September 21, 1956, after several infractions of the conditions of his probation, he was again suspended by the Dean. After each such suspension he appealed to the President of Brooklyn College, whose decision in cases involving appeals from suspensions is final. The President sustained the Dean in each case.

Following his second suspension the plaintiff and his parents wrote several letters to the President and other officials of Brooklyn College respecting his suspension, requesting his reinstatement. He continued, however, to engage in many of the practices and activities which had been the basis of his suspensions, included among which was the deposit by him on December 6, 1956, in staff and student mail boxes at the College, of a letter, many thousands of words in length, bearing his signature and addressed to "To Whom It May Concern," containing uncomplimentary comment concerning several officers of Brooklyn College and their official conduct in the matter of his suspensions.

On December 10, 1956, the plaintiff sent an application to the Dean by registered mail, requesting his reinstatement. The application was referred to the Faculty Committee on Orientation and Guidance of the College for consideration and advice. That Committee held a hearing thereon on December 13, 1956, at which the plaintiff was present. He was permitted to make a statement in his behalf. The Committee, after considering the application and plaintiff's activities and conduct since his first suspension, unanimously recommended to the Faculty Council, of which the President is Chairman, that the plaintiff be dismissed from Brooklyn College.

On December 18, 1956, the Faculty Council approved the recommendation of the Committee on Orientation and Guidance that the plaintiff be dismissed from the College, effective at the end of that semester, and on December 20 the President wrote him, informing him of his dismissal, and advising him that the by-laws of The Board provided that an appeal may be made to it from the decision dismissing him from the College. On January 26, 1957, the plaintiff appealed to The Board.

It should be noted here that the public colleges of The City of New York, of which Brooklyn College is one, constitute a unit of the public school system of the State of New York. Under Section 6202 of the Education Law of the State of New York The Board, a body corporate separate and distinct from the Board of Education of The City of New York, which administers the affairs of the public elementary and secondary school system, is authorized to govern and control those educational institutions in the City which are of collegiate grade. Included among the powers and duties of The Board provided by Section 6202 of said Law is the power to "prescribe conditions of student admission, attendance and discharge." The Board has prescribed such conditions, which, so far as they are here pertinent, are contained in Sections 214a, 216 and 217 of its by-laws. Section 214a provides, *inter alia*, that each student obey all the rules, regulations and orders of the duly established college authorities, and shall conform to the requirements of good manners and good morals. Section 216 provides that, in the event of the violation of such rules, regulations or requirements, the Dean may reprimand the student involved, suspend him for a period not exceeding one term, or deprive him of certain college privileges. He may also *recommend* the dismissal of the student, but such disciplinary action may be *imposed* only by the President, or by the votes of a majority of the members of the Faculty Council. Section 217 provides that the student involved in disciplinary action by the Dean or the Faculty Council may appeal to the President, whose decision is final, except in the case of a dismissal, in which event appeal may be made to The Board.

On February 4, 1957, the then Chairman of The Board, the late

Joseph B. Cavallaro, wrote the plaintiff, informing him that pursuant to Section 217, supra. The Board would consider his appeal at its next meeting to be held on February 18, 1957, suggesting that the plaintiff appear on that occasion, and enclosing a copy of the report of the Faculty Committee on Orientation and Guidance, on the basis of which he had been dismissed. The plaintiff and his mother, who asked for leave to speak in his behalf, were afforded a hearing, and on February 19, 1957, The Board, after a review of the matter, rendered its decision denying his appeal.

Under the Education Law, supra, the Education Department of the State of New York is charged with the general management and super-vision of all the public schools in the State, and The Commissioner is the chief executive and administrative officer of the Department. Section 310 of said Law provides that in a case such as the instant case a "person conceiving himself aggrieved may appeal or petition to the commissioner of education who is hereby authorized and required to examine and decide the same . . . and his decision in such appeals, petitions or proceedings shall be final and conclusive, and not subject to question or review in any place or court whatever."

Pursuant to the authority vested in him by Section 311 of said Law, the Commissioner promulgated rules and practice relating to appeals. In accordance with such rules and practice the plaintiff filed his petition on appeal on May 3, 1957. An answer thereto was filed by the Dean of Brooklyn College, and the plaintiff then filed his reply to said answer, together with a number of other documents. In conformity with the privilege granted by Rule 18 of the Commissioner's afore-mentioned rules and practice, the plaintiff and representative of The Board were permitted to and did argue their respective contentions orally on June 13, 1957. On August 29, 1957, the Commissioner rendered his decision, sustaining the action of The Board and dismissing the appeal.

On October 3, 1957, the plaintiff made an application to reopen his appeal, based on what he claimed to be "new evidence and positive proof of misapprehension in the original decision," and, in support of his application, submitted rather voluminous documents, in large measure repetitious of those previously filed herein. That application was denied on the ground that the plaintiff had failed to present a sufficient basis therefor.

(2) The question to be determined, then, is: Was the plaintiff deprived, under color of the applicable State statute, of any right guaranteed to him under the Constitution of the United States, more particularly the Fourteenth Amendment thereof.

The plaintiff, aggrieved, as he stated he was, by the action of The Board, had three remedies available to him. He could have (1) sought relief from this Court, or (2) commenced a proceeding under Article 78 of the Civil Practice Act of the State of New York to review his dismissal, or (3) appealed to The Commissioner pursuant to the provisions of Section 310, supra, the constitutionality of which, it may be added, has been sustained. . . . He chose the last-mentioned course.

Copies of all documents filed by The Board, including the charges made against the plaintiff by the Brooklyn College authorities, were served upon him. He was permitted to, and did, file numerous documents and exhibits in his own behalf and argued orally at the hearing on his appeal. In summary, as the record clearly indicates, the plaintiff has been granted hearings by or interviews with the Dean, the Faculty Committee on Orientation and Guidance, the Faculty Council and the President of Brooklyn College, The Board and the Commissioner. In each such step he was informed of the nature of the charges made against him, and was afforded an opportunity to file papers and argue orally in opposition thereto. At the hearing before the Commissioner the same rights and privileges prescribed by the rules which were available to The Board were equally available to the plaintiff.

In the case of *Beam* v. *Wilson* . . . the Court said,

> The commissioner is authorized and required to examine appeals and petitions by persons conceiving themselves aggrieved . . . and his decision in such appeals, petitions and proceedings is final and conclusive and not subject to question or review in any place or court whatever . . . except when it has shown purely to have been arbitrary or palpably illegal.

(3) In the proceeding *O'Brien* v. *Commissioner of Education of State of New York* . . . decided March 27, 1958, the Court of Appeals of the State of New York, in passing upon an appeal, brought on alleged constitutional grounds, seeking to annul a decision of the Commissioner, said:

> The Commissioner of Education held a hearing at which, though no one was called to testify or give evidence, an opportunity was accorded for full oral argument, the submission and exchange of briefs and the filing of any and all affidavits, exhibits and other materials the parties desired.

The Court further said:

> Quite obviously, and we recently so held in a case very similar to the present one, the Commissioner of Education's resolution of a dispute on conflicting affidavits without an oral hearing neither directly involves the construction of the constitution nor poses a constitutional question of any kind. . . . The Court dismissed the

appeal. The procedure followed in the hearing before The Commissioner in the case at bar was substantially similar to that employed in the O'Brien-Murphy appeal, supra.

(4) It should be noted, too, that the plaintiff failed to exhaust *all* remedies available to him in the State. If he believed that the decision of the Commissioner was arbitrary, capricious or palpably illegal he could have filed a petition . . . for a review of the decision of the Commissioner. . . .

I have read all the cases cited by the plaintiff. None of them is apposite.

Accordingly, judgment is granted dismissing the complaint herein.

7
Publications

Dickey v. Alabama State Board of Education

Dickey v. *Alabama State Board of Education*
273 F.Supp. 613
Sept. 8, 1967
JOHNSON, Chief Judge

Gary Clinton Dickey, a citizen of the United States and a resident of this district, was, for the 1966–1967 school year, a student in good standing at Troy State College, a state-operated public institution of higher learning located at Troy, Alabama, which is controlled and supervised by the Alabama State Board of Education. Dickey had earned as of the end of the school year in June, 1967, 147 quarter hours toward a degree in English, which degree requires 192 quarter hours, according to Troy State standards. He made known his wishes to attend Troy State College for the school year 1967–1968, commencing September, 1967, by giving written notice as required by the institution. On July 18, 1967, Dickey received "Official Notice of Admission" from the college, admitting him to the undergraduate division of said college for the fall quarter 1967. On August 11, 1967, Dickey received a certified letter from Troy State College, signed by the Dean of Men, advising him that the Student Affairs Committee of said college had voted not to admit him "at this time."

Upon the verified complaint filed with this Court on August 16, 1967, and the matters alleged therein, this Court observed that, in cases involving suspension or expulsion of students from a tax-supported college or university (due process requires notice and some opportunity for a hearing before suspension or expulsion. *Dixon* v. *Alabama State Board of Education,* 294 F.2d 150. . . . It was further observed in said order that, upon Dickey's verified allegations of deprivation of constitutionally guaranteed rights and where there is factual evidence of a clear and imminent threat of irreparable injury, judicial action

149

was required. Accordingly, the defendants were, by formal order made and entered on August 17, 1967, directed to rescind the action suspending or expelling Dickey without any notice of hearing and to afford him an administrative hearing as required by the constitutional principle of due process. Following the order of this Court, the defendants on August 21, 1967, caused to be rescinded the action taken by the Student Affairs Committee that resulted in Dickey's suspension, and at that time advised Dickey that he would be afforded an opportunity to be heard "on the charge of insubordination resulting from his refusal to comply with specific instructions of his Faculty Advisor in defiance of such instructions" and that such a hearing would be conducted on Friday, August 25, 1967. A full hearing was afforded Dickey before the Student Affairs Committee on that date. Dickey was present with his attorney, and witnesses appeared and were examined. On August 28, 1967, Troy State College, acting through its Dean of Men, advised Dickey that it was the decision of the Student Affairs Committee that he not be admitted to Troy State College for one academic year (nine months), beginning with the fall quarter of 1967. Upon receipt of this notice, Dickey moved for a preliminary injunction on the theory that his substantive rights of due process had been and were being deprived by reason of his expulsion and/or suspension from Troy State College. . . . Due notice of the hearing upon the plaintiff's motion was given the defendants, and the matter is now submitted to this Court upon the pleadings and the evidence taken orally before the Court.

During the early part of the 1966–1967 school year, Gary Clinton Dickey, while a full-time student at Troy State College, was chosen as an editor of the Troy State College student newspaper, The Tropolitan. It appears that Dickey was an outstanding student, as he was also chosen as editor-in-chief of the Troy State College literary magazine, was copy editor of the college's annual student yearbook, and was editor-in-chief of the student handbook. He was also a member of a national honorary journalism fraternity.

In early April 1967, Dr. Frank Rose, President of the University of Alabama, came under attack by certain Alabama state legislators for his refusal to censor the University of Alabama student publication, "Emphasis 67, A World in Revolution." "Emphasis 67," as published for the University of Alabama, served as the program for a series of guest speakers and panel discussions held in March at the University of Alabama. The publication contained brief biographical sketches of the participants, which included Secretary of State Dean Rusk, James Reston of *The New York Times,* and Professor Robert Scalapino, a leading authority on Asian politics. The theme of the "Emphasis" program was a "World in Revolution." In carrying out this theme,

"Emphasis" published excerpts from the speeches of Bettine Aptheker, a Communist who gained notoriety at the University of California, and Stokely Carmichael, President of the Student Nonviolent Coordinating Committee and an incendiary advocate of violent revolution. To give a balanced view of a "World in Revolution," "Emphasis" carried articles by leading anti-revolutionaries such as General Earl G. Wheeler, Chairman of the Joint Chiefs of Staff. After public criticism by certain Alabama legislators, Dr. Rose, in the exercise of his judgment as President of the University of Alabama, took a public stand in support of the right of the University students to academic freedom. Criticism of Dr. Rose for this position by certain state legislators became rather intense. The newspapers widely publicized the controversy to a point that it became a matter of public interest throughout the State of Alabama.

Editor Dickey determined that the Troy State College newspaper, The Tropolitan, should be heard on the matter. He prepared and presented to the faculty adviser an editorial supporting the position taken by Dr. Rose. He was instructed by his faculty adviser not to publish such an editorial. Dickey then took the editorial to the head of the English Department at Troy State College. The head of this department approved the publication of Dickey's proposed editorial. Upon returning to the faculty adviser, Dickey was again informed that the editorial could not be published. Dickey then went directly to the president of the college, Ralph Adams, who also determined that the editorial could not be published. It is without controversy in this case that the basis for the denial of Dickey's right to publish his editorial supporting Dr. Rose was a rule that had been invoked at Troy State College to the effect that there could be no editorials written in the school paper which were critical of the Governor of the State of Alabama or the Alabama Legislature. The rule did not prohibit editorials or articles of a laudatory nature concerning the Governor or the Legislature. The rule has been referred to in this case as the "Adams Rule." The theory of the rule, as this Court understands it, is that Troy State College is a public institution owned by the State of Alabama, that the Governor and the legislators are acting for the owner and control the purse strings, and that for that reason neither the Governor nor the Legislature could be criticized. The faculty adviser furnished substitute material concerning "Raising Dogs in North Carolina" to be published in lieu of Dickey's proposed editorial. Upon being furnished the editorial on the North Carolina dogs, Dickey, as editor of The Tropolitan, determined that it was not suitable, and, acting against the specific instructions of his faculty adviser and the president of the college, arranged to have—with the exception of the title, "A Lament for Dr. Rose"—the space ordinarily occupied by the editorial left blank, with the word "Censored" diagonally across the blank space. In addition to this conduct, Dickey mailed the censored editorial* to a Montgomery newspaper. All parties in this case concede that the editorial is well written and in good taste. However, the evidence in this case reflects that solely because it violated the "Adams Rule," Dickey's conduct, in acting contrary to the advice of the faculty adviser and of President Adams, was termed "willful and deliberate insubordination." This insubordination is the sole basis for his expulsion and/or suspension.

(1–5) It is basic in our law in this country that the privilege to communicate concerning a matter of public interest is embraced in the First Amendment right relating to freedom of speech and is constitutionally protected against infringement by state officials. The Fourteenth Amendment to the Constitution protects these First Amendment rights from state infringement . . . and these First Amendment rights extend to school children and students insofar as unreasonable rules are concerned. *West Virginia State Board of Education* v. *Barnette,* 319 U.S. 624 . . . . Boards of education, presidents of colleges, and faculty advisers are not excepted from the rule that protects students

---

* The complete text of the editorial, "A Lament for Dr. Rose," is as follows:

Dr. Frank Rose, president of the University of Alabama, is currently under attack by certain state legislators for his refusal to censor a student publication. The publication, entitled, "Emphasis 67, A World in Revolution," served as the program for a series of guest speakers and panel discussions held on March 16 and 17 at the University. The publication contained brief biographical sketches of each of the participants, which included Secretary of State Dean Rusk, James Reston of the New York Times, and Professor Robert Scalapino, a leading authority on Asian politics.

The theme of the "Emphasis" program was a "World in Revolution." In keeping with this theme, the publication carried excerpts from the speeches of Bettina Aptheker, a Communist who gained notoriety at the University of California, and Stokely Carmichael, president of the Student Non-Violent Coordinating Committee, and the incendiary advocate of violent revolution and "black power."

To give a balanced view of "A World in Revolution," the "Emphasis" publication carried articles by leading anti-revolutionaries such as Gen. Earl G. Wheeler, chairman of the Joint Chiefs of Staff, and Roy Wilkins, president of the NAACP and a supporter of non-violent moderate change.

Some of the legislators have read into this publication an attempt by President Rose to condone and abet revolutionary and subversive activity at the University.

The Tropolitan feels that these legislators have sadly misinterpreted the intent of the publication.

Surely, they cannot seriously consider Gen. Wheeler, the highest military official in the United States, a subversive. Surely, Secretary of State Dean Rusk, who was brought to the University as the keynote speaker on the "Emphasis" program, and who is currently conducting a war of diplomacy and bullets against Communist subversion in Asia, cannot be labeled a subversive. The very purpose of including excerpted speeches by revolutionaries Carmichael and Aptheker was not to endorse their views, but to present a backdrop against which the phenomenon of revolution could be studied and the problems and the role of the United States in a world in revolution could be defined.

The Tropolitan, therefore, laments the misinterpretation of the "Emphasis" program by members of the legislature, and the considerable harassment they have caused Dr. Rose. It is our hope that this episode does not impair his effective leadership at the University or discourage him in his difficult task.

against unreasonable rules and regulations. This Court recognizes that the establishment of an educational program requires certain rules and regulations necessary for maintaining an orderly program and operating the institution in a manner conducive to learning. However, the school and school officials have always been bound by the requirement that the rules and regulations *must be reasonable*. Courts may only consider whether rules and regulations that are imposed by school authorities are a reasonable exercise of the power and discretion vested in those authorities. Regulations and rules which are necessary in maintaining order and discipline are always considered reasonable. In the case now before this Court, it is clear that the maintenance of order and discipline of the students attending Troy College had nothing to do with the rule that was invoked against Dickey. As a matter of fact, the president of the institution, President Adams, testified that his general policy of not criticizing the Governor or the State Legislature under any circumstances, regardless of how reasonable or justified the criticism might be, was not for the purpose of maintaining order and discipline among the students. On this point, President Adams testified that the reason for the rule was that a newspaper could not criticize its owners, and in the case of a state institution the owners were to be considered as the Governor and the members of the Legislature.

(6–9) With these basic constitutional principles in mind, the conclusion is compelled that the invocation of such a rule against Gary Clinton Dickey that resulted in his expulsion and/or suspension from Troy State College was unreasonable. A state cannot force a college student to forfeit his constitutionally protected right of freedom of expression as a condition to his attending a state-supported institution. State school officials cannot infringe on their students' right of free and unrestricted expression as guaranteed by the Constitution of the United States where the exercise of such right does not "materially and substantially interfere with requirements of appropriate discipline in the operation of the school." . . . The defendants in this case cannot punish Gary Clinton Dickey for his exercise of this constitutionally guaranteed right by cloaking his expulsion or suspension in the robe of "insubordination." The attempt to characterize Dickey's conduct, and the basis for their action in expelling him, as "insubordination" requiring rather severe disciplinary action, does not disguise the basic fact that Dickey was expelled from Troy State College for exercising his constitutionally guaranteed right of academic and/or political expression.

The argument by defendants' counsel that Dickey was attempting to take over the operation of the school newspaper ignores the fact that there was no legal obligation on the school authorities to permit Dickey to continue as one of its editors. As a matter of fact, there was no legal obligation on the school authorities to operate a school newspaper. However, since this state-supported institution did elect to operate

The Tropolitan and did authorize Dickey to be one of its editors, they cannot as officials of the State of Alabama, without violating the First and Fourteenth Amendments to the Constitution of the United States, suspend or expel Dickey from this state-supported institution for his conduct as that conduct is reflected by the facts presented in this case.

(10) As the Supreme Court stated in *West Virginia State Board of Education* v. *Barnette,* supra:

> The Fourteenth Amendment, as now applied to the States, protects the citizen against the State itself and all of its creatures—Boards of Education not excepted. These have, of course, important, delicate, and highly discretionary functions, but none that they may not perform within the limits of the Bill of Rights. That they are educating the young for citizenship is reason for scrupulous protection of Constitutional freedoms of the individual, if we are not to strangle the free mind at its source and teach youth to discount important principles of our government as mere platitudes.

(11) Defendants' argument that Dickey's readmission will jeopardize the discipline in the institution is superficial and completely ignores the greater damage to college students that will result from the imposition of intellectual restraints such as the "Adams Rule" in this case. The imposition of such a restraint as here sought to be imposed upon Dickey and the other students at Troy State College violates the basic principles of academic and political expression as guaranteed by our Constitution. Dr. Rose recognized the importance of this academic and constitutional principle when he determined that as to the University of Alabama, such freedoms must be permitted to flourish. As the Supreme Court stated in *Sweezy* v. *State of New Hampshire,* 354 U.S. 234, 250:

> We believe that there unquestionably was an invasion of petitioner's liberties in the areas of academic freedom and political expression—areas in which government should be extremely reticent to tread.
>
> The essentiality of freedom in the community of American universities is almost self-evident. No one should underestimate the vital role in a democracy that is played by those who guide and train our youth. To impose any strait jacket upon the intellectual leaders in our colleges and universities would imperil the future of our Nation. No field of education is so thoroughly comprehended by man that new discoveries cannot yet be made. Particularly is that true in the social sciences, where few, if any, principles are accepted as absolutes. Scholarship cannot flourish in an atmosphere of suspicion and distrust. Teachers and students must always remain free to inquire, to study and to evaluate, to gain new maturity, and understanding; otherwise our civilization will stagnate and die.

In accordance with the foregoing, it is the order, judgment and decree of this Court that the action taken by Troy State College, acting through its Student Affairs Committee, on Friday, August 25, 1967, which action denies to Gary Clinton Dickey admission to Troy State College beginning with the fall quarter of 1967, be and the same is hereby declared unconstitutional, void, and is rescinded.

It is further ordered that the defendants immediately reinstate Gary Clinton Dickey as a student in Troy State College, commencing September 11, 1967.

It is further ordered that the defendants, and each of them, their agents, servants, employees, and others acting in concert or participation with them, be and each is hereby enjoined and restrained from denying, upon the basis of his conduct as herein discussed, Gary Clinton Dickey admission to Troy State College as a student and from refusing to allow him to attend as such for the academic year commencing September 11, 1967.

It is further ordered that the costs incurred in this proceeding be and they are hereby taxed against the defendants, for which execution may issue.

Antonelli v. *Hammond*
308 Fed. Supp. 1329
February 5, 1970

GARRITY, J.

Plaintiff is John Antonelli, a student at Fitchburg State College, a state-supported school of higher education in the Commonwealth of Massachusetts. He was the editor-in-chief of The Cycle, the campus newspaper, when a dispute as to the control of the newspaper arose between the student editorial staff and the college president, defendant James J. Hammond. The complaint in substance is that the defendant Hammond through his power over the purse is censoring the material for publication by subjecting it to the prior approval of a faculty advisory committee. It is also alleged that president Hammond refused to release the usual funds to pay for the printing of an issue of The Cycle containing an article the defendant felt was obscene. Contending that this action is in violation of the First and Fourteenth Amendments to the Constitution of the United States, plaintiff is seeking injunctive relief and a declaratory judgment. . . .

FINDINGS OF FACT

1. In the spring of 1969 plaintiff Antonelli was duly elected by the

student body of Fitchburg State College to serve for one year as the editor-in-chief of the campus newspaper. At the start of the fall semester in September 1969 Antonelli changed the name of the paper from Kampus Vue to The Cycle. The change in name was indicative of a change in policy and format. While Kampus Vue's focus had been primarily on student news and events on campus, The Cycle sought to explore and comment upon areas of broader social and political impact.

2. The Cycle is not financially independent. It depends on an allocation of a portion of revenues derived from compulsory student activity fees. In accordance with Mass. G.L. c. 73, § 1B, these fees and any receipts from the student activities themselves are retained in a revolving fund to be expended "as the president of the college may direct in furthering the activities from which the fees and receipts were derived . . . ." Prior to the present dispute, the publication costs and other bills of the student newspaper at Fitchburg State College had been consistently paid from this fund. Without this money the campus newspaper cannot be published on a regular basis.

3. On September 21, 1969, an article entitled "Black Moochie," written by Eldridge Cleaver and originally appearing in Ramparts Magazine, Vol. 8, No. 4, October 1969, was included in the material for Vol. 1, No. 3, of The Cycle submitted to Raymond Plante, the paper's usual printer. Mr. Plante, whose daughter is a student at the college, strenuously objected to the theme of and four-letter words generously used in the text of "Black Moochie." He refused to print the article, preferring to smash his presses first, and he telephoned president Hammond to inform him of the content of the edition which the students were asking him to print. Soon thereafter the defendant came to Plante's office and expressed his own displeasure at the proposed issue of The Cycle. He felt that the "Black Moochie" article was "garbage" and obscene and not fit for publication in the campus newspaper. President Hammond had not been pleased with the change in the focus and format that previous issues of The Cycle had brought to the campus newspaper. He stated that publication should provide an opportunity for students to develop skills in journalism, should not consist primarily of compilations published previously elsewhere and should not serve as a vehicle for the dissemination of obscene material. On this occasion and thereafter the defendant indicated to the plaintiff and others that he felt morally obligated to use his powers over the allocation of funds for student activities under G.L. c. 73, 1B, to see that the money was spent properly and to prevent its expenditure on the publication of such "trash" as "Black Moochie." He stated that therefore he would not consider paying for articles like "Black Moochie" and would refuse to allow future editions of The Cycle to be published unless he or someone acting with his authority approved of all the matter to be included in the newspaper prior to its being printed.

4. In order that some form of student publication continue during the pendency of these proceedings, and under protest, plaintiff agreed to cooperate with an advisory board of two faculty members, Drs. Greene and Quigley, who were appointed by the defendant to exercise their judgment as to the "responsible freedom of the press" in the student newspaper. Under president Hammond's plan, funds from student fees would not be forthcoming for future issues until the issues were approved by the advisory board. Drs. Greene and Quigley were authorized by the defendant to certify the necessary expenditures and approve their payment only after they exercised their judgment as to the "responsible freedom of the press" in the student newspaper. President Hammond expressed his willingness to abide by the judgment of the advisory board.

5. The primary function of the advisory board is to pass on the acceptability of material intended to be published in The Cycle and to prevent the printing of articles which the administration feels are not fit for the campus newspaper. No guidelines of acceptability were established and no standards limit the discretion of the two faculty members as they pass judgment on the material submitted to them. No procedure was designed whereby the reasonableness or validity of a board decision might be tested or reviewed.

6. Prior to the present controversy, the officials at Fitchburg State College had left control over the content of the campus newspaper entirely to the student editors. Only with the attempted publication of "Black Moochie" did president Hammond feel it necessary to interpose administrative control in the form of the advisory board.

7. The issue of The Cycle containing the article entitled "Black Moochie" was in fact printed and widely circulated both at Fitchburg State College and elsewhere. A different printer did the printing and the costs were not paid for from student activity funds. President Hammond never authorized payments relating to this issue of The Cycle. The publication came about through the combined efforts of the editors of the newspapers of five Massachusetts state colleges, including Fitchburg. There was no evidence that any of the funds expended in connection with this issue belonged to plaintiff or that he has any legal liability with respect to them.

8. On November 7, 1969, plaintiff repudiated his agreement to cooperate with the advisory board and he and the entire editorial board submitted their resignations. This action was announced in the one issue of The Cycle published under the control of the advisory board, Vol. 1, No. 4. It was prompted by disputes with the two faculty members as to the newspaper's financial responsibilities and budgetary mechanics.

9. Although the conflict leading to the resignations did not concern material submitted for publication and although the board neither rejected nor censored in any way any of the material actually proposed for the one issue printed under its auspices, the controversy over censor-

ship still colored the relationship of the student editors and representatives of the administration.

10. On November 20, 1969, the resignations were accepted by the
student government association of the college. However, in an attempt
to avoid the threat of mootness, a special meeting of the student
government was called on November 25, 1969, and the previous recognition of the resignations was unanimously withdrawn. The acceptance
of the resignations was now to be deemed effective December 17, 1969
rather than November 20.

11. This is not the only indication of support that the student government association has shown for The Cycle and the plaintiff in the
dispute over the control of the content of the campus newspaper. On
October 14, during a time of cessation in publication, an open meeting
of the student government association was held and a motion was de-
bated that another publication, edited by one who opposed The Cycle,
be given funds from the newspaper budget to publish a weekly news-
letter until the fate of The Cycle was decided. This motion was
virtually unanimously defeated.

12. The Cycle has not been published since the announcement of
the resignations on November 7. The office of editor-in-chief will have
been officially vacant since December 17, 1969. Although he would have
to be reelected by the student body, Antonelli testified that he would be
willing to run again and serve as editor-in-chief if the advisory board
were eliminated.

13. At no time has any disciplinary action been taken by Fitchburg
State College against the plaintiff or any other student in connection
with the publication of The Cycle.

CONCLUSIONS OF LAW

The first question for decision is whether the case is moot. "Simply
stated, a case is moot when the issues presented are no longer 'live' or the
parties lack a legally cognizable interest in the outcome." . . . As argued
by the defendant, there has been full publication and circulation of
Vol. 1, No. 3, of The Cycle including Eldridge Cleaver's "Black
Moochie"; plaintiff did not spend any of his own money and is not
liable in law to anyone for the expenses of such publication; the advisory board has not in fact censored any material submitted to it nor
denied funds concerning the printing of any article; plaintiff has re-
signed as editor-in-chief and The Cycle has not functioned since the
announcement of his resignation. Under these circumstances, the court
rules that plaintiff has no legally cognizable interest in a decision by this
court as to the constitutionality of president Hammond's efforts to
prevent publication of the issue of The Cycle containing "Black
Moochie."

However, plaintiff asserts a further and continuing interest, i.e., the right to be free from the burden of submitting future issues of The Cycle to the advisory board for its prior approval. The nature of the legal interest inherent in this claim is such that it is not affected by the factors which moot his other claims. This is true notwithstanding plaintiff's resignation, which was largely due to his unwillingness to "clear" the contents of The Cycle with the advisory board. The prospect of his reelection as editor is not at all insubstantial, considering that he was unopposed last year and has enjoyed the overwhelming support of the student government association. "There is and there ought to be no rule of constitutional standing that, in order to construct a justiciable 'case,' a plaintiff must submit to the very burden whose validity he wishes to attack." . . . We conclude that plaintiff has a continuing personal stake in the outcome of these proceedings and that the case is not moot.

Turning to the merits of the plaintiff's claim to freedom from censorial supervision by the advisory board, we note first the absence of any express limitation on the board's powers to review and approve. All manner of intended publication must be submitted; there is no exception, so there is nothing that does not come within the censor's purview. Therefore, the powers actually conferred could presumably be used, without change in form or need for expansion, to achieve complete control of the content of the newspaper. However, there is no indication of an intention to go beyond excising obscenity, and in any event, for purposes of this case, we must construe the powers conferred upon the advisory board by the defendant in the narrowest light possible, i.e., censorial only over the obscene. This is essential because the plaintiff claims freedom from an obligation to submit anything for prior approval.

No matter how narrow the function of the advisory board, it constitutes a direct previous restraint of expression and as such there is a "heavy presumption against its constitutional validity." . . . The general rules are clear, ". . . [L]iberty of the press, historically considered and taken up by the Federal Constitution, has meant, principally although not exclusively, immunity from previous restraints or censorship." . . . Any limitation on the constitutional immunity from prior restraints "is the exception; it is to be closely confined so as to preclude what may fairly be deemed licensing or censorship." . . .

It is true that the advisory board proposes to suppress only obscene writings and that obscenity does not fall within the area of constitutionally protected speech or press. . . . However, the manner and means of achieving the proposed suppression are of crucial importance. . . . Whenever the state takes any measure to regulate obscenity it must conform to procedures calculated to avoid the danger that protected expression will be caught in the regulatory dragnet. . . . Such procedures are constitutionally required themselves—going to the very nature of the First Amendment rights.

It is characteristic of the freedoms of expression in general that they are vulnerable to gravely damaging yet barely visible encroachments. Our insistence that regulations of obscenity scrupulously embody the most rigorous procedural safeguards . . . is therefore but a special insistence of the larger principle that the freedoms of expression must be ringed about with adequate bulwarks. . . .

The type of procedural safeguards required by the First Amendment was indicated in *Freedman* v. *Maryland,* 1965, 380 U.S. 51. There the appellant had been convicted for exhibiting a motion picture without submitting it to the Maryland State Board of Censors for prior approval. In sustaining the challenge to the constitutionality of the licensing system because of procedural inadequacies, the Supreme Court listed three minimal requirements: first, that the censor bear the burden of showing the film to be obscene; second, that the requirement of advance submission not be so administered as to give an effect of finality to the censor's adverse determination; and third, that the procedure ultimately assure a prompt final judicial determination.[*]

Nothing of the sort is included in the system devised by the defendant for passing upon the contents of The Cycle. It lacks even the semblance of any of the safeguards the Supreme Court has demanded.[**] The advisory board bears no burden other than exercising its judgment; there is no appeal within the system from any particular decision; and there is no provision for prompt final judicial determination. . . . Indeed, final responsibility rests with two faculty members, serving at the pleasure of the defendant, who so far as the evidence showed are wholly unfamiliar with the complex tests of obscenity established by the Supreme Court. . . . Accordingly, the court concludes that the defendant's establishment of the advisory board is prima facie an unconstitutional exercise of state power.

If the advisory board of The Cycle is to withstand constitutional challenge, it can only be because there is something either in the institutional needs of a public university or in the nature of a newspaper funded from student activity fees that justifies a limitation of free expression and thereby permits an exercise of state power plainly unwarranted if applied to the press generally.

Free speech does not mean wholly unrestricted speech and the con-

---

[*] If anything, safeguards are more essential to protect publishers of a student newspaper than distributors of a motion picture. There the substantial investment involved in producing a movie provides an obvious impetus for the pressing of constitutional claims which is absent in the context of a student newspaper. Therefore the effective finality of a censor's decision regarding the content of a student newspaper is all the more probable and consequently so is the danger that protected expression will be suppressed.

[**] Under the circumstances, we need not decide whether adequate procedural safeguards could ever be formulated supporting prior restraint of a weekly newspaper. It is extremely doubtful. Newspaper censorship in any form seems essentially incompatible with freedom of the press.

stitutional rights of students may be modified by regulations reasonably designed to adjust these rights to the needs of the school environment. The exercise of rights by individuals must yield when they are incompatible with the school's obligation to maintain the order and discipline necessary for the success of the educational process. However, any infringement of individual constitutional freedoms must be adequately related to this legitimate interest. . . .

No such justification has been shown in the instant case. Obscenity in a campus newspaper is not the type of occurrence apt to be significantly disruptive of an orderly and disciplined educational process. Furthermore, assuming that a college administration has a sufficient educationally oriented reason to prevent the circulation of obscenity on campus, there has been no showing that the harm from obscenity in a college setting is so much greater than in the public forum that it outweighs the danger to free expression inherent in censorship without procedural safeguards. If anything, the contrary would seem to be true. The university setting of college-age students being exposed to a wide range of intellectual experience creates a relatively mature marketplace for the interchange of ideas so that the free speech clause of the First Amendment with its underlying assumption that there is positive social value in an open forum seems particularly appropriate. . . .

There is an added element in the present case: the expenses of publishing The Cycle are payable by the college from funds received from compulsory student activity fees. Does this circumstance significantly alter either the rights of the students or the powers of the college president over the campus press? We think not. Contrary to the defendant's contention, Mass. G.L. c. 73, § 1B, does not make him ultimately responsible for what is printed in the campus newspaper. Under that section, student activity fees "shall be expended as the president of the college may direct in furthering the activities from which the fees and receipts were derived. . . ." This imposes no duty on the president to ratify or to pass judgment on a particular activity. The discretion granted is in the determination whether the funds to be expended actually further the activities to which they are intended to be applied. Once that determination has been made, the expenditure is mandatory.

We are well beyond the belief that any manner of state regulation is permissible simply because it involves an activity which is a part of the university structure and is financed with funds controlled by the administration. The state is not necessarily the unrestrained master of what it creates and fosters. Thus in cases concerning school-supported publications or the use of school facilities, the courts have refused to recognize as permissible any regulations infringing free speech when not shown to be necessarily related to the maintenance of order and discipline within the educational process.

These decisions do not stand for the proposition that a state college administration has no more control over the campus newspaper than it would have over a private publication disseminated on campus. In the very creation of an activity involving media of communication, the state regulates to some degree the form of expression fostered. But the creation of the form does not give birth also to the power to mold its substance. For example, it may be lawful in the interest of providing students with the opportunity to develop their own writing and journalistic skills, to restrict publication in a campus newspaper to articles written by students. Such a restriction might be reasonably related to the educational process. See generally, *Developments in The Law— Academic Freedom,* 1968, 81 Harv. L. Rev. 1045, 1128–1134. But to tell a student what thoughts he may communicate is another matter. Having fostered a campus newspaper, the state may not impose arbitrary restrictions on the matter to be communicated. . . . What was said in *Tinker* v. *Des Moines School Dist.,* supra, where the form of expression was the wearing of black armbands, is equally applicable here. "In our system, students may not be regarded as closed-circuit recipients of only that which the state chooses to communicate. They may not be confined to the expression of those sentiments that are officially approved. In the absence of a specific showing of constitutionally valid reasons to regulate their speech, students are entitled to freedom of expression of their views." . . .

Because of the potentially great social value of a free student voice in an age of student awareness and unrest, it would be inconsistent with basic assumptions of First Amendment freedoms to permit a campus newspaper to be simply a vehicle for ideas the state or the college administration deems appropriate. Power to prescribe classroom curricula in state universities may not be transferred to areas not designed to be part of the curriculum.*

Accordingly, since (a) there is no right to editorial control by administration officials flowing from the fact that The Cycle is college sponsored and state supported, and (b) defendant has not shown that circumstances attributable to the school environment make necessary more restrictive measures than generally permissible under the First Amendment, the court holds and declares that the prior submission to the advisory board of material intended to be published in The Cycle, in order that the board may decide whether it complies with "responsible freedom of the press" or is obscene, may not be constitutionally required either by means of withholding funds derived from student activity fees or otherwise.

The court declines at this time to issue any injunctive relief. Defendant is a highly placed and responsible public official, and there is no

---

* There is, of course, no occasion here to examine the nature and extent of the power of a state university over its curriculum. See generally, *Developments in the Law—Academic Freedom,* supra at 1051–1054.

reason to believe that he will not abide by the law as herein declared. . . .

United States District Judge

State v. *Buchanan*
Supreme Court of Oregon
436 P.2d 729
Jan. 24, 1968

GODWIN, Justice

(1) This is an appeal from a judgment of contempt of court. The only issue is whether freedom of the press gives a newspaper reporter the constitutional right to preserve the anonymity of an informer in the face of court order requiring disclosure.

Conceding that neither she nor her informers had statutory* or common-law privileges,** Annette Buchanan, a writer for a student newspaper, asserted on constitutional and professional-ethics*** grounds that she had the right, after a publication, to refuse to disclose the identity of her source of information.

The issue arose upon a court order in aid of a grand jury investigation into the use of marijuana in Lane County. Miss Buchanan had promised seven persons who claimed to be marijuana users that if they permitted her to interview them for publication she would under no circumstances reveal their names. Miss Buchanan reported the results of the interviews, using fictitious names. This publication produced a well-publicized**** confrontation with the then district attorney culminating in the proceedings which led to this appeal.

---

* "There are particular relations in which it is the policy of the law to encourage confidence, and to preserve it inviolate; therefore a person cannot be examined as a witness in the following cases . . . ." ORS 44.040. (List includes husband and wife, attorney and client, priest and penitent, physician and patient, public officer and official communication, stenographer and employer, professional nurse and patient, certified psychologist and client.)

** At common law only the priest, physician, and lawyer were recognized for testimonial purposes as parties to privileged communications, and each could be released only by the other party to the communication or by law in certain situations. It was not the identity of the privileged party that was to be protected, but the contents of the communication. At common law each of the privileged professionals was subject to rigorous intraprofessional discipline and, except for the priest in modern times, to governmental licensing and discipline as well.

*** "Though there is a canon of journalistic ethics forbidding the disclosure of a newspaper's source of information—a canon worthy of respect and undoubtedly well founded—it is subject to a qualification: it must yield when in conflict with the interests of justice; the private interests involved must yield to the interests of the public."

**** "The public interest at stake in this contempt case is not that persuasive. If the district attorney and other law enforcement officers had done their own investigative work competently, they would not have had to try to coerce a college student to turn unwilling informer. It is to her credit that she refused to play their childish game." *New York Times*, June 29, 1966.

In the trial court, testimony and argument were addressed to the social value and professional desirability of the asserted privilege. The trial court, however, was of the opinion that the asserted privilege was not a right of constitutional stature and that the public-policy questions were of a kind that should be left to the Legislative Assembly. A fine of $300 was imposed.

Miss Buchanan seeks reversal on the ground that the constitutionally protected freedom of the press necessarily includes freedom to gather news. Since certain news stories cannot be obtained unless the reporter can promise anonymity to a confidential informer, she argues that a judicial order requiring disclosure abridges a protected freedom. The social values which favor a free press, she argues, should be judicially balanced against those which favor the discovery and prosecution of law violators. It may be true, as the defendant argues, that some balancing of values occurs when district attorneys ignore the reports in the popular press based upon anonymous confessions concerning drug use, abortions, and other activities in which law violations may have played a part. This social phenomenon, however, is not relevant to the defendant's underlying assumption that the "press" has a right to gather information superior to that which other members of society can assert. While the government from time to time extends to selected representatives of news media privileges (such as access to war zones and seats on a presidential aircraft) not accorded the general public, it has not been suggested that these privileges are necessarily rights conferred by the Constitution solely upon those who can qualify as members of the press.

On the contrary, it has been held that those claiming to be news gatherers have no constitutional right to information which is not accessible to the public generally.

In the decisions dealing with the reporter's asserted right to refuse to disclose his source of information, the courts have held that rights of privacy, freedom of association, and ethical convictions are subordinate to the duty of every citizen to testify in court.

(2) Indeed, it would be difficult to rationalize a rule that would create special constitutional rights for those possessing credentials as news gatherers which would not conflict with the equal-privileges and equal-protection concepts also found in the Constitution. Freedom of the press is a right which belongs to the public; it is not the private preserve of those who possess the implements of publishing.

Apart from the definitional difficulties in attempting to give constitutional status to a privilege for qualified news gatherers which presumably would be denied to less favored classes, there is another objection to discrimination between news gatherers and other persons. Such a practice would be potentially destructive of the very freedom that is sought to be preserved by this appeal. After the lessons of colonial times,* the First Amendment required the federal government to resist the normal temptation of rulers to regulate, license, or otherwise pass upon the credentials of those claiming to be authors and publishers. An invitation to the government to grant a special privilege to a special class of "news gatherers" necessarily draws after it an invitation to the government to define the membership of that class. We doubt that all news writers would want the government to pass upon the qualifications of those seeking to enter their field.

The scope-of-employment test contemplated by typical statutes creating such privileges appears to approach the problem from two sides: (a) the person claiming the privilege is "engaged in the work of gathering," and (b) the material being gathered is "news." Statutory distinctions may or may not be made among the media to be used for dissemination. The statutes generally omit any guidance as to what is "work" and what is "news."

Assuming that legislators are free to experiment with such definitions, it would be dangerous business for courts, asserting constitutional grounds, to extend to an employe of a "respectable" newspaper a privilege which would be denied to an employe of a disreputable newspaper; or to an episodic pamphleteer; or to a free-lance writer seeking a story to sell on the open market; or, indeed, to a shaggy nonconformist who wishes only to write out his message and nail it to a tree. If the claimed privilege is to be found in the Constitution, its benefits cannot be limited to those whose credentials may, from time to time, satisfy the government.

Since we decline to attempt a constitutional definition of "news" and "news reporters," we have not discussed a secondary argument advanced in this appeal: that we should fashion for those eligible to enjoy it a privilege limited to cases in which secrecy is an aid to social criticism aimed at reforming the law.

(3) We hold that there is no constitutional reason for creating a qualified right for some, but not others, to withhold evidence as an aid to newsgathering. We do not hold that the Constitution forbids the legislative enactment of reasonable privileges to withhold evidence.**

---

* The licensing acts, which prevailed in England during most of the period from Charles I until William and Mary, influenced the colonies by way of instructions to the royal governors. The following is representative:

And forasmuch as great inconvenience may arise by the liberty of printing within our said territory under your government you are to provide by all necessary orders that no person keep any printingpress for printing, nor that any book pamphlet or other matters whatsoever be printed without your especial leave and license first obtained.

** Our attention has been directed to the enactment in thirteen states of legislation which appears to create a statutory right of newspaper, radio, and television employes to reveal the contents of a communication without being required to reveal the name of its author:

Ala. Cod. tit. 7, § 370 (1958);
Ariz. Rev. Stat. Amm. § 12-2237 (Cum.Supp.1966);

That question is not before us. We hold merely that nothing in the state or federal constitution compels the courts, in the absence of statute, to recognize such a privilege.

Affirmed.

Arvins v. *Rutgers State University*
385 F.2d 151
Nov. 2, 1967

MARIS, Circuit Judge

The plaintiff, Alfred Arvins, brought suit in the District Court for the District of New Jersey against the defendant, Rutgers, The State University of New Jersey, for declaratory and injunctive relief. The plaintiff alleged that he had submitted to the editors of the Rutgers Law Review for publication in the Review an article which reviewed the legislative history of the Civil Rights Act of 1875 as it pertained to school desegregation and which concluded that, in the light shed by the Congressional debates, the United States Supreme Court had erred in *Brown* v. *Board of Education,* 1954 . . . in holding that "although these sources cast some light, it is not enough to resolve the problem with which we are faced. At best, they are inconclusive." The articles editor of the Review had rejected the article, stating in his letter of rejection "that approaching the problem from the point of view of legislative history alone is insufficient." The plaintiff asserted that the editors of the Law Review had adopted a discriminatory policy of accepting only articles reflecting a "liberal" jurisprudential outlook in constitutional law, an outlook which, he said, rejects the primacy of legislative history and the original intent of the framers of a constitutional provision. The plaintiff stated that his article represented the "conservative" approach to constitutional law and he contended that its rejection, which he said was solely because of its conservative tenor, violated his constitutional right to freedom of speech. Both the plaintiff and the defendant moved for summary judgment. After hearing, the trial judge, in an oral opin-

Ark. Stat. Ann § 43-917 (1964) ;
Cal. Evidence Code, § 1070 (1966) ;
Ind. Ann Stat. § 2-1733 (Cum.Supp.1966) ;
Ky. Rev. Stat. § 421.100 (1963) ;
La. Rev. Stat. §§ 45:1451 to 45:1454 (Cum.Supp.1965) ;
Md. Code Ann. § 28.945 (1) C.L.Mich.1948 767.5a [P.A.1961,No. 276] (1954) ;
Mont. Rev. Code, §§ 93-601-1, 93-601-2 (1964) ;
N.J. Stat. Amm. §§ 2A:84A-21, 2A·84A-29 (Cum.Supp.1966) ;
Ohio Rev. Code Ann. §§ 2739.04,2739.12 (Supp. 1966) ;
Pa. Stat. Ann. tit. § 330 (Cum.Supp.1965) .

ion, stated, inter alia, that he had "serious doubt as to whether the right of freedom of speech embraces a privilege to use a law school review publication as a medium. Freedom of speech is guaranteed by the Constitution, but the right to have others listen is not guaranteed, nor is anyone obligated to read articles that an author is able to publish. It could not be contended reasonably that the Editorial Board of Rutgers Law Review must accept for publication every treatise on law which is submitted to it. There must necessarily be a broad area for the exercise of discretion." The judge concluded that the plaintiff had not shown that he had been deprived of a federally protected right. Summary judgment was accordingly entered for the defendant and this appeal by the plaintiff followed.

(1) The plaintiff's basic contention on this appeal is that a law review published by a state-supported university, such as the defendant, is a public instrumentality in the columns of which all must be allowed to present their ideas, the editors being without discretion to reject an article because in their judgment its nature or ideological approach is not suitable for publication. In considering this contention it must be borne in mind that the validity of a restraint on speech in each case depends on the particular circumstances. . . . It is essential, therefore, to scrutinize the procedure by which it is claimed that Rutgers, as an instrumentality of the State of New Jersey, has restrained that freedom. For "Differences in circumstances beget appropriate differences in law." . . . As Justice Black remarked: "The First and Fourteenth Amendments, I think, take away from government, state and federal, all power to restrict freedom of speech, press, and assembly, *where people have a right to be for such purposes.*"

Our inquiry, therefore, is whether in the setting of this case the refusal of the editors of the Rutgers Law Review to permit the review to be the medium for the expression of the plaintiff's ideas abridged his right of free speech. It appears that the publication is part of the educational program of the Law School of Rutgers University for its law students, that the editorial work is done by law students under general faculty guidance, and that the material published consists of "lead" articles contributed by outside authors, in addition to students' writing. The plaintiff does not assert that the operation of the Rutgers Law Review, or the work of the student editors, deviates in any way from that which is customarily followed in the publication of similar law reviews by nonpublic law schools. Traditionally, a law review is student edited and the student editors determine the policies and decide which of the submitted articles and other material are to be published. In this regard, the trial judge stated:

. . . the Editorial Board must be selective in what it publishes, and a selective process requires the exercise of opinion to what particular subject matter of the law will at a given time be of educational value, not only to the student body, but also to the subscribers.

The plaintiff in this case seems to feel that the subject matter of his article is of paramount significance and should be published to the exclusion of other articles that were apparently selected to fill the space that this article would have taken in the Law Review.

In this respect he seeks to intrude his opinion upon that of the Editorial Board.

The trial judge found as a fact "that the reasons for rejection as stated by Mr. Calligaro [the student articles editor] were valid and that this particular article was one which it would not be unreasonable for any editorial review board of a Law Review to reject."

(2, 3) We agree. The right to freedom of speech does not open every avenue to one who desires to use a particular outlet for expression. On the contrary, each particular avenue for expression presents its own peculiar problems. . . . Nor does freedom of speech comprehend the right to speak on any subject at any time. . . . "True, if a man is to speak or preach he must have some place from which to do it. This does not mean, however, that he may seize a particular radio station for his forum." . . .

(4, 5) Thus, one who claims that his constitutional right to freedom of speech has been abridged must show that he has a right to use the particular medium through which he seeks to speak. This the plaintiff has wholly failed to do. He says that he has published articles in other law reviews and will sooner or later be able to publish in a law review the article here involved. This is doubtless true. Also, no one doubts that he may freely at his own expense print his article and distribute it to all who wish to read it. However, he does not have the right, constitutional or otherwise, to commandeer the press and columns of the Rutgers Law Review for the publication of his article, at the expense of the subscribers to the Review and the New Jersey taxpayers, to the exclusion of other articles deemed by the editors to be more suitable for publication. On the contrary, the acceptance or rejection of articles submitted for publication in a law school law review necessarily involves the exercise of editorial judgment and this is in no wise lessened by the fact that the law review is supported, at least in part by the State.

The plaintiff's contention that the student editors of the Rutgers Law Review have been so indoctrinated in a liberal ideology by the faculty of the law school as to be unable to evaluate his article objectively is so frivolous as to require no discussion.

The judgment of the district court will be affirmed.

8
Military Service

Hanauer v. *Elkins*
217 Md. 213 (141 A.2d 903)
June 3, 1958
HENDERSON, Judge

The Appellants, Kenneth George Hanauer and Jack A. Crabill, claiming to be conscientious objectors, filed petitions in the Circuit Court for Prince George's County on January 16, 1957, for writs of mandamus directing the President and Board of Regents of the University of Maryland to allow them to continue as students in the University without conforming to the general requirement that all able-bodied male undergraduates take basic military training. The petitions were denied by the trial court and the petitioners appealed. Both cases involve the same constitutional questions and substantially the same facts and were consolidated for the purpose of hearing the appeals. The writ was denied in the Hanauer case and judgment entered in favor of the appellees after full hearing and consideration of testimony. In the Crabill case, judgment was entered for the appellees by order of the trial court sustaining a demurrer to the petition, without leave to amend.

The material facts established by the evidence in the Hanauer case and alleged in the petition in the Crabill case are substantially similar. The Board of Regents of the University of Maryland adopted as a part of the curriculum of the University a course in the Reserve Officer Training Corps, which is conducted by United States Air Force personnel. The University, as a land-grant college, received federal funds under the Morrill Act. . . . Pursuant to the provisions of that Act, the University is required to offer a course in Reserve Officer Training Corps, which may be either elective or mandatory in the discretion of the University. The regulations concerning this course which have been adopted by the Board of Regents require that all male students under thirty years of age, who are citizens of the United States, except those specifically exempted by the regulations, take the basic two-year course during their first two years after matriculation. Included in the exemptions are those students who have completed the basic course in other approved units of the Army, Navy or Air Force R.O.T.C., or have served in the Army, Navy, Marine Corps, Coast Guard, or Air Force, for a period of time long enough to be considered equivalent to the basic training in the AFROTC course. Conscientious objectors are not expressly exempted.

The basic course was described as being "designed as a course training a man to better perform his duties as a citizen of the United States and of his community, to understand the impact of international tensions, world organization, the place of the United States in the family of nations, and his responsibility as a citizen to support his country." The training includes instruction in the nature of a military force, that is, how the Army, Navy and Air Force combine together to form the defense force of the nation and their mission and responsibility as a combined defense force. The basic course involves learning to engage in military drill as a unit, and the wearing of an Air Force uniform, but completion of the basic course does not impose any subsequent military obligations. The purpose of the elective advanced course of two years, following the basic course, is to instruct Junior Officers of the United States Air Force and provide a major source of officer personnel for the regular Air Force. Insofar as the basic course is necessary in order to take the advanced course, the objectives of the advanced course are reflected in the basic course. United States Air Force officers conduct all classroom academic work and supervise drill on the field. Regulations covering the type of training offered by the course are the regulations of the United States Air Force which have been adopted by the University.

Both Hanauer and Crabill claimed to be conscientious objectors. Both profess to be followers of the teaching of Jesus Christ and believe from his teaching that violence and the killing of human beings is against the principles of the Christian religion. They are opposed to war or military training in preparation for war, as being contrary to their religious beliefs. Hanauer is a member of the Evangelical Reformed Church. Crabill is a member of the Church of the Brethren. The tenets of neither of these denominations require that its members be conscientious objectors, but it is their policy to show consideration to those members who are conscientious objectors and support them in their conviction. The sincerity of this religious belief by Hanauer and Crabill is not questioned by the officials of the University in either case. Prior to their enrollment, both Hanauer and Crabill were classified by their local draft board as conscientious objectors under the provisions of the Universal Military Training and Service Act. . . . This section of the Act provides for exemption from military training of conscientious objectors who are opposed to participation in war in any form and their assignment to work of national importance under civilian direction. Pursuant to this classification, each of the appellants served two years in civilian work after being inducted into service under the Selective Service Act and received their certificates of discharge as draftees.

Hanauer is twenty-four years of age and a citizen of Maryland. He enrolled as a third-year student in the College of Education in September 1965. He desired to become a student at the University because the cost is lower than a private school and he could receive the training required to become a high school teacher. At the time of his admission, he informed the officials he was a conscientious objector and that he could not take the required two-year basic AFROTC course because it was against his religious beliefs. The officials of the University, through inadvertence, neglected to consider his case until after he had been admitted as a student and had entered upon the first semester. After consideration they advised him he must take the course or leave the University at the end of the first semester in January 1957.

Crabill is twenty-five years of age and a citizen of Maryland. He enrolled as a first-year student in the College of Education in September 1956. At the time of his enrollment he likewise advised the University officials that he was a conscientious objector. Upon being informed that he could not become a student unless he agreed to take the prescribed two-year, basic course in AFROTC, he agreed to take the course under written protest. After experiencing the requirements of the course he notified the officials, prior to the end of the first semester, that he could not continue, as experience showed it was a military program in violation of his religious beliefs. The officials then notified him he must leave the University at the end of the semester because of his failure to take this required course. We think no distinction should be drawn between Crabill and Hanauer for present purposes, although the appellees argue that there is evidence of a waiver on Crabill's part.

(1) The appellants' first contention is that the mandatory requirement that they take the basic course is contrary to the charter of the University and the Maryland Constitution. The charter of the University provides, in part, that " 'no sectarian or partisan test shall be allowed or exercised . . . in the admission of students thereto, or for any purpose whatever . . .' and that the University shall be maintained for students of . . .' every religious denomination who shall be freely admitted to equal privileges of education and to all the honors of the college according to their merit without requiring or enforcing any religious or civil test.' " Article 36 of the Maryland Declaration of Rights provides that "all persons are equally entitled to protection in their religious liberty; wherefore, no person ought, by any law to be molested

in his person or estate, on account of his religious persuasion or profession, or for his religious practice, unless, under the color of religion, he shall disturb the good order, peace or safety of the State, or infringe the laws of morality, or injure others in their natural, civil or religious rights. . . ." Article 37 forbids a religious test as a qualification for public office. It seems clear that the University, in requiring the basic course as a part of the curriculum, is not imposing a religious test. . . . The question is . . . simply whether the policy of the University must yield to the views of the petitioners that the prescribed course is at variance with their personal and pacifist beliefs. The test of eligibility to attend the University is not directed at these petitioners. They are asserting a right to attend the University without compliance with a general condition which they are unwilling to meet, because of religious convictions personal to them. We think the Regulations adopted by the Board of Regents are well within any limitations imposed by the Constitution and laws of this State.

(2, 3) The appellants invoke the protection of the First and Fourteenth Amendments of the federal Constitution. We entertain no doubt that the University of Maryland is a branch or agency of the State government. . . . If its exclusionary policy toward persons who are otherwise qualified, but who refuse to take the prescribed basic course, is a violation of rights guaranteed by the federal Constitution, then the policy of the State must yield. But we are not persuaded that such rights exist. . . . In *Hamilton* v. *Regents of University of California*, 293 U.S. 245, 55 S.Ct. 197, 79 L.Ed. 343, it was held by a unanimous court that a conscientious objector was properly excluded from the State University because of his refusal to take the required course in the R.O.T.C. Mr. Justice Butler, for the court, said:

> Taken on the basis of the facts alleged in the petition, appellants' contentions amount to no more than an assertion that the due process clause of the Fourteenth Amendment as a safeguard of 'liberty' confers the right to be students in the State University free from obligation to take military training as one of the conditions of attendance. Viewed in the light of our decisions that proposition must at once be put aside as untenable." Mr. Justice Cardozo, concurring "to say an extra word," and joined by Justices Brandeis and Stone, said: "The First Amendment, if it be read into the Fourteenth, makes invalid any state law 'respecting an establishment of religion, or prohibiting the free exercise thereof.' Instruction in military science is not instruction in the practice or tenets of a religion. Neither directly nor indirectly is government establishing a state religion when it insists upon such training. Instruction in military science, unaccompanied here by any pledge of military service, is not an interference by the state with the free exercise of religion when the liberties of the Constitution are read in the light of a century and a half of history during days of peace and war. . . . Manifestly a dif-

ferent doctrine would carry us to lengths that have never yet been dreamed of. The conscientious objector, if his liberties were to be thus extended, might refuse to contribute taxes in furtherance of a war, whether for attack or defense, or in furtherance of any other end condemned by his conscience as irreligious or immoral. The right of private judgment has never yet been so exalted above the powers and the compulsion of the agencies of government. One who is a martyr to a principle—which may turn out in the end to be a delusion or an error—does not prove by his martyrdom that he has kept within the law.

* * *

The appellants also rely upon the case of *West Virginia State Board of Education* v. *Barnette,* 319 U.S. 624 ... and holding unconstitutional a state act requiring a flag salute. But the Hamilton case was not overruled. In fact, it was cited and distinguished in the majority opinion by Mr. Justice Jackson, on the grounds that attendance in the Hamilton case was not compulsory, and because the State "has power to raise militia and impose the duties of service therein upon its citizens." There were also intimations that the requirement had no substantial or apparent relation to the public welfare, and that the flag salute was a form of utterance compelling the students to declare a belief. Mr. Justice Frankfurter in his dissent, conceded that the Hamilton case was not overruled, but found it impossible to distinguish it, at least upon the first ground assigned. We need not speculate as to where the line may ultimately be drawn or redrawn. Unless and until the Hamilton case is overruled, we think it is controlling, so far as the interpretation of the federal Constitution is concerned, in its application to the facts of the instant case.

(4, 5) The appellants further contend that since they have completed their obligation to serve under the Universal Military Training and Service Act, by performance of "civilian work contributing to the maintenance of the national health, safety, or interest," it is a violation of their "privileges or immunities," under the Fourteenth Amendment to require them to take the AFROTC basic course. But we think the answer is that the Act of Congress according the exemption was a matter of grace, not conferring any federal right that would preclude this State from refusing to accord an equivalent exemption to students applying for admission to the State University. .... If we assume, without deciding, that Congress has any Constitutional power to supersede the State policy in the training of its youth, it is sufficient to say that Congress has not yet attempted to do so. Nor do we think that the requirement is discriminatory, or denies the equal protection of the laws to these appellants. The appellants have not taken the prescribed course elsewhere, and the Regulations of the University require all persons in their age group to take the course if they have not taken it elsewhere. ....

Judgments affirmed, with costs.

9
Domicile

Newman v. *Graham*
52 Idaho 90 (349 P2d 716)
Feb. 24, 1960
* * *

KNUDSON, Justice

The facts in this case have been stipulated to be:
That respondent (Plaintiff) is twenty-five years of age and self-supporting, and that he has been continuously in the State of Idaho since September, 1957; that immediately prior to his coming to Idaho he had been in the military service of the United States where he had served for a period of four years; that prior to his entry into the military service he had been a resident of and domiciled in the State of Vermont; that in September, 1957, shortly after his arrival in the State of Idaho, he enrolled as a regular student at Idaho State College at Pocatello, Idaho, for the school year 1957–1958 and was required to and did pay nonresident, out-of-state tuition for the academic school year commencing September, 1957, and ending June, 1958:
That since his arrival in the State of Idaho in September, 1957, respondent has maintained continuous residence in and has not departed from this State;
That in September, 1958, respondent registered as a regular student at Idaho State College for the school year 1958–1959, commencing in September, 1958, and ending June, 1959; that respondent was required upon registration in September, 1958, for each school year, to pay out-of-state tuition as a nonresident student; that respondent protested the assessment of such out-of-state, nonresident tuition, claiming he was a resident of the State of Idaho; that each protest was forwarded to the State Board of Education and by said Board disallowed by reason of the following regulation which has been adopted by said State Board of Education acting as trustees of Idaho State College, to wit:

174

Special Fees. Non-resident fee (per semester). . . . $125.00.

A student who has not been domiciled in Idaho more than six months preceding his first enrollment at Idaho State College is required to pay a tuition of $125.00 a semester in addition to the uniform schedule of fees of $69.25, making a total of $194.25.

. . . . Any person who is properly classified as a non-resident student retains that status throughout continuous regular term attendance at any institution of higher learning in Idaho.

That by reason of said regulation respondent has been classified as a nonresident student, and retains that status throughout continuous regular term attendance at Idaho State College;

That respondent has had no domicile or residence other than in Idaho since September, 1957; that he did register and vote in the Idaho 1958 election, and by reason of his continuous residence and domicile in the State of Idaho since September, 1957, has complied with all the requirements for the establishment of residence in the State of Idaho, by both intent and actual residence, for all purposes except to qualify as a resident student under existing regulations of the State Board of Education (as set forth above) acting as Trustees for Idaho State College.

It is stipulated and agreed by the parties that the sole question for determination by the Court is:

Whether the plaintiff who was properly classified as a nonresident student when he first enrolled at Idaho State College in September, 1957, can be required by regulations of the State Board of Education acting as Trustees for Idaho State College, to retain such status throughout continuous regular term attendance at Idaho State College, as prescribed by the regulation of the Board quoted hereinabove, it being stipulated and agreed the plaintiff has been and has become a resident of and domiciled in the State of Idaho for all other purposes?

The trial court adopted the stipulation of facts as and for its findings of fact and as conclusions of law found that the regulation, in part, is:

Arbitrary, capricious and unreasonable and is an attempt on the part of the State Board of Education by regulation to assume and usurp the power vested only in the Legislature of the State under its constitutional authority.

and entered judgment accordingly. This appeal is from said judgment.

Appellant assigns as error the action of the trial court in making its conclusions of law and the entry of the judgment based upon said conclusions.

(1) The Legislature of this State not having provided who shall be admitted to the Idaho State College and having delegated the power

to make rules and regulations necessary to the government of the College to the Board of Trustees, the Board is invested with the power of determining what qualifications shall be required of persons who may be admitted to the College, providing the rules and regulations in that regard are reasonable and not arbitrary. The reasonableness of such regulations is a question of law for the courts. . . .

Pursuant to the provisions of said I.C. § 33-3008, supra, the Board ordained the regulation designated "Special Fees" hereinbefore set out in the stipulated facts. Validity of the following quoted portion of said regulation is questioned by this action, towit:

> Any person who is properly classified as a non-resident student retains that status throughout continuous regular term attendance at any institution of higher learning in Idaho.

(2) The regulation specifically provides that a student who has not been domiciled in Idaho more than six months preceding his first enrollment at the College is required to pay a tuition in addition to the uniform schedule of fees. It is clear that, under said regulation, more than mere residence is intended and required in order to entitle a student to a classification which will exempt him from the payment of tuition. While the words "residence" and "domicile" are frequently used interchangeably, the distinction is aptly noted in the following from Bouvier's Law Dictionary. . . :

> A residence is different from a domicile, although it is a matter of great importance in determining the place of domicile. The essential distinction between residence and domicile is that the first involves the intent to leave when the purpose for which one has taken up his abode ceases. The other has no such intent; the abiding is animus manendi. One may seek a place for the purpose of pleasure, of business or of health. If his intent be to remain, it becomes his domicile; if his intent be to leave as soon as his purpose is accomplished, it is his residence.

Since the Board exercises delegated power, its rules and regulations are of the same force as would be a like enactment of the Legislature, and its official interpretation placed upon the rule so enacted becomes a part of the rule. . . .

Under the interpretation placed upon the foregoing quoted regulation by the Board it would necessarily follow that a student who is a nonresident of the State at the time of initial enrollment at the College would, if he attends each regular term, retain such status throughout his entire college career irrespective of the fact that he may have become a bona fide resident and domiciled more than six months in the State during the intervening time. Under such interpretation it does not afford any opportunity to show a change of residential or domiciliary status and does in effect deny equality of opportunity to persons of the same class who are similarly situated and for that reason it is an unreasonable regulation. The authority of the Board, through its authorized agency or representative, to inquire into and ascertain an applicant's residential or domiciliary status is unquestioned. It is the denial to the applicant of an opportunity to be heard in the matter, within a reasonable time, that constitutes the objectionable feature of the regulation here considered.

It being stipulated that respondent has continuously resided and been domiciled in the State of Idaho since September, 1957, it is clear that he was improperly classified as a nonresident student upon registration for the regular term commencing in September, 1958. At that time (September, 1958) respondent had been domiciled in the State for more than six months and was entitled to be classified as other bona fide residents who had been domiciled in the State for the required six months period.

(3) We conclude that the regulation as interpreted by the Board is arbitrary, capricious and unreasonable. To the extent that the judgment appealed from is in favor of respondent it is affirmed; however, the following quoted portion of the conclusions of law as determined by the trial court, to wit:

and is an attempt on the part of the State Board of Education by regulation to assume and usurp the power vested only in the Legislature of the State under its constitutional authority

is in error. The cause is remanded with instructions to enter judgment in accordance herewith. Costs to respondent.

TAYLOR, C.J., and SMITH, McQUADE and McFADDEN, J.J., concur.

Matter of Robbins v. *Chamberlain*
297 N.Y. 108
Oct. 30, 1947

DESMOND, J.

Section 4 of article II of the State Constitution and section 151 of the Election Law say that, for purposes of registering and voting, no person shall be deemed to have gained or lost a residence "by reason of his presence or absence . . . while a student of any seminary of learning." Those enactments have been construed by the courts, and held to mean at least this: that a student who moves into residence on the campus of an educational institution does not, without more, accomplish a change of voting residence. . . . But the quoted constitutional and statutory enactment "disqualifies no one; confers no rights upon any one." . . . It means only that such presence at a seat of learning is not "a test of a right to vote, and is not to be so regarded. The person offering to vote must find the requisite qualifications elsewhere." . . . No case (except the present ones) goes so far as to hold that a married student, moving with his wife from their former residence to one nearer his studies, automatically loses his right to vote by force of the constitutional-statutory edict.

The petitioners here, whose votes have been successfully challenged in the election districts in Rockland County wherein they now reside, occupy apartments at a housing development called "Shanks Village." Those buildings were formerly part of the wartime Camp Shanks, but after the war they came under the control of the Federal Public Housing Administrator who leased them to Columbia University or, at least, put them under the control of that university. The agreement between Columbia and the administration authorizes the former to rent the apartments to students only, and only to such students as are war veterans. All the petitioners are such students or their wives or relatives, all occupy these apartments as separate family domiciles, and each male petitioner is actually the head of a family unit, consisting in most cases of himself and his wife. (Anomalously enough, the wives have been permitted to vote by these same adjudications.) Many of these student-veterans are gainfully employed, part-time, elsewhere than at the schools they attend. Shanks Village is many miles from any of those educational institutions and the residential facilities there are a part of the Columbia campus only to the limited extent above described.

Our Constitution and our statutes, for sufficient reasons, have decreed that those who attend colleges and seminaries away from their family homes and live in college residential halls during the college year in the fashion conventional before the war, do not, thereby and without more, become qualified to vote in the communities in whose life and doings these students had so limited a part and so limited an interest. The mischief against which the law was aimed was "the participation of an unconcerned body of men in the control through the ballot-box of municipal affairs in whose further conduct they have no interest, and from the mismanagement of which by the officers their ballots might elect, they sustain no injury." . . . However, that old concept of semi-cloistered college life has little to do with the way these petitioners are getting their education. They are married men who have left their parental firesides and gone out on their own, with their wives and children. Their living arrangements at Shanks Village bear small resemblance to an old-fashioned college community, but are more like the kind of new-fashioned company-owned housing projects, which great industries build near their factories to attract and serve their employees and their employees' families. These students are family men, not college boys away from their parental homes. True, their tenure of occupancy at Shanks Village can continue only while they are students, but, since they have no other homes, their tenure is "temporary" or "indefinite" only in the same sense as the tenure of the occupant of a city apartment house.

There is no substantial dispute of fact here. These petitioners have shown their eligibility to vote from the only residences they have. As to the right to vote of the petitioners who are wives or parents of veteran-students, we cannot see that there is any doubt whatever.

The orders should be modified so as to grant the petitions of the student petitioners, and as so modified affirmed, without costs.

THACHER and DYE, JJ., concur with DESMOND, J.; LOUGHRAN, Ch.J., CONWAY and FULD, JJ., concur in result; LEWIS, J., taking no part.

Ordered accordingly.

Clarke v. *Redeker*
259 F. Supp. 117
Sept. 15, 1966
STEPHENSON, District Judge
* * *

THE CONTROVERSY

The principal question before the Court involves a determination of whether the plaintiff, George Clarke, is being deprived of certain constitutional rights because he is charged a nonresident rather than a resident tuition fee while attending the College of Law at the State University of Iowa. Plaintiff seeks to enjoin state officials from charging him nonresident tuition at the University.

The plaintiff entered the State University of Iowa (hereinafter referred to as SUI) in September, 1961. Prior to that time he had resided in Illinois. Since the plaintiff enrolled at SUI, he has been continuously attending the University and, at the age of 22, is presently a student in the College of Law. During August 1964, the plaintiff married Joan Weaver. Mrs. Clarke has lived in Iowa all of her life.

During his entire tenure as a student at SUI, the plaintiff has been charged the nonresident tuition fee, which is approximately twice as much as the tuition fee charged students who are classified as residents. The plaintiff is now contending that there is no basis for charging him a nonresident tuition fee and seeks to enjoin SUI from doing so. The plaintiff premises his contention upon the following allegations: (1) It is a violation of the equal protection and privileges and immunities clauses of the Fourteenth Amendment to the Constitution for a state-operated university to charge a nonresident student a higher rate of tuition than that charged a resident student. (2) The tuition regulations applied by SUI unreasonably discriminate between a nonresident male whose wife is a resident of Iowa and a nonresident female whose husband is a resident of Iowa. (3) He is a resident and citizen of the State of Iowa.

The regulations concerning the classification of residents and nonresidents for admission and tuition fee purposes are attached to the application for admission which must be filled out by all individuals seeking admission to SUI. The regulations which resulted in the plaintiff's being classified as a nonresident student are as follows.

Students enrolling at The University of Iowa, Iowa City, shall be classified as Resident or Nonresident for admission, fee, and tuition purposes by the Registrar. The decision shall be based upon information furnished by the student and all other relevant information. The Registrar is authorized to require such written documents, affidavits, verifications, or other evidence as are deemed necessary to establish the domicile of a student, including proof of emancipation, adoption, award of custody, or appointment of a guardian. The burden of establishing that a student is exempt from paying the nonresident fee is upon the student.

*   *   *

Regulations regarding residence for admission, fee, and tuition payment are generally divided into two categories—those that apply to students who are minors and those that apply to students who are over 21 years of age. The requirements in these categories are different. Domicile within the state means adoption of the state as fixed permanent home and involves personal presence within the state. The two categories are discussed in more detail below.

*   *   *

A resident student 21 years of age or over is (1) one whose parents were residents of the state at the time he reached his majority and who has not acquired a domicile in another state or (2) who, while an adult, has established a bona fide residence in the state of Iowa by residing in the state for at least 12 consecutive months immediately preceding registration. Bona fide residence in Iowa means that the student is not in the state primarily to attend a college; that he is in the state for purposes other than to attempt to qualify for residence status.

Any nonresident student who reaches the age of 21 years while a student at any school or college does not by virtue of such fact attain residence in this state for admission or tuition payment purposes.

The residence of a wife is that of her husband. A nonresident female student may attain residence through marriage, and correspondingly, a resident female student may lose residence by marrying a nonresident. Proof of marriage should be furnished to the Registrar at the time change of status is requested.

* * *

Ownership of property in Iowa, or the payment of Iowa taxes, does not in itself establish residence.

A student from another state who has enrolled for a full program, or substantially a full program, in any type of educational institution will be presumed to be in Iowa primarily for educational purposes, and will be considered not to have established residence in Iowa. Continued residence in Iowa during vacation periods or occasional periods of interruption to the course of study does not of itself overcome the presumption.

All students not classified as resident students shall be classified as nonresidents for admission, fee, and tuition purposes. A student who willfully gives incorrect or misleading information to evade payment of the nonresident fees and tuition shall be subject to serious disciplinary action and must also pay the nonresident fees for each session attended.

* * *

The decision of the Registrar on the residence of a student for admission, fee, and tuition purposes may be appealed to a Review Committee. The finding of the Review Committee shall be final.

(5, 6) The Fourteenth Amendment to the Constitution provides that a state cannot deny to any person within its jurisdiction the equal protection of the law. This constitutional provision, however, does not prohibit classifications by the states. Any classification by a state which is not palpably arbitrary and is reasonably based on a substantial difference or distinction is not a violation of the equal protection clause so long as the classification is rationally related to a legitimate state object or purpose. In this instance then, the Court must determine whether the classification of students as residents or nonresidents for the purpose of paying tuition is reasonable and whether that classification is rationally related to a legitimate object of the State of Iowa.

* * *

(8–10) The students at SUI who are classified as nonresidents are charged a higher tuition than resident students. The defendants justify the discrimination primarily on the basis that resident students or their parents pay taxes to the State of Iowa which, in turn, supports and maintains SUI. The higher tuition charged nonresident students tends to distribute more evenly the cost of operating and supporting SUI between residents and nonresidents attending the University.* Although there is no way for this Court to determine the degree to which the higher tuition charge equalizes the educational cost of residents and non-residents, it appears to be a reasonable attempt to achieve a partial cost equalization. The regulation classifying students as residents or non-residents for tuition payment purposes is not arbitrary or unreasonable and bears a rational relation to Iowa's object and purpose of financing, operating and maintaining its educational institutions.

The plaintiff further contends that SUI's tuition regulations constitute an unconstitutional discrimination against him on the basis of his sex. The regulation which gives rise to this contention is as follows:

> The residence of a wife is that of her husband. A nonresident female student may attain residence through marriage, and correspondingly, a resident female student may lose residence by marrying a nonresident. Proof of marriage should be furnished to the Registrar at the time change of status is requested.

Plaintiff contends that this regulation discriminates against him on the basis of his sex because it permits a nonresident female to acquire residence through marriage and does not give a nonresident male the same opportunity. This regulation is obviously an attempt to adhere to the well-established legal concept that the domicile of a wife is the same as that of her husband. Classification under this regulation is not automatic. The regulation merely serves as a guideline for the classification of both nonresident females marrying Iowa residents and resident Iowa females marrying nonresidents.

(11) This Court is convinced that, when a resident marries a non-resident, it is reasonable for SUI to classify both the husband and wife as residents of the same state. This does not mean, however, that it is required to do so. Such classifications should be left to the sound discretion of the appropriate University officials.

(12, 13) Although it is reasonable to classify a husband and wife as residents of the same state, it does not necessarily follow that they must be classified as residents of the state where the husband was a resident prior to the marriage. The marriage of a resident and a nonresident should merely be a factor in determining the residency classification. While it is by no means controlling, such a marriage is a relevant consideration in determining a student's residency for tuition purposes. The regulation of SUI on this point pertains only to female students.

---

* It must be recognized that most students who are classified as nonresidents pay taxes to the State of Iowa in one form or the other. There is still a valid basis for distinguishing between a student who is paying taxes while temporarily residing in the State and one who pays taxes and plans to reside in Iowa indefinitely. Although payment of state taxes is one factor to consider when classifying students as residents or nonresidents, it is not controlling.

It is not expressed in absolute terms requiring reclassification of the female student if a resident marries a nonresident. The regulation serves only as a guideline for the possible reclassification of the female student. The fact that there is not a similar guideline for male students involved in such a marriage does not prevent the appropriate University officials from considering his marriage when he is attempting to overcome the rebuttable presumption of nonresidency. Although it is possible that the University regulations on this point could be clarified, they do not presently constitute a constitutional violation.

(14) Plaintiff further contends that he is a resident of Iowa and has been improperly classified as a nonresident for tuition payment purposes. In reviewing a determination of an administrative body, a Court is normally limited to ascertaining whether the administrative action was arbitrary, unreasonable, or capricious or unlawful. This Court is thus somewhat limited in considering the plaintiff's contention that he should be classified as a resident.

(15) While the administrative rules and regulations pertaining to classification of residents and nonresidents for tuition payment purposes are slightly confusing and could be improved in some aspects, they are not unlawful and any determination in conformity with them which is not unreasonable or arbitrary must be upheld by the courts. As previously discussed, a student from another state attending SUI is presumed to be a nonresident. The presumption is by no means conclusive. If a proper showing is made, a student originally from out of state should be reclassified as a resident. Although the Registrar at SUI does not appear to be applying the regulations as creating only a rebuttable presumption, the Review Committee, as final arbiter of residency classifications at SUI, correctly interprets those regulations in this regard. The Review Committee recognizes that a student originally classified as a nonresident may, under appropriate circumstances, be reclassified as a resident even though he has been enrolled in a full program at SUI or another Iowa educational institution since his arrival in the State.

(16) While the Review Committee's interpretation of the regulations is correct, its application of them in this instance appears to be unduly rigid. It is the view of the Court that the plaintiff herein has established a substantial basis for being classified as a resident for tuition payment purposes. The Review Committee should be given an opportunity to reconsider the plaintiff's classification in light of this opinion. This cause is therefore remanded to the Review Committee for appropriate action.

Jurisdiction of this cause will be retained by the Court pending action by the Review Committee, and for such further relief as either party may request.

10
Dormitories

Jones v. *Vassar College*
299 NYS 283
April 15, 1969
W. VINCENT GRADY, Justice

Student protests and demonstrations are prevalent in many colleges and universities today. The instant case presents a related facet of the student-college relationship.

Vassar College, for over 100 years, has been an all-female institution. In January of this year, it received approximately 80 male exchange students from various colleges. On March 5, a code of regulations and enforcement was passed unanimously by the student senate established under the terms of the new constitution of the Vassar College Student Government Association. It had been given the responsibility for enacting and enforcing undergraduate social regulations. These new rules and regulations changed the college's parietal regulations to permit the female students living in each corridor of the residential halls to decide whether or not they wished limitations to be placed upon the hours during which they might receive male guests in their rooms. An election was held on the proposed change, and 1,453 students voted. 1,375 voted for "no restrictions" on visiting hours and 68 students voted for a "limitation" on visiting hours without moving from their corridor. Ten students voted in favor of living in a corridor with "limited visiting hours," even if they would be required to move to a different corridor. It appears that the wishes of these ten students have been followed.

The president of Vassar College did not exercise his power of veto over the student-enacted legislation, thereby giving approval to the change in rules and regulations voted upon by the students and enacted by the Vassar College Student Government Association.

Plaintiff, Edna W. Jones, the mother of a Vassar College female student and on behalf of all parents of Vassar College students "similarly affected," commenced this action for a declaratory judgment that Vassar owed a duty to the plaintiffs to continue the former rules and regulations as pertains to parietals and for an injunction restraining the defendants from changing such rules and regulations. Plaintiffs herein seek an order to show cause, a temporary injunction and stay, although they demand the relief prayed for in the complaint. Thereafter, defendants moved for summary judgment, and this application is now before the court.

Plaintiffs' motion for "an order granting the relief prayed for in the . . . summons and verified complaint" is treated as a cross-motion for summary judgment.

There are three basic issues involved in this controversy:

1. Does Vassar College owe a legal obligation to the plaintiffs now to change its rules and regulations pertaining to social conduct on the college campus?

2. Have plaintiffs shown that there are issues of fact with regard to irreparable damage to their legal interests which require a trial on the merits?

3. Are there any issues of fact with respect to whether a declaratory judgment should be granted?

A review of the case law involving the student-college relationship does not reveal any case dealing with the issue as to whether a college has a contractual obligation not to change its rules and regulations governing social conduct.

* * *

Plaintiffs herein claim that there was an abuse of discretion on the part of Vassar College in permitting its students to make new rules and regulations with no restrictions on the visiting hours of males. Plaintiffs allege that this was a drastic change which constituted a breach of contract entitling the plaintiffs to the relief sought.

There is no genuine dispute as to any of the material facts surrounding the adoption and application of the new rules and regulations and the defendants concede that such change is drastic. However, does a drastic change in social rules and regulations, by a college, constitute a breach of its implied contract with a student or her parents? It is not controverted that all of the rules and regulations of Vassar, whether disciplinary, social, or academic, are subject to constant review. The Bulletin of Vassar College, Student Handbook Issue 1968–1969, states with respect to such regulations:

These regulations have been kept to the minimum deemed necessary to secure and maintain decent and orderly conditions of living and working for all the members of this residential college. Within this basic framework, the individual student shall be as free as possible to conduct her own academic and non-academic life. This assumes that individual decisions will be accompanied by careful consideration of the standards maintained by the group. The privilege of making independent decisions involves the acceptance of a penalty should such choices violate either the spirit or the letter of the regulations (p. 31)

The Vassar Catalogue for 1968–1969 also states that the

College expects students to uphold its standards of personal and social conduct at all times when they are associated with Vassar (p. 193)

The position of the plaintiffs is that the above statements in the Bulletin and Catalogue of Vassar College do not permit the college to change its rules and regulations as it has done herein.

As the court so aptly stated in *Sweezy* v. *State of New Hampshire*:

The essentiality of freedom in the community of American universities is almost self-evident. No one should underestimate the vital role in a democracy that is played by those who guide and train our youth. To impose any straitjacket upon the intellectual leaders in our colleges and universities would imperil the future of our Nation. No field of education is so thoroughly comprehended by man that new discoveries cannot yet be made. Particularly is that true in the social sciences, where few, if any, principles are accepted as absolutes. Scholarship cannot flourish in an atmosphere of suspicion and distrust. Teachers and students must always remain free to inquire, to study and to evaluate, to gain new maturity and understanding; otherwise our civilization will stagnate and die.

(1) In academic communities greater freedoms may prevail than in society at large and the subtle fixing of these limits should, to a great degree, be left to the educational institution itself (*Goldberg* v. *Regents of University of California*, 248 Cal. App.2d 867, 57 Cal. Rptr. 463). The judiciary must exercise restraint in questioning the wisdom of specific rules or the manner of their application, since such matters are ordinarily in the prerogative of school administrators rather than the courts (*Barker* v. *Hardway*, D.C., 283 F. Supp. 228).

(2) There has been no showing by plaintiffs that there was an abuse of discretion by defendants in approving and adopting the new rules and regulations and this court will not interfere with defendant's discretion.

(3, 4) The plaintiffs urge that the court should interfere to protect alleged invasions of the students' right of privacy by forbidding unlimited visiting hours for males; however, as a matter of law, the plaintiffs are not entitled to an injunction since the complaint and other affidavits do not show that the plaintiffs have suffered or will suffer immediate and irreparable damage. Mere speculation as to the possible consequences of conduct complained of in the complaint is insufficient . . .

(5, 6) The plaintiffs also seek a declaratory judgment, but the court cannot substitute its judgment as to the propriety of the new rules and regulations governing visiting hours of males for that of the administrative body which formulates such rules and regulations. Plaintiffs have failed to show a breach of the implied contract with the student or parent causing the plaintiffs irreparable injury; therefore, there are no legal rights of the plaintiffs which have been violated and declaratory judgment does not lie.

(7) Private colleges and universities are governed on the principle of academic self regulation, free from judicial restraints (See Developments in the Law—Academic Freedom, 81 Harv. L. Rev. 1045) . Vassar College, like other previously all-female institutions, has succumbed to the trend of coeducation and with the advent of males, new difficulties will be encountered by the college administration. It is the privilege of a college, through its Student Government Association, to promulgate and enforce rules and regulations for the social conduct of students without judicial interference.

Defendants' motion for summary judgment is granted and the relief requested by plaintiffs is denied in all respects.

Moore v. Student Affairs Committee of Troy State University
284 F. Supp. 725
May 14, 1968

JOHNSON, Chief Judge

On February 28, 1968, plaintiff, Gregory Gordon Moore, was a student in good standing at Troy State University and resided in a dormitory on the campus which he rented from the school. A search of his room on that day, conducted by the Dean of Men and two agents of the State of Alabama Health Department, Bureau of Primary Prevention, in plaintiff's presence, revealed a substance which upon analysis proved to be marijuana. Following a hearing on March 27, 1968, by the Student Affairs Committee of Troy State University, plaintiff was "indefinitely suspended" from that institution on March 28.

This action was commenced on March 30, 1968, seeking reinstatement of plaintiff as a student in good standing. At a hearing in this court conducted on April 26, 1968, it was determined that plaintiff had exhausted his administrative remedies at Troy State University and that he "was denied his right to procedural due process of law in the hearing conducted at Troy State University on March 27, 1968, as a result of which he was indefinitely suspended." On motion of the defendants, jurisdiction of this cause was retained pending remand to the Student Affairs Committee of Troy State University for the purpose of conducting a hearing comporting with procedural due process of law. Pending those proceedings, plaintiff was ordered reinstated.

(1) On May 1, 1968, a second hearing was held before the Student Affairs Committee and plaintiff was again indefinitely suspended. He again challenges, from a procedural point of view, the action taken in suspending him. He does not challenge the underlying substantive basis for the action of the Student Affairs Committee. If plaintiff while a student possessed marijuana in a dormitory on campus in violation of state law, then indefinite suspension from his status as a student is clearly justified.

(2) Plaintiff now seeks relief in this court. First, he seeks readmission as a student at Troy State University on the ground of denial of procedural due process in the proceedings which resulted in his suspension; second, he seeks a declaratory judgment that none of the evidence seized in the search of his room "may be admitted in any criminal proceedings . . .; and third, he alleges the admission in the University's hearing of the evidence obtained through a search of his dormitory room violates his Fourth Amendment rights prohibiting illegal search and seizure. The second part of the relief sought is clearly unavailable.

On the morning of February 28, 1968, the Dean of Men of Troy State University was called to the office of the Chief of Police of Troy, Alabama, where a conference was held regarding "the possibility of there being marijuana on the campus." Two narcotics agents, the Chief of Police, and two students were present. A second meeting was held later that morning at which a list was procured of the names of students whose rooms the officers desired permission to search. This information came from unnamed but reliable informers. About 1 P.M., the officers received additional information that some of the subjects they were interested in were packing to leave the campus for a break following the end of the examination period. Upon receipt of this information, and fearing a "leak," two narcotics agents, accompanied by the Dean of Men, searched six dormitory rooms in two separate residence halls. The search of the room which plaintiff occupied alone occurred between approximately 2:30 and 2:45 P.M., in his presence, but without his permission.

At the second hearing before the Student Affairs Committee, the following stipulation was entered concerning the search:

That no search warrant was obtained in this case, that no consent to search was given by the defendant, that the search was not incidental to a legal arrest, that no other offense was committed by the defendant in the arresting officers' presence, that Troy State University had in force and effect at the time of the search and subsequent arrest of the defendant the following regulation,

"The college reserves the right to enter rooms for inspection purposes. If the administration deems it necessary the room may be searched and the occupant required to open his personal baggage and other personal material which is sealed."

This language appears in the Troy State College current bulletin of the year 1967–68. The quoted language also appears . . . in the Troy State Bulletin for the year 1967–68. . . . This language also appears in the current publication of the Oracle, which is a student handbook. . . . This language further appears on the reverse side of a leaflet entitled "Residence Hall Policies" which is also made available to all students of Troy State University.

It is further stipulated that the defendant's room was searched at the invitation or consent of Troy State University by the law enforcement officials acting under the above-quoted regulations.

The search revealed a matchbox containing a small amount of vegetable matter, which a state toxicologist who examined it testified was marijuana. All this testimony was received over plaintiff's objection that the evidence was seized as a result of a search in violation of the Fourth Amendment. He also challenges the constitutionality, facially and as applied, of the regulation under which the search was conducted.

This Court has previously expressed itself on the question of campus regulations, and the duty of school administrations to maintain order and discipline on their campuses in an environment suited to education, in *Dickey* v. *Alabama State Board of Education,* 273 F. Supp. 613, 617–618.

This Court recognizes that the establishment of an educational program requires certain rules and regulations necessary for maintaining an orderly program and operating the institution in a manner conducive to learning. However, the school and school officials have always been bound by the requirement that the rules and regulations *must be reasonable* [emphasis in original]. Courts may only consider whether rules and regulations that are imposed by school authorities are a reasonable exercise of the power and discretion vested in those authorities. *Regulations and rules which are necessary in maintaining order and discipline are always considered reasonable.* . . . State school officials cannot infringe on their students' right of free and unrestricted expression as guaranteed by the Constitution of the United States where the exercise of such right does not "materially and substantially interfere with requirements of appropriate discipline in the operation of the school" [emphasis added].

* * *

(5–9) College students who reside in dormitories have a special relationship with the college involved. Insofar as the Fourth Amendment affects that relationship, it does not depend on either a general theory of the right of privacy or on traditional property concepts. The college does not stand, strictly speaking, *in loco parentis* to its students, nor is their relationship purely contractual in the traditional sense. The relationship grows out of the peculiar and sometimes the seemingly competing interests of college and student. A student naturally has the right to be free of unreasonable search and seizures, and a tax-supported public college may not compel a "waiver" of that right as a condition precedent to admission. The college, on the other hand, has an "affirmative obligation" to promulgate and to enforce reasonable regulations designed to protect campus order and discipline and to promote an environment consistent with the educational process. The validity of the regulation authorizing search of dormitories thus does not depend on whether a student "waives" his right to Fourth Amendment protection or on whether he has "contracted" it away; rather, its validity is determined by whether the regulation is a reasonable exercise of the college's supervisory duty. In other words, if the regulation—or, in the absence of a regulation, the action of the college authorities—is necessary in aid of the basic responsibility of the institution regarding discipline and the maintenance of an "educational atmosphere," then it will be presumed facially reasonable despite the fact thtat it may infringe to some extent on the outer bounds of the Fourth Amendment rights of students.

(10–12) In *Englehart* v. *Serena,* a civil action for alleged wrongful expulsion, the Supreme Court of Missouri defined the dormitory student-college relationship in real property terms as follows:

> One of the grounds on which appellant seeks a recovery of damages is that he was deprived of the "possession" of the room he was occupying in the dormitory before the expiration of the period for which he had paid "rent." He was not, however, a tenant in any sense of the word. He did not have even the full and unrestricted rights of a lodger, because Albert Hall was not an ordinary lodging house. It was an auxiliary of the college, and was maintained and conducted in furtherance of that institution's general purposes. When appellant took up residence there, he impliedly agreed to conform to all reasonable rules and regulations for its government which were then in force or which might thereafter be adopted by the proper authorities.

That definition is equally apt when measuring the relationship of this plaintiff and Troy State University by the Fourth Amendment. The student is subject only to reasonable rules and regulations, but his rights must yield to the extent that they would interfere with the institution's fundamental duty to operate the school *as an educational institution.* A reasonable right of inspection is necessary to the institution's performance of that duty even though it may infringe on the outer boundaries of a dormitory student's Fourth Amendment rights. ... The regulation of Troy State University in issue here is thus facially reasonable.

(13, 14) The regulation was reasonably applied in this case. The constitutional boundary line between the right of the school authorities to search and the right of a dormitory student to privacy must be based on a reasonable belief on the part of the college authorities that a student is using a dormitory room for a purpose which is illegal or which would otherwise seriously interfere with campus discipline. Upon this submission, it is clear that such a belief existed in this case.*

(15–16) This standard of "reasonable cause to believe" to justify a search by college administrators—even where the sole purpose is to seek evidence of suspected violations of law—is lower than the constitutionally protected criminal law standard of "probable cause." This is true because of the special necessities of the student-college relationship and because college disciplinary proceedings are not criminal proceedings in the constitutional sense. It is clearly settled that due process in college disciplinary proceedings does not require full-blown adversary hearings subject to rules of evidence and all constitutional criminal guaranties. "Such a hearing, with the attending publicity and disturbance of college activities, might be detrimental to the college's educational atmosphere and impractical to carry out." ...

(17, 18) Assuming that the Fourth Amendment applied to college disciplinary proceedings, the search in this case would not be in violation of it. It is settled law that the Fourth Amendment does not prohibit reasonable searches when the search is conducted by a superior charged with a responsibility of maintaining discipline and order or of maintaining security. A student who lives in a dormitory on campus which he "rents" from the school waives objection to any reasonable searches conducted pursuant to reasonable and necessary regulations such as this one.

(19) Plaintiff also alleges that he was denied procedural due process of law in the hearing in that the hearing was not open to the press, other students, and the public generally. Pursuant to a long-standing policy of the school, the hearing was attended only by the Student Affairs Committee—whose membership contains two students—the witnesses, plaintiff and his counsel, and plaintiff's parents. Over plaintiff's objection, a newspaper reporter was forbidden to attend, but a full record of the proceedings was made by a court reporter.

---

* The school authorities in this case not only had information sufficient to form "reasonable cause to believe" plaintiff was using his room in a manner inconsistent with appropriate school discipline, but they also had enough information to amount to probable cause to believe the conduct was criminal.

(20, 21) This Court has recently expressed its opinion that such hearings should be open to the press when this is possible without interference with the orderly operation of the educational institution. But this Court at the same time ruled that "an open hearing in the sense that a defendant in a criminal case is entitled to a hearing in open court is not contemplated by the law insofar as the compliance with the procedural rights of students are concerned. . . . The evidence in this case reflects that the school authorities at Troy State University considered it necessary in the exercise of their duty to conduct a relatively closed hearing in order to maintain order and discipline on campus and to avoid interference with the educational function. Any possible prejudice in this case was ameliorated by the fact that plaintiff was given the right to have his counsel attend and the opportunity to confront and fully cross-examine all witnesses against him. In addition, a full transcript of the hearing was made by a court reporter and is a part of the record in this cause.

This Court recognizes that presently in our society, education is no longer a luxury but a necessity. The privilege of attending public educational institutions must be recognized as a right for those qualified to meet the academic requirements and whose conduct does not interfere with the orderly operation of an educational institution. But this does not mean that a disciplinary proceeding held for the purpose of preserving an orderly educational environment through the discipline of those students whose conduct interferes with the educational function is such a proceeding in which all constitutional safeguards are applicable. The Constitution requires only that "rudimentary elements of fair play" be observed and this must be determined on a case-by-case basis. *Dixon,* supra. The hearing afforded Moore by Troy State University in this case was in all respects fair and none of Moore's constitutional rights were infringed by reason of the University's action in suspending him.

In accordance with the foregoing, it is the order, judgment and decree of this Court that plaintiff's claim for relief be and is, in each instance, hereby denied. It is ordered that this cause be and the same is hereby dismissed.

It is further ordered that the costs incurred in these proceedings be and the same are hereby taxed against the plaintiff, for which execution may issue.

11
Societies

People ex rel. Pratt v. *Wheaton College*
40 Ill. 186
April 1866

* * *

Mr. JUSTICE LAWRENCE delivered the opinion of the Court:

E. Hartley Pratt, a student in Wheaton college, joined a secret society known as the Good Templars, in violation of the college rules. For this the faculty "suspended him from the privileges of the institution until he should express a purpose to conform to its rules." His father thereupon applied for a mandamus to compel the college to reinstate him as a student. The mandamus was refused, and the relator has brought the case here.

Wheaton college is an incorporated institution, resting upon private endowments, and deriving no aid whatever from the State or from taxation. Its charter gives to the trustees and faculty the power "to adopt and enforce such rules as may be deemed expedient for the government of the institution," a power which they would have possessed without such express grant, because incident to the very object of their incorporation, and indispensable to the successful management of the college. Among the rules they have deemed it expedient to adopt, is one forbidding the students to become members of secret societies. We perceive nothing unreasonable in the rule itself, since all persons familiar with college life know that the tendency of secret societies is to withdraw students from the control of the faculty, and impair to some extent the discipline of the institution. Such may not always be their effect, but such is their general tendency. But whether the rule be judicious or not, it violates neither good morals nor the law of the land, and is therefore clearly within the power of the college authorities to make and enforce. A discretionary power has been given them to regulate the discipline of their college in such manner as they deem proper, and so long as their rules violate neither divine nor human law, we have no more authority to interfere than we have to control the domestic discipline of a father in his family. It is urged that the Good Templars are a society established for the promotion of temperance, and incorporated by the legislature, and that any citizen has a right to join it. We do not doubt the beneficent objects of the society, and we admit that any citizen has a right to join it if the society consents. But this right is not of so high and solemn a character that it cannot be surrendered, and the son of the relator did voluntarily surrender it when he became a student of Wheaton college, for he knew, or must be taken to have known, that by the rules of the institution which he was voluntarily entering, he would be precluded from joining any secret society. When it is said that a person has a legal *right* to do certain things, all that the phrase means is, that the law does not forbid these things to be done. It does not mean that the law guarantees the right to do them at all possible times and under all possible circumstances. A person in his capacity as a citizen may have the right to do many things which a student of Wheaton college cannot do without incurring the penalty of college laws. A person as a citizen has a legal right to marry, or to walk the streets at midnight, or to board at a public hotel, and yet it would be absurd to say that a college cannot forbid its students to do any of these things. So a citizen, as such, can attend church on Sunday or not, as he may think proper, but it could hardly be contended that a college would not have the right to make attendance upon religious services a condition of remaining within its walls. The son of the relator has an undoubted legal right to join either Wheaton college or the Good Templars, and they have both an undoubted right to expel him if he refuses to abide by such regulations as they establish, not inconsistent with law or good morals.

Judgment affirmed.

Webb v. *State University of New York*
125 F. Supp. 910
June 7, 1954
* * *

AUGUSTUS N. HAND, Circuit Judge

(1) The plaintiffs and intervenors, as members and affiliates of national fraternities and sororities, seek to void the resolution adopted by the Board of Trustees of the State University of New York on October 8, 1953. The resolution in effect bans social organizations having a

direct or indirect affiliation with any national or other organization outside the particular unit of the State University where such social organization is located. The resolution in its entirety is quoted below.* Since the local chapters will have to forego affiliation with the national organization of their fraternity or sorority if they wish to continue functioning at the state units, the plaintiffs claim that the resolution deprives them of their civil rights. Specifically they charge that the resolution was adopted without due process of law, encroaches on their freedom to assemble, denies them equal protection of the law, and adversely affects existing contract rights. Accordingly a judgment is sought declaring the resolution unconstitutional and enjoining its enforcement. . . .

(2, 3) At the hearing plaintiffs introduced evidence to show the beneficial aspects of national affiliation, the lack of discriminatory clauses in their constitutions, and generally the relationship between the national organization and the local chapters. Testimony was introduced to the effect that no notification of the pending resolution or a chance for a hearing was given. However, we find little merit in the numerous contentions made by the plaintiffs as it is clear that the constitutionality of the action taken here cannot be questioned. A state may adopt such measures, including the outlawing of certain social organizations as it deems necessary to its duty of supervision and control of its educational institutions. . . . Moreover, the incidental effect of any action or policy adopted upon individuals or organizations outside the university is not a basis for attack. . . . The plaintiffs have cited no authority contrary to these decisions and since we consider them controlling in the case before us, further discussion becomes unnecessary.

(4, 5) Plaintiffs argue that they were not notified of the pending action, but lack of notice and hearing before adoption of a resolution by an administrative body is not a denial of due process where legislative action of a prospective nature is taken under a valid delegation of powers from the legislature. . . . Moreover, the Board of Trustees seems clearly within its supervisory powers . . . in making the decision that social organizations, other than strictly local autonomous ones subject without question to local control by the University, are detrimental to the educational environment at units of the State University.

---

* Resolved that no social organization shall be permitted in any state-operated unit of the State University which has any direct or indirect affiliation or connection with any national or other organization outside the particular unit; and be it further

Resolved that no such social organization, in policy or practice, shall operate under any rule which bars students on account of race, color, religion, creed, national origin or other artificial criteria; and be it further

Resolved that the President be, and hereby is, authorized to take such steps as he may deem appropriate to implement this policy, including the determination of which student organizations are social as distinguished from scholastic or religious, and his decision shall be final.

(6) Accordingly, we find that plaintiffs here have not shown that they have been deprived of any civil rights. Since the resolution adopted by the Board of Trustees does not encroach on any constitutional rights, the action is dimissed.

Judgment for the defendants.

Eisen v. *Regents of the University of California*
75 Cal. Reptr. 45
Feb. 17, 1969

TAYLOR, Associate Justice

Plaintiff, Michael Eisen, appeals from a judgment of dismissal entered on an order sustaining, without leave to amend, the demurrer of defendants, The Regents, and certain officers of the Berkeley campus of the University of California (hereafter collectively referred to as University) . Plaintiff contends that the University's policy that registration statements filed by student organizations are records open to inspection by the public, violates his rights of free speech and association under the First and Fourteenth Amendments to the Constitution of the United States. In the alternative, he also contends that his complaint for injunctive relief stated sufficient facts to warrant an opportunity to amend.

The basic facts are not in dispute. Plaintiff was a law student at the University's Berkeley campus and an officer of a student organization engaged in the advocacy of dissident ideas. This organization was fully qualified as a student organization "registered" by the University. An organization that has complied with registration procedures and attained the status of a "registered" student organization, is entitled to several privileges on campus, including the use of University facilities for meetings, fund raising, recruiting participants, posting and distributing literature, as well as the privilege of inviting non-University speakers to address campus meetings. As a condition of "registration" the University required that the organization submit to the appropriate campus officer a statement of its purpose and the names of its officers. Plaintiff's name was submitted under this requirement.

In October 1966, a member of the public, Patricia Atthowe, filed a suit against the officers of the Berkeley campus praying, *inter alia*, the disclosure of the names of the officers and stated purposes of all student campus organizations "registered" for the spring semester of the 1965–1966 academic year. On October 17, 1966, the University made public a letter written to Patricia Atthowe indicating that on advice of its counsel, the University would allow her to examine the documents containing the information she demanded.

On October 25, the University adopted a policy "that registration statements filed with the University by student organizations are records open to inspection by University students and staff and members of the public." This action ensued, and a temporary restraining order issued. After a hearing, the trial court found "that public policy as framed within the law of this state requires disclosure of the subject records such public policy being dominant and controlling to the right of associational privilege," and entered its orders dissolving the temporary order and dismissing the action.

(1) The parties agreed that the University's rule-making powers and its relationship with its students and student organizations are subject to federal constitutional guarantees . . . and that ideas, no matter how unpopular or erroneous in their dissemination, including the formation of groups and associations to advance such ideas are fully protected by the First Amendment.

* * *

Consequently, we deal, as we did in *Goldberg,* supra, pages 876–877, 57 Cal. Rptr. 463, with the issue presented in the constitutional framework of whether here, the University's policy of annexing limited disclosure conditions to the privilege of becoming a registered campus organization entitled to use campus facilities, is justified by a sufficient state interest to outweigh the alleged impairment of plaintiff's constitutional rights. . . .

Plaintiff argues that he is entitled to a constitutional right of anonymity and that the disclosure* of the "registration" statements to inspection by members of the public has a deterrent effect on his rights of free speech and association.

* * *

(2) . . . just as the People of the state have a right to know how their elected officials conduct the public business, they are entitled to know the identity and responsible officers of organizations that are granted the privileges of becoming campus organizations and using the public property and facilities of the University. Nor can it be successfully argued that the protection of plaintiff's First Amendment rights requires complete anonymity. The U.S. Supreme Court has held that First Amendment freedoms are not violated by legislation requiring "a modicum of information" of lobbyists. . . .

We question the consistency of plaintiff's assertion of a right to keep anonymous his relationship as an officer of the organization (a rela-

---

* Plaintiff does not challenge the reasonableness of the University's requirement of these "registration" statements for its own administrative purpose. His argument is limited to the disclosure to the public of the information acquired.

tionship and responsibility he presumably sought and assumed voluntarily) in the absence of any immediate and direct threats of physical or other danger, in N.A.A.C.P. . . . Thus, it can reasonably be inferred that the disclosure sufficient to identify the organization and the officers responsible for its activities is not equally repugnant to First Amendment freedoms.

Nor here . . . can it be said that the identification requirement of the University's policy and the disclosure of this limited information to a member of the public would unduly deter the freedom of expression of dissident organizations and their officers. In fact, it appears well designed to promote that freedom of expression in a manner consistent with the University's interest in insuring the orderly enjoyment of its facilities together with the public's right to ascertain the identity of organizations and the responsible officers* who are using public property. The Regents' policy here in issue is like a time, place and manner regulation of free speech enacted to maintain the integrity of the extracurricular aspects of the educational process at a public university (cf. *Goldberg* v. *Regents,* supra) . . . .

(3–5) Impairments of First Amendment rights are "balanced" by determining whether there is a reasonable relationship between the impairment and a subject of overriding and compelling state interest. . . . There can be no doubt that disclosure requirements may impair rights of free speech and association and that First Amendment rights are primarily intended to protect minority views. . . . We conclude, however . . . that here the compelling interest of the public in being able to ascertain the information contained in the registration statement outweighs any minimal infringement of plaintiff's First Amendment rights.

It may be contended that even though the overriding purpose is legitimate and substantial, the purpose can be achieved by means more narrow that the University's policy in question. . . . The only information made available to the public is the purpose of the organization and the names of its officers found on the registration statement submitted to the appropriate campus officer. We think this modicum of information is far from overly broad.

* * *

The judgment appealed from is affirmed.

SHOEMAKER, P.J., and AGEE, J., concur.

---

* At oral argument, plaintiff conceded that the identity of the organization could be made public, as well as the name of some person related to the organization who was responsible for the use of a University facility at any particular time. He argued that the officers should not be made public, as the officers were not necessarily the particular persons responsible for each use made by the organization of a University facility. Carrying plaintiff's argument to its logical conclusion, it would appear to us to lead to the disclosure of many more names than those of the current officers.

City of Baltimore v. Poe
224 Md. 428 (168 A.2d 193)
March 10, 1961

SYBERT, Judge

A successful application was made by the appellant, Phi Sigma Delta
Alumni Association, Johns Hopkins University Chapter, Inc., to the
Bureau of Building Inspection of Baltimore City to use the property
at 3904 Canterbury Road, Baltimore City, for a fraternity house. The
Board of Municipal and Zoning Appeals affirmed the granting of the
permit on appeal by the appellees (neighbors, nearby property owners,
and a neighborhood improvement association). Upon appeal to the
Baltimore City Court by the appellees the decision of the Board was
reversed, whereupon Baltimore City and the fraternity brought this
appeal.

The fraternity purchased the property in August, 1959, for use as
the fraternity house of its local chapter, The Johns Hopkins University
Chapter of Phi Sigma Delta Fraternity. Prior thereto, the local chapter
had occupied property at 3801 Canterbury Road, where it had carried
on its activities, including provision of sleeping facilities for some of
its members. The record shows that the local chapter has about fifty-nine
members, approximately one-third being Baltimoreans and the remainder being students from out of town.

In the fraternity house there are meeting rooms, study rooms, a
television room, a card room and a ping-pong room. In addition, there
are a dining room, a kitchen and eleven sleeping rooms, presently occupied, according to the testimony, by eleven or thirteen students.
Present plans contemplate housing a total of eighteen or nineteen when
the necessary alterations are completed. Two persons are employed by
the fraternity for cooking and cleaning purposes. The various facilities
are available to all members of the fraternity and activities are financed
by dues paid into a common fund, the amount of the dues being
determined by whether a member is a resident or a nonresident of the
house.

The record details the activities carried on in the fraternity house.
Each year the members of the local chapter elect officers and designate
various committees, including a social committee, a house committee,
a rushing committee, a scholarship committee, an athletic committee
and a charitable activities committee. The regular bi-weekly meetings
of the fraternity, social activities of the chapter, whether it be a smoker,
a rush affair for freshman students, a formal initiation ceremony, a
dance or other function, committee meetings and committee activities
all take place at the fraternity house, except occasionally when an affair
may be held at a hotel or other location. The chapter has a system of

tutoring by proficient members, who make a charge for such service.

The property is a three-story-and-basement brick building, located in a Class E Residential Use District, and prior to its acquisition by the fraternity it was used as a four-apartment dwelling. The planned use of the house for the activities of the fraternity has given rise to the present litigation.

Appellants contend that the fraternity is a nonprofit, social and scholastic organization. They cite its objectives, as set forth in its charter: . . . "the non-commercial, social, educational and fraternal purposes of the Phi Sigma Delta Fraternity . . . and for the non-profit purpose of upholding the general welfare, social, scholastic and educational interests of The Johns Hopkins University Chapter of Phi Sigma Delta Fraternity." They argue that the finding of the Board that occupancy of this house by the fraternity would not constitute a business or club such as is excluded from a residential use district under the Baltimore City Zoning Ordinance, was the correct interpretation of the law.

In the opinion of the lower court, however, since the major portion of the house was devoted to living quarters, the providing of room and board was the chief activity, and such use was, therefore, prohibited under the Ordinance as a business activity. The lower court felt the word "club" in the Ordinance referred not to the organization, but rather to the use of the property itself.

Article 40, § 10, Baltimore City Zoning Ordinance (1958 Rev.), sets forth uses excluded from Residential Use Districts. Among them are uses excluded from Residential and Office Use Districts. These are delineated in § 9, which reads in part as follows:

> 9. Residential and Office Use Districts. In a Residential and Office Use District, no use of land or building shall be excluded, except that
> (a) no land or building shall be used; . . . for—
> 32. Club, the chief activity of which is a service customarily carried on as a business, provided, however, that nothing in this ordinance shall be construed to exclude the sale of beverages or food products such as are customarily served to members only, but such permissive use shall not be construed to authorize the construction of any building or alteration of any building, which indicates that the building was used or is intended to be used for commercial purposes, and it is hereby declared that such club use shall not be construed to be classified as a commercial use, nor may such club use be changed to a commercial use which is excluded from a Residential and Office Use District or Residential Use District by any other provisions of this Section.

The Zoning Ordinance of 1931 originally couched Exception 32 only in the following language: "Club, the chief activity of which is a service customarily carried on as a business." Apparently question was raised as to the scope of this language with respect to the activities of private clubs and it appears significant that the more extensive language hereinbefore quoted was added by ordinance in 1933. Obviously it was inserted in order to protect the traditional activities of private clubs, so long as they were confined to the use of members only and not made available to the public generally. Some private clubs have always provided sleeping quarters for some of their members and, since such practice has been traditional, it apparently was not regarded as a service necessary to be mentioned in the amendment.

The other forty-five exceptions in § 9 have not required clarification over the years. The obvious activity of a baker or a tailor needs no further investigation to merit its exclusion from a residential neighborhood. Thus the word "bakery" or "tailoring establishment" in the ordinance is enough to make the exclusion of all bakers and tailors clear. However, the word "club" covers an extensive field and the Legislators did not intend to exclude all clubs, but only clubs whose chief activity was of a business nature.

Appellants contend that this fraternity is not a "Club, the chief activity of which is a service customarily carried on as a business" and that, since it is not excluded by the Ordinance, it has a permissible use. They argue that the word "club" refers to the organization or association of persons and not to the use of the property. They further claim that even if the trial court's interpretation is correct, the manner of use of the property by the fraternity does not constitute a business activity.

Appellees . . . argue that the chief activity at the fraternity house was the providing of living quarters to members and that such use would result in a profit and thereby constitute a business in the nature of a rooming house. They would have the Court look solely to the use of the property and not to the objects and purposes of the organization.

(1) It is settled law in this State that the zoning ordinance is concerned with the use of property and not with ownership thereof nor with the purposes of the owners or occupants. . . .

Accordingly, the question with respect to Exception 32 as to clubs is whether the dominant use of the property, or, in the words of the ordinance, the "chief activity" carried on thereon, is such as is "customarily carried on as a business."

In support of their contention that the principal use of the premises is as a boarding house, appellees point out that eleven members of the fraternity are already housed on the premises, and that plans are being made to provide facilities for eighteen or nineteen members eventually at one hundred dollars per month each for dues, room and board. (Members who do not "live in" pay dues of fifteen dollars per month only.) Appellees argue that this clearly establishes the dominant use to be a rooming-house operation which is a service customarily carried on as a business. They discount the other activities of the fraternity on the premises.

* * *

The chief activities carried on at this fraternity house, hereinbefore mentioned, have clearly been established to be social and educational functions for the benefit of the whole membership. The fact that rooming facilities are provided for some members as an accessory or incidental use does not make the dominant use of the house a business proposition. This fraternity is exempt from federal taxation as a nonprofit organization, and we may assume that any excess income over and above that which is needed for the upkeep of the house will be used to further the nonprofit, nonbusiness objectives of the fraternity.

* * *

(2) We conclude therefore that the principal use which this fraternity is making of the premises in question does not constitute a "service customarily carried on as a business" under the zoning ordinance.

The Court recognizes the problem that neighborhoods in proximity to a college campus face when, as sometimes happens, youth tends to overflow with exuberance to the point of creating disturbance and disorder. While "young blood must run its course," it must also be restrained, when necessary, by resort to local police enforcement or injunctive relief. This then is the legal remedy available and not the present zoning ordinance.

The finding of this Court, therefore, is that the Board's interpretation of Art. 40, § 9) a) 32, is the correct one and the order of the lower court must therefore be reversed. In view of this holding, it is unnecessary to pass upon the procedural question raised by appellants.

Order reversed, with costs to appellants, and case remanded for entry of an order affirming the board.

City of Memphis v. *Alpha Beta Welfare Ass'n*
174 Tenn. 440 (126 S.W.2d 323)
1 April 1939

DeHAVEN, Justice

The Alpha Beta Welfare Association is a nonprofit corporation organized under the laws of the State of Tennessee. The Association, in the year 1930, purchased a house and lot in the City of Memphis for the use of the local chapter of the Phi Chi Medical Fraternity of Memphis. The property was assessed for taxation for the year 1936 by the City of Memphis and, the taxes remaining unpaid, a distress warrant was issued to enforce collection of the taxes and funds of the Association sufficient to pay the taxes were impounded. The trial judge dismissed the garnishment proceeding upon the ground that the Association is a general welfare corporation and that the real estate owned by it, and involved in the case, is used by it exclusively for educational purposes and is, therefore, exempt from taxation.

On the city's appeal, the Court of Appeals affirmed the judgment of the trial court. Thereupon the city filed its petition for certiorari to this court, which was granted and argument has been heard.

The one question presented for determination is whether or not the property in question is used exclusively for educational purposes, within the meaning of the Constitution and statutes of the State of Tennessee.

Section 28, Article 2, of the Constitution of this State provides, in part, as follows:

> All property, real, personal or mixed, shall be taxed, but the Legislature may except such as may be held by the State, by counties, cities or towns, and used exclusively for public or corporation purposes, and such as may be held and used for purposes purely religious, charitable, scientific, literary or educational.

Chapter 602, Acts 1907 . . . provides tax exemption for:

> All property belonging to any religious, charitable, scientific, or educational institutions, when used exclusively for the purpose for which said institution was created, or is unimproved and yields no income.

The specific purpose for which the Alpha Beta Welfare Association was created, as stated in its charter, is the "promoting and providing for medical and scientific education of young men, and for the purpose of owning property, both real and personal, to be used exclusively in furthering the aforesaid purposes."

The only witnesses who testified on the trial of the case were three physicians introduced by the Association. Thus the facts of the case are not in controversy.

The Alpha Beta Chapter of the Phi Chi Medical Fraternity in the Medical School of the University of Tennessee, at Memphis, is unincorporated. Its membership is made up of the alumni of the Phi Chi Fraternity residing in the City of Memphis, who are in good standing, and the active members of the chapter are the undergraduates of the Medical School.

The specific purpose of the Phi Chi Medical Fraternity is to promote the welfare of medical students morally and scientifically. For admission to the active chapter, a student must be desirable from a scholastic and moral standpoint. No one is eligible for membership in the active chapter except matriculants in the University of Tennessee Medical Department.

Prior to the organization of the Association, in 1930, the student members of the Alpha Beta Chapter of the Phi Chi Fraternity were living in boarding houses, scattered around over the city, the University being without dormitories. As the result of the appeal of the then undergraduate members of the Fraternity, a number of the leading doctors of Memphis interested themselves in organizing the Welfare Association in order that suitable property might be acquired and the student members of the Fraternity housed under one roof. This was considered very essential to the welfare of these members and to the successful carrying out of the purposes of the Fraternity.

It appears that about fifty students live in the house in question and each one pays $37.50 per month, which covers board, lodging and Fraternity dues. They maintain a mess, with which the Association has nothing to do. Supervision is exercised by the Association over the physical condition of the premises and over the conduct of the student residents. A high standard of moral and ethical conduct is demanded.

It is shown that the alumni of the Phi Chi Chapter have furnished the students with a considerable number of books, the majority of which are medical in their scope, but others are upon subjects of general information and interest. Additional books are being added to this library from time to time.

No teaching staff is maintained by the Association or by the Fraternity. No classes of any kind are conducted on the premises. However, other things of a cultural and educational nature are relied on as entitling the Association to tax exemption. One of the witnesses was asked:

Q. State what supervision, if any, is exercised by the older members of the active chapter over the younger members, both as to morals and scholastic work?

A. Well, you might say that the older men, in a measure, act as tutors to the young man. It must be borne in mind that the study of medicine is a pretty hard subject to embrace, and that it takes a man about two years, even though he be a college graduate, to learn to study medicine. Now, that is an accepted fact, and the advantages that the younger men receive through contact and the so-called tutoring from the older men is, without question, very beneficial.

Asked for what purpose the property in question is used, the witness replied that it was used to house the active members of the Fraternity and elaborated by stating:

Its purpose is to provide better housing conditions, to bring the members into a group where each and all of them may benefit from the contact with one another, the purpose of this being to turn out a more finished product of a doctor. Now, to be more specific, these men are grouped according to classes. In other words, the first quarter men are grouped together where they will have the benefit of exchange of thought and ideas relative to the subject matter of their studies. This applies to the four different groups that occupy the house. The younger men also enjoy the benefit of counsel and advice on the part of the older men.

Another witness states:

The real purpose of the association is to make it possible for medical students in whom we could take a personal interest because of their contacts in the house with the alumni, to become better doctors.

Q. In other words, to learn more of medicine and science pertaining to medicine?

A. Well, I think that in this connection these boys learn something that they can't get in their ordinary work in the college. There they are taught the science of medicine. All of their work is science. By their associations here, and by their associations with us, and of other men, of national and international repute in our particular profession, they are enabled to acquire the art of medicine, and that is many times more essential in the practice of the profession than science.

Again:

I would say in addition to the primary purpose of having a decent place in which to live, we have a place in which it is possible for these boys to make contacts with local men, practicing physicians and faculty men, that they could not make at a boarding house, because they have facilities there for having these men at the time that is convenient for the men. Sometimes it is just a dinner, or just a social visit, and many times they are combined with that and a rather formal talk or lecture afterwards. And many times they have a rather informal talk in the evening, without any dinner. That has been done many times, without any dinner, or anything. They have a room there, a ballroom, which makes a very nice room, gathering room, or chapter room, any way you want to look at it, and these men can address the boys there very formally, or informally, with or without lantern slides, with or without motion. And, in addition, to my mind, one of the main reasons is that by having a place large enough to house a good number of boys, they are able to take advantage of the stand-out students in their groups, and obtain from them knowledge of their course in reviews and checkups, that enable them to make better marks themselves. And as I understand the idea, scholarship is one of the paramount things for which the thing was started, and the paramount reason for the University being here.

It is shown in proof that some twenty-five or thirty men have delivered lectures to the students since the property was acquired; that men who are outstanding in their specialties go there and give discourses on their particular branch of the profession, sometimes with motion pictures and sometimes with lantern slide projections and thus enable the students to form an idea of whether or not they would be interested in some particular branch of medicine rather than in general practice itself. That the Association encourages the presence at the fraternity house of any outstanding medical men who may happen to visit Memphis, or who may be returning to renew their collegiate associations and these, it is said, contribute something to the cultural and intellectual welfare of the student members of the Fraternity.

It is further shown that a code of high morality, or culture and general refinement, and a knowledge of the amenities of polite society, are prime requisites in the success of a doctor; that the alumni associates seek to inculcate these things in the minds of the students by active supervision over the men in the chapter and all of its functions.

The Association is operated in accordance with the purposes set forth in its charter, not for profit, but for the better education of the student members of the Fraternity, and its real property, sought to be taxed, is devoted solely and exclusively to such purposes.

(1) The fact that a corporation is organized under a general welfare charter which authorizes educational activities does not of itself exempt the property of the corporation from taxation; the use it makes of the property is the test for determining whether or not its property is taxable. . . .

In *State et al* v. *Rowan et al.,* 171 Tenn. 612 . . . it was held that a club for university men was not an educational institution whose property was exempt from taxation under Constitution and statute, where social and athletic activities of the club so greatly exceeded educational and literary activities that the latter were merely incidental to the former. The court said in the course of its opinion: "So far the exemption authorized by that section of the Constitution to educational institutions has not been extended to any institutions save schools or institutions where actual instruction was given as from teacher to pupil," citing a number of our cases.

The instant case can be readily distinguished from *State et al.* v. *Rowan et al.,* supra, on its facts. In the instant case no physical activities whatever appear to be conducted by the Association, or by the Fraternity, except that some six or eight dances a year are allowed to be given under careful supervision. There is direct instruction given by eminent doctors to the students by means of lectures. Furthermore, it is shown that the lowerclassmen are tutored by the upperclassmen. Thus there exists a system of instruction approximating that of teacher to pupil. In addition to all this, it is shown that a rigid code of ethics is laid down and enforced.

(2, 3)   It is contended for the city that under the great weight of authority tax exemptions have not been granted to college Greek letter fraternities, except under express statutory authority. This appears to be true. . . . In our opinion no blanket rule can be laid down and made applicable to all fraternities. Whether or not the property of a fraternity is exempt from taxation is dependent, as in all other cases, on the use made of the property. Each case must be determined on its own facts. In the instant case, both the trial judge and the Court of Appeals have determined that the property in question is used exclusively for educational purposes and with this finding we feel constrained to concur. The result is that the decree of the Court of Appeals is affirmed at the cost of the City of Memphis.

Alford v. *Emory University*
216 Ga. 391   (116 S.E.2d 596)
October 18, 1960

On October 19, 1959, Emory University filed a petition in equity in the Superior Court of DeKalb County, alleging itself to be an educational and charitable institution, in which it named as defendants Luther F. Alford, J. C. Johnson and Fred J. Wilson, in their capacity as Tax Assessors of DeKalb County, Fred Nash, in his capacity as Tax Commissioner, and Robert K. Broome, in his capacity as Sheriff. The petition sought to enjoin the defendants Nash and Broome from the collection of taxes already assessed and to enjoin the Tax Assessors from assessing any similar taxes on thirteen parcels of property which Emory University claimed it owned and on which had been erected chapter houses occupied by Greek Letter Fraternities.

The defendants filed a plea of nonjoinder, alleging that the assessments complained of were made against certain named fraternities, which were not made parties to the action, and that they were necessary parties, and the failure to include them constituted nonjoinder of parties plaintiff.

Defendants also filed general and special demurrers, and their plea and answer, in which they admitted that the assessments were made against the fraternity houses described in the petition, but denying that the property assessed was owned by Emory University, and denying that the property is used for educational purposes. By way of further plea and answer, defendants alleged that plaintiff was not entitled to equity because it had not come into court with clean hand in that it had not paid or tendered into court all taxes lawfully due DeKalb County on property owned by it subject to taxation.

On January 5, 1960, the plaintiff filed its reponse to the defendants' plea of nonjoinder, alleging that the tax assessments were not made against the fraternities, but were made against Emory University, and that the property was owned in fee simple by Emory University, the fraternities having no interest in the property.

On February 19, 1960, the trial judge entered an order on defendants' special demurrers overruling certain grounds and sustaining others. Thereafter, the plaintiff amended its petition by striking the pleaded paragraphs of its petition in their entirety and substituting a new petition, with exhibits attached thereto, which was filed on February 24, 1960. This amended petition sought to enjoin the defendants tax commissioner and sheriff from collecting taxes assessed, and the defendant tax assessors from assessing taxes on the property occupied by thirteen Greek Letter Fraternity Chapter Houses as named in paragraph 4 of the petition. Petitioner alleged that the property in question was owned by Emory University, and its only income received in connection with said property comes from the interest on loans which have from time to time been made to the separate groups in said buildings, interest income as referred to amounting to $10,744.99 during the fiscal year ending August 31, 1959; and that all income from said loans is used exclusively for maintenance, operation, enlarging its charitable and educational facilities, and for furtherance of its charitable and educational purposes, with no part of the income being distributable to anyone having an interest therein. The amended petition further alleged that the Board of Trustees of Emory University had permitted the operation on the campus of the college Greek Letter Fraternities, which were student organizations, limited in membership to students at Emory University; that the chapter houses, built on the property listed in paragraph 4, were built under contract between Emory and a separate builder for each of said houses; that the land on which they were constructed was owned in fee simple by Emory University; that the said houses contain sleeping, eating, and study accommodations, and are located on the campus for the purpose of providing housing and dining-hall facilities for students and facilitating the exercise of supervision and control of deportment by the faculty and administrative staff of Emory University. It was further alleged that membership in Greek Letter Fraternities on the Emory University campus is by invitation from the members of such organizations to a student in the university whom that organization wishes to become one of its members, and each group controls the building which it occupies within the limitations of the general rules of Emory University. Attached to the petition as Exhibit "E" are the regulations on which Emory University claims it exercises supervision of the fraternities. A set of rules of the Emory Chapter House of Sigma Chi Fraternity and a copy of the Code of National Chapter House rules of Sigma Nu Fraternity were attached to the amendment as typical rules of the local and national groups of the fraternities. . . .

The plaintiff alleged that the assessment of taxes against the property in question is violative . . . of the Constitution of Georgia . . . and the acts of the General Assembly, pursuant to the authority of the said constitutional provisions, implementing the same . . . in that said assessment is an imposition of a tax upon buildings and property of the petitioner erected for and used as a college, because the property in question is located in the geographical center of the college campus, provides housing and eating facilities for students in the college, and by its location enables the college faculty and administrative staff to exercise closer control over the deportment and studies of the students at Emory University.

The prayers of the amendment were that the court declare the assessment, levy, and collection of taxes against the property to be unlawful and violative of the Constitution of the State of Georgia; and that the defendants be permanently enjoined and restrained from levying, assessing, or collecting taxes on the property referred to, and that petitioner have such other and further relief as the court deems meet and proper.

To this petition as amended the defendants, on February 25, 1960, filed their renewed general demurrer, and the matter came on to be heard on April 4, 1960. After hearing argument on the general demurrer and plea of nonjoinder, the trial judge took these matters under consideration, and proceeded to hear evidence on the interlocutory injunction. Thereafter, the general demurrer was overruled, the plea of nonjoinder was denied, and the following order was entered: "It is further ordered, after hearing evidence presented by the parties, that the restraining order heretofore issued is continued until further order of the court." To these judgments the defendants excepted.

* * *

HAWKINS, Justice (after stating the foregoing facts)

* * *

(2, 3) 2. The petition alleged that the property here involved belongs to Emory University, and that Emory University is the owner thereof; that the residential buildings were erected on lands to which Emory University held fee-simple title under described deeds, copies of which are attached to the petition; and that the buildings were erected for and used as a college, Emory University being a duly incorporated university open to the general public; and that the property was not used for purposes of private or corporate profit or income. These allegations, which must be taken as true on demurrer, state a cause of action, and the trial judge did not err in overruling the general demurrer. . . .

(4) 3. Does the evidence adduced on the interlocutory hearing support the allegations of the petition and judgment of the trial court that

the property is exempt from taxation under the constitutional and statutory provisions heretofore referred to, because they are "buildings erected for and used as a college"? The contract between the university and the trustees of one of the fraternities was introduced in evidence. It recites: "Whereas, Emory University is desirous of having additional buildings erected on its campus for housing of its students," and provides that the fraternity house shall be constructed according to plans and specifications, and at a point on the campus agreed to by the university and the trustees of the fraternity; that the university shall enter into a contract with the builders for the construction of a house within the cost range specified by the contract, and is to pay the contractor, upon certification from the architect, from funds made available to the university by the fraternity, forty percent of the contract price to be furnished from funds of the fraternity, and the remaining sixty percent from funds furnished by the university, which the fraternity agrees to repay in monthly or annual installments at an agreed rate of interest; that, upon completion, the house shall always be known as the named fraternity house, and shall always be occupied by students of Emory University who are members or pledges of the fraternity, said students to be selected, and the house to be occupied, managed, and maintained entirely and exclusively by the house committee or other authorities of the fraternity; that until the university has been paid the entire amount invested by it in said house, fire insurance shall be carried thereon at the expense of the fraternity payable to Emory University; that in the event of any damage to the house the amount of insurance collected shall be used to repair and restore the house, but if the destruction of the house is complete, the fraternity may elect not to rebuild the house and may at its option receive the amount of the insurance in excess of a sufficient amount to repay Emory University for the amounts that it may have invested in said property, with simple interest at an agreed rate. The contract prohibits specified conduct in the house in violation of law, or the general rules of Emory University for the discipline of its student body (which rules were also introduced in evidence), and confers upon the university the right at any and all times, through any designated member of its faculty, to enter upon and inspect the house and each and every room thereof to see that the house is being managed and conducted in accordance with the agreement; that the fraternity, at any time when it continues to have any interest in the house under the contract, may transfer and assign its right to name, occupy, and control said house to any other fraternity maintaining a regular licensed charter at Emory University, or to any other organization of the students or faculty recognized by the university, provided the transferee shall agree to thereafter comply with the fraternity's obligations under the contract, including the payment of any arrearages; that upon default by the fraternity in the repayment of the loan to the university, the university reserves the right, upon sixty days' notice, (a) to suspend the license granted and take over operation of the house, and operate it as it does other dormitories, and if at any time the fees collected by the university (in excess of the expenses incurred by it in operating and maintaining said house) shall equal the amount due to that date under the contract, then the control and right of exclusive occupancy shall be restored to said fraternity so long as it shall comply with its obligations under the contract, but subject to the same remedy for subsequent default; or (b) refund to said fraternity the amount invested by it in said house, without interest, less a fair depreciation, and that, if the amount of depreciation cannot be agreed upon, it shall be fixed by arbitration; that after said refund shall have been made, any further interest of the fraternity in the house shall cease, and the same shall thereafter be controlled by the university as all of its other dormitories are owned and controlled; that, in the event Emory University should at any time exercise option "a," it may thereafter, while the default continues, by additional notice of thirty days to the fraternity of its intention to do so, exercise option "b." Each fraternity collects its own dues, pays its own bills, employs its own house mother with the approval of the university, and either the university or the fraternity can discharge her as they see fit. The evidence further discloses that no fraternity or other organization is allowed upon the campus unless it is the holder of a regular license charter issued by the university, which, by its terms, "may be recalled at any time by order of the Board of Trustees upon the recommendation of the Committee on Student Activities and Organizations."

While this court has held that, where the owner of land grants to another the perpetual possession and use of land and of a house to be erected thereon by the grantee so long as the grantee shall comply with the covenants contained in the agreement, such grantee holds a base or determinable fee, and the property should be taxed to the grantee as owner . . . and counsel for the plaintiffs in error contend that such ruling is controlling here, we cannot agree with this contention. There is no such leasing of the property under the contract here as was true under the contract referred to in those decisions. There the property was leased for the exclusive use of the grantee, and for a stipulated rental payable to the grantor. Here the use of the property by the fraternities is to provide housing for the students of the university; only students of the university may reside therein; it is a permissive use only, subject to the control, supervision and cancellation by the university, with the obligation on its part in the event of cancellation to pay the fraternity the cost of the construction of the house, less depreciation. As pointed out . . . under the contract here involved, no rental is paid by the fraternity to the university, the right to the use of the fraternity house is not inheritable, and is assigned only by consent of the university to another fraternity maintaining a regular license charter issued by the university, or to an organization of the students or faculty recognized by the university. . . . "It is the use made of the property . . . which determines the matter of taxation." Under the evidence in this case, these fraternity buildings were built by the university; they are regulated and supervised by the university; they are located in the heart of the campus, upon property owned by the university, required to be so located and to be occupied only by students of the university; adopted as a part of the dormitory and feeding system of the college, and an integral part of the operation of the college. In our opinion these fraternity houses are buildings erected for and used as a college, and not used for the purpose of making either private or corporate income or profit for the university, and our law says that they shall be exempt from taxes. . . .

The fact that the local fraternity collects initiation fees and dues from its members and remits a portion thereof to the national organization does not require a different result, since fees and dues are required of all members of the fraternity, whether they reside in the fraternity house or not, and no part of these is received by the university. . . . Under the evidence in this case, the trial judge was authorized to find that the fraternity houses here involved were exempt from taxation.

Judgment affirmed.

State v. *State Board of Education et al.*
97 Mont. 121 (33 P.2d 516)
May 24, 1934
MR. JUSTICE MATTHEWS delivered the opinion of the court.

* * *

Turning next to the plan adopted by the board for the (7, 8) construction of the students' union building at Missoula, it is first contended that the State Board of Education has no power or authority to charge a student union fee to each student, or, if such authority exists, this cannot be done without the consent of the student body, and that the attempt to do so violates section 11 of Article XI of the Constitution and the Code provisions enacted pursuant thereto. This constitutional provision merely vests control over the state educational institutions in the board, and authorizes the legislature to define and circumscribe the powers and duties of the board.

Section 836, Revised Codes of 1921, declares that the board shall have general control and supervision over the institutions named and over their buildings, grounds and other property; it authorizes the board to adopt rules and regulations for its own government "and proper and necessary for the execution of the powers and duties conferred upon it by law," and for the "regulations for the government of the affairs of the . . . institutions." This section also authorizes the board to receive from the United States, from "state boards or persons," funds, income, and property to which the institutions are entitled, and "to use and appropriate" the same for the specific purpose "of the grant or donation, and none other," and to have general control and supervision over all receipts and disbursements of the institutions.

The legislative grant of power contains no direct authorization to the board to impose fees of any kind upon the students, but it contains the restriction that "tuition shall ever be free to all students who shall have been residents of the state for one year." (Sec. 866, *Id.*)

The express power to manage and control the business and finances of the institutions carries with it the implied power to do all things necessary and proper to the exercise of the general powers, which would include the exaction of fees, not prohibited, if fees are necessary to the conduct of the business of the institutions. The very fact that the legislature deemed it necessary to prohibit the charge for tuition to the class of students classified, discloses the legislative intent that the board should exact tuition fees from students other than those specified, and could, without the prohibition, exact tuition fees from all students in conjunction with other fees collected for the maintenance of the institutions. The granted powers are sufficiently broad to include the exaction of fees from students, except as expressly limited. . . .

Unless these fees are for "tuition," they stand on no different footing than matriculation, registration and other fees heretofore exacted, and require no vote of the student body for their exaction. In the orderly conduct of the business of the institution the board cannot be embarrassed by requiring it to submit such a matter to a vote; nor, if this fee can be pledged for the repayment of the loan secured, can it be possible for the students in some future year to disrupt the plan by staging an election and voting against the payment of the fees.

"Tuition" is from the Latin and has the same derivation as "tutor," from "tuto," to guard; "tutela," watching over, protection; "tutio," care over, guardianship. Thus a tutor is one who teaches, usually a private instructor; "tuition," "the act or business of teaching the various branches of learning." . . . This definition is in accord with that given by the several lexicographers and with the common acceptation and use of the term.

The expense of conducting an institution of learning embraces many items having nothing to do with the business of teaching or the cost of instruction, among which are the cost of heating, lighting and care of buildings, which are remotely connected with teaching, as they are necessary in order to have a fit and proper place in which to give instruction; an item of expense in the conduct of such an institution, not even remotely connected with instruction, is the upkeep of the campus.

The question as to whether fees charged students in order to defray such incidental expenses were fees charged for tuition, and thus within the prohibition of such a statute as ours, has been before the courts of a number of the states. The most recent case on the subject, and the one most nearly paralleling the present case, is *Rheam* v. *Board,* 161 Okl. 268, 18 Pac. (2d) 535, wherein the power of the board of regents of the University of Oklahoma to require the payment of a fee for construction, equipment, and maintenance of a student union building, and for the retirement of bonds issued for such construction, as a condition precedent to admission to the University, was upheld as not within the prohibition against a charge for "tuition." . . .

In Wisconsin, the board of regents of the University had for years charged a tuition fee and divers fees to aid in defraying incidental expenses, when the legislature passed an Act providing that "no fee for tuition" should be exacted; that court held that the Act did not affect the right to continue the exaction of fees other than for "tuition." (*State ex rel. Priest* v. *Regents of University,* above.) And where the matter has come before the courts, generally it is held that the provisions respecting "tuition" have no relation to fees collected in aid of defraying incidental expenses of colleges and schools, such as for heat, light, cleaning or interest on bonds. . . .

Under the authorities and on principle, the provision respecting free tuition does not bar the state board from collecting the fee fixed here, as a condition precedent to entry into the University, from each student in each year until the bonds are all paid, unless the board, composed of members appointed for a definite period of years, is barred from binding their successors by its pledge of the fees.

If the proposed building was to be for the housing of classrooms, study-rooms, library facilities and the like, necessary space for the imparting and acquiring of instruction, we might not be disposed to so hold, but the main purpose of the erection of this building is to house extracurriculum activities of the student body; special accommodations to which they may be assessed a fee without infringing upon the provision that they shall be given free tuition. The fact that a small portion of the building may be devoted to classes in the dramatic arts and kindred subjects does not militate against this holding.

* * *

The writ of injunction for which relator prays is denied and the proceeding dismissed.

MR. CHIEF JUSTICE CALLAWAY and ASSOCIATE JUSTICES ANGSTMAN, STEWART and ANDERSON concur.

PROFESSORS

1

Appointment

Sittler v. *Board of Control*
333 Mich. 681 (53 N.W.2d 681)
June 2, 1952

NORTH, Chief Justice

This is an appeal from an order dismissing plaintiff's suit entered in the Michigan court of claims. On December 13, 1950, Edward V. Sittler, plaintiff and appellant herein, filed a verified petition stating a claim against the board of control of the Michigan college of mining and technology, a defendant and appellee herein. The claim was based on an alleged contract of employment as assistant professor of German for the school year September 19, 1949, to June 10, 1950, at a salary of $4,000. Plaintiff alleged that this contract was executed by B. B. Bennett, who was head of the department of languages; that Professor Bennett had authority to make the contract on behalf of the board of control, and that the contract was also ratified by the board of control. The petition further alleged that plaintiff had performed his duties as assistant professor of German from September 19, 1949, to November 10, 1949, at which time his employment was terminated without justification. Plaintiff claims damages of $3,186.60, this being the amount he would have received if his employment had not been terminated. The claimed contract which plaintiff relies upon for recovery is contained in a letter written to plaintiff by Professor Bennett, dated September 12, 1949, the pertinent portions of which we quote:

> This letter will confirm our telephone conversation of September 10.
> The position which you have accepted is an assistant professorship of German with a salary of $4000 for the three-term year approximating nine months. As I indicated Saturday raising the salary above the budgeted amount may make it impossible to grant you a salary increase for the 1950–51 academic year. I believe it was our under-

standing that the appointment is for a one-year period but will become a permanent one if both you and the administration of the college are quite satisfied at the end of the first year.

* * *

I am enclosing a formal application blank which you may complete and return to me by mail. If you have available two small gloss prints of yourself, please send them along. I shall send to you within the next day or two copies of the texts that have been used in the German work.

Perhaps some information concerning our payroll procedures would help you in your personal planning. You will go on our payroll on September 19. Our salary checks always have a two-week lag. That means that you will receive your first salary check on October 20. Your checks thereafter you will receive at two-week intervals. The college pays salary over a full calendar year. That means that you will continue to receive salary checks throughout the summer of 1950. The details of the various deductions we can clarify after you arrive. . . .

(1, 2) Defendants point out that by the statute which sets up the board of control, the authority to enter into such contracts is vested in the board of control.

* * *

(3) Plaintiff asserts that the power to contract with teachers may be delegated, and in the instant case that it is at least a question of fact if such power were not delegated by the board of control to Professor Bennett. . . . But the instant case involved the right by contract to bind the State in the operation of one of its educational institutions over a period of time and to expend public funds in greater or less amounts. Powers of the character vested by the above statutory provisions in a board of control of an educational institution maintained by the State cannot be delegated to some subordinate or representative.

The board of supervisors cannot delegate such powers as the law requires to be submitted to their corporate discretion and judgment.

* * *

(4–8) It follows that plaintiff did not possess a contract under which he could assert rights. Even the letter written by Professor Bennett does not purport on its face to be a contract. We are mindful that it appears in plaintiff's opposition to the motion to dismiss that on other occasions heads of departments have hired assistant teachers; but such usage or custom, if it ever prevailed, cannot be availed of to enlarge the statutory powers of the board of control so as to include or justify acts which are unauthorized and contrary to the applicable statutory law. . . .

The extent of the authority of the people's public agents is measured by the statute from which they derive their authority, not by their own acts and assumption of authority.

* * *

Public officers have and can exercise only such powers as are conferred on them by law, and a State is not bound by contracts made in its behalf by its officers or agents without previous authority conferred by statute or the Constitution. . . . Nor is a State bound by an implied contract made by a State officer where such officer had no authority to make an express one.

* * *

The powers of State officers being fixed by law, all persons dealing with such officers are charged with knowledge of the extent of their authority or power to bind the State, and are bound, at their peril, to ascertain whether the contemplated contract is within the power conferred.

(9, 10) Plaintiff did not have a contract with the board of control of the Michigan college of mining and technology, nor were the negotiations between plaintiff and Professor Bennett such as to constitute a contract binding upon the defendants in the instant case. Because of an absolute lack of power vested in Professor Bennett to consummate a contract with plaintiff which would be binding upon defendants, nothing appearing in this record would or could constitute ratification of an alleged contract as asserted by appellant. While there are presented by the record some controverted issues of fact, nonetheless there are presented questions of law herein considered which are decisive of plaintiff's right to recover. We are of the opinion that the trial judge correctly granted defendants' motion to dismiss. Affirmed, with costs to appellees.

* * *

Kay v. Board of Higher Education
18 N.Y.S.2d 821
Mar. 30, 1940

McGEEHAN, Justice

In this application . . . the petitioner seeks to review the action of the Board of Higher Education in appointing Bertrand Russell to the chair of philosophy at City College. Petitioner contends that the action of the Board of Higher Education was illegal and an abuse of such powers as the Board of Higher Education had in making such appointments, because (a) Bertrand Russell was not a citizen and had not declared his intention to become a citizen; (b) the appointment did not comply with . . . the Constitution of the State of New York with reference to appointments in civil service on the basis of merit and fitness; and, finally, (c) because the appointment was against public policy because of the teachings of Bertrand Russell and his immoral character.

The corporation counsel, appearing on behalf of the Board of Higher Education of the City of New York, moved to dismiss the petition upon the ground that it did not state facts sufficient to constitute a cause of action. The corporation counsel's motion was based solely upon the ground that the provisions in the Education Law with respect to citizenship were not binding on the Board of Higher Education.

Three organizations appeared through their attorneys and asked leave to file briefs as amici curiae in support of the appointment of Bertrand Russell. Permission was granted on the argument for the filing of these briefs as amici curiae. These three parties contend that the appointment is lawful, that citizenship was not an issue and the appointment should not be disturbed because it would be an interference with "academic freedom."

(1) The motion of the corporation counsel to dismiss the petition upon the ground that the Board of Higher Education is not required to employ citizens is denied. It is not necessary to pass upon this question to deny the motion because the application is based on two additional grounds to which the motion of the corporation counsel was not addressed. The court has afforded the respondent an opportunity to interpose an answer, but the respondent has declined to interpose an answer though counsel has informed the court that its defense is to be limited to the question of law raised by the cross-motion to dismiss the petition.

(2) Petitioner contends, in the first place, that section 550 of the Education Law requires that "No person shall be employed or authorized to teach in the public schools of the state who is: . . . 3. Not a citizen. The provisions of this subdivision shall not apply, however, to an alien teacher now or hereafter employed, provided such teacher shall make due application to become a citizen and thereafter within the time prescribed by law shall become a citizen." It is conceded that Bertrand Russell is not a citizen and that he has not applied to become a citizen. The corporation counsel contends that he has a reasonable time after appointment to make the application. He further contends that the section does not apply to teachers in the colleges of the City of New York, contending that if section 550 did apply, most of the teachers in the colleges of the City of New York would be holding their appointments illegally because they are neither graduates of a state normal school nor have they licenses from the commissioner of education. It requires in subdivision 2 that they must either be in possession of a Teacher's Certificate issued under the authority of the Education Law, or a diploma from a state normal school or the state normal college, and certainly, if they have been appointed and received a Certificate

of Appointment from the Board of Higher Education, they have been appointed and hold a Teacher's Certificate under the authority of the Education Law. It does not seem logical that the section was ever intended to cover a case similar to the case of Bertrand Russell who has been in this country for some time and who has never made any application for citizenship and who apparently, as shall hereafter appear, would be denied citizenship. The section applies generally to "teachers and pupils" and is not limited to elementary and secondary schools, and the court therefore holds that Bertrand Russell is not qualified to teach by reason of the provisions of this section, but the decision herein made is not based solely upon this ground.

The second contention of the petitioner is that no examination of any kind was given to Bertrand Russell at the time of his appointment, and this is borne out by the minutes of the Administrative Committee of the City College of the City of New York and of the Board of Higher Education at the time of his appointment. . . . "We need not at this time undertake to say how far the Legislature may go in exempting all positions under the Board of Higher Education from competitive examinations. Until it is determined by the Legislature or some other body that such examinations are impracticable, the Constitution . . . is to be enforced."

* * *

In *Matter of Carow* v. *Board of Education* . . . the Court of Appeals said:

> The Constitution, article 5, § 6, in part provides that "appointments and promotions in the civil service of the state, and of all the civil divisions thereof, including cities and villages, shall be made according to merit and fitness to be ascertained, so far as practicable, by examinations, which, so far as practicable, shall be competitive." The Legislature may not disregard, evade, or weaken the force of that mandate. It applies to every position in the civil service of the state, but within limits which we have attempted to define in other cases, the Legislature may determine whether it is practicable to ascertain merit and fitness for a particular position by competitive examination, or, indeed, by any examination. . . .
> Even casual consideration of the offices comprised in the unclassified civil service leaves little doubt that the Legislature in most cases determined that it was not practicable to ascertain merit and fitness by examination, and intended that both in appointment and removal the appointing officers should be free to pass upon the merit and fitness of those appointed by them; and in most cases the legislative determination may hardly be challenged as unreasonable. In the case, however, of teachers in the public schools in large cities, it might well be argued that a determination by the Legislature that appointments and promotions according to merit and fitness ascertained by competitive examination is impracticable, would be arbitrary.

(3) While it is not necessary for this court to adjudicate the action of the Board of Higher Education in proceeding by assuming that a competitive examination for the position of Professor of Philosophy in City College was impracticable, such assumption on the part of the Board of Higher Education is held to be unwarranted, arbitrary and capricious and in direct violation of the plain mandate of the Constitution of the State of New York. If there were only one person in the world who knew anything about philosophy and mathematics and that person was Mr. Russell, the taxpayers might be asked to employ him without examination, but it is hard to believe, considering the vast sums of money that have been spent on American education, that there is no one available, even in America, who is a credit both to learning and to public life. Other universities and colleges, both public and private, seem to be able to find American citizens to employ and to say that the College of the City of New York could not employ a professor of philosophy by an examination of some sort, is an assumption by the Board of Higher Education of the power which was denied to them by the People of the State of New York in the constitution and no Legislature and no board can violate this mandate.

The foregoing reasons would be sufficient to sustain the petition and to grant the relief prayed for but there is a third ground on which the petitioner rests and which, to the court, seems most compelling. The petitioner contends that the appointment of Bertrand Russell has violated the public policy of the state and of the nation because of the notorious immoral and salacious teachings of Bertrand Russell and because the petitioner contends he is a man not of good moral character.

It has been argued that the private life and writings of Mr. Russell have nothing whatsoever to do with his appointment as a teacher of philosophy. It has also been argued that he is going to teach mathematics. His appointment, however, is to the department of philosophy in City College.

(4) In this consideration I am completely dismissing any question of Mr. Russell's attacks upon religion, but there are certain basic principles upon which this government is founded. If a teacher who is a person not of good moral character is appointed by any authority, the appointment violates these essential prerequisites. One of the prerequisites of a teacher is good moral character. In fact, this is a prerequisite for appointment in civil service in the city and state, or political subdivisions, or in the United States. It needs no argument here to defend this statement. It need not be found in the Education Law. It is found in the nature of the teaching profession. Teachers are supposed not only to impart instruction in the classroom but by their example to teach the students. The taxpayers of the City of New York spend millions to maintain the colleges of the City of New York. They are not spending that money nor was the money appropriated for the

purpose of employing teachers who are not of good moral character. However, there is ample authority in the Education Law to support this contention.

Section 556 in the same general article, Article 20, entitled "Teachers and Pupils," reads as follows:

> A school commissioner shall examine any charge affecting the moral character of any teacher within his district, first giving such teacher reasonable notice of the charge, and an opportunity to defend himself therefrom; and if he find the charge sustained, he shall annul the teacher's certificate, by whomsoever granted, and declare him unfit to teach; and if the teacher holds a certificate of the commissioner of education or of a former superintendent of public instruction or a diploma of a state normal school, he shall notify the commissioner of education forthwith of such annulment and declaration.

(5) It has been argued that this section does not apply. Assuming it does not apply to the Board of Higher Education specifically, it is a declaration of the public policy of this state. It is inconceivable that the Board of Higher Education would dare to contend that they had the power to appoint persons of bad moral character as teachers in the colleges of the City of New York. If that is their contention, then this proceeding is properly and timely brought. We do not have to go far to find authority for this contention in the decisions of the courts.

* * *

(6) The contention of the petitioner that Mr. Russell has taught in his books immoral and salacious doctrines, is amply sustained by the books conceded to be the writings of Bertrand Russell, which were offered in evidence. It is not necessary to detail here the filth which is contained in the books. It is sufficient to record the following:

> from *Education and the Modern World,* pages 119 and 120: "I am sure that university life would be better, both intellectually and morally, if most university students had temporary childless marriages. This would afford a solution of the sexual urge neither restless nor surreptitious, neither mercenary nor casual, and of such a nature that it need not take up time which ought to be given to work." From *Marriage and Morals,* pages 165 and 166: "For my part, while I am quite convinced that companionate marriage would be a step in the right direction, and would do a great deal of good, I do not think that it goes far enough. I think that all sex relations which do not involve children should be regarded as a purely private affair, and that if a man and a woman choose to live together without having children, that should be no one's business but their own. I should not hold it desirable that either a man or a woman should enter upon the serious business of a marriage intended to lead to children without having had previous sexual experience." ("The peculiar

importance attached, at the present, to adultery, is quite irrational."
From *What I Believe,* page 50.)

(7, 8) The Penal Law of the State of New York is a most important
factor in the lives of our people. As citizens and residents of our city
we come within its protective scope. In dealing with human behavior
the provisions of the Penal Law and such conduct as therein condemned
must not be lightly treated or completely ignored. Even assuming that
the Board of Higher Education possesses the maximum power which
the Legislature could possibly confer upon it in the appointment of
its teachers, it must act so as not to violate the Penal Law or to encourage
the violation of it. Where it so acts as to sponsor or encourage violations
of the Penal Law, and its actions adversely affect the public health,
safety and morals, its acts are void and of no legal effect.

* * *

(9, 10) When we consider the vast amount of money that the taxpayers are assessed each year to enforce these provisions of the law, how
repugnant to the common welfare must be any expenditure that seeks
to encourage the violation of the provisions of the Penal Law. Conceding
arguendo that the Board of Higher Education has sole and exclusive
power to select the faculty of City College and that its discretion cannot
be reviewed or curtailed by this court or any other agency, nevertheless,
such sole and exclusive power may not be used to aid, abet or encourage
any course of conduct tending to a violation of the Penal Law. Assuming that Mr. Russell could teach for two years in City College without
promulgating the doctrines which he seems to find necessary to spread
on the printed pages at frequent intervals, his appointment violates
a perfectly obvious canon of pedagogy, namely, that the personality
of the teacher has more to do with forming a student's opinion than
many syllogisms. A person we despise and who is lacking in ability
cannot argue us into imitating him. A person whom we like and who
is of outstanding ability, does not have to try. It is contended that
Bertrand Russell is extraordinary. That makes him the more dangerous.
The philosophy of Mr. Russell and his conduct in the past is in direct
conflict and in violation of the Penal Law of the State of New York.
When we consider how susceptible the human mind is to the ideas
and philosophy of teaching professors, it is apparent that the Board of
Higher Education either disregarded the probable consequences of their
acts or were more concerned with advocating a cause that appeared to
them to present a challenge to so-called "academic freedom" without
according suitable consideration of the other aspects of the problem
before them. While this court would not interfere with any action of
the board insofar as a pure question of "valid" academic freedom is
concerned, it will not tolerate academic freedom being used as a cloak
to promote the popularization in the minds of adolescents of acts for-

bidden by the Penal Law. This appointment affects the public health, safety and morals of the community and it is the duty of the court to act. Academic freedom does not mean academic license. It is the freedom to do good and not to teach evil. Academic freedom cannot authorize a teacher to teach that murder or treason are good. Nor can it permit a teacher to teach directly or indirectly that sexual intercourse between students, where the female is under the age of eighteen years, is proper. This court can take judicial notice of the fact that students in the colleges of the City of New York are under the age of eighteen years, although some of them may be older.

Academic freedom cannot teach that abduction is lawful nor that adultery is attractive and good for the community. There are norms and criteria of truth which have been recognized by the founding fathers. We find a recognition of them in the opening words of the Declaration of Independence, where they refer to the laws of nature and of Nature's God. The doctrines therein set forth, which have been held sacred by all Americans from that day to this, preserved by the Constitution of the United States and of the several states and defended by the blood of its citizens, recognizing that the inalienable rights with which men are endowed by their Creator must be preserved, and a man whose life and teachings run counter to these doctrines, who teaches and practices immorality and who encourages and avows violations of the Penal Law of the State of New York, is not fit to teach in any of the schools of this land. The judicial branch of our government under our democratic institutions has not been so emasculated by the opponents of our institutions . . . [as] to render it impotent to act to protect the rights of the people. Where public health, safety and morals are so directly involved, no board, administrative or otherwise, may act in a dictatorial capacity, shielding their actions behind a claim of complete and absolute immunity from judicial review. The Board of Higher Education of the City of New York has deliberately and completely disregarded the essential principles upon which the selection of any teacher must rest. The contention that Mr. Russell will teach mathematics and not his philosophy does not in any way detract from the fact that his very presence as a teacher will cause the students to look up to him, seek to know more about him, and the more he is able to charm them and impress them with his personal presence, the more potent will grow his influence in all spheres of their lives, causing the students in many instances to strive to emulate him in every respect.

(11) In considering the power of this court to review the determination and appointment of Dr. Russell by the Board of Higher Education this court has divided the exhibits in this proceeding into two classes, namely, those exhibits which dealt with controversial measures not malum in se as far as the law is concerned, even though abhorrently repulsive to many people, and those considered malum in se by the

court. . . . If the standards of the Board of Higher Education in these respects are lower than common decency requires, the remedy is with the appointing power who may be held responsible for appointing individuals with moral standards below that required for the public good. But as to such conduct this court is powerless to act because of the power conferred by law on the Board of Higher Education. But where the matter transcends the field of controversial issues and enters the field of criminal law then this court has the power and is under a duty to act. . . .

Considering Dr. Russell's principles, with reference to the Penal Law of the State of New York, it appears that not only would the morals of the students be undermined, but his doctrines would tend to bring them, and in some cases their parents and guardians, in conflict with the Penal Law, and accordingly this court intervenes.

(12) The appointment of Dr. Russell is an insult to the people of the City of New York and to the thousands of teachers who were obligated upon their appointment to establish good moral character and to maintain it in order to keep their positions. Considering the instances in which immorality alone has been held to be sufficient basis for removal of a teacher and mindful of the aphorism "As a man thinketh in his heart, so is he," the court holds that the acts of the Board of Higher Education of the City of New York in appointing Dr. Russell to the Department of Philosophy of the City College of the City of New York, to be paid by public funds, is in effect establishing a chair of indecency and in doing so has acted arbitrarily, capriciously and in direct violation of the health, safety and morals of the people and of the petitioner's rights herein, and the petitioner is entitled to an order revoking the appointment of the said Bertrand Russell and discharging him from his said position, and denying to him the rights and privileges and the powers appertaining to his appointment. Settle final order accordingly.

McConnell v. *Anderson et al.*
316 Fed. Supp. 809
Sept. 9, 1970

NEVILLE, District Judge

Squarely presented to the court for decision is a case where the University of the State of Minnesota, acting through its Board of Regents, rejected as an employee an otherwise qualified male applicant because of his public profession that he is a homosexual. The question raised is whether under the 1871 Civil Rights Act, 42 U.S.C. 1983, the Board of Regents, acting "under color of any statute, ordinance, regulation, custom, or usage, of any State . . ." deprived plaintiff as a homosexual and as a citizen of the United States "of any rights, privileges or immunities secured by the Constitution and laws," specifically the due process, privileges and immunities, and equal protection clauses of the Fourteenth Amendment to the United States Constitution and collaterally the freedom of speech or "expression" clause of the First Amendment. The court has found no authority directly bearing on the question and none of the cases presented by either counsel are directly on point. The case at bar thus appears to be one of first impression.

The facts are largely undisputed. Plaintiff, 28 years of age, is a librarian holding a Master's degree. He was last employed during the 1969–70 school year at the Park College Library in Missouri. In late December of 1969 he sent a number of letters of inquiry to prospective employers and received a favorable response from the librarian at the University of Minnesota. An interchange of correspondence and a personal interview followed, an employment application was submitted and by letter dated April 27, 1970, plaintiff was advised "This is to confirm the telephone conversation . . . in which we agreed to your appointment to the position of Head of the Cataloging Division in our St. Paul Campus Library . . . carrying an annual salary of $11,000 . . . to begin on or about July 1, 1970." Despite the language of this letter, it is acknowledged by plaintiff that no contract of employment was ever perfected, since the formal necessary approval by the Board of Regents was never forthcoming.

Plaintiff moved to Minneapolis and on or about May 18, 1970, publicly applied to the appropriate authority for a marriage license, seeking marriage to another man, one Jack Baker, a University of Minnesota law student. Both men freely admitted to the news media that they were and are homosexuals. This rather bizarre occurrence drew substantial publicity, including pictures in the newspapers of the two men, though no reference was made to plaintiff's connection with or future employment by the University.

Plaintiff's appointment was scheduled to come routinely before the University Board of Regents for consideration at its July 1970 meeting. Prior thereto, a committee of the Regents was appointed which met twice, the latter time on July 9, 1970, at which meeting eleven of the twelve Regents were in attendance. The committee accorded plaintiff and his lawyers a personal interview and hearing. The following recommendation was thereinafter adopted unanimously:

that the appointment of Mr. J. M. McConnell to the position of the Head of the Cataloguing Division of the St. Paul Campus Library at the rank of Instructor not be approved on the grounds that his personal conduct, as represented in the public and University news media, is not consistent with the best interest of the University.

Under the Board's rules no appearance is permitted by anyone at its meetings, but the committee's recommendation was duly adopted by the Regents at its regular meeting the next day.

Plaintiff testified that he is presently receiving no earnings whatsoever; that he declined a tendered position elsewhere in reliance on his University of Minnesota employment, which position has now been filled; that he has approximately $200 in total assets. He professes publicly his homosexuality. He is a member of an organization known as FREE, standing for "Fight Repression of Erotic Expression," though apparently its name recently has been changed. This organization is comprised of homosexuals and maintains headquarters in the University of Minnesota Student Union. Plaintiff is in no way clandestine about his homosexuality. On cross-examination he denied that he had ever practiced or committed the crime of sodomy within the State of Minnesota, though he is presently living at the same address as his intended "spouse," Jack Baker. He stated unequivocally that he has never advocated the practice of homosexuality by anyone else nor induced any other person to engage in its pursuits.

The chairman of the Regents' aforesaid committee was a witness at the trial. Counsel for the University stated to the court that this is the first case in at least ten years where a rejection has occurred against the favorable recommendation of the academic staff. The Regents' position, with no dissenting vote, is that even though plaintiff may be a very capable librarian, his professed homosexuality connotes to the public generally that he practices acts of sodomy, a crime under Minnesota law; that the Regents have a right to presume that by his applying for a license to marry another man plaintiff intended, were the license to be granted, to engage in such sodomous criminal activities; that the Regents cannot condone the commission of criminal acts by its employees and thus plaintiff has rendered himself unfit to be employed.

Several observations are in order:

* * *

(2) No claim is made by plaintiff that he actually has or had an enforceable employment contract and thus he claims no tenure rights of the type which under the University rules would require a showing of good cause before termination of employment.

(3) No claim is asserted under the 1964 Civil Rights Act, 42 U.S.C. 2000e-2, which makes it an unlawful employment practice for any employer, private or public "to fail or refuse to hire or to discharge any individual . . . because of such individual's race, color, religion, sex or natural origin." The term homosexual is significantly omitted from this statute and thus it is of no assistance to a decision of the case except generally to indicate to the court the adoption of a national policy by the Congress against discriminatory hiring and employment practices and for equal employment opportunities.

(4) No medical or other expert witnesses were called by either party to opine on the habits, proclivities, attitudes or attributes of a homosexual person. The court is therefore left with but the dictionary definition of the term.

(5) No attack was made on plaintiff's competency as a librarian, nor was there any attempt to show that his homosexual tendencies might affect the performance of his duties or his efficiency as a librarian.

(6) Nowhere in the rules and regulations adopted by the University is there any mention of homosexuals nor does the application form in any way inquire into an applicant's sexual habits or practices, hetero-sexual or otherwise.

(7) Plaintiff will not be in a position to handle or be exposed to information involving national security or so called "classified" information important to the national interest.

In the absence of any controlling statute, the question remains as to whether it is a violation of plaintiff's constitutional rights to refuse him public employment because he proclaims that he is a homosexual.

No case in the United States Supreme Court has been found where a person was either discharged or the prospective employer refused to hire him on the grounds that he was a homosexual or that specific acts of homosexuality were committed. In the Circuit courts two cases have been found in the District of Columbia involving the same plaintiff. They hold that an admission that one is a homosexual, stand-ing alone and without evidence of any practice thereof, will not justify the Civil Service Commission in refusing to certify him as eligible for employment based on a determination of "immoral conduct." . . . These cases come as close as any to a refusal to hire for homosexuality as distinguished from a discharge from existing employment. There appear to be no Circuit court cases where a government employee has been discharged for homosexuality per se. There are several cases where employees have been discharged for homosexual acts which are specified by the discharging agency and either clearly supported in the evidence before it, or simply not contested by the employee. Most of the cases reviewing such discharges for reasonableness have simply deferred to the agency determination thereof.

* * *

(1, 2) The courts have abandoned the concept that public employ-ment and the opportunity therefor is a mere privilege and not a con-stitutionally protected right. As stated in this court's opinion in *Olson* v. *Regents of University of Minnesota*:

> It was once held that a citizen has no "constitutional right to be a policeman" and that governmental employment was an unprotected privilege and not a right. . . . More recently, however, this right-privilege distinction as a limitation on substantive or procedural due

process affecting employment in the public sector has been seriously eroded if not virtually rejected. . . . "The focus of inquiry has shifted from identification of individual rights to an examination of the reasonableness of governmental action."

* * *

Particularly apropos here is the language of Chief Circuit Judge Bazelon in *Scott* v. *Macy*:

> Appellant is an applicant for public employment, and thus may have less statutory protection against exclusion than an employee. But he is not without constitutional protection. The Constitution does not distinguish between applicants and employees; both are entitled, like other people, to equal protection against arbitrary or discriminatory treatment by the Government. . . .

(3–5) Though by current standards many persons characterize a homosexual as engaging in "immoral conduct,' "'indecent" and "disgraceful," it seems clear that to justify dismissal from public employment, or, as the court finds in this case, to reject an applicant for public employment, it must be shown that there is an observable and reasonable relationship between efficiency in the job and homosexuality. In the case at bar, of course, since plaintiff never has been permitted to enter on his duties, there is no history as to his performance or the possible claimed effect of his homesexuality. The Regents are of necessity speculating and presuming. Plaintiff's position will not expose him to children of tender years who conceivably could be influenced or persuaded to his penchant. What he does in his private life, as with other employees, should not be his employer's concern unless it can be shown to affect in some degree his efficiency in the performance of his duties. . . .

> But the notion that it could be an appropriate function of the federal bureaucracy to enforce the majority's conventional codes of conduct in the private lives of its employees is at war with elementary concepts of liberty, privacy, and diversity. . . .

(6) A homosexual is after all a human being, and a citizen of the United States despite the fact that he finds his sex gratification in what most consider to be an unconventional manner. He is as much entitled to the protection and benefits of the laws and due process fair treatment as are others, at least as to public employment in the absence of proof and not mere surmise that he has committed or will commit criminal acts or that his employment efficiency is impaired by his homosexuality. Further, the decided cases draw a distinction between homosexuality, i.e., sexual propensity for persons of one's own sex, and the commission of homosexual criminal acts. Homosexuality is said to be a broad term involving all types of deviant sexual conduct with one of the same sex but not necessarily criminal acts of sodomy.

(7–9) Plaintiff does not have an inalienable right to be employed by the University but he has a right not to be discriminated against under the Fourteenth Amendment due process clause. He has a constitutional right that the terms of his public employment which he must meet be "reasonable, lawful and non-discriminatory." . . .

The "purges" of the late 1940s and 1950s of homosexuals in the federal government service, particularly in the Department of State, are not authority in the case at the bar. There clandestine homosexuals, when discovered, were claimed to have become the subject of possible blackmail. See 82 Harv.L.Rev. 1738 (1969). Here plaintiff is very open about his deviation, and in any event is not dealing with classified or secret information important to the national security.

* * *

A separate order granting an injunction has been entered. This memorandum opinion will serve in lieu of findings of fact as provided by Rule 52 (a) of the Federal Rules of Civil Procedure.

Trustees of State Normal School v. Wightman
93 Colo. 226 (25 P.2d 193)
Sept. 11, 1933

BOUCK, Justice

The defendant in error, E. Russell Wightman, recovered judgment for $1,333.33 against the plaintiff in error, the trustees of the state normal school for services as head of the department of physics in the state normal school at Gunnison, Colo., better known as the Western State College. The trustees claim that they owe Wightman nothing, and ask that the judgment be reversed.

(1) 1. At the outset, the trustees contend that this action is against the state in its governmental capacity, and that the state has not consented to be sued. By section 8164 of C. L. 1921, the plaintiff in error, which is a board consisting of six trustees, is constituted a body corporate by the name and style of "the trustees of the state normal school," and it is therein provided that "as such and by its said name" it "may hold property for the use of said school, be party to all suits and contracts, and do all things thereto lawfully appertaining, in like manner as municipal corporations of this state." These powers and those conferred by section 8168 are ample. By the plain meaning of the language used, these sections subject the trustees to an action on such a contract as is relied upon here, inasmuch as the powers and duties of the trustees are made applicable in full force to the Western State College by section 8179. This special defense of the trustees, which is in effect a plea to the jurisdiction, is therefore overruled.

(2–6) 2. The real issue here is whether a resignation tendered by Wightman was duly accepted before it was withdrawn. To determine this it becomes necessary to examine the facts in considerable detail. On April 29, 1929, at a regular meeting held in Greeley, the trustees approved the recommendation of Aspinall, president of the college, that a salary of $4,000 be offered Wightman as professor of physics for the ensuing year. Wightman, who had been a member of the same faculty continuously since September of 1920, accepted the offer. This clearly constituted a contract of employment. On September 12, 1929, Aspinall dispatched a letter to Wightman. It was based ostensibly upon the former's alleged discovery that, contrary to a representation claimed to have been made to the college by Wightman (but denied by him), the latter did not possess the degree of a doctor of philosophy. The letter contained an urgent request for Wightman's resignation. On September 20 Wightman gave his resignation, addressed to the president, as follows: "I wish to tender my resignation as head of the department of physics of Western State College of Colorado to take effect as soon as the vacancy caused by my leaving can be filled." A doubt exists as to whether the vacancy, if any, was ever filled; but, owing to the views we are about to express, it will not be necessary to discuss that question. The resignation was accompanied by a letter stating that the resignation was being made "with no strings whatever," and expressing regret at having caused embarrassment. Thereafter, however, Wightman informed the president by a telegram of October 3 that he was recalling his resignation, that a letter of explanation would follow, and that he was ready to fulfill his contract. The letter arrived the next day. It called attention to the fact that the resignation was not to take effect until the vacancy should be filled, and declared that he was withdrawing his resignation because he had discovered the request therefor to have been actuated by a different reason from the one assigned. According to the testimony of Wightman, the demand for his resignation was due to the pressure of some unnamed personal enemy of his. In this Wightman was corroborated. Copies of the aforesaid telegram and explanatory letter were promptly transmitted by Wightman to the trustees. Up to that time the trustees had taken no official action relative to the resignation. What had been done was done by Aspinall as president of the college, without the official cognizance of the board, though the evidence shows that one of its officers knew of Aspinall's acts and informally approved of them.

We need not consider whether, as a matter of educational policy, a doctor's degree ought to be regarded as important or indispensable for the head of a department of physics. As a matter of fact, at least two other heads of departments in the college, among about ten departments, were possessed of no higher degree than a master's. In 1920, when first appointed, Wightman had all but completed the work for his Ph.D. in a university of the highest standing. After many delays due at least in part to circumstances beyond Wightman's control, he received this degree during the very college year here involved. He claims to have kept the college informed of some of these delays, and we must accept the finding of the trial court on that issue. From the record before us we must infer, as the trial court expressly found, that Wightman's services were satisfactory, for they continued unbroken during a period of nine years and under at least two presidents of the college. In the absence of a positive and recognized rule requiring the degree, and in the absence of an express condition to like effect in the contract of employment, the failure to hold a Ph.D. could not, under the facts here found, be a legitimate ground either for removal or for deeming the position vacant; nor could the matter of a particular degree be significant except in inducing or withholding the original appointment, as a mere matter of administrative policy.

A contract of employment becomes effective when the appointee has accepted. So also an offer by the appointee to terminate or surrender an appointment by resignation is effectual only when the resignation is duly accepted by the body whose duty it is to make or terminate the appointment. Probably the trustees here could have avoided this controversy had they previously adopted a general rule, and expressly incorporated it in the contract of employment, that a resignation should be deemed accepted whenever it is lodged with the president or other named official of the college or of the trustees themselves. However, there being no rule to govern such a contingency, the trustees alone have the power to accept a resignation and thus to sever the contractual relation between the college and a member of its faculty, even as they alone have the power to establish that relation. An effort was made by the trustees to show that they had given instructions to the president to employ and discharge members of the faculty, but the lower court properly ruled out all evidence of such unauthorized delegation of the trustees' statutory powers and duties. From what has been said, we may draw the conclusion that the resignation of Wightman was not legally accepted. Not having been legally accepted, the resignation could be and was legally withdrawn; therefore the Wightman contract for the college year 1929–30 remained in full force and effect. The district court was right in its view of the law, and its findings are supported by the evidence. There was no prejudicial error.

Judgment affirmed.

ADAMS, C.J., and HOLLAND, J., concur.

2
Dismissal

Keleher v. *La Salle College*
394 Pa. 545 (147 A.2d 835)
Jan. 15, 1959
BENJAMIN R. JONES, Justice

This appeal involves a question of the applicability of the parol evidence rule.

James F. Keleher, appellant, taught philosophy and religion at LaSalle College, Philadelphia, from 1948 to 1953. On June 15, 1951, appellant and appellee, the latter acting through its then President, Brother Paul, entered into a written contract of employment, the summarized terms of which are: (1) appellant was employed as a full-time member of appellee's instructional staff with the rank of "Assistant Professor of Philosophy in the Area of Philosophy and Religion" for the academic year 1951–1952; (2) appellant agreed to (a) serve "faithfully, diligently and according to his best ability," (b) to accept at appellee's request certain administrative and nonteaching duties such as student consultation, etc., (c) by his conduct to uphold appellee's ideals and (d) not to engage, directly or indirectly, in any activity detrimental to appellee; (3) appellant was to be paid a salary—for a minimum semester teaching load of 12 semester credit hours and a maximum teaching load of 16 semester credit hours—of $3,950, provided that if the appellee requested a teaching load in excess of 16 semester credit hours per semester, appellant's compensation would be the sum, per hour, which the maximum semester teaching load multiplied by thirty established academic weeks bears to $3,950, multiplied by fifteen established academic weeks for each semester.

On June 15, 1952, appellant and appellee, the latter again through its then President, Brother Paul, entered into another written contract identical with the 1951 contract in all respects except that it covered the academic year 1952–1953 and appellant's salary was fixed at $4,160.

On March 2, 1953, Brother E. Stanislaus, then appellee's President, wrote appellant to the effect that appellee could not offer him a new contract upon the expiration of the 1952–1953 contract, assigning as the reason therefor the necessity that appellee curtail its expenditures because of rising costs and diminishing enrollment. On March 7, 1953, the appellant wrote Brother Stanislaus questioning his authority to revoke "academic tenure" which appellant stated had been given him in June 1951 by Brother Paul and requesting of Brother Stanislaus an appeal to appellee's Board of Managers. On March 11, 1953, Brother Stanislaus wrote appellant: ". . . Please be advised that, inasmuch as this [academic] tenure was extended to you by authority of the President, it can, likewise, be revoked under the same authority . . .", and since as President of the Board of Managers, Brother Stanislaus had full authority to act, no question of an appeal to the Board of Managers was involved. In the same letter Brother Stanislaus offered to continue appellant's services until June 1954 subject to the conditions that appellant would not act as head of the Department of Religion and Philosophy and that his salary would be cut to its previous level, which offer, in the absence of an acceptance by appellant, was dithdrawn on April 23, 1953.

On September 18, 1953, appellant instituted an assumpsit action against appellee for an alleged breach of an *oral* contract of employment. In this action appellant alleged that in June of 1951, Brother Paul, appellee's President, entered into an *oral* contract with appellant increasing his salary to $4,160, assigning him as "Acting Chairman of the Area of Philosophy and Religion" and giving him "tenure of academic employment," and that the revocation, without cause, of his tenure and employment by appellee, violated and breached this oral contract. Appellee's answer denied the existence of any oral contract and averred that appellant's employment arose solely under the two written contracts of June 15, 1951, and June 15, 1952.

When the matter came for trial before Judge John Morgan Davis and a jury and after appellant's counsel's opening address, the first day of the trial apparently was consumed in conferences between the court and counsel. The next day, apparently as the result of a stipulation between counsel, appellee's counsel offered in evidence the written contract of June 15, 1952, and, in response to a question addressed to him by appellee's counsel, appellant acknowledged that the signature on this written contract was his signature. After appellant's counsel had placed in evidence the March and April 1953 correspondence between appellant and Brother Stanislaus, the trial court granted "a motion for a nonsuit on the pleadings." Appellant presented a motion to set aside this nonsuit which motion was subsequently denied and a judgment entered for appellee on April 1, 1958. Subsequent to the perfection of this appeal, Judge Davis in a written opinion directed the Prothonotary to correct the docket entries made April 1, 1958, which showed the entry of a nonsuit and to enter in place thereof judgment for the defendant upon the pleadings.

(1) The instant record is far from satisfactory. *Apparently,* after conferences between counsel and the court, an agreement was reached as to the manner of presentation of the evidence so as to raise the fundamental issue in the lawsuit, to wit, the applicability of the parol evidence rule.

* * *

(2) *Walker* v. *Saricks* . . . well states the Pennsylvania Parol Evidence Rule:

> Where parties, without any fraud or mistake, have deliberately put their engagements in writing, the law declares the writing to be not only the best, but the only, evidence of their agreement. . . . All preliminary negotiations, conversations and verbal agreements are merged in and superseded by the subsequent written contract . . . and unless fraud, accident, or mistake be averred, the writing constitutes the agreement between the parties, and its terms cannot be added to nor subtracted from by parol evidence. . . .

the test is

> whether parties, situated as were the ones to the contract, would naturally and normally include the one in the other if it were made. If they relate to the same subject-matter, and are so interrelated that both would be executed at the same time, and in the same contract, the scope of the subsidiary agreement must be taken to be covered by the writing. This question must be determined by the court.

The written contract of June 15, 1952, is clear and free of any ambiguity. It purports to encompass all the terms and conditions of the relationship between appellant and appellee concerning the former's employment as a teacher during the academic year 1952–1953. Appellant now seeks to prove an oral agreement which would clearly alter and vary the terms of this written contract in a most material instance, to wit the length of appellant's employment. The written contract distinctly and unambiguously sets forth that appellant is employed for the academic year 1952–1953. What appellant wants to prove is that, as the result of an oral contract, he acquired "academic tenure" by which we understand permanent tenure. That appellant's oral contract would vary and alter the written contract is clear beyond any peradventure and doubt.

(3, 4) Appellant neither alleges nor does he seek to prove any fraud, accident or mistake, but simply contends that the parol evidence rule is inapplicable because the written contract did not constitute an integration of the alleged oral contract and that both the oral and the written contract are coexistent. A comparison of the subject-matter of the written contract with that of the alleged oral contract clearly indicates an integration of the latter by the former. To allow appellant to prove an oral contract under these circumstances would violate the parol evidence rule, a rule to which this Court requires rigid adherence. . . .

For the reasons stated, judgment is directed to be entered for the appellee.

Raney v. Board of Trustees, Coalinga Junior College District
48 Cal. Rptr. 555
Jan. 7, 1966
* * *

CONLEY, Presiding Justice

Joseph F. Raney, a former probationary school teacher of the Coalinga Junior College District, was denied a writ of mandate directing respondent to reemploy him and to pay his back salary for the 1964–65 school term. The superior court found that Mr. Raney had been a probationary teacher of the Coalinga Junior College District for two previous years and was teaching for the third year when on or about May 11, 1964, the board of trustees of the college district caused written notice to be given him that his services would not be required for the 1964–65 school year; that upon request the board gave him a written statement of the reasons for not hiring him and that on or about June 11, 1964, it served him with a formal accusation; that following the filing of his notice of defense and request for a hearing, such hearing was regularly held by the school board on July 9, 1964, and that thereafter the board made findings of fact and rendered a decision, copies of which are attached to the petition for the writ of mandate. The trial court found that the matters set forth in paragraphs 1, 2, and 3 of the board's findings of fact are supported by substantial evidence in the light of the whole record, as follows:

1. That the philosophy of the said Joseph F. Raney with respect to grading is unsuitable for the junior college level and is contrary to the accepted practices of the administration of the Coalinga College in that he has an extremely "tough" attitude toward his students which causes excessive dropouts during the semester and between semesters; that his severity of grading as aforesaid, his tough philosophy, his sarcasm toward his students, particularly those who may

disagree with his philosophy, results in many students either failing to take his course or failing to complete it, resulting in said students missing an important basic course.

2. That originally employed as a counselor, he proved ineffective as such with extremely poor rapport with his students, necessitating his reassignment to classroom work; that he would not ever be suitable for counseling.

3. That he has a general reputation among students, faculty and the community as a contentious person, which lessens their respect for him, thereby reducing his effectiveness as a teacher.

The trial court determined that said reasons "relate solely to the welfare of the school and the pupils thereof." In his conclusions of law, the trial judge held that the respondent board duly and regularly acted within the authority granted by sections of the Education Code, as they then existed.

The judgment is ". . . that the petitioner take nothing by this action, and that each party shall bear his own costs of suit herein."

The decision is in accordance with the law. . . .

The inquiry [of judicial review] extends to the questions whether the board has proceeded without or in excess of jurisdiction, whether there was a fair trial, and whether there was any prejudicial abuse of discretion. An abuse of discretion is established if the board has not proceeded in the manner required by law, the order or decision is not supported by the findings, or, with regard to local boards like the one before us, the findings are not supported by substantial evidence in the light of the entire record. [Citations.] However . . . the Education Code specifically limits the scope of judicial review, stating, "[T]he determination of the board as to the sufficiency of the cause for dismissal shall not be subject to judicial review," and "[T]he determination of the board as to the sufficiency of the cause for dismissal shall be conclusive, but the cause shall relate solely to the welfare of the schools and the pupils thereof."

* * *

In 1965, section 13444 of the Education Code was repealed, and the pertinent subject matter thereof is covered in section 13443, which provides:

The governing board's determination not to reemploy a probationary employee for the ensuing school year shall be for cause only. The determination of the governing board as to the sufficiency of the cause pursuant to this section shall be conclusive, but the cause shall relate solely to the welfare of the schools and the pupils thereof.

It will thus be seen that notwithstanding frequent amendments of the code sections involved, the same rule has at all times applied, namely, that the sufficiency of the cause adopted by the board of trustees for failing to reemploy a teacher for a fourth year, thus giving him permanent status, is conclusive within specified limits, and the courts cannot interfere with the judgment of the school board with respect to reemployment.

(2) The trial judge correctly determined that there was substantial evidence before the board of trustees supporting the findings which they made. It is not within our power to substitute our own judgment of the character and ability of the petitioner or his worthiness as a teacher; we are powerless to pass judgment on the "sufficiency of the cause for dismissal."

(3) It would be a useless consumption of time and space for us to discuss in detail the evidence at the hearing before the board of trustees. The board believed the evidence, which was countered by other testimony, that Mr. Raney was too strict in his insistence that his students should attain a high degree of efficiency approximating a university level of scholarship, and that the grades given by him were not in line with the customary relaxed attitude of certain other teachers. Some of his students found his comments disagreeable. As a counselor, during part of his three years of teaching, he did not meet with unanimous approval, and some of the students and faculty and the school community believed that he was a contentions person, and that such belief tended to reduce his effectiveness as a teacher.

If this court were at liberty to supervise the judgment of the members of the school board and to reverse their decision as to the retention of appellant on the basis of his ability and merits as a teacher, we might well reach an opposite conclusion. As remarked by the learned trial judge, who had been both a teacher and a school trustee prior to his elevation to the bench, Mr. Raney ". . . is a highly intelligent [and] courageous . . . individual," and the record evidences qualities of the petitioner which are desirable in the profession. If education is to achieve its asserted end of causing young people to think and to reach independent conclusions about the issues that agitate the world, there must be afforded to their teachers a sufficient independence to permit them to inculcate these virtues. Ideally, a teacher should be a little contentious, rather than stodgy and lethargic, but our theory of government gives to the school trustees, for better or for worse, an almost absolute choice either to "hire or fire" teachers who have not yet attained tenure. It might will be argued that the Legislature has created a mirage for probationary teachers by seeming to assure them that they may demand a hearing if they are not retained for a fourth year. In practice, such an official inquiry does not result in a reinstatement of the teacher but only produces a possibly expanded assignment of reasons why the board does not wish to give him permanent status by rehiring him for a fourth year. This is how it is, and probationary teachers should clearly understand the way of the world insofar as their jobs are concerned.

The judgment is affirmed.

RALPH M. BROWN and STONE, JJ., concur.

Scott v. *Joint Board of Education, etc.*
258 Ky. 449 (258 S.W. 2d 449)
March 20, 1953

CAMMACK, Judge

Lena Mae Scott sued the appellees, alleging that they "have wrongfully, unlawfully and unethically refused to act fairly by her, and have arbitrarily and without lawful reason refused to re-employ her" as a teacher of English at Kentucky Wesleyan College, a position which she held for four years, from 1947 to 1951. She asked for a judgment "for damages and salary in the sum of $5,000" and a decree "restoring her to her position as an associate professor of English on the faculty of Kentucky Wesleyan College" and for a declaration of rights. An amended petition added allegations that the appellee had made statements injurious to her professional and moral standing. Special and general demurrers were sustained to the petition, and Miss Scott having declined to plead further now appeals.

Miss Scott states in her brief that: "This is not a suit for performance of a contract, but is for a tortious violation of a right resulting from it."

Whatever the nature of the claim asserted, the complaint is based on the alleged violation of some right grounded in a contract relationship. Nowhere in the 25 pages of the petition and amended petition do we find facts pleaded which state a case of legal duty on the part of the appellees to reemploy Miss Scott. She argues that the Statement of Principles of the American Association of University Professors, of which she is a member, provides that a college teacher is entitled to permanent or continuous tenure after a three-year probationary period. Miss Scott's Exhibit A seems to contradict this allegation, however, since it provides for the maximum of seven years' probation. In any event, she does not allege that the Statement of Principles was accepted by the Board as a binding part of contracts of employment. However, she does allege that continuous tenure after a three-year probationary period is "usual" in member colleges of the Southern Association of Schools and Colleges, by which Kentucky Wesleyan is accredited. This also falls short of an allegation that contracts of the Board provide for continuous tenure after a three-year probationary period. In fact, Miss Scott specifically alleges that the Board had not set up any period of probationary teaching as necessary for tenure. Her allegations concerning what the American Association of University Professors and the Southern Association regard as desirable tenure policies do not amount to an assertion that faculty members of Kentucky Wesleyan actually had any legal rights to tenure at the time of her discharge.

Miss Scott also asserted in her original petition that, when she began her fourth year's work, the Board promised that tenure would be established for her at the end thereof. This allegation of a specific promise of tenure was contradicted, however, by her allegation that the promise was conditioned that she serve "satisfactorily." Although the petition further alleges that her service was satisfactory to 90 percent of the faculty and 100 percent of the students, this does not amount to an allegation that her service during the fourth year of employment was satisfactory to the Board. We conclude, therefore, that Miss Scott has failed also to allege a specific contractual promise by the Board to give her tenure or even to rehire her for 1951–1952. In the face of this fundamental defect, we need not consider the question of what Miss Scott's rights might have been if she had alleged facts making out a case of tenure status.

Under the circumstances, we think the chancellor properly sustained the general demurrer to the petition as amended.

Judgment affirmed.

Worzella v. *Board of Regents of Education*
77 So. Da. 447 (93 N.W.2d 411)
Dec. 10, 1958

HANSON, Judge

The petitioner, Dr. W. W. Worzella, seeks a writ of mandamus compelling the State Board of Regents to reinstate him as professor of agronomy or as head of the agronomy department at South Dakota State College. The circuit court refused relief and he appeals.

Dr. Worzella was first employed as a professor of agronomy at State College on October 1, 1943. Thereafter he served continuously on that faculty until discharged by the Board of Regents on January 11, 1958. He was dismissed after an extensive investigation into the personnel and administrative affairs of State College by the Board. After the investigation the Board prepared a written report. With reference to Dr. Worzella the Board found he ". . . wittingly or unwittingly, permitted himself and his name to become involved in serious personal disputes and activities in the many years above referred to, and has . . . been guilty of insubordination; that by virtue of the controversial character he has become, it would not be to the best interests of South

Dakota State College for him to be retained." The Board concluded "the retention of Dr. W. W. Worzella as head of the Department of Agronomy is incompatible to the best interest and welfare of State College, its students, and the State of South Dakota as a whole, and that he should be summarily dismissed and relieved from all further duties under his current contract; his compensation, however, to continue as therein provided during the remainder of this fiscal year." His summary dismissal followed.

Dr. Worzella contends he has permanent tenure under a tenure policy approved by the Board of Regents and could be dismissed only in compliance with its substantive and procedural provisions. It is conceded that no complaint was filed, notice given, or hearing held pursuant thereto. However, the Board maintains the tenure policy did not, and could not, abrogate its constitutional and statutory power to dismiss all officers, instructors and employees under its control.

The advisability of establishing and the merits of academic tenure are not involved. We are concerned only with the validity and enforceability of the tenure policy approved for State College by the Board of Regents.

The exact meaning and intent of this so-called tenure policy eludes us. Its vaporous objectives, purposes, and procedures are lost in a fog of nebulous verbiage. We gather from it, in general, that a faculty member who is retained on the staff at State College for over three years gains permanent tenure. He cannot thereafter be divested of tenure unless a complaint against him is filed by the president of the college. He is then entitled to have notice of hearing, and a hearing before a Tenure Committee consisting of seven faculty members. It further provides that "since the final decision must be made by the President" it is desirable that he sit with the Tenure Committee during the formal hearing as an auditor. At the conclusion of the hearing the committee makes its recommendations to the president. The president must then decide whether to recommend the dismissal of the accused faculty member to the Board of Regents. The faculty member whose dismissal is recommended may appeal for a hearing before the Board. The concluding paragraph states that the tenure policy is based "upon good faith between the college administration and the individual faculty member."

The policy statement is silent as to the Board of Regents' authority. By inference we may assume the Board would have power to discharge a faculty member having tenure when recommended by the Tenure Committee and President. Otherwise the Board would have no authority to act. Apparently the Board could not discharge or remove a faculty member with tenure for any reason if the President failed or refused to recommend dismissal. We believe this to be an unlawful abdication of the Board's exclusive prerogative and power.

The Board of Regents is a constitutionally created administrative body charged with the control of all institutions of higher learning "under such rules and restrictions as the legislature shall provide." § 3, art. XIV. With reference to the issue involved the legislature has provided:

The Board of Regents is authorized to employ and dismiss all officers, instructors, and employees of such institutions, necessary to the proper management thereof, to determine their number, qualifications, and duties, fix the term of their employment, and rate and manner of their compensation, and provide for sabbatical leave on part pay; provided, that no person shall be employed or dismissed by reason of any sectarian or political opinions held.

The Board of Regents shall have power to enact and enforce all rules and regulations not in conflict with any law and deemed necessary by it for the wise and successful management of the institutions under its control and for the government of students and employees therein.

The Board may delegate provisionally to the president, dean, principal, or faculty of any school under its control, so much of the authority conferred by this section as in its judgment seems proper and in accordance with the usual custom in such cases. . . .

(1, 2) The above statutory provisions merely confirm and clarify the Board of Regents' constitutional power to employ and dismiss all officers, instructors, and employees at all institutions under its control. These provisions become a part of every contract of employment entered into by the Board. . . . It cannot be restricted, surrendered, or delegated away. Our constitution prescribes that our state university and colleges "shall be under the control" of the Board of Regents. Without the right to employ, and the power to discharge, its employees the Board loses its constitutional right of control. . . .

(3) . . . the Board of Regents "may delegate provisionally to the president, dean, principal, or faculty of any school under its control, so much of the authority conferred by this section as in its judgment seems proper. . . ." This is a limited power. It does not empower the Board to delegate away all of its powers or its constitutional duty of control. Under its provisions the Board may only delegate the limited authority conferred on it by the same section.

* * *

(4, 5) In South Dakota, under the present tenure policy at State College, the Board of Regents cannot remove a faculty member for any reason or cause on its own volition. Without the prior action and approval of the President and Tenure Committee the Board is powerless to act. The President and Tenure Committee do not serve in an advisory

THE LAW AND HIGHER EDUCATION

capacity only. Their action and approval are conditions precedent to any dismissal of college personnel by the Board. Such delegation of authority to subordinates is an unlawful encroachment upon the Board of Regents' constitutional and statutory power of control over such college. A writ of mandamus was, therefore, properly denied by the trial court.

Affirmed.

All the Judges concur.

Board of Trustees of Mt. San Antonio Jr. Coll. Dist. v. *Hartman*
55 Cal. Rptr. 144
Dec. 1, 1966

FORD, Justice

This is an appeal from a judgment permitting plaintiff to dismiss defendant and to terminate his employment as a permanent teacher of the Mount San Antonio Junior College District. The contentions of the defendant are that the matters stated in various charges are barred by the provisions of section 13436 of the Education Code, that the evidence is insufficient to support the findings of fact, that the findings of fact do not sustain the conclusions of law, and that the trial court erred in certain rulings as to the admissibility of evidence. In the light of the record and the governing law we have reached the conclusion that the judgment must be affirmed.

On January 18, 1963, charges were formulated by plaintiff in which it was alleged that causes existed for defendant's dismissal. Written notice of plaintiff's intention to dismiss defendant, together with a copy of the charges, was served upon him. Thereupon defendant demanded a hearing. Plaintiff, pursuant to section 13412 of the Education Code, elected to file this action asking that the superior court inquire into the charges, determine whether or not they were true, and if true whether they constituted sufficient ground for his dismissal.

On May 10, 1963, further charges were formulated in like manner, notice of which was given to the defendant, and it was subsequently stipulated that such charges should be deemed to be charges attached to the complaint. Thereafter, pursuant to leave of court, plaintiff filed a supplemental complaint with respect to additional charges which had been formulated by plaintiff on September 3, 1963, and as to which notice had been given to defendant.

The matter was tried and the court determined that the evidence in support of the charge as to the defendant's relationship with a woman, herein designated as Patricia, constituted cause for defendant's dis-

missal on the grounds of immoral conduct and evident unfitness for
service (Ed. Code, § 13403). The court found that the various times,
commencing on or about December 12, 1961, and during much of the
calendar year 1962, defendant cohabited with Patricia, who was married to a man other than the defendant, that such relationship commenced on the day that Patricia left her husband, that the defendant's
wife had died less than thirty days prior thereto, and that Patricia had
been a student of defendant at Mount San Antonio Junior College.
The court further found that neither Patricia nor defendant "believed
in good faith that their activities in Tijuana, Mexico, on December 19,
1961, had resulted in that day or at any time later in a valid divorce
[sic] between Patricia . . . and her husband, or in a valid marriage
between defendant and Patricia. . . ."

The trial court further determined that, "when considered in combination with the actions of the defendant found to be true" as set forth
hereinabove, the relationship of defendant and another woman, herein
designated as Frances, constituted cause for the dismissal of defendant
on the grounds of immoral conduct and evident unfitness for service.
The charge involving Frances, which the court found to be true, was
formulated as follows: "During the fall of 1960 he lived in an apartment with said Frances . . . under the name of Mr. and Mrs. Hartman.
At that time he was married to Barbara Jean Hartman."

* * *

(1) The evidence was sufficient to sustain the finding of fact of the
trial court. . . .

(2) Defendant contends that the findings of fact with respect to the
relationship between him and Patricia do not support the conclusion
of law that such "activities . . . under all the circumstances of this case,
constitute cause for the dismissal of the defendant on the grounds of
1) immoral conduct and 2) evident unfitness for service." The argument is in essence that a finding of cohabitation is not a finding that
there were sexual relations between defendant and Patricia. In *Boyd* v.
Boyd, . . . the court stated: "The accepted California concept of cohabitation is the mutual assumption of those marital rights, duties and
obligations which are usually manifested by married people, including
but not necessarily dependent upon sexual relations." But, in any event,
under circumstances such as are present in this case the evil at which
the statutory provision is directed is the harmful impression on others,
particularly students, arising from the fact of a teacher and a woman
to whom he is not married living together openly as man and wife. If
adherence to a code of proper personal conduct is not essential in all
callings, it is in the teaching profession. . . .

A teacher, and more particularly a principal, in the public school
system is regarded by the public and pupils in the light of an exem-

plar, whose words and actions are likely to be followed by the children coming under her care and protection.

* * *

The judgment is affirmed.

Thomas v. *Catawba College*
248 NC 609 (104 SE 2d 175)
June 30, 1958
* * *

Plaintiff's employment was terminated as of February 23, 1952. Thereafter, he had no connection with Catawba College.

Plaintiff instituted this action on July 16, 1954. Meanwhile defendant issued to plaintiff, as directed by its Board of Trustees, and plaintiff received, endorsed and accepted, checks aggregating $4,175.00, plaintiff's salary for the year following notification of dismissal. The last of these salary payments, a check for $289.52, bearing the notation "Final Payment," was issued February 21, 1953.

Plaintiff's allegations, apart from allegations referred to in the opinion, may be summarized as follows:

* * *

4. His discharge was without adequate cause, was not for age, and was not for financial exigencies, but was in breach of defendant's contract with plaintiff.

Plaintiff prayed (1) "that for purposes of this and subsequent suits between the parties for accrued salary, the discharge of the plaintiff be adjudged wrongful," (2) that he recover all unpaid salary to date of the trial, (3) that he recover punitive damages in the amount of $50,000, and (4) that he recover costs.

Answering, defendant alleged, in summary, that plaintiff's discharge was for adequate cause, in good faith, and after hearing in strict compliance with paragraph (a) (4) of the statement of tenure; and that plaintiff was estopped to maintain this action for alleged wrongful discharge by his acceptance of his salary for the year following his dismissal.

At the conclusion of plaintiff's evidence, the court, allowing defendant's motion therefor, entered judgment of involuntary nonsuit and dismissed the action. Plaintiff excepted and appealed, assigning errors.

* * *

BOBBITT, Justice

No evidence was offered to support plaintiff's further allegations that defendant, after plaintiff's discharge, made statements, false, willful, malicious or otherwise, to prospective employers of plaintiff, and thereby interfered with plaintiff's efforts to obtain other employment; and no evidence was offered to support plaintiff's allegations that the Board of Trustees acted "maliciously, tortiously and wilfully" to carry out a preconceived and deliberate scheme to ruin plaintiff. Indeed, a witness for plaintiff testified that each member of the Board of Trustees was "a man of outstanding reputation and character" and undertook to serve the college in the capacity of Trustee "with absolute faithfulness and honesty" and in obedience to what he conceived to be his conscientious duty." Without further comment, we pass from these unsupported allegations of the complaint.

The Board of Trustees terminated plaintiff's employment as of February 23, 1952. Conceding the *power* of the Board of Trustees to discharge him, thus severing his connection with Catawba College, plaintiff denies the *right* of the Board of Trustees to discharge him otherwise than for "adequate cause." He contends that "adequate cause" for his discharge did not exist. Hence, he contends he was discharged wrongfully.

Consideration of the record leaves the impression that the proceedings before the hearing committee and Board of Trustees were in good faith and in substantial compliance with paragraph (a) (4) of the tenure policy. However, the basis of decision, stated below, renders unnecessary the discussion or decision of questions raised as to whether the action of the Board of Trustees *when rendered* was a final determination that plaintiff's dismissal was for "adequate cause."

Plaintiff had full notice and knowledge that his dismissal was based on the determination by the hearing committee and the Board of Trustees that "adequate cause" for his dismissal existed. Moreover, he had full notice and knowledge that the resolution of the Board of Trustees, quoted in the notification of dismissal, contained this provision: "Further, as provided in the tenure policy of the college his salary shall be continued for one year from date of this notice. Payments thereunder are to be made in accordance with the standard pay schedule of the college." Thus, he was advised plainly that the $4,175 paid to him during the year following notification of dismissal was paid to him *as salary*.

Obviously, the provision in paragraph (a) (4) of the tenure policy, regarding payment of salary for one year following notification of dismissal, is applicable only when "adequate cause" for dismissal has been determined after proceedings conducted in accordance with its terms; and, in such cause, the payment of the discharged employee's salary for one year is both the measure and *the limit* of defendant's obligation. It does not bear upon the respective rights of the parties in case of wrongful discharge in breach of contract. In the latter case, the discharged employee's remedy is an action to recover damages for defendant's breach of contract.

(1) The wrongful discharge of plaintiff by defendant, if such occurred, would constitute a breach of defendant's contract with plaintiff and give rise to a cause of action in favor of plaintiff and against defendant; but in such action the measure of the damages recoverable would be the actual loss or damage sustained on account of the breach. The maximum amount recoverable would be the difference, if any, between the agreed compensation and the amount plaintiff earned or by reasonable effort could earn during the contract period. . . .

Thus, if plaintiff elected to acquiesce in his dismissal by the Board of Trustees, as expressed in its resolution, he was entitled thereunder to salary payments aggregating $4,175 for the year following notification of his dismissal and, *in addition*, was entitled to whatever he earned from other employment during that year. On the other hand, if plaintiff elected to treat his dismissal as wrongful and sue for damages for breach of contract, and obtained other employment in which he earned compensation equal to or in excess of his compensation as a member of the faculty of Catawba College, his recovery would be limited to nominal damages.

If plaintiff were wrongfully discharged, he could elect to pursue either course but not both; for his rights and remedies under the alternatives available to him were essentially different and inconsistent.

(2) "The whole doctrine of election is based on the theory that there are inconsistent rights or remedies of which a party may avail himself, and a choice of one is held to be an election not to pursue the other." . . . this statement expresses succinctly the well established rule in this jurisdiction.

(3) Plaintiff made his election when he accepted, endorsed and collected the salary checks aggregating $4,175.00, paid as directed by the resolution of the Board of Trustees, for the year following notification of his dismissal. The law will not permit him now to assert different rights or pursue a different remedy. Perhaps, when he made his election, his impression was that he could and would earn equal or greater compensation in other employment. Be that as it may, having made his election, whether he earned more or less than $4,175.00 from other employment during the year following notification of his dismissal has no bearing upon his right to maintain this action for alleged wrongful discharge.

Having reached the conclusion that plaintiff's said election constitutes a complete bar to his right to maintain this action, the judgment of nonsuit is affirmed.

Affirmed.

Jones v. *Hopper*
410 F.2d 1323
May 19, 1969

PER CURIAM

This appeal is from a judgment dismissing with prejudice the complaint of appellant Jones, an associate professor of philosophy. The basis of the dismissal was that the complaint failed to state a claim upon which relief could be granted. Appellees, who are the President and members of the Board of Trustees of Southern Colorado State College, filed the motion to dismiss upon which the judgment is based.

The dismissal of the complaint, drawn as a civil rights pleading, presents the issue of whether a claim is stated under the Civil Rights Act.

The complaint alleges jurisdictional facts, identity of parties, their residence and citizenship, and the status of the college.

The complaint alleges the powers of the Board of Trustees are as follows:

The Board of Trustees is vested by [§§ 124-17-1 and 124-5-1 Colo. Rev. Stats. (1963)] with the entire control and management of the affairs of the College, has general supervision of said College and the control and direction of the funds and appropriations made thereto, with power to appoint and remove all subordinate officers, professors, associate professors, teachers, assistants, employees or agents, in, about, or concerning said College, to appoint or employ, discharge and suspend, contract and fail to renew contracts of employees and other subordinates, and to fix the salaries of each and prescribe their several duties. They further have the power and authority to prescribe the various books and texts to be used in the Colleges, the courses of study and instruction and to make all needful rules, regulations and By Laws for the good government and management of the same. The actions of President Hopper, hereinafter described, were approved, authorized and ratified by said Board of Trustees, and each of them.

It is further alleged the acts complained of are exercised under color of the statutes, regulations, customs and usages vesting the power above averred.

The complaint further alleges that Jones was given notice that his services would be terminated at the end of the academic year by a letter sent from the President and authorized by the Board which is attached to the complaint as Exhibit A.*

---

* Exhibit A: "February 25, 1966 Dr. George Jones, Jr. 1401 Greenwood Pueblo, Colorado 81003 Dear Dr. Jones: I regret to inform you that at the end of this academic year, your services with Southern Colorado State College will be terminated.

The complaint then continues with a partial description of the "John Dean case" referred to in the above exhibit.

The *curriculum vitae* of appellant Jones is set forth in the complaint as well as the details of his association and status with Southern Colorado State College. In this description of his status with the college, Jones points out that the duration of each appointment under which he served was one year and that it was at the end of his second appointment that the appellees determined he would not be reappointed.

The allegations then conclude that the reason Jones was not reappointed was because he had exercised his constitutionally protected rights in the following manner:

(a) He objected to the disqualification of an applicant for his department because the applicant was an Oriental.

(b) He attacked an English department textbook in a student newspaper.

(c) He founded an independent faculty-student publication which contained articles criticizing the war in Viet Nam, commenting on labor problems and pacifism, and an article objecting to monitored classrooms.

(d) He supported the student, John Dean, referred to above in Exhibit A, who had been committed to a hospital pursuant to a court order obtained by his parents as a result of the student's attempt to register with his draft board as a conscientious objector.

Jones averred he was a pacifist by a religious conviction and that his views expressed orally and by writing on this subject were an exercise of his religious freedom.

He concluded that because of the above conduct and actions an expectancy of continued employment was terminated which was an injury to an interest which the law will protect against invasion by acts in violation of the Civil Rights Act.

Jones alleges he was damaged as a result of the failure to renew his teaching contract, and relief is prayed for in the amount of $300,000.00.

The second claim of Jones's complaint by reference adopts the foregoing allegations describing them as a conspiracy to punish him for exercising his constitutional rights granted by the First and Fourteenth Amendments. He further concludes he was denied equal protection under the law.

"So that there will be no misunderstanding, I wish to point out that this decision was arrived at before the publicity surrounding the John Dean case. Prior to the John Dean case, the Chairman of the Division and the Dean of the College and I agreed upon this decision. The Chairman of the Executive Committee of the College from the Trustees of State Colleges in Colorado was likewise informed at that time.

"I trust and hope that you will find future employment which will be satisfying to you. Yours truly, /s/ J. V. Hopper, President."

(1, 2) The basic requirements of a complaint based upon 42 U.S.C. § 1983 are: (1) that the conduct complained of was engaged in under color of state law, and (2) that such conduct subjected the plaintiff to a deprivation of rights, privileges, or immunities secured by the Federal Constitution and laws. The allegations necessary to state such a claim, as in the case of any other civil action in the federal courts, are not to be held insufficient unless it appears beyond doubt that the plaintiff can prove no set of facts in support of his claim which would entitle him to relief.

When we examine the complaint herein in the light of the foregoing rules, we are directed to ask: What guaranteed right, privilege or immunity was denied Jones which is protected under the Constitution and laws?

The complaint alleges the refusal of the appellees to reappoint Jones after the term of his current appointment expired.

Jones contends the appellees, authorized by the Colorado statutes to administer the college, have denied him a right of expectancy to continued employment because he exercised freely his constitutional rights of speech, publication and religion. Jones cites only *Bomar* v. *Keyes* as authority recognizing this expectancy interest.

* * *

(3) The complaint in our case makes no allegation or inference that a contract existed. Jones's complaint expressly concedes that his "termination was not a breach of contract," thereby admitting that a contract did not exist. Accordingly, the interest which Jones seeks to assert cannot be derived from a contract.

We now look to the Federal Constitution and laws for the source of the interest secured.

The Supreme Court has consistently held, "the interest of a government employee in retaining his job, can be summarily denied." It has become a settled principle that government employment, in the absence of legislation, can be revoked at the will of the appointing officer. The principle stated teaches that public employment may be denied altogether subject, however, to the restriction that unreasonable conditions may not be imposed upon the granting of public employment. There is nothing in the complaint to warrant an inference or conclusion that the Colorado statute or its application herein went "beyond what might be justified in the exercise of the State's legitimate inquiry into the fitness and competency of its teachers."

(4) As a matter of fact, there are no allegations relating to conditions of employment of professors or assistant professors at Southern Colorado State College. The complaint merely alleges the duties and authority of the administrators. Therefore, we can find nowhere in the complaint an allegation of any identified interest which is secured by the Federal Constitution or laws.

The complaint alleges a Colorado institution involved, governed by the laws of Colorado identified in the pleading. Appellant was a professor at this institution of learning. "It is clear that a professor is not an officer, but an employe under contract to fill a chair of learning."

The complaint alleges Jones was appointed for an academic year and then reappointed and served the entire second appointment. He was notified he would not be reappointed for a third academic year. The alleged interest deprived was in the appointment for a third year. It is admitted he did not have a tenure privilege either by Colorado law or contract. "Among the most fundamental rules of the law of master and servant is that which recognizes that, absent an applicable statutory or contractual provision to the contrary, an employer enjoys an absolute power of dismissing his employee, with or without cause."

Southern Colorado State College is a state academic institution organized and existing under Colorado law which vests the government and management of its affairs in a board of trustees which has among other vestitures "power to appoint and remove all subordinate officers, professors, associate professors, teachers, assistants, employees or agents, in, or about, or concerning said college, to appoint or employ, discharge and suspend contract and fail to renew contracts of employees and other subordinates." (recited in complaint as set forth, supra)

(5) We think this provision precludes Jones from having the relief he seeks in this proceeding. His claimed interest must find its source in his expired appointment which constituted whatever contract existed. The provision above acknowledged became a part of any contract that may have existed between him and the college.

(6) The provision specifically denies an expectancy to continued employment; therefore, absent an expectancy, there could be no interest. "One has no constitutional right to a 'remedy' against the lawful conduct of another."

(7) As demonstrated above the right, privilege or immunity Jones alleges he was deprived of is nonexistent.

(8) We believe the appellees herein were exercising a discretion given them by the power vested under the Colorado statute set forth in the complaint. The exercise of this discretion cannot, under the facts alleged in the complaint, become unlawful conduct which would justify its falling within the ambit of the Civil Rights Act.

> Because of the special needs of the university, both public and private, great discretion must be given it in decisions about the renewal of contracts during the probationary period. In deciding whether to rehire or grant tenure, the considerations involved go well beyond a judgment about general teaching competence.
> "Will the interests of an institution of learning be promoted by dispensing with the services of a particular professor?" And yet if we assume that the statute of the state is of any virtue, it is just such a

question that the plaintiff in error sought to have determined in the Circuit Court. It is a question which, in our opinion, the Legislature intended to commit to the sound judgment of the regents who are selected because of an especial fitness for the performance of such duties, and who, by their experience and their intimate familiarity with the institution, are qualified to exercise that discretion in a far sounder manner than any court or jury could be qualified by evidence adduced through witnesses. It is elementary that no cause of action can arise from the lawful exercise of a statutory power in the absence of an express provision conferring it. It is also a principle of law as securely founded that an exercise of a power by an administrative board or officer to whose judgment and discretion it is committed is not a proper subject of review by the courts when fraud or conditions equivalent thereto do not exist.

It would be intolerable for the courts to interject themselves and to require an educational institution to hire or to maintain on its staff a professor or instructor whom it deemed undesirable and did not wish to employ. For the courts to impose such a requirement would be an interference with the operation of institutions of higher learning contrary to established principles of law and to the best traditions of education.

* * *

The trial court concluded that under the Colorado statutes the exercise of discretion was authorized and justified. We agree and affirm. Affirmed.

SETH, Circuit Judge, with whom HOLLOWAY, Circuit Judge, joins (dissenting) :

This case comes to us on the dismissal of plaintiff's complaint for failure to state a claim. The majority has held that the complaint is legally insufficient because the plaintiff has asserted no "right" or "interest" to be protected by the Constitution. I must disagree because in my opinion the allegations are sufficient under the decisions of the Supreme Court for the case to be brought to trial.

The complaint describes plaintiff's two contracts of employment each for a year and asserts an expectancy of continued employment thereafter. He further alleges that he received a notice of termination. This letter advised him in part: "I regret to inform you that at the end of this academic year, your services with Southern Colorado State College will be terminated." There was no reference to any contract, but his services were terminated at the expiration date of his contract then in force. The plaintiff alleges that his services were so terminated solely because of his exercise of First Amendment rights.

The majority bases its opinion on the proposition that there was no "expectancy" of further employment, and thus the plaintiff had no "interest" to be protected by the First Amendment to entitle him to relief. The majority finds no "expectancy" by referring to the statutory powers of the trustees of the school to hire and fire (Colo. Rev. Stat. 1963, §§ 124-17-1 and 124-17-5), and states that:

> The provision specifically denies an expectancy to continued employment, therefore, absent an expectancy, there could be no interest . . .

The majority then holds that there is no "interest," therefore no cause of action was alleged. The majority thus holds that under this Colorado statute, and apparently in the absence of a contractual provision or of tenure specifically provided by statute, the board has unlimited power to discharge teachers. It holds that "beyond doubt" plaintiff could not prove otherwise. This is in error on two grounds; the first is that plaintiff could very well prove an "expectancy of continued employment to exist outside any specific contractual or statutory provision, if this be necessary, and secondly, the board's power to discharge cannot be unlimited as the holding of the majority assumes."

To consider first the power to discharge, it appears that college professors may be "employees," as the majority says, as contrasted to "public officers"; but nevertheless they have many additional and unique prerequisites, privileges, rights and concurrent burdens, obligations, and ethical standards which have been added, assumed, and accepted over a long period of time as part of their professorial positions. To categorize them as "employees" is not helpful, nor is it really descriptive because it is incomplete. The majority then quotes from authorities to say that the fundamental rule of the master-servant relationship is that ". . . an employer enjoys an absolute power of dismissing his employee, with or without cause." As a practical matter, this again hardly fits the relationship between trustees or regents of a college or university and the professors or the lesser teachers at such an institution. . . . Under this prevailing case law, I cannot agree that the Board here concerned had an unlimited discretion to discharge plaintiff. To include within the Board's discretion by statute, practice, or employment status the right to discharge for the exercise of First Amendment rights is certainly to attach unreasonable conditions to plaintiff's employment.

The Board certainly has broad discretion over the teaching staff and administrators, and is charged with the duty of operating the school in an orderly, effective, and professional manner. They can discipline and discharge those whose actions and words unduly interfere with teaching programs or with the teaching by others on the staff, or otherwise seriously disrupt the operation of the school. . . . But no matter how broad their discretion may be by statute or by custom it cannot be used to deprive teachers of their constitutional rights. This is what plaintiff has alleged, and this is sufficient. Whether he can prove it is indeed another matter, and a matter which has not yet been reached in this case.

* * *

The exercise of constitutional rights cannot create for a teacher or be used as some sort of a protection or insulation against discharge for proper and adequate reasons, nor can it be under Pickering without limit any more than can the exercise of discretion by the Board. As to the position of the majority that plaintiff could not prove as a fact and beyond doubt an "expectancy" of continued employment, it must be observed that consideration is given in the opinion only to possible contractual and statutory provisions. The expectancy, if one is required, could very well arise from other sources or be based on school rules, practice, or custom as observed above. The plaintiff has alleged as a fact that there was such an expectancy. This is probably a mixed fact and law assertion, but we must assume on this appeal that the fact elements are capable of proof unless there is some legal bar. The majority says that the statutory powers of the trustees are such a bar, and also says that nothing arises by contract or statute.

The power bar has been considered above, but it is intertwined with the tenure or expectancy matter, and is mentioned again. But what is this "interest" or "expectancy" requirement? It would appear that a tenure requirement as a basis for asserting a cause of action has been long abandoned. . . . Teachers of whatever status do not give up First Amendment rights by reason of their employment. Pickering expressly so holds. Nontenure teachers cannot be held to have more limited constitutional rights than do others. They are on a temporary basis not for reasons related to the problems before us, but instead on the quality of their teaching. Tenure is not the status which gives rise to the right to be protected. Tenure as a requirement for standing or to assert a cause of action has disappeared. The "expectancy" requirement of the majority does not seem greatly different from tenure. Some "interest" in continued employment or "expectancy" is an essential ingredient of both. This "expectancy" is perhaps a tenuous sort of tenure, but it is nevertheless such a requirement, and in my opinion can no longer be made.

I would thus hold that the complaint is sufficient as measured by the standards in the recent decisions of the Supreme Court, and the case should come on for trial.

3
Conflict of Interest

Jones v. *Board of Control*
131 Fla. 713 (131 So.2d 713)
June 23, 1961

THORNAL, Justice

Appellant Jones seeks reversal of a final judgment denying to him recovery for an alleged breach of his contract of employment as a professor at the University of Florida.

Numerous points for reversal are assigned but the principal contention revolves around the validity of a rule of the appellee Board which prohibits its employees from seeking election to public office.

The appellee, Board of Control, which supervises the operations of the State Universities, employed the appellant Jones as an interim associate professor of law at the University of Florida for the academic year 1959–1960. Compensation was to be paid monthly over a ten-month period, although appellee's teaching duties started on September 6, 1959 and would have terminated in normal course on June 6, 1960. The contract between the parties was evidenced by a document designated "notice of contract for academic staff," which was approved and accepted by the appellant. The notice of contract likewise included the provisions of the Constitution of the University of Florida, as well as the rules promulgated by appellee Board of Control.

On February 18, 1960, the dean of academic affairs, by letter, informed Mr. Jones that the filing of qualifying papers establishing eligibility and intention to run for public office would be considered as conclusive evidence of the breach of a Board of Control rule which prohibited its employees from seeking election to public office. On February 29, 1960, Professor Jones filed with the Secretary of State his papers qualifying to seek the nomination for the office of circuit judge in the next ensuing primary to be held May 5, 1960. On the next day

Mr. Jones was called to the office of the President of the University and was informed of his dismissal because of his violation of the rule which we shall later quote in full. He was paid through March 1, 1960. Two days later Mr. Jones demanded a hearing by a faculty committee, which he claimed to be a privilege granted to him by the University Constitution. In consequence of a hearing held March 9, 1960, the faculty committee found that the President had acted within the authority of the rule in question. Thereafter on March 25, 1960, appellant was accorded a hearing by the appellee Board of Control, which thereupon also affirmed the President's action. Claiming a breach of the employment contract for various reasons, which we shall discuss, Mr. Jones brought this action seeking compensation allegedly due him for the remainder of the contract term subsequent to March 1, 1960. For all practical purposes, the parties stipulated to the salient facts. The trial judge entered a judgment upholding the validity of the rule in dispute and sustaining the action of the University officials in dismissing appellant Jones. Reversal of this judgment is now sought.

We shall undertake to dispose of a number of the incidental questions preliminary to our ultimate discussion of the constitutional question raised by the appellant.

Article XV, Section 5, of the Constitution of the University of Florida provides as follows:

> Dismissal of a member of the Academic staff as distinguished from termination of appointment as defined in Article XVI may not be effected except for serious cause and on the basis of written and specific charges filed by an administrative officer of the part of the University directly concerned or by the President. In answer to such charges the faculty member shall have a hearing before a committee of the faculty appointed by the President. Opportunity shall be given the accused to challenge for cause the appointment of any faculty member to this committee. At this hearing and at any hearings of its own that the Board of Control may wish to conduct, the defendant shall be allowed the benefit of counsel of his own choosing at his own expense. Except in cases of flagrant offense, dismissal shall not become effective until at least sixty days after action by the Board of Control.
>
> In case of flagrant offense the President may suspend a member of the academic staff from performance of his duties and, after an expeditious hearing, recommend immediate dismissal to the Board of Control. When dismissal is ordered in such cases by the Board of Control it shall be effective at once.

The Board of Control rule which prohibits its employees from seeking election to public office provides as follows:

> 1. Employees under the jurisdiction of the Board of Control are

prohibited from seeking election to public office. Any employee desiring to engage in a political campaign for public office shall first submit his resignation to the Board.

(1) The trial judge concluded that applicable statutes, the University Constitution, the valid regulations of the appellee Board of Control and the faculty handbook, specifically referred to in the notice of contract, together with the provisions of the last-mentioned document, comprised the composite contractual arrangement between Professor Jones and the Board of Control. In so holding, the trial judge ruled correctly. . . .

(2, 3) Professor Jones insists that he was denied procedural due process because of the alleged failure of the University officials to meet the requirements of Article XV, Section 5, University Constitution, supra. He claims that they failed to comply with the rule regarding the filing of specific charges, the hearing before a faculty committee and the postponement of ultimate dismissal until at least sixty days after final action by the appellee Board of Control. We find little merit in this contention. In the first place, if the rule pursuant to which the appellant was dismissed is valid, then he breached his contract by qualifying to seek election to public office. When he filed his papers and paid his qualifying fee, which was substantial, he certainly proclaimed his desire and intention to engage in a political campaign for public office. The rule in effect required that he submit his resignation to the Board before doing so. Inasmuch as this is an action on the contract, Mr. Jones will not be permitted to recover for his own breach. We agree further with the trial judge when he concluded that the willful conduct of the appellant in announcing his specific and well-planned intention to violate the rule of the appellee Board constituted not only a "serious cause" but actually a "flagrant offense," within the provisions of Article XV, Section 5, of the University Constitution, supra. As we read the applicable provision, such an offense justified immediate suspension by the President and a prompt hearing with immediate dismissal by the appellee Board. So far as procedural due process is concerned, we have little difficulty in concluding that the appellant has enjoyed a full measure in the instant matter.

(4) It is next asserted that the rule regarding the political activities of employees of the appellee Board was beyond the contemplation of the Legislature in the enactment of Section 240.04, Florida Statutes, F.S.A. That legislative act provides in part, "the Board of Control has jurisdiction over the complete management and control of all the said several institutions, and each and every of them, to wit: The University of Florida . . . ." The statute further provides that the Board is "invested with full power and authority to make all rules and regulations necessary for their governance, nor inconsistent with the general rules

and regulations . . . made at any joint meeting of the said board with the state board of education." The appellee Board by the same statute is empowered "to appoint all the managers, faculty, teachers, servants, and employees, and to remove the same as in their judgment and discretion may be best." A more comprehensive legislative authorization to an administrative agency, such as the appellee, could hardly be conceived. It is perfectly clear that the Legislature has endowed the appellee Board with extensive powers to operate the State's institutions of higher learning subject only, of course, to the specific limitations of the authorizing statute. Assuming the rule in question to be constitutionally valid, as we hereafter find it to be, there is no doubt whatever but that it is well within the limits of the legislative prescriptions announced in Section 240.04, supra.

* * *

(6) We now proceed to the assault on the rule on the basis of appellant's constitutional claims. It appears to be the position of Professor Jones that the restriction imposed upon college professors prohibiting them from seeking public office encroaches on their rights as citizens to run for public office and impinges on their liberty generically described as "academic freedom."

Nowhere in the briefs are we supplied with a definition of the term "academic freedom" or the outer limits thereof if any are recognized to exist. This apparent shortcoming in the otherwise excellent briefs is quite understandable for the simple reason that in none of the authorities mentioned and in none of the authorities discovered by our own research is the term given any definitive meaning. As contended for by the appellant, however, we understand the expression "academic freedom" to comprehend a claimed privilege of scholars and academicians and teachers generally to teach without restriction either to subject matter or as to limitation on collateral activities. Should we adopt literally the position of the appellant, it appears to us that we would be compelled to concede that a license to teach in a public school system is subject to no regulations whatsoever regarding either the nature of the subject matter to be taught or the time and effort that may be required to be devoted to the classrooms.

We should not lose sight of the fact that Professor Jones is insisting upon continued public employment in a public institution in the face of a violation of a rule apparently in full force and effect when he was engaged for the service and which we must assume that he knew, or should have known, particularly in view of his professional stature as a lawyer and a law professor.

Although we might appropriately do so, we find it unnecessary to approach a solution through the narrow corridor suggested by Justice Holmes in his descriptive dictum that "The petitioner [a policeman] may have a constitutional right to talk politics, but he has no constitutional right to be a policeman." . . . To this end, we do not find it necessary to restrict our perspective to the limited concept, in a measure now outmoded, that a person has no constitutional right to government employment. We think that we can dispose of our problem on a much broader plateau of reasoning with the view that any right which an individual does have to work for the government or to continue in the public employ or to seek public office must necessarily be subject to all reasonable rules and regulations promulgated by the government in the interest of the public and for the well-being of the public services. The appellant claims the right to teach in a State institution pursuant to his contract. The appellee simply replies with the assertion of the power to promulgate reasonable regulations of the appellant's conduct of his employment in the interest of the public and particularly the students who depend upon the professor for their instruction.

(7) Here the appellant contends that the rule of the appellee Board which prohibits its employees from seeking election to public office denied to him substantive due process, contrary to the provisions of the First and Fourteenth Amendments to the Constitution of the United States, and Sections 12 and 13 of the Declaration of Rights, Florida Constitution, F.S.A. To this end it is contended that the Board's rule, when applied to the plaintiff, unreasonably interferes with his right to seek work in a capacity for which he had been professionally trained, to wit: the position of circuit judge. Likewise, asserts the appellant, the rule unreasonably interferes with his right to work and earn a living as a teacher. Implicit in these contentions is a recognition of the limitations thereof. In each instance the plaintiff contends that there has been an "unreasonable" interference with the asserted right. Necessarily this leads to a conclusion that if the rule does not unreasonably interfere with the ascertained right, then the rule must be upheld. Appellant's argument necessarily recognizes a truism to the effect that the right to teach or the right to seek public office is not a constitutional absolute. Each of the privileges is subject to reasonable restraint and reasonable conditions. The test of reasonableness in either situation involves a consideration of the nature of the right asserted by the individual and the extent that it is necessary to restrict the assertion of the right in the interest of the public.

* * *

The holding . . . however, is far removed from the rule applicable in the case at bar. Here, the rule promulgated by the Board of Control had no relevancy whatever to the subjects which Professor Jones might teach. It dealt merely with his right to teach and simultaneously carry on a political campaign for an elective public office. The rule prohibits no one from teaching. Neither does it prohibit a teacher from running for public office. It merely provides that he cannot do both simultaneously. There is adequate justification for the rule in the public

interest, as well as in the interest of the University student body which
looks to its professors for instruction. As the circuit judge points out,
there are many reasons why the appellee Board would be justified in
placing restrictions on the University faculty in connection with political campaigns. The demands upon the time and energies incident to
a warmly contested campaign for an important public office would necessarily affect the efficiency of the candidate; the potential effect upon
the students, not only as the result of such inefficiency, but also in the
nature of the political influences that might be brought to bear upon
them would be further justification; the potential involvement of the
State University, which is dependent upon public support from all
political elements, would be another major consideration supporting
the reasonableness of the rule. Although appellant suggests that he
might well have conducted his campaign in the evening so as not to
interfere with his professorial duties, the reasons which we have
epitomized above would still apply. Moreover, anyone who has ever
been associated with a heated political campaign well knows that it
involves handshaking, speech making, telephone calling, letter writing,
and door-to-door campaigning from morning well into the night. To
anyone familiar with the practical aspects of American politics, it is
asking too much to expect him to agree that success in a strenuous political campaign can be achieved merely by appearances at Saturday afternoon fish fries or early evening precinct rallies. The result simply is
that it would be extremely difficult for a university professor to conduct
his classroom courses with efficiency over a period of eight to ten weeks
while simultaneously "beating the bushes" in search of votes to elevate
him to the position of a circuit judge.

* * *

We hold that the rule of the appellee Board here under assault is
constitutional. When appellant willfully ignored the rule, he breached
his preexisting contract with appellee. Having breached the contract
himself, appellant is not entitled to the recovery sought. The judgment
in favor of the appellee is affirmed.

THOMAS, C.J., and TERRELL, HOBSON, ROBERTS, DREW
and O'CONNELL, JJ., concur.

Colorado School of Mines v. *Neighbors*
119 Colo. 399 (203 P.2d 904)
March 7, 1949

HILLIARD, Chief Justice

Originally this was an action by Colorado School of Mines, hereinafter
identified as the School, against W. Doy Neighbors and Mary Doe

Neighbors, husband and wife, for certain rentals alleged to be due from them. That feature of the litigation, however, was amicably adjusted in the trial court and is not considered on this review. What does require our attention grows out of a counterclaim by defendant in error, W. Doy Neighbors, against the School for damages, in which his wife, the other defendant in error, is not interested. The counterclaim is based on the alleged breach of a contract of employment between Neighbors and the School, evidenced, as presently will be stated, and on which he enjoyed judgment below in the sum of $1,148.61.

It appears that Neighbors received a letter from the School, in which it was stated that he had been appointed "director of physical education for the regular or academic school year at a salary of $2,750.00 to be paid in twelve equal monthly installments . . . beginning as of September 1, 1945, and ending August 31, 1946." He accepted the appointment, entered upon the discharge of the duties of the position, and, without complaint or criticism in relation to his services, as such, he served until February 9, 1946, when, pursuant to a resolution of the board of trustees of the School, his employment as director of physical education was terminated, and, as stated in the notice of dismissal, he was to be paid "that proportion of your full annual salary which your period of service during the school year 1945–46 up to February 9, 1946, bears to the full school year." On that basis he was paid the sum of $1,601.39. For the remainder of the term of his employment, and but for such discharge, Neighbors would have earned $1,148.61 additional, which was the sum the jury found constituted his damages, and for which he was given judgment, as already stated.

Counsel for the School make two contentions: One, that since Neighbors "elected to take outside work," it "acted within its power and authority in terminating the . . . employment contract." Two, that, in any event, Neighbors earned otherwise during the period he was not permitted to discharge the duties of his contracted employment as much or more than the sum of his alleged loss, hence, as argued by counsel for the School, "the result is zero."

The letter of dismissal does not assign the reason therefor, but other evidence indicated that it was premised on the fact that that during hours not in conflict with those to be devoted to his duties as physical director, Neighbors was employed as "manager of a cocktail lounge in the LaRay Hotel in Golden." He was advised that "You must give up your employment in connection with the dispensing of liquors if you wish to remain on the Faculty at this institution." Neighbors freely admitted the extra employment, but maintained, nevertheless, that since he had not failed in the discharge of his contractual obligation, validity did not attend the order of dismissal in the sense that thereby he would be despoiled of the compensation provided in the contract of his employment. It is important to note that Neighbors was not a stranger on the campus of the School. On the contrary, it appears that beginning in September, 1937, and until February 9, 1946, when he was discharged, as we have seen, he had been employed by the School, first as assistant coach, second, as coach, and from September 1, 1945 to August 31, 1946, as contracted, but terminated earlier, as already stated, as director of physical education. A further significant fact, although not originally known by the board of trustees of the School, is that, at the time Neighbors and the School entered into the contract of his reliance, he was engaged in the activity emphasized by the School in justification of its order of dismissal.

(1, 2) 1. It is understandable that the board of trustees of the School would not look with favor on Neighbors's employment in a cocktail lounge in the very midst of the School's activities, even though such employment did not conflict with the hours of his contractual employment, or otherwise impair his services in that regard. Since Neighbors would not consent to desist in the cocktail employment, the trustees of the School worked a separation of what they considered an intolerable situation, and dismissed Neighbors from the faculty. None will say, we think, that moral justification did not attend the action of the trustees in the premises. But did legality attend? The School had the power to exclude Neighbors from the service contemplated in the contract of his employment, which it exercised, as already stated. But does it follow that its formal order of dismissal worked legal termination of its contractual obligation to pay salary for the term, and in the sum set forth in the contract? We think not. "When a servant is discharged, without a sufficient legal excuse, before the expiration of his term . . . he may defer suit until the end of the term [as here], and sue for the actual damages he has sustained, which, however, can in no case exceed the wages for the entire term." . . . At no time of importance here was it illegal to serve or be employed in dispensing liquors. . . . Considering the foregoing, and that the contract of employment involved here contained no provision in relation to how Neighbors should employ his time when not engaged in his contractual duties, nor that he should not engage in dispensing liquors during such time, plus the fact that in relation to the discharge of his duties under the contract there was no complaint, we think that in the sense of its liability for salary as contracted, the School breached its obligation.

2. We proceed now on the claim of the School's counsel that for the period between February 9, 1946, the date of his dismissal, to September 1, 1946, when by its terms the contract of employment would have terminated, Neighbors earned otherwise, and received, a sum in excess of his adjudged recovery. Concededly for the period involved, as our study of the record convinces, Neighbors, proceeding in other employment, earned and received money greatly in excess of the sum adjudged in his favor. In operating the "Golden Nugget Cafe," Neighbors testified

that through June, July and August, 1946, he enjoyed a net income of "around $1,500," and he engaged in other activities to his considerable profit. The entire story in mind, Neighbors suffered no substantial damage.

(3) 3. Since there was a breach of the contract, however, and regardless of what Neighbors otherwise earned and received during the period of his enforced separation from his employment with the School, he is "entitled to nominal damages and his costs." . . .

Let the cause be remanded, and on receipt of our formal remittitur the trial court will vacate its former judgment as to sum, and in lieu thereof adjudge recovery in a nominal sum, together with costs, as originally judged.

ALTER, J., does not participate.

4
Academic Freedom

Sweezy v. *New Hampshire*
354 U.S. 234, 257
June 17, 1957
(Majority opinion of WARREN, C.J., omitted)
FRANKFURTER, J., concurring in result

Pursuant to an investigation of subversive activities authorized by a joint resolution of both houses of the New Hampshire Legislature, the State Attorney General subpoenaed petitioner before him on January 8, 1954, for extensive questioning. Among the matters about which petitioner was questioned were: details of his career and personal life, whether he was then or ever had been a member of the Communist Party, whether he had ever attended its meetings, whether he had ever attended meetings that he knew were also attended by Party members, whether he knew any Communists in or out of the State, whether he knew named persons with alleged connections with organizations either on the United States Attorney General's list or cited by the Un-American Activities Committee of the United States House of Representatives or had ever attended meetings with them, whether he had ever taught or supported the overthrow of the State by force or violence or had ever known or assisted any persons or groups that had done so, whether he had ever been connected with organizations on the Attorney General's list, whether he had supported or written in behalf of a variety of allegedly subversive, named causes, conferences, periodicals, petitions, and attempts to raise funds for the legal defense of certain persons, whether he knew about the Progressive Party, what positions he had held in it, whether he had been a candidate for Presidential Elector for that Party, whether certain persons were in that Party, whether Communists had influenced or been members of the Progressive Party, whether he had sponsored activities in behalf of the candidacy of Henry A. Wallace, whether he advocated replacing the capitalist system with another eco-

265

nomic system, whether his conception of socialism involved force and violence, whether by his writings and actions he had ever attempted to advance the Soviet Union's "propaganda line," whether he had ever attended meetings of the Liberal Club at the University of New Hampshire, whether the magazine of which he was coeditor was "a Communist-line publication," and whether he knew named persons.

Petitioner answered most of these questions, making it very plain that he had never been a Communist, never taught violent overthrow of the Government, never knowingly associated with Communists in the State, but was a socialist believer in peaceful change who had at one time belonged to certain organizations on the list of the United States Attorney General (which did not include the Progressive Party) or cited by the House Un-American Activities Committee. He declined to answer as irrelevant or violative of free speech guarantees certain questions about the Progressive Party and whether he knew particular persons. He stated repeatedly, however, that he had no knowledge of Communists or of Communist influence in the Progressive Party, and he testified that he had been a candidate for that Party, signing the required loyalty oath, and that he did not know whether an alleged Communist leader was active in the Progressive Party.

Despite the exhaustive scope of this inquiry, the Attorney General again subpoenaed petitioner to testify on June 3, 1954, and the interrogation was similarly sweeping. Petitioner again answered virtually all questions, including those concerning the relationship of named persons to the Communist Party or other causes deemed subversive under state laws, alleged Communist influence on all organizations with which he had been connected including the Progressive Party, and his own participation in organizations other than the Progressive Party and its antecedent, the Progressive Citizens of America. He refused, however, to answer certain questions regarding (1) a lecture given by him at the University of New Hampshire, (2) activities of himself and others in the Progressive political organizations, and (3) "opinions and beliefs," invoking the constitutional guarantees of free speech.

The Attorney General then petitioned the Superior Court to order petitioner to answer questions in these categories. The court ruled that petitioner had to answer those questions pertaining to the lectures and to the Progressive Party and its predecessor but not those otherwise pertaining to "opinions and beliefs." Upon petitioner's refusal to answer the questions sanctioned by the court, he was found in contempt of court and ordered committed to the county jail until purged of contempt.

The Supreme Court of New Hampshire affirmed the order of the Superior Court. It held that the questions at issue were relevant and that no constitutional provision permitted petitioner to frustrate the State's demands. 100 N.H. 103, 121 A. 2d 783.

The questions that petitioner refused to answer regarding the university lecture, the third given by him in three years at the invitation of the faculty for humanities, were:

What was the subject of your lecture?
Didn't you tell the class at the University of New Hampshire on Monday, March 22, 1954, that Socialism was inevitable in this country?
Did you advocate Marxism at that time?
Did you express the opinion, or did you make the statement at that time that Socialism was inevitable in America?
Did you in this last lecture on March 22 or in any of the former lectures espouse the theory of dialectical materialism?
I have in the file here a statement from a person who attended your class, and I will read it in part because I don't want you to think I am just fishing. "His talk this time was on the inevitability of the Socialist program. It was a glossed-over interpretation of the materialist dialectic." Now again I ask you the original question.

In response to the first question of this series, petitioner had said at the hearing:

I would like to say one thing in this connection, Mr. Wyman. I stated under oath at my last appearance that, and I now repeat it, that I do not advocate or in any way further the aim of overthrowing constitutional government by force and violence. I did not so advocate in the lecture I gave at the University of New Hampshire. In fact I have never at any time so advocated in a lecture anywhere. Aside from that I have nothing I want to say about the lecture in question.

The New Hampshire Supreme Court, although recognizing that such inquiries "undoubtedly interfered with the defendant's free exercise" of his constitutionally guaranteed right to lecture, justified the interference on the ground that it would occur "in the limited area in which the legislative committee may reasonably believe that the overthrow of existing government by force and violence is being or has been taught, advocated or planned, an area in which the interest of the State justifies this intrusion upon civil liberties." . . . According to the court, the facts that made reasonable the Committee's belief that petitioner had taught violent overthrow in his lecture were that he was a Socialist with a record of affiliation with groups cited by the Attorney General of the United States or the House Un-American Activities Committee and that he was coeditor of an article stating that, although the authors hated violence, it was less to be deplored when used by the Soviet Union than by capitalist countries.

When weighed against the grave harm resulting from governmental intrusion into the intellectual life of a university, such justification for compelling a witness to discuss the contents of his lecture appears grossly inadequate. Particularly is this so where the witness has sworn that neither in the lecture nor at any other time did he ever advocate overthrowing the Government by force and violence.

Progress in the natural sciences is not remotely confined to findings made in the laboratory. Insights into the mysteries of nature are born of hypothesis and speculation. The more so is this true in the pursuit of understanding in the groping endeavors of what are called the social sciences, the concern of which is man and society. The problems that are the respective preoccupations of anthropology, economics, law, psychology, sociology and related areas of scholarship are merely departmentalized dealing, by way of manageable division of analysis, with interpenetrating aspects of holistic perplexities. For society's good—if understanding be an essential need of society—inquiries into these problems, speculations about them, stimulation in others of reflection upon them, must be left as unfettered as possible. Political power must abstain from intrusion into this activity of freedom, pursued in the interest of wise government and the people's well-being, except for reasons that are exigent and obviously compelling.

These pages need not be burdened with proof, based on the testimony of a cloud of impressive witnesses, of the dependence of a free society on free universities. This means the exclusion of governmental intervention in the intellectual life of a university. It matters little whether such intervention occurs avowedly or through action that inevitably tends to check the ardor and fearlessness of scholars, qualities at once so fragile and so indispensable for fruitful academic labor. One need only refer to the address of T. H. Huxley at the opening of Johns Hopkins University, the Annual Reports of President A. Lawrence Lowell of Harvard, the Reports of the University Grants Committee in Great Britain, as illustrative items in a vast body of literature. Suffice it to quote the latest expression on this subject. It is also perhaps the most poignant, because its plea on behalf of continuing the free spirit of the open universities of South Africa has gone unheeded.

> In a university knowledge is its own end, not merely a means to an end. A university ceases to be true to its own nature if it becomes the tool of Church or State or any sectional interest. A university is characterized by the spirit of free inquiry, its ideal being the ideal of Socrates—"to follow the argument where it leads." This implies the right to examine, question, modify or reject traditional ideas and beliefs. Dogma and hypothesis are incompatible, and the concept of an immutable doctrine is repugnant to the spirit of a university. The concern of its scholars is not merely to add and revise facts in relation to an accepted framework, but to be ever examining and modifying the framework itself.
>
> Freedom to reason and freedom for disputation on the basis of observation and experiment are the necessary conditions for the

advancement of scientific knowledge. A sense of freedom is also necessary for creative work in the arts which, equally with scientific research, is the concern of the university.

. . . It is the business of a university to provide that atmosphere which is most conducive to speculation, experiment and creation. It is an atmosphere in which there prevail " the four essential freedoms" of a university—to determine for itself on academic grounds who may teach, what may be taught, how it shall be taught, and who may be admitted to study. The Open Universities in South Africa 10–12. (A statment of a conference of senior scholars from the University of Cape Town and the University of the Witwatersrand, including A. v d.S. Centlivres and Richard Feetham, as Chancellors of the respective universities.)

I do not suggest that what New Hampshire has here sanctioned bears any resemblance to the policy against which this South African remonstrance was directed. I do say that in these matters of the spirit inroads on legitimacy must be resisted to their incipiency. This kind of evil grows by what it is allowed to feed on. The admonition of this Court in another context is applicable here. "It may be that it is the obnoxious thing in its mildest and least repulsive form; but illegitimate and unconstitutional practices get their first footing in that way, namely, by silent approaches and slight deviations from legal modes of procedure."

Petitioner stated, in response to questions at the hearing, that he did not know of any Communist interest in, connection with, influence over, activity in, or manipulation of the Progressive Party. He refused to answer, despite court order, the following questions on the ground that, by inquiring into the activities of a lawful political organization, they infringed upon the inviolability of the right to privacy in his political thoughts, actions and associations:

Was she, Nancy Sweezy, your wife, active in the formation of the Progressive Citizens of America?
Was Nancy Sweezy then working with individuals who were then members of the Communist Party?*
Was Charles Beebe active in forming the Progressive Citizens of America?
Did he work with your present wife—Did Charles Beebe work with your present wife in 1947?
Did it [a meeting at the home of one Abraham Walenko] have anything to do with the Progressive Party?

* Inclusion of this question among the unanswered questions appears to have been an oversight in view of the fact that petitioner attempted to answer it at the hearing by stating that he had never to his knowledge known members of the Communist Party in New Hampshire. In any event, petitioner's brief states that he is willing to repeat the answer to this question if the Attorney General so desires. This is consistent with his demonstrated willingness to answer all inquiries regarding the Communist Party, including its relation to the Progressive Party.

The Supreme Court of New Hampshire justified this intrusion upon his freedom on the same basis that it upheld questioning about the university lecture, namely, that the restriction was limited to situations where the Committee had reason to believe that violent overthrow of the Government was being advocated or planned. It ruled:

> That he [the Attorney General] did possess information which was sufficient to reasonably warrant inquiry concerning the Progressive Party is evident from his statement made during the hearings held before him that "considerable sworn testimony has been given in this investigation to the effect that the Progressive Party in New Hampshire has been heavily infiltrated by members of the Communist Party and that the policies and purposes of the Progressive Party have been directly influenced by members of the Communist Party."

For a citizen to be made to forego even a part of so basic a liberty as his political autonomy, the subordinating interest of the State must be compelling. Inquiry pursued in safeguarding a State's security against threatened force and violence cannot be shut off by mere disclaimer, though of course a relevant claim may be made to the privilege against self-incrimination. (The New Hampshire Constitution guarantees this privilege.) But the inviolability of privacy belonging to a citizen's political loyalties has so overwhelming an importance to the well-being of our kind of society that it cannot be constitutionally encroached upon on the basis of so meagre a countervailing interest of the State as may be argumentatively found in the remote, shadowy threat to the security of New Hampshire allegedly presented in the origins and contributing elements of the Progressive Party and in petitioner's relations to these.

* * *

And so I am compelled to conclude that the judgment of the New Hampshire court must be reversed.

Goldberg v. *Regents of University of California*
57 Cal. Rptr. 463
April 26, 1967

TAYLOR, Associate Justice

In this action, plaintiffs, Arthur L. Goldberg, Michael L. Klein, David A. Bills and Nicholas Zveginitzov (hereafter referred to by their last names), challenge, upon constitutional grounds, their suspension and dismissal from the University of California on April 20, 1965. This appeal is from a judgment of dismissal entered on an order sustaining the general demurrer of defendants, The Regents of the University of California (hereafter University), without leave to amend, to plaintiff's petition for a writ of mandate seeking reinstatement to the University. Plaintiffs contend that their petition states a cause of action as the action of the University, through its disciplinary committee, was an unconstitutional limitation of their First Amendment Rights, was taken pursuant to a constitutionally vague regulation, deprived them of procedural due process, and constituted an invasion of an area exclusively operated by state law. We have concluded that there is no merit in any of these contentions.

The basic facts are not in dispute. Until April 20, 1965, all plaintiffs were students in good standing at the Berkeley campus* of the University of California. Each of them participated in a different manner in rallies held on March 4 and March 5 on the campus to protest the March 3 arrest of John Thomson (hereafter Thomson), a nonstudent who had displayed on campus a sign reading: "Fuck! Verb." Three of the plaintiffs (Goldberg, Klein and Bills) were also arrested and charged on March 4, 1965, with violations of the obscenity statutes . . . and disturbing the peace (Pen. Code, § 415) on the basis of the same facts that led to the University disciplinary proceedings. These criminal prosecutions were still pending on April 20, 1965.

On March 17, the Dean of Men wrote to each plaintiff that he had been charged with violating the University-wide policy on student conduct and discipline (as set forth below) ** and quoted the pertinent portion of the General Catalogue of the Berkeley campus (quoted below).*** The letters detailed the acts charged against each plaintiff (likewise set forth below).****

---

* Goldberg, Klein and Zvegintzov were graduate students; Bills (then a minor appearing through Patricia Surry, his guardian ad litem), an undergraduate student.

** "It is taken for granted that each student . . . will adhere to acceptable standards of personal conduct; and that all students . . . will set and observe among themselves proper standards of conduct and good taste. . . . This presumption in favor of the students . . . continues until, . . . by misconduct, it is reversed, in which case the University authorities will take such action as the particular occurrence judged in the light of the attendant circumstances, may seem to require. . . ."

*** "The University authorities take it for granted that a student enters the University with an earnest purpose and will so conduct himself. Unbecoming behavior . . . will result in curtailment or withdrawal of the privileges or other action of the University authorities that they deem warranted by the student's conduct."

**** Goldberg was charged with· having organized and participated in the March 4 rally held on the steps of Sproul Hall to protest the arrest of Thomson, acting as moderator for the rally and in the course thereof addressing the persons assembled by repeatedly using the word "fuck" in its various declensions; on Friday, March 5, with moderating and speaking at another rally conducted from the steps of the Student Union Building utilizing the terms "fuck, bastard, asshole and pissed off." Klein was charged with addressing the March 4 rally by using the word "fuck" in the course of his remarks; and on the same afternoon in Room 2 of Sproul Hall, repeatedly reading aloud several paragraphs from D. H. Lawrence's "Lady Chatterly's Lover" in which the term "fuck" appears. Bills was charged with acknowledging to University police officers that about 1:30 P.M. on March 4, he was manning a table at Bancroft and Telegraph for the purpose of raising money for the de-

The letters informed plaintiffs that a special Ad Hoc Committee (hereafter Committee) had been appointed to hear the matter;* that plaintiffs might wish to obtain counsel to represent them at the hearing; and that they should plan to be present at a prehearing conference scheduled for the afternoon of Friday, March 19. Plaintiffs were not personally present at the prehearing conference but were represented by their attorney who raised several objections. The Committee considered and denied these objections, formulated the issues to be considered and procedures to be followed, and indicated that the hearings would begin on Monday, March 29. On Friday, March 26, the Committee was served with an alternative writ of prohibition issued by the Superior Court of Alameda County on behalf of Klein and Bills who were accordingly excluded from the March 29 hearings. The peremptory writ was denied and the temporary restraining orders were dissolved on Friday, April 2, and the hearing resumed as to all plaintiffs on Tuesday, April 6.

After unsuccessfully attempting to obtain a stipulation concerning the factual matters charged, the Committee held further hearings. At one of these hearings, plaintiffs' counsel took offense at something said and walked out, followed by plaintiffs. The hearings were continued and resumed on the evening of April 8, when plaintiffs were represented by another counsel, as their original counsel was unavailable. Klein became dissatisfied with that representation and after making a short and polite statement of his reasons, withdrew. All later hearings were set for times convenient to plaintiffs' original counsel. The three plaintiffs present did not testify at the hearings but presented witnesses on their behalf. The final hearing was postponed until April 15 so that the Committee could hear the testimony of Lieutenant Chandler, who had made the arrests on March 4 and was personally present at all the events involved.

The Committee's findings of fact acknowledged that the substantial differences between the conduct of the four plaintiffs necessitated separate findings, but noted that the charges against each had been abundantly proved. The Committee concluded that plaintiffs had en-

---

fense of Thomson; a container on the table was labeled "Fuck Fund..; also displayed was a large sign that Bills reportedly helped to prepare, reading: "Support the Fuck Defense Fund. Raise money for the bail and legal defense of John Thomson. Combat hypocrisy. Sponsored by Student Committee for a Good Fuck." Zvegintzov was charged with participating in the March 4 rally by leading a yell or cheer consisting of first spelling and then shouting the word "fuck."

* This committee was specially appointed by the Acting Chancellor at the request of the then-existing Committees on Student Conduct and Student Political Activity and consisted of two members of each of the existing committees with a chairman selected from nominations submitted by the Berkeley Academic Senate's Committee on Committees. A student member was also added and participated in all hearings and meetings but did not vote on the final recommendations.

gaged in a clear pattern of planned and coordinated activity that had as one of its purposes a test of University reaction. The Committee also rejected the contention that the disciplinary hearings should not have proceeded as to Goldberg, Klein and Bills until their court cases were completed, reasoning that both for the good of the students and the University community, student disciplinary matters should be resolved as soon as practicable.

The Committee agreed unanimously that plaintiffs had committed the acts charged and concluded that their actions "did constitute violations of the University's Regulations on Student Conduct and Discipline. [quoted above] Whether motivated by social protest or not, the members [of the Committee] agreed that the loud use and prominent display of the words in question in a public place such as the Sproul-Student Union Plaza is a violation of the regulation."

(1) Because of the substantial differences between the seriousness of the individual offenses, the Committee recommended different disciplinary measures as to each plaintiff. Goldberg was dismissed from the University, effective April 20, 1965; Klein and Zvegintzov were suspended until September 13, 1965; and Bills suspended until June 10, 1965.* The disciplinary actions were reviewed by the Acting Chancellor of the Berkeley campus and the President of the University, and on August 6, 1965, plaintiffs were informed that there would be no interference with the discipline imposed.

* * *

(5, 6) Article IX, section 9 of the state Constitution, provides that the University of California shall constitute a public trust to be administered by the existing corporation known as The Regents of the University, with full powers of organization and government, subject only to such legislative control as may be necessary to insure compliance with the terms of the endowment of the University and the security of its funds. Accordingly, the University is a constitutional department or function of the state government. . . . The Regents have the general rule-making or policy-making power in regard to the University . . . and are (with exceptions not material here) fully empowered with respect to the organization and government of the University . . . including the authority to maintain order and decorum on the campus and the enforcement of the same by all appropriate means, including suspension or dismissal from the University. Pursuant to this authority, the previously quoted regulations concerning student conduct were adopted.

---

* Although the record indicates that by the fall of 1965, the suspensions of Bills and Klein had expired while Goldberg was a student at Howard University Law School and Zvegintzov at the Carnegie Institute of Technology, no contentions concerning the mootness of these proceedings have been raised, nor can be. The dismissals and suspensions are on plaintiffs' academic records.

Also pertinent are the particular resolutions set forth below.*

The parties agree that the University's rule-making powers and its relationship with its students are subject to federal constitutional guarantees. Before discussing the contentions raised, we will briefly describe our approach to the application of these guarantees. The case is one of first impression in this state and requires the drawing of fine lines of demarcation between matters that involve the legitimate interests of the University and those that involve constitutionally protected rights.** The facts here presented relate to on-campus conduct expressing criticism and disapproval by highly visible and provocative means.

The more recent federal cases stress the importance of education to the individual and conclude that attendance in a state university is no longer considered a privilege as in *Hamilton* v. *Regents of University of California* (1934), 293 U.S. 245, 55 S.Ct. 197, 79 L.Ed. 343.*** but is now regarded as an important benefit. . . . (*Dixon* v. *Alabama State*

---

*   REGENTS RESOLUTION
                November 20, 1964
    (a) The Regents restate the long-standing University policy as set forth in Regulation 25 on student conduct and discipline that "all students and student organizations . . . obey the laws of the State and community."
    (b) The Regents adopt the policy effective immediately that certain campus facilities, carefully selected and properly regulated, may be used by students and staff for planning, implementing, raising funds or recruiting participants for lawful off-campus action, not for unlawful off-campus action.
                REGENTS RESOLUTION
                December 18, 1964
    (a) The Regents direct the Administration to preserve law and order on the campuses of the University of California, and to take the necessary steps to insure orderly pursuit of its educational functions.
    (b) The Regents reconfirm that ultimate authority for student discipline within the University is constitutionally vested in The Regents, and is a matter not subject to negotiation. Implementation of disciplinary policies will continue to be delegated, as provided in the By-Laws and Standing Orders of The Regents, to the President and Chancellors, who will seek advice of appropriate faculty committees in individual cases.
    (c) The Regents will undertake a comprehensive review of University policies with the intent of providing maximum freedom on campus consistent with individual and group responsibility. A committee of Regents will be appointed to consult with students, faculty and other interested persons and to make recommendations to the Board.
    (d) Pending results of this study, existing rules will be enforced. The policies of The Regents do not contemplate that advocacy or content of speech shall be restricted beyond the purview of the First and Fourteenth Amendments to the Constitution.
** We note that the problem presented has recently been the subject of many thoughtful comments (see the Bibliography on Student Rights and Campus Rules, 54 Cal.L.Rev., 177). For help in our analysis, we are particularly indebted to the symposium on the subject in this volume of the California Law Review and wish to commend the publication for such an outstanding collection of viewpoints on such a timely subject.
***. . . . See W. W. Van Alstyne, Student Academic Freedom and the Rule-Making Powers of Public Universities: Some Constitutional Considerations, 2 Law In Transition Quarterly 1; H. A. Linde, Constitutional Rights in the Public Sector, 40 Washington Law Review 10.
                    *   *   *

Board of Education (5 Cir., 1961), 294 F.2d 150, cert. denied 368 U.S. 930, 82 S.Ct. 368, 7 L.Ed.2d 193; *Knight v. State Board of Education* (D.C. 1961), 200 F.Supp. 174.)

In the Dixon and Knight cases, it was held that procedural due process required a hearing before students who participated in demonstrations violating laws concerning the separation of the races in public places could be dismissed or suspended from the state university. As stated in Dixon: "The precise nature of the private interest involved in this case is the right to remain at a public institution of higher learning in which the plaintiffs were students in good standing. It requires no argument to demonstrate that education is vital and, indeed, basic to civilized society. Without sufficient education the plaintiffs would not be able to earn an adequate livelihood, to enjoy life to the fullest, or to fulfill as completely as possible the duties and responsibilities of good citizens." (P. 157 of 294 F.2d.) The court noted in Knight that: "Whether the interest involved be described as a right or a privilege, the fact remains that it is an interest of almost incalculable value, especially to those students who have already enrolled in the institution and begun the pursuit of their college training. Private interests are to be evaluated under the due process clause of the Fourteenth Amendment, not in terms of labels or fictions, but in terms of their true significance and worth." (P. 178 of 200 F.Supp.)

(7–9) For constitutional purposes, the better approach, as indicated in Dixon, recognizes that state universities should no longer stand in loco parentis in relation to their students.* Rather, attendance at publicly financed institutions of higher education should be regarded a benefit somewhat analogous to that of public employment.** Accordingly, we deal with the question here presented within the same constitutional framework as that applied in the recent public employment cases. . . . The test is whether conditions annexed to the benefit reasonably tend to further the purposes sought by conferment of that benefit and whether the utility of imposing the conditions manifestly outweighs any resulting impairment of constitutional rights.

(10, 11) Plaintiffs first contend that they were engaged in the exer-

---

* The classic case applying the loco parentis approach is *Anthony* v. *Syracuse University* (1928) . . . 231 N.Y.S. 435. In earlier decades in loco parentis had some superficial appeal because the vast majority of college students were below 18. Today, in contrast, there are more students between the ages of 30 and 35 in universities than there are those under 18, and the latter group account for only seven percent of the total college enrollment (54 Cal.L.Rev., 28, note 13). See also, Rosemary Park, Alma Mater, Emerita in The University in America, An Occasional Paper on the Role of Education in the Free Society, Center for Democratic Institutions (1967). . . .

** In the cases dealing with public employment, there has also been a change from no constitutional right to public employment . . . to a recognition that the power of government to withhold benefits from its citizens does not encompass a supposed "lesser" power to grant such benefits upon an arbitrary deprivation of constitutional rights. . . .

cise of their First Amendment rights of free speech* and assembly in protesting the arrest of Thomson, and that the University's disciplinary action taken as the result of their conduct on March 4 or March 5 constituted a denial of these rights. Their argument has as its major unarticulated premise that since their purpose was to protest, they had a constitutional right to do so whenever, however, and wherever they pleased. That concept of constitutional law was vigorously and forthrightfully rejected by the United States Supreme Court. . . . These cases recognize that it is not enough for the plaintiffs to assert they are exercising a "right" to claim absolute immunity against any form of social control or discipline, for it is well recognized that individual freedoms and group interests can and do clash. . . . An individual cannot escape from social constraint merely by asserting that he is engaged in political talk or action. . . .

The applicable principles were stated in *Konigsberg* v. *State Bar*, 366 U.S. 36 at pages 49–51, 81 S.Ct. 997 at page 1006, 6 L.Ed.2d 105:

> Throughout its history this Court has consistently recognized at least two ways in which constitutionally protected freedom of speech is narrower than an unlimited license to talk. On the one hand, certain forms of speech, or speech in certain contexts, has been considered outside the scope of constitutional protection. . . . *On the other hand, general regulatory statutes, not intended to control the content of speech but incidentally limiting its unfettered exercise, have not been regarded as the type of law the First or Fourteenth Amendment forbade Congress or the States to pass, when they have been found justified by subordinating valid governmental interests, a prerequisite to constitutionality which has necessarily involved a weighing of the governmental interest involved"* [emphasis added].

(12, 13) Thus, reasonable restrictions on the freedoms of speech and assembly are recognized in relation to public agencies that have a valid interest in maintaining good order and proper decorum. . . . Conduct, even though intertwined with expression and association, is subject to regulation. . . . As the purposes and functions of a public university are markedly different from the public institutions involved in the cases mentioned above, we must examine the interest the University was protecting in disciplining plaintiffs.

(14, 15) Broadly stated, the function of the University is to impart

---

* Plaintiffs erroneously contend that their dismissal was based on their use of obscene language and that the standards used to determine obscenity did not conform to constitutional requirements. The University (relying on its answer) compounds the error by arguing that plaintiffs were subsequently convicted of using obscene language which is not within the purview of constitutionally protected speech. However, as we have indicated above, the question is whether in determining that plaintiffs should be disciplined for the manner in which they exercised their rights, the University imposed any unconstitutional conditions on plaintiffs' continued attendance at the University.

learning and to advance the boundaries of knowledge. This carries with it the administrative responsibility to control and regulate that conduct and behavior of the students which tends to impede, obstruct or threaten the achievements of its educational goals. Thus, the University has the power to formulate and enforce rules of student conduct that are appropriate and necessary to the maintenance of order and propriety, considering the accepted norms of social behavior in the community, where such rules are reasonably necessary to further the University's educational goals.

(16) Unquestionably, the achievement of the University's educational goals would preclude regulations unduly restricting the freedom of students to express themselves.* . . .

[A] function of free speech under our system of government is to invite dispute. It may indeed best serve its high purpose when it induces a condition of unrest, creates dissatisfaction with conditions as they are, or even stirs people to anger. Speech is often provocative and challenging. It may strike at prejudices and preconceptions and have profound unsettling effects as it presses for acceptance of an idea.

(17) Historically, the academic community has been unique in having its own standards, rewards and punishments. Its members have been allowed to go about their business of teaching and learning largely free of outside interference. To compel such a community to recognize and enforce precisely the same standards and penalties that prevail in the broader social community would serve neither the special needs and interests of the educational institutions, nor the ultimate advantages that society derives therefrom. Thus, in an academic community, greater freedoms and greater restrictions may prevail than in society at large, and the subtle fixing of these limits should, in a large measure, be left to the educational institution itself.

The question here is whether the University's requirement that plaintiffs conform to the community's accepted norms of propriety with respect to the loud, repeated public use of certain terms was reasonably necessary in furthering the University's educational goals. We note that plaintiffs were not disciplined for protesting the arrest of Thomson, but for doing so in a particular manner. The qualification imposed was

---

* As so aptly put in *Sweezy* v. *State of New Hampshire*, 354 U.S. 234, 250 . . . . "The essentiality of freedom in the community of American universities is almost self-evident. No one should underestimate the vital role in a democracy that is played by those who guide and train our youth. To impose any straightjacket upon the intellectual leaders in our colleges and universities would imperil the future of our Nation. No field of education is so thoroughly comprehended by man that new discoveries cannot yet be made. Particularly is that true in the social sciences, where few, if any, principles are accepted as absolutes. Scholarship cannot flourish in an atmosphere of suspicion and distrust. Teachers and students must always remain free to inquire, to study and to evaluate, to gain new maturity and understanding; otherwise our civilization will stagnate and die."

simply that plaintiffs refrain from repeatedly, loudly and publicly using certain terms which, when so used, clearly infringed on the minimum standard of propriety and the accepted norm of public behavior of both the academic community and the broader social community. Plaintiffs' contention that the words were used only in the context of their demonstration is not borne out by the record which indicates that the terms were used repeatedly, and often out of context, or when used in context given undue emphasis. The conduct of plaintiffs thus amounted to coercion rather than persuasion.

(18–20) The association with an educational institution as a student requires certain minimum standards of propriety in conduct to insure that the educational functions of the institution can be pursued in an orderly and reasonable manner. The limitation here imposed was necessary for the orderly conduct of demonstrations, not unlike reasonable restrictions on the use of loudspeakers. . . . The irresponsible activity of plaintiffs seriously interfered with the University's interest in preserving proper decorum in campus assemblages. . . . Conduct involving rowdiness, rioting, the destruction of property, the reckless display of impropriety or any unjustifiable disturbance of the public order on or off campus is indefensible whether it is incident to an athletic event, the advent of spring, or devotion, however sincere, to some cause or ideal.

(21) We hold that in this case, the University's disciplinary action was a proper exercise of its inherent general powers to maintain order on the campus and to exclude therefrom those who are detrimental to its well-being. . . . Thus, for the purposes of this appeal, it is not necessary to discuss plaintiffs' contention that any particular regulation was unconstitutionally vague.

* * *

(25) Plaintiffs further contend that they were denied procedural due process because certain newspaper articles (incorporated in the petition) quoting the President of the University and the Acting Chancellor of the Berkeley campus, who reviewed the disciplinary action, indicate that their cases had been prejudged. This argument is preposterous. The newspaper articles simply indicate that the conduct described had occurred on the campus and the personal reactions of those administrative officers to this type of conduct. The Committee's careful procedures and evaluations of the evidence and thorough findings, along with the final differences of opinion among its members reflected by their various recommendations concerning the discipline appropriate to each plaintiff, evidence its fairness. The record indicates that the administrative officers of the University accepted, without modification, the recommendations of the Committee as to the discipline to be imposed.

Rather than indicating any bias, we note that one newspaper article indicates that the Acting Chancellor and President of the University rejected the demands for summary and immediate dismissals of plaintiffs made by some other University officials. Both subsequently submitted their resignations unless the orderly disciplinary procedures of the University were allowed to proceed. Thus, the record indicates that whatever their personal reactions were to the type of conduct here involved, the Acting Chancellor and President of the University did everything in their power to perfect and assure plaintiffs' rights of procedural due process.

(26) Finally, plaintiffs argue that they were deprived of procedural due process* because the University proceeded with its disciplinary hearings and actions before the final termination of the off-campus formal judicial proceedings relating to their arrest for the same acts. While recognizing that the disciplinary measures that were imposed may have a very serious effect upon the careers of the individual plaintiffs,** the disciplinary measures, as we have indicated above, amounted to a denial of a benefit and can by no stretch of the imagination be classified as criminal proceedings. Furthermore, we cannot accept the contention that where certain conduct is violative of both rules and regulations of the University and the statutes of the state that the discipline imposed by the academic community must wait the outcome of the other proceedings.

(27–29) As we have previously indicated, the University, as an academic community, can formulate its own standards, rewards and punishments to achieve its occasional objectives. In this context, violations of certain rules of the outside community (parking, for example) are of little significance to the University's functions and objectives. Similarly, certain conduct that violates no laws of the external community, such as cheating on an examination, is properly proscribed by and disciplined by the University as it interferes with the University's basic educational purpose. Thus, except for the applicable constitutional limitations, the relationship between appropriate University rules and laws of the outside community is entirely coincidental. The validity of one does not establish the validity of the other.

As indicated above, we have determined here that the Committee was operating properly within constitutional limitations. Its recognition of the interest of the academic community in resolving its disciplinary matters swiftly does not invade any area occupied by state law. As noted in *Dixon*, supra, any other approach would be highly impractical*** and inconsistent with the functions of an educational institution.

---

* In plaintiffs' mistaken conception of the issues previously noted, they characterize this question as one of obscenity laws fully occupied by state law.

** See W. A. Seavey, Dismissal of Students: "Due Process," 70 Harvard Law Review, 1406–1407.

*** For instance, here, the criminal proceedings against plaintiffs would not be finally determined in the legal sense until all the appeals to higher courts were completed, a matter of years.

(30) We conclude, upon the application of all pertinent constitutional requirements, that plaintiffs' complaint does not state a cause of action on any theory.

The answer is stricken from the record and the judgment is affirmed.

AGEE, Acting P.J., and BRAY, J., concur.

Close v. *Lederle*
424 F. 2d 988 (1970)
ALDRICH, Chief Judge

Plaintiff, an art instructor at the University of Massachusetts, was asked by a superior if he would care to have an exhibition of his paintings on the walls of a corridor used from time to time for such purposes in the Student Union, a university building. He said that he would. The exhibition, which had been arranged for but not seen by the superior in charge, proved to be controversial. Several administrative meetings were held, attended by the university president, the provost, and other officials, and after it had been up for five of the twenty-four days scheduled, the exhibition was removed. Claiming that this was an invasion of his constitutional rights, plaintiff sued for a mandatory injunction ordering the officials to make the space available for the equivalent of the unexpired period. The district court, after trial, granted the relief and defendants appeal.

Basically, the district court held that "embarrassment" and "annoyance," causing defendants to conclude that the exhibition was "inappropriate" to the corridor, was insufficient to warrant interference with plaintiff's right of free speech. This holding was not grounded upon finding that defendants were unreasonable in their opinion. The court refused autoptic profference of the exhibition, apparently taking the position that, at least in the absence of express regulations as to what was impermissible, defendants had no right to censor simply on the basis of offensiveness which fell short of unlawful obscenity.

We disagree. We first consider the nature and quality of plaintiff's interest. Plaintiff makes the bald pronouncement, "Art is as fully protected by the Constitution as political or social speech." It is true that in the course of holding a motion picture entitled to First Amendment protection, the Court said . . . that moving pictures affect public attitudes in ways "ranging from direct espousal of a political or social doctrine to the subtle shaping of thought which characterizes all artistic expression." However, this statement in itself recognizes that there are degrees of speech.

(1, 2) There is no suggestion, unless in its cheap titles, that plaintiff's art was seeking to express political or social thought. . . . Cases dealing with students' rights to hear possibly unpopular speakers . . . involve a medium and subject matter entitled to greater protection than plaintiff's art. Even as to verbal communication the extent of the protection may depend upon the subject matter. . . . We consider plaintiff's constitutional interest minimal.

(3, 4) In this posture we turn to the question whether defendants have demonstrated a sufficient counterinterest to justify their action. The corridor was a passageway, regularly used by the public, including children. Several of the paintings were nudes, male or female, displaying the genitalia in what was described as "clinical detail." A skeleton was fleshed out only in this particular. One painting bore the title, "I'm only 12 and already my mother's lover wants me." Another, "I am the only virgin in my school."

The defendants were entitled to consider the primary use to which the corridor was put. . . . On the basis of the complaints received, and even without such, defendants were warranted in finding the exhibit inappropriate to that use. Where there was, in effect, a captive audience, defendants had a right to afford protection against "assault upon individual privacy."

There are words that are not regarded as obscene, in the constitutional sense, that nevertheless need not be permitted in every context. Words that might properly be employed in a term paper about Lady Chatterley's Lover or in a novel submitted in a creative writing course take on a very different coloration if they are bellowed over a loudspeaker at a campus rally or appear prominently on a sign posted on a campus tree.

Freedom of speech must recognize, at least within limits, freedom not to listen.

In hyperconcern with his personal rights plaintiff would not only regard his interest in self-expression as more important than the interests of his unwilling audience, but asks us to add nearly three weeks of such exposure to the five days he has already received. With all respect to the district court, this is a case that should never have been brought.

Judgment reversed. Complaint dismissed.

Siegel v. *Regents of University of California*
308 Fed. Supp. 832
Jan. 19, 1970
SWEIGERT, District Judge

The facts shown by the record are in substance and effect that plaintiff Siegel is a student enrolled at the School of Law on the Berkeley Campus of the University of California. On May 15, 1969, he was president-elect of the Associated Students, University of California, designated by the Chancellor of the Berkeley Campus as the student government organization at the campus.

As of May 15, 1969, certain real property belonging to defendant The Regents, and situated in the vicinity of the Berkeley Campus, had been forcibly seized and occupied by persons not acting under the control and direction of defendant Regents. On the morning of May 15, 1969, The Regents caused a fence to be erected on the perimeter of said property.

On the same day a rally was held at the noon hour in Sproul Plaza on the Berkeley Campus. Several thousand persons were in attendance. Plaintiff Siegel addressed the rally and concluded his remarks as follows:

> Now, we have not yet decided exactly what we are going to do. But there is some plans, I have a suggestion, let's go down to the Peoples Park, because we are the people. But a couple of things, a couple of points I would like to make. If we are to win this thing, it is because we are making it more costly for the University to put up its fence than it is for them to take down their fence. What we have to do then is maximize the cost to them, minimize the cost to us. So what that means, is people be careful. Don't let those pigs beat the shit out of you, don't let yourselves get arrested on felonies, *go down there and take the park.* [emphasis added] [Ex. A, Plaintiff's Complaint].

Immediately thereafter, several thousand persons proceeded from the rally down Telegraph Avenue toward the aforementioned property, where they were met by law enforcement officers. Violence ensued, resulting in the next few days in one death, numerous injuries and many arrests.

Plaintiff was also advised that a hearing had been set before the Berkeley Committee on Student Conduct for May 29, 1969, and he was asked to state whether or not he would be represented by legal counsel. At Plaintiff Siegel's request the hearing was reset for June 5, 1969. Defendants refused an additional postponement.

On May 29, 1969, a preliminary hearing was held by defendant Williams, Dean of Students, at which University counsel and plaintiff and his counsel were present. Plaintiff and his counsel reviewed video-tapes and audiotapes taken of plaintiff's speech of May 15, 1969.

The hearing was held on June 5, 1969, before the Berkeley Campus Student Faculty Committee. Plaintiff was represented by his counsel and presented witnesses.

The Committee on Student Conduct found and concluded:

. . . that the action of Mr. Siegel did constitute violations of the University's regulations on the Standard of Conduct by exposing the University and its people to mob formation and its attendant potential consequence of violence. Therefore the Committee as a whole agrees that disciplinary action is warranted. (Plaintiff's Exhibit L, 13.)

A majority of the Committee also concluded that Siegel:

. . . knowingly spoke at a rally in reckless disregard of the tense and angry nature of the crowd without regard to the foreseeable consequences. At best, his conduct exhibits inexcusable ignorance of the dangerous circumstances.

A majority of the Committee also decided that Siegel:

. . . by his initiation of the march to the "Park" through his reckless words, greatly inflamed the situation at Haste and Telegraph by sending a great crowd to join another smaller one which was described in great detail by the defense counsel in such words as "unruly," "hostile," "aggressive," "undisciplined," "angry," etc.

A majority of the Committee also found that Siegel's:

. . . reckless choice of words spoken in an angry and highly excited tone, nevertheless loses significance as an appeal to reason or aggressive persuasion. They become instead part of the instrument of force and violence. Such disorderly and disruptive conduct, which endangers the welfare and safety of any members of the campus community, is a violation of University regulations.

The Committee recommended that the Chancellor approve the placing of Siegel on disciplinary probation, including exclusion from participation in all privileges or extracurricular activities and specifically from serving as President of the student government.

By letter dated July 2, 1969, defendant Williams advised plaintiff of the Chancellor's acceptance of the recommendations of the Committee on Student Conduct and informed Siegel that he was placed on probation for a one-year period, the terms of probation permitting plaintiff the privileges of a student and privileges incidental to his studies, but prohibiting him from holding student government office or engaging in other extracurricular activities.

The preliminary injunction sought by plaintiff would enjoin defendants from imposing any discipline on plaintiff for his speech of May 15, 1969, and would require defendants to restore plaintiff forthwith to full student status with all rights to hold and occupy the office of President of the Associated Students.

Plaintiff contends that the University regulations promulgated by the University, an agency of the State of California, are constitutionally invalid in that they are "overbroad and vague" restrictions upon the right of free speech protected by the First Amendment.

Upon this ground, plaintiff moves for the convening of a three-judge court.

Since the requirement for a three-judge court is not applicable unless the court determines that the constitutional issues are substantial, we must first examine the record to make a determination of substantiality.

The regulations under which plaintiff was disciplined and which are attacked upon constitutional grounds by plaintiff are as follows:*

SUBSTANTIALITY OF CONSTITUTIONAL CONTENTIONS

(1) Although First Amendment rights of expression, applied in the light of the special characteristics of school environment, are available to teachers and students (who, of course, do not shed their constitutional rights to freedom of speech or expression at the schoolhouse gate), school officials, nevertheless, have comprehensive authority to prescribe and control, consistently with constitutional safeguards, conduct which in-

---

* (1) University of California Policies Relating to Students and Student Organizations, Use of University Facilities and Non-Discrimination (March 17, 1969) . . . *Section II, Part A, Standard of Conduct,* provides that a student enrolling in the University assumes an obligation to conduct himself in a manner compatible with the University's functions as an educational institution, and that misconduct for which students are subject to discipline falls into the following categories:

Paragraph 3, prohibits obstruction or disruption of administration or other University activities, including its public service functions, or of other authorized activities on University premises.

Paragraph 4, prohibits physical abuse of any person on University owned or controlled property or conduct which threatens or endangers the health or safety of any such person.

Paragraph 7, refers generally to violation of University policies or of campus regulations concerning the use of University facilities . . . .

Paragraph 10, prohibits disorderly conduct on University owned or controlled property.

Paragraph 12, prohibits conduct which adversely affects the student's suitability as a member of the academic community.

(3) Emergency Regulations, Office of the Chancellor, 2/24/69. This emergency regulation recites a declaration of the Regents that interim suspension shall be imposed immediately in all cases where there is reasonable cause to believe that during a campus disturbance a student has violated University or campus regulations by acts such as physical violence or threats thereof, willful destruction of University property, wrongful blocking of access to University facilities or other disruptive activities, and further, the regulation recites a policy of the Regents and of the University, that in the light of an emergency University facilities shall not be used for the purpose of organizing or carrying out unlawful activity. The regulation concludes to the effect that the use or threat of physical force to coerce persons using University facilities or engaged in administration or University related activities on campus is a fundamental violation of conditions of membership in an academic community and that any student found to have engaged in such misconduct shall be disciplined.

trudes upon the work of the school. *Tinker* v. *Des Moines Independent Community School District . . .*

(2) It is well settled that even speech or expression, which materially and substantially intrudes upon the work of the school by interfering with the requirements of appropriate discipline in its operation may be prohibited. *Tinker,* supra . . .

(3) Regulations for these purposes, which reasonably set forth what conduct is expected from students, are sufficient and need not be tested by the strict standards applicable to criminal statutes or proceedings. *Esteban* v. *Central Missouri State College. . . .*

It will be noted that the regulations in question here are on their face directed, not to speech or mere expression of opinion, but to conduct.

(4) There is nothing in these regulations that could be fairly said to have a "chilling effect" upon a student's exercise of First Amendment rights of free speech or expression because of "vagueness" or "overbreadth" or otherwise.

Nor is the record such as to show that the regulations have been applied with the effect as to this particular plaintiff.

The complaint itself sets forth the exhortation by plaintiff at the close of his speech to "Go down and take the park," and the circumstances under which these words were uttered. . . .

(5, 6) Although the complaint alleges that this exhortation by plaintiff was intended by him as mere rhetoric, and not for the purpose of directing a physical seizure of the park,* the complaint, nevertheless, discloses that plaintiff, President-elect of the Associated Students addressing 2,000 students already aroused over the park situation, told them to "Go down and take the park."

The record also shows that plaintiff has admitted by his own testimony at the hearing (as set forth in the hearing transcript . . . and as quoted in the Committee Report . . .) that he attempted to make his comments sound militant so he wouldn't be tuned off; that he couldn't say simply, "Now stay away from the police," because they would have told him to sit down; that he couldn't say it in those words because a moderate-sounding statement "wouldn't have any effect on them, whereas a statement made in their own language would have a modifying effect on them, I hoped."

(7) Under the circumstances shown by the record that statement transcends mere expression of opinion and becomes *conduct*—a distinct,

* We have well in mind that plaintiff's suit cannot be and should not be, treated as a mere petition for reviewing of the University's proceedings . . . . However, the issue raised by this civil rights complaint is, not whether plaintiff was in fact guilty of violating university rules or any other law, nor whether his subjective intent, was in fact, innocent and therefore, a defense to the charges, nor whether the university hearing board's findings were correct, but, rather, and only whether the university in charging, trying and disciplining plaintiff the circumstances shown on the face of the complaint, deprived plaintiff of any federally protected constitutional right.

affirmative *verbal act*—overt conduct for which plaintiff could be properly called to account under the regulations, whatever might be his claim as to his subjective purpose and intent.

(8, 9) Illegal conduct is not protected merely because it is in part initiated, evidenced or carried out by language. Utterance in a context of violence, involving a clear and present danger, can lose its significance as an appeal to reason and become part of an instrument of force and as such unprotected by the Constitution.

Obviously, such conduct, according to any reasonable, educational standard, would materially and substantially intrude upon University administration within the meaning of *Tinker,* supra.

Tinker is clearly distinguishable in its facts and ultimate result in that, as pointed out by the Supreme Court, it involved merely the silent, passive wearing of black armbands by the student, a symbolic act, entirely divorced from actual or potentially disruptive conduct and closely akin to pure speech, and, as such, protected by the First Amendment even as to teachers and students.

(10) The court concludes that the constitutional issues raised by plaintiff concerning the regulations in question are insubstantial. . . .

Accordingly, plaintiff's motion for a preliminary injunction should be and is hereby denied, and defendants' motion to dismiss the action should be and is hereby granted upon the ground that the complaint, considered as a whole and with the exhibits attached thereto, fails to state a claim upon which relief could be granted in this action.

* * *

Dickson v. *Sitterson*
280 F.Supp. 486
Feb. 19, 1968
EDWIN M. STANLEY, District Judge

The plaintiff seeks to declare unconstitutional and enjoin the enforcement of § 116–199 and § 116–120, General Statutes of North Carolina, statutes regulating the appearance of visiting speakers at State-supported colleges and universities. . . .

* * *

From the pleadings, and stipulated facts and other documents, the following material facts are found:

FACTS

1. At all times pertinent, the plaintiffs, except Wilkinson and Aptheker, were students duly enrolled and in good standing at the

University of North Carolina at Chapel Hill, North Carolina. The student body consisted of approximately twelve thousand students and the plaintiff, Dickson, was the duly elected president of the student body.

* * *

3. Each of the student organizations designated in the preceding paragraph exists at the University of North Carolina, and each is composed of a number of students.

4. The plaintiff, Frank Wilkinson, is a citizen and resident of the State of California, and is Executive Director of the National Committee to Abolish the House Un-American Activities Committee.

5. The plaintiff, Herbert Aptheker, is a citizen and resident of the State of New York, and is Director of the American Institute for Marxist Studies.

* * *

8. The 1963 General Assembly of North Carolina enacted Chapter 1207 of the Session Laws (codified as G.S. § 116–199 and § 116–200), regulating visiting speakers at State-supported colleges and universities, as follows:

§ 116–199. No college or university, which receives any State funds in support thereof, shall permit any person to use the facilities of such college or university for speaking purposes, who:
(A) Is a known member of the Communist party;
(B) Is known to advocate the overthrow of the Constitution of the United States or the State of North Carolina;
(C) Has pleaded the Fifth Amendment of the Constitution of the United States in refusing to answer any question, with respect to Communist or subversive connections, or activities, before any duly constituted legislative committee, any judicial tribunal, or any executive or administrative board of the United States or any state.

§ 116–200. This Act shall be enforced by the Board of Trustees, or other governing authority, of such college or university, or by such administrative personnel as may be appointed therefor by the Board of Trustees or other governing authority of such college or university.

9. Thereafter, on July 8, 1963, the Executive Committee of the Board of Trustees of the University of North Carolina adopted the following regulation and policy statement:

The facilities of the Consolidated University of North Carolina shall be denied to any visiting speaker who is known to be a member of any Communist Party; or is known to advocate the overthrow of the Constitution of the United States or the State of North Carolina; or is known to have pleaded the Fifth Amendment of the Constitution of the United States in refusing to answer any question, with respect to Communist or subversive connections, or activities, before any duly constituted legislative committee, any judicial tribunal, or any executive or administrative board of the United States or any state.

This policy shall be enforced by student representatives of student organizations authorized to invite visiting speakers and by any member of the faculty or administrative official who invites a visiting speaker to the campus.

10. After the enactment of Chapter 1207 of the Session Laws of 1963, commonly referred to as the "Speaker Ban" law, the statute became a matter of widespread public concern. As a consequence, the 1965 General Assembly, by resolution adopted on June 16, 1965, created a Commission to study the statutes and report the results of its study to the Governor of North Carolina. The Commission members consisted of five lawyers, two industrial manufacturers, one newspaper editor, and one Baptist minister, and their residence was distributed over the several geographical areas of the State.

11. The aforesaid Study Commission filed its report on November 5, 1965, which report included the following recommendations:

1. Subject to Recommendation No. 2, we recommend that Chapter 1207 of the 1963 Session Laws be amended so as to vest the trustees of the institutions affected by it not only with the authority but also with the responsibility of adopting and publishing rules and precautionary measures relating to visiting speakers covered by said Act on the campuses of said institutions. We submit as a part of this report a proposed legislative bill to accomplish this purpose.

2. We recommend that each of the Boards of Trustees of said institutions adopt the Speaker Policy hereto attached and made a part of this Report.

3. In order that this important matter might be settled forthwith, we recommend that you, The Governor of North Carolina, request the boards of trustees of the affected institutions to assemble as soon as practicable for purpose of giving consideration to the aforementioned Speaker Policy, and at such time as it has been adopted by the said boards of all of said institutions, that you cause to be called an extraordinary Session of the General Assembly for purpose of considering amendments to Chapter 1207 of the 1963 Session Laws as hereinbefore set forth.

12. The Speaker Policy, attached to and made a part of the report of the Study Commission, provided as follows:

The Trustees recognize that this Institution, and every part thereof, is owned by the people of North Carolina; that it is operated by duly selected representatives and personnel for the benefit of the people of our state.

The Trustees of this Institution are unalterably opposed to Communism and any other ideology or form of government which has as its goal the destruction of our basic democratic institutions.

We recognize that the total program of a college or university is committed to an orderly process of inquiry and discussion, ethical and moral excellence, objective instruction, and respect for law. An essential part of the education of each student at this Institution is the opportunity to hear diverse viewpoints expressed by speakers properly invited to the campus. It is highly desirable that students have the opportunity to question, review and discuss the opinions of speakers representing a wide range of viewpoints.

It is vital to our success in supporting our free society against all forms of totalitarianism that institutions remain free to examine these ideologies to any extent that will serve the educational purpose of our institutions and not to the purposes of the, enemies of our free society.

We feel that the appearance as a visiting speaker on our campus of one who was prohibited under Chapter 1207 of the 1963 Session Laws (The Speaker Ban Law) or who advocates any ideology or form of government which is wholly alien to our democratic institutions should be infrequent and then only when it would clearly serve the advantage of education; and on such rare occasions reasonable and proper care should be exercised by the institution. The campuses shall not be exploited as convenient outlets of discord and strife.

We therefore provide that we the Trustees together with the administration of the Institution shall be held responsible and accountable for visiting speakers on our campuses. And to that end the administration will adopt rules and precautionary measures consistent with the policy herein set forth regarding the invitations to and appearance of visiting speakers. These rules and precautionary measures shall be subject to the approval of the Trustees.

13. On November 12, 1965, the Board of Trustees of the University of North Carolina, acting within their statutory authority, adopted a policy regarding visiting speakers in the identical words as recommended by the Study Commission.

14. Thereafter, in an extra Session, the North Carolina General Assembly, on November 17, 1965, amended G.S. § 116–199 and § 116–200 to read as follows:

§ 116–199. Use of facilities for speaking purposes.—The board of trustees of each college or university which receives any State funds in support thereof, shall adopt and publish regulations governing the use of facilities of such college or university for speaking purposes by any person who:
(1) Is a known member of the Communist Party;
(2) Is known to advocate the overthrow of the Constitution of the United States or the State of North Carolina;
(3) Has pleaded the Fifth Amendment of the Constitution of the United States in refusing to answer any question, with respect to Communist or subversive connections, or activities, before any duly constituted legislative committee, any judicial tribunal, or any ex-

ecutive or administrative board of the United States or any state.
§ 116–120. Enforcement of article.—Any such regulations shall be enforced by the board of trustees, or other governing authority, of such college or university, or by such administrative personnel as may be appointed therefor by the board of trustees or other governing authority of such college or university.

15. On January 3, 1966, the plaintiffs Matthews and Waller invited the plaintiff Wilkinson to speak on the campus of the University of North Carolina at Chapel Hill on March 2, 1966, and the plaintiff Aptheker to speak on March 9, 1966, under the sponsorship of the Students for a Democratic Society. These invitations were personally approved by the defendant Friday and by Chancellor Paul Sharp, who was then the Chancellor of the University of North Carolina at Chapel Hill, but no official action was taken.

* * *

17. On January 14, 1966, the Executive Committee of the Board of Trustees, meeting on one of the campuses of the University of North Carolina, acting within their statutory authority and pursuant to G.S. § 116–119 and § 116–200, adopted the following procedures to apply to visiting speakers:

1. All statutes of the State relating to speakers and the use of facilities for speaking purposes are to be obeyed (1941 law and others).
2. Only recognized student, faculty and University organizations are authorized to invite speakers.
3. Non-University organizations authorized through official channels (e.g., Extension Division) to meet on the campus are to be routinely informed that the use of facilities must conform to State laws.
4. Student attendance at campuswide occasions is not compulsory.
5. The appearance of speakers on campus does not imply approval or disapproval of them or what is said by the speaker.
6. As a further precaution and to asure free and open discussion as essential to the safeguarding of free institutions, each Chancellor, when he considers it appropriate, will require any or all of the following:
a. That a meeting be chaired by an officer of the University or a ranking member of the faculty;
b. That speakers at the meeting be subject to questions from the audience;
c. That the opportunity be provided at the meeting or later to present speakers of different points of view.

18. On January 14, 1966, Roy James McCorkle, Jr., who was then the president of Students for a Democratic Society, made a written request for reservation of space to the Reservations Secretary at the Central

Reservations Office of the University of North Carolina at Chapel Hill, requesting Carroll Hall Auditorium from 8 P.M. to 10 P.M. on February 28, or March 2, 1966, for a speech by the plaintiff Wilkinson, and Memorial Hall Auditorium from 8 P.M. to 10 P.M. on March 9, 1966, for a speech by the plaintiff Aptheker. The Reservations Secretary confirmed the fact that space was available at each of these places on the dates requested.

19. On January 28, 1966, the Executive Committee of the Board of Trustees of the University met in the office of the Governor of North Carolina and discussed the pending appearances of the plaintiffs Wilkinson and Aptheker. The defendants Friday and Sitterson, and Chancellor Paul Sharp, who was then the Chancellor of the University of North Carolina at Chapel Hill, supported these invitations in statements to the Executive Committee of the Board of Trustees. Chancellor Sharp set up the format of a panel discussion, with a former dean of the University Law School presiding, and with other faculty members on the panel, to be able, if appropriate, to rebut anything that might be said. Following the meeting the Governor of North Carolina issued the following statement:

February 1, 1966

STATEMENT BY GOVERNOR DAN MOORE

I am calling a meeting of the Executive Committee of the Trustees of the University of North Carolina in the Governor's Office for 3:30 P.M., Monday, February 7, 1966, to settle the question of whether Herbert Aptheker and others will be permitted to speak on the University campus.

* * *

As Chairman of the Board of Trustees, I realize it is important that we measure up to the responsibilities given us as trustees by the General Assembly in dealing with the matter of speakers who will be permitted to speak on the University campus.

It should be obvious to everyone that the invitation under consideration was made in an effort to create controversy for the sake of controversy and not for any legitimate educational purpose. For this reason, I do not think the Trustees should permit this request to be granted.

20. On or about February 1, 1966, the plaintiffs Dickson, Nicholson and McCrary invited the plaintiff Aptheker to speak on the University campus on March 9, 1966, under the sponsorship of the Student Government, the Carolina Forum, and *The Daily Tar Heel*. The invitation was accepted by plaintiff Aptheker on February 3, 1966.

21. On February 3, 1966, the faculty, and on February 6, 1966, the

Faculty Advisory Committee, endorsed the recommendation of the Chancellor and President that plaintiff Aptheker be permitted to speak on March 9, 1966.

22. On February 7, 1966, the Executive Committee of the Board of Trustees of the University reconvened in the office of the Governor of North Carolina, at which time the following resolutions were adopted:

RESOLUTION No. 1
   The Executive Committee of the Board of Trustees of the University of North Carolina deny the use of University facilities for speaking purposes for the scheduled appearances of Herbert Aptheker and Frank Wilkinson.
RESOLUTION No. 2
   The Executive Committee of the Board of Trustees of the University of North Carolina here suspends all invitations to speakers who are under the terms of G.S. 116–119 until formal action is taken by the Board of Trustees establishing rules and regulations governing visiting speakers, as required by law.

23. Shortly after the action of the Executive Committee of the Board of Trustees on February 7, 1966, Chancellor Sharp stated publicly: "In view of the commitments of a great university, this was an unfortunate action."

* * *

25. On February 10, 1966, the student government of the University of North Carolina at Chapel Hill unanimously adopted a resolution supporting the invitation to plaintiff Aptheker to speak on the campus on March 9, 1966, "on the basis of the principle of freedom of speech and academic freedom."

* * *

27. On February 28, 1966, the Board of Trustees, acting pursuant to G.S. § 116–199 and § 116–200, adopted the following procedures and regulations regarding the appearance of visiting speakers:

Procedures Regarding Invitations to Speakers
Affected by G.S. 116–199 and 200.

In order to provide the Chancellors with an opportunity to exercise the responsibilities imposed upon them by trustee regulations respecting visiting speakers, the following procedures shall be observed prior to extending an invitation to any visiting speaker covered by G.S. 116–199 and 200.
   1. The officers of a recognized student club or society desiring to use University facilities for a visiting speaker shall consult with the club's faculty adviser concerning the proposed speaker.
   2. The head of the student organization shall submit to the Chancel-

lor a request for reservation of a meeting place along with the
following information:

(a) Name of the sponsoring organization and the proposed speaker's topic.

(b) Biographical information about the proposed speaker.

(c) Request for a date and place of meeting.

3. Upon receipt of the above information, the Chancellor shall refer
the proposed invitation to a joint student-faculty standing committee on visiting speakers for advice. He may consult such others
as he deems advisable.

4. The Chancellor shall then determine whether or not the invitation
is approved.

Once a speaker affected by G.S. 116–199 and 200 has been invited
and his acceptance received, his appearance on the campus shall be
governed by these regulations:

*Regulations Regarding the Appearance of Visiting
Speakers Affected by G.S. 116–199 and 200.*

1. All statutes of the State relating to speakers and the use of facilities
for speaking purposes are to be obeyed.

2. Student attendance at campuswide occasions is not compulsory.

3. The appearance of speakers on the campus does not imply either
approval or disapproval of the speakers or what is said by them.

4. As a further precaution and to assure free and open discussion as
essential to the safeguarding of free institutions, each Chancellor,
when he considers it appropriate, will require any or all of the
following:

(a) That a meeting be chaired by an officer of the University or a
ranking member of the faculty;

(b) That speakers at the meeting be subject to questions from the
audience;

(c) That the opportunity be provided at the meeting or later to
present speakers of different points of view.

The Chancellor shall keep the President informed of the application of these regulations covering the invitation to and the appearance
of visiting speakers affected by G.S. 116–199 and 200.

28. On March 1, 1966, plaintiffs Dickson, Nicholson, Powell, Medford, Greenbacker, Van Loon, McCrary, Waller and Matthews, along
with Eunice Minton, delivered to the defendant Sitterson a written
request for permission for the plaintiff Aptheker to speak on the campus
of the University of North Carolina at Chapel Hill on March 9, 1966,
and for the plaintiff Wilkinson to speak on the campus on March 2,
1966. For each proposed speaker, the written request was accompanied
by the name of the sponsoring organization, the topic of the proposed
speech, and biographical information concerning the speaker. These
requests complied with the requirements of the procedures and regulations which had been adopted by the Board of Trustees governing in-

vitations to visiting speakers. The topic on which the plaintiff Wilkinson was to speak was the House Un-American Activities Committee, and the topic on which the plaintiff Aptheker was to speak was the war in Viet Nam.

29. The joint Student-Faculty Committee on visiting speakers, appointed pursuant to the procedures and regulations adopted by the Board of Trustees on February 28, 1966, met on the night of March 1, 1966, to consider what recommendations to make to Chancellor Sitterson in regard to the invitation to Frank Wilkinson to speak on the University campus on March 2, 1966. The Committee was sharply divided with respect to the action they should take, but a majority of the members recommended that the invitation to Wilkinson be rejected.

* * *

31. On March 2, 1966, the defendant Sitterson denied the request for approval of the invitation to the plaintiff Wilkinson to speak on the subject of the House Un-American Activities Committee on the campus of the University on March 2, 1966, and stated publicly:

> On March 1, 1966, I received a request from the officers of several student organizations for a speaking appearance of Mr. Frank Wilkinson on the campus on March 2.
>
> As soon as possible, I set up the faculty-student committee, provided for in Trustee regulations of February 28, and this committee gave the most careful and thorough consideration to the proposed invitation. I have also had the benefit of the thoughtful and thorough consideration of this matter by the faculty elected Advisory Committee. As would be expected, not everyone was of one mind and it should be clearly understood that while I greatly appreciate their helpful advice, the decision is entirely my own.
>
> The Executive Committee of the Board of Trustees on February 7, 1966, cancelled the scheduled appearances in March of Mr. Frank Wilkinson and Mr. Herbert Aptheker. Consequently, even though prior to the Executive Committee action I recommended that the earlier invitation should be approved, I regard the Executive Committee's action as in effect binding in these two instances, and I do not at this time think I should grant permission for the use of the University facilities for Mr. Wilkinson on March 2. I have informed President Friday of this decision and he concurs in the action taken.
>
> J. Carlyle Sitterson
> Acting Chancellor

32. On March 3, 1966, Chancellor Sitterson advised the Student-Faculty Committee that it was useless for them to meet concerning the invitation to Aptheker to speak on March 9 since the reason for denying the invitation to Wilkinson to speak on March 2, 1966, applied equally to the invitation to Aptheker to speak on March 9, 1966, and there was no use for them to have a useless meeting about Aptheker.

* * *

35. On March 4, 1966, the defendant Sitterson, by letter, denied the request for the plaintiff Aptheker to speak on the campus on the subject of the war in Viet Nam.

36. Shortly after noon on March 9, 1966, more than 1,000 students assembled at McCorkle Place in front of the Confederate Memorial on the campus of the University of North Carolina at Chapel Hill for the purpose of hearing the plaintiff Aptheker, who was present for the purpose of making a speech on the subject of the war in Viet Nam. When Plaintiff Dickson undertook to introduce Aptheker, a police officer, acting on his own initiative and without specific instructions from anyone, but within the scope of his authority as an agent of the defendants, interrupted and stated that if Aptheker spoke he would be breaking the law and would be arrested. The police officer further instructed the plaintiff Dickson that he would prefer charges against him before the Honor Council of the University for deliberately disobeying a directive of Chancellor Sitterson.

* * *

40. The plaintiffs Wilkinson and Aptheker had previously spoken on many university campuses throughout the country on the subjects on which they were invited to speak at the University of North Carolina at Chapel Hill. During the month of March, 1966, they both spoke on these subjects on the campus of Duke University, Durham, North Carolina.

* * *

43. The plaintiff Aptheker has been a member of the Communist Party of the United States since 1939, and has served on the National Committee of the Communist Party U.S.A. He has been editor of *Political Affairs,* the official theoretical organ of the Communist Party U.S.A., and has made trips to the Soviet Union. In 1965, Aptheker made a trip to North Viet Nam, and upon his return, published a book highly favorable to the North Vietnamese. Bettina Aptheker, who has been a member of the DuBois Club, is Aptheker's daughter.

44. Plaintiff Wilkinson has been convicted of unlawfully refusing to answer inquiries before a sub-committee of the House Un-American Activities to determine whether or not he was at any time a member of any Communist Party. By reason of said conviction, Wilkinson served a term in Federal prison.

45. Because Wilkinson has pleaded the Fifth Amendment in refusing to answer any questions with respect to Communist or subversive connections or activities before a duly constituted legislative committee, and because Aptheker admits being a member of the Communist Party of the United States, both are within the classifications set forth in G.S. § 116–199 and § 116–200, and the rules and regulations established by the defendants pursuant to said statutes.

46. Since the passage of G.S. § 116–199 and § 116–200 in their present form, and the adoption on February 28, 1966, of procedures and regulations pursuant to said statutes, three members of the Communist Party have appeared and spoken at the University of North Carolina at Chapel Hill, one upon invitation of a student group and two upon the invitation of faculty groups. Chancellor Sitterson did not consider the invitations by faculty groups to be subject to the statute.

* * *

DISCUSSION

This Court is not blind to world affairs, and can understand and appreciate the vital concern of the people of the State of North Carolina over the unregulated appearance of dedicated members of the Communist Party on the campuses of its State-supported institutions. The record in this case clearly establishes that the Communist conspiracy is dedicated to the destruction of freedom, and attempts to achieve its goals of world conquest through discord, deceit and untruths. The record further establishes that the use of college campuses affords the Communist Party an optimum chance of reaching and influencing a maximum number of young people. Certainly the State is under no obligation to provide a sanctuary for the Communist Party, or a platform for propagandizing its creed.

(1) It is beyond question that boards of trustees of State-supported colleges and universities have every right to promulgate and enforce rules and regulations, consistent with constitutional principles, governing the appearance of all guest speakers. Institutions of higher learning are engaged in the education of students, rather than satisfying their whimsical curiosity. There are undoubtedly many speakers, both as individuals and with respect to the causes they espouse, who add nothing whatever to the educational process. No one has an absolute right to speak on a college or university campus, but once such institution opens its doors to visiting speakers it must do so under principles that are constitutionally valid.

We are also aware that when student groups have the privilege of inviting speakers, the pressure of considerations of audience appeal may impel them to so prefer sensationalism as to neglect academic responsibility. Such apparently motivated the plaintiff students during the spring of 1966. If the offering of the sensational becomes their primary objective, the resulting program may not complement the educational purposes of the university. One does not acquire an understanding of important racial problems by listening successively to a Stokely Carmichael or an R. Rap Brown and an officer of the Ku Klux Klan. Countering a Herbert Aptheker with an official of the American Nazi Party may furnish excitement for young people, but it presents no rational alternatives and has but dubious value as an educational experience. University students should not be insulated from the ideas of extremists, but there is danger that the voices of reason, throughout the broad spectrum they cover, will remain unheard if the clamor of extremists is disproportionately amplified on university platforms. A more balanced program, unenslaved by sensationalism, but reaching it, too, would not be calculated to evoke legislative response.

(2) We do not doubt that the 1963 and 1965 Sessions of the General Assembly, and the Commission appointed to study the vexing problems relating to the appearance of guest speakers, acted in utmost good faith and out of a genuine concern for the welfare of the students enrolled in State-supported institutions. Neither do we doubt the assertion that academic freedom, to be meaningful, demands a high degree of academic responsibility. Nevertheless, gauged by constitutional standards, our view is that the 1965 enactment of G.S. § 116–199 and § 116–200, and the procedures and regulations adopted by the Board of Trustees on February 28, 1966, pursuant to these statutes are facially unconstitutional because of vagueness. This is true even though the statutes and regulations, unlike their 1963 counterparts, only regulate, rather than prohibit, the appearance of a special group of speakers.

(3, 4) It is firmly established that a statute "which either forbids or requires the doing of an act in terms so vague that men of common intelligence must necessarily guess at its meaning and differ as to its application" violates the due process clause of the Fourteenth Amendment because of vagueness. . . . Moreover, standards of permissible statutory vagueness are particularly strict when First Amendment rights are involved. . . . While the question of vagueness has most frequently arisen in criminal prosecutions, it has been applied in a variety of other situations where the obedience to a rule or standard has been exacted. . . .

The first provision of the statute under attack covers a "known member of the Communist Party." "Known" to whom, and to what degree of certainty? "Known" according to what standard? A "member" in what sense? Does it include membership in a Communist "front" organization? Is it a matter of general reputation or rumor, or the personal knowledge of the Chancellor? The statutes and regulations provide no clues to any of these questions. Without such answers, neither those who must obey nor those who must enforce the statutes and regulations can determine the extent of their obligation.

The next provision of the statute requires regulations covering visiting speakers who are "known to advocate the overthrow of the Constitution of the United States or the State of North Carolina." Does it mean with force and arms or is the advocacy of ideas sufficient? Must the advocacy be public or private? Is the advocacy of peaceful change included? It is sufficient to say that reasonable men might differ on the answers to these questions.

The third section of the statute covers speakers who have "pleaded the Fifth Amendment of the Constitution of the United States." Presumably, this means the "self-incrimination" class, although this is a matter of conjecture. What is meant by "subversive connections"? Here again, since reasonable men might differ, the statute is unconstitutionally vague. Moreover, the imposition of any sanction by reason of the invocation of the Fifth Amendment is constitutionally impermissible. . . .

The statement of policy and the procedures and regulations adopted by the Board of Trustees suffer from the same infirmities. In order to withstand constitutional attack, they must impose a purely ministerial duty upon the person charged with approving or disapproving an invitation to a speaker falling within the statutory classifications, or contain standards sufficiently detailed to define the bounds of discretion. Neither criteria has been met with respect to the procedures and regulations in question.

. . . Similarly, in *Keyishian* v. *Board of Regents*, 385 U.S. 589 . . . the Supreme Court, in striking down certain New York statutes and administrative regulations dealing with the employment or retention of State employees because of vagueness, stated:

> There can be no doubt of the legitimacy of New York's interest in protecting its educational system from subversion. But "even though the governmental purpose be legitimate and substantial, that purpose cannot be pursued by means that broadly stifle fundamental personal liberties when the end can be more narrowly achieved."

* * *

> We emphasize once again that "[p]recision of regulation must be the touchstone in an area so closely touching our most precious freedoms . . . [f]or standards of permissible statutory vagueness are strict in the area of free expression. . . . Because First Amendment freedoms need breathing space to survive, government may regulate in the area only with narrow specificity." . . . New York's complicated and intricate scheme plainly violates that standard. When one must guess what conduct or utterance may lose him his position, one necessarily will "steer far wider of the unlawful zone." . . . For "[t]he threat of sanctions may deter . . . almost as potently as the actual application of sanctions." *N.A.A.C.P.* v. *Button,* supra. . . . The danger of that chilling effect upon the exercise of vital First Amendment rights must be guarded against by sensitive tools which clearly inform teachers what is being proscribed. . . .

> The regulatory maze created by New York is wholly lacking in "terms susceptible of objective measurement. . . . [M]en of common intelligence must necessarily guess at its meaning and differ as to its application." . . . Vagueness of wording is aggravated by prolixity and profusion of statutes, regulations, and administrative machinery, and by manifold cross-references to interrelated enactments and rules.

When the statutes and regulations in question are applied to the un-broken line of Supreme Court decisions respecting the necessity for clear, narrow and objective standards controlling the licensing of First Amendment rights, the conclusion is inescapable that they run afoul of constitutional principles.

CONCLUSIONS OF LAW

1. The Court has jurisdiction of the parties and of the subject matter.

2. The plaintiffs are entitled to an order declaring § 116–119 and § 116–200, General Statutes of North Carolina, and the procedures and regulations adopted by the Board of Trustees of the University of North Carolina pursuant thereto, to be unconstitutional and null and void.

3. The plaintiffs are further entitled to an order enjoining the defendants from further acting under said statutes, procedures and regulations.

Clemson University Vietnam Moratorium Committee v. *Clemson University*
306 Fed. Supp. 129
Nov. 11, 1969
DONALD RUSSELL, District Judge

The plaintiffs, styling themselves the Steering Committee of the Clemson University Vietnam Moratorium Committee filed this action against the President, Executive Committee and Trustees of Clemson University, seeking primarily a Temporary Restraining Order, requiring the defendants to allow the plaintiffs "to host a regional Vietnam Moratorium Day Observance" on November 13 and 14 on the campus of the University, using such facilities of the University as may be agreed upon between the Committee and the University administration. The request of the Committee for permission to "host" the proposed regional conference was submitted orally; the exact nature of the program to be had at the conference is indefinite. It is intended, however, that invitations to participate should be extended to student bodies of colleges and universities in Florida, Alabama, Arkansas, Georgia, North and South Carolina, and Tennessee. The number who might attend is indefinite, though it was hoped, according to the Committee, that three thousand students outside the Clemson body, would attend. It was proposed that the real observance should extend over a twelve-hour period from twelve o'clock noon on November 14 to twelve o'clock midnight of the same day. Space and facilities for registration were desired by the Committee. In addition, there would be refreshment stands set up and booths where badges and other mementoes of the occasion would be sold. From six o'clock on there would be meetings. Some of these would be small panel discussions, for which appropriate accommodations would be required. Later, a debate or confrontation between a "dove" and a "hawk" on the Vietnam involvement would be had. The Committee, through cooperation with the National Committee for the observance of a Vietnam Moratorium Observance would supply the "dove" and an auxiliary of the John Birch Society was expected to supply the "hawk." The National Committee had agreed to support financially the observance.

The plaintiffs, through their counsel, conceded that, if the hosting of the regional observance was authorized, the University should take steps to provide police protection for the meetings. To aid in this, one who was cooperating with the Committee-plaintiff stated it was planned to create for those interested in the observance a group of so-called marshals to the number of one hundred twenty-five. The number of highway patrolmen which it was thought the University should secure from the State Highway Department to afford proper protection for the observance was never precisely stated; it was plain, however, that a substantial force was believed to be necessary. It is accordingly clear that the Committee itself felt that the observance would involve very real danger of riot and commotion. It seems likely, however, that, as the plaintiffs argue, the spark for such commotion would be struck by those opposed to the observance. It cannot be overlooked, though, that, in an hour of extreme tension and apprehension on both sides it is difficult to anticipate just what will fire an explosion.

The University, fearing a campus disruption, refused to approve the request that it approve the hosting of the regional observance. It did state to the Committee that it would happily approve a local observance, to be participated in by the students of Clemson, and to have such speakers as the Committee might like. It took the position that it could provide security for such an observance through its ability to discipline the members of its own student body. This permission, which apparently the Committee spurned, provided those members of the Clemson student body with the freest possible right of assembly and of speech, according to the University authorities.

On a few occasions since 1964, the University, at the instance of recognized student organizations, has permitted meetings for University students to hear political speakers. While, as said, meetings have been held on University premises for University students and sponsored by a recognized student organization, there was no restriction on public attendance. There was no public announcement of the meeting as one for the general public but the meeting was advertised as one sponsored by Clemson students for Clemson students.

The plaintiffs refer in their affidavits to two meetings held in University facilities, with the permission of the University authorities, at which representatives from colleges within the State were invited, for the purpose of conducting "Black Identity" studies. The purpose of such meetings was seemingly to bring together black and white students so that the two groups could better understand one another and live together more harmoniously. So far as the record shows, despite the fact that the subject for discussion at such meetings was one that in the past would have been regarded as explosive in the South, no difficulties were encountered and no threat of violence had.

On the basis of these facts, the plaintiffs assert that the University, in denying them the right to host the regional meeting, has illegally curtailed their constitutional rights of free speech and assembly and has denied them the equal protection of the laws. The defendants deny any such infringement of the plaintiff's rights and have moved to dismiss the proceeding for want of federal question.

(1) I am of opinion that, on this record, the temporary restraining order sought by the plaintiffs should be denied.

The claim of an infringement of the constitutional right of free speech and assembling is novel. Unlike the situation in *Hammond* v. *South Carolina State College* . . . 272 F. Supp. 947, the plaintiffs have not been denied the right to assemble in protest; that right, it is conceded, the University has offered the plaintiffs. Unlike *Tinker* v. *Des Moines Independent Community School Dist.* (1969) 393 U.S. 503, 89 S.Ct. 733, L.Ed.2d 731, the plaintiffs are not strained in their right to demonstrate support of their views through an observance program; that right, too, the University has recognized and permitted. Unlike *Dickson* v. *Sitterson* (D.C.N. 1968) 280 F.Supp. 486, and *Brooks* v. *Auburn University* (D.C.Ala.1969) 2 F.Supp 188, the University has imposed no ban on any speaker; the plaintiffs have been given the right to invite to the campus for an observance of a Vietnam Moratorium any speaker they desire.

All that the plaintiffs are denied, according to their own statement of the complaint in their own brief, is the right "to host a regional Vietnam Moratorium Day Observance" on the Clemson campus, utilizing for such purposes University grounds and facilities and operating under at least the semi-official auspices of the University. In fact, they claim that this is a right any group, however informal, has, because the University property is State property. I do not think constitutional rights extend so far. As the Court said . . . the right of free speech does not mean that the right may be exercised on public property any way one pleases in any place one chooses. When a public college or university extends its students the right to assemble, demonstrate and to speak, using such speakers as they select, it has accorded to its students free speech. It does not have to make of its campus, dedicated to educational pursuits for its own students, a "donnybrook" or a "Woodstock" for students, drawn from a widely distributed area and in no wise subject to the control of its own disciplinary procedures, in order for them to have a meeting on its premises using its facilities, especially when it is conceded that such meeting involves dangers of rioting, against which the University should with proper caution (as the plaintiffs by their counsel concede in this case) guard by importing onto its campus a considerable body of outside policemen. The very presence of such outside policemen, as recently experienced at other universities and colleges, is an incitement to violence by the students. For this reason, wise counselors have suggested that, if at all possible, such outside forces should never be brought on the campus. Yet, as I have said, the plaintiffs herein express the opinion that, because of the circumstances attending the earlier observance of the University, a substantial body of these outside forces should be stationed on the campus as a precautionary measure.

The plaintiffs contend that, to deny them the right here sought would be to deny them equal protection of the law. This claim of infringement rests on the fact that the University has permitted other groups to have meetings on the campus. Three of these meetings were sponsored by local campus groups for the benefit of the student population. They were local or University affairs, though a few members of the public may have attended. They were the same as the observance the University permitted the plaintiff group to have on October 13 and have offered to permit on November 14. There is no difference in treatment between that accorded the rights of the plaintiffs and those given these three groups.

The only type of meeting authorized by the University having any analogy to that proposed by the plaintiffs is the "Black Identity" meetings. These have not been confined to Clemson students. Students from other colleges in the State of South Carolina have been invited to attend. But, it is conceded that there has never been either any violence or even threat of violence at such meetings—and this represents an important difference between such meetings and that proposed by the plaintiffs. Too, these meetings were far smaller than that proposed by the plaintiffs. They posed none of the problems of housing and feeding created by the proposed meeting. To bring thousands of visitors on a college campus for a midnight vigil is almost an invitation to violence. And this would be especially true in a small, remote college community such as Clemson.

The plaintiffs suggest that the defendants have denied them the right to "host" the regional conference because of the fear of public resentment. They picture the action of the defendants as a craven truckling to majority opinion on the part of the "Establishment." This argument lacks persuasiveness. If, in approving or disapproving a meeting, the defendants were motived by considerations of public approval, they would hardly have authorized the "Black Identity" meetings. These dealt with a subject fraught with far more combustible features than that involved in the proposed observance. The very fact that the University authorities have authorized and supported these "Black Identity" meetings is cogent proof of their good faith in seeking fairly to secure to their students their rights of free speech and assembly and the opportunity to discuss candidly subjects on which there are strong feelings still in South Carolina. For this reason I cannot take lightly their expressions of fear of violence and commotion that would attend the proposed regional meetings.

The plaintiffs argue that the only threat of violence comes from those of the Clemson students who are hostile to the demonstration; and that it is unfair to permit them, by their threat of violence, to prevent the regional observance. . . . There is much merit in this point if the issue was protection of the right of the Clemson student himself to free speech; and, if the threat was permitted by the defendants to prevent the plaintiffs from having a demonstration of their views on Vietnam or from exercising free speech, appeal to this Court might well be appropriate. But this is not the situation. The University accepts its responsibility to assure to its students the right to free speech as to the Vietnam involvement and it is prepared to provide protection for the exercise of such rights. It does not accept, however, the responsibility for sponsoring a gathering of students from over five or six states, students for whose conduct it cannot be responsible and whose conduct it cannot restrain by the threat of disciplinary action. Some of those students may come for purposes of disrupting the meeting; some may come for using it as a means of creating hostility and for generating an environment ripe for violence. The University is entitled to protect itself from such difficulties, created by persons to whom it owes no responsibility. Its requirement to accord constitutional rights may well be deemed to extend merely to its own students.

Finally, even the plaintiffs are at some loss on the nature of the order they seek. They have no real plans for their proposed conference. They admit that the parties were proceeding in good faith, to maintain almost continuous surveillance of the cooperation between the plaintiffs and the defendants. In fact, it is very doubtful that given the small amount of time intervening before the observance, any regional meeting could be had. Invitations could hardly reach most of the student groups before the date of the observance. The security arrangements which the plaintiffs themselves assert would be necesary, at this stage cannot be assured on such short notice. All in all, this application comes so late that, if any affirmative action were taken, this Court would likely be required to supervise every detail of the planning. That is not a proper role for the judiciary.

Under all the circumstances and given proper regard to all the facts, I feel the application for a temporary restraining order herein should be denied.

And it is so ordered.

Matter of Buckley v. *Meng*
35 Misc.2d 467
June 25, 1962

JACOB MARKOWITZ, J.

"[C]ourage [is] the secret of liberty" (*Whitney* v. *California,* 274 U.S. 357, 375, concurring opinion of BRANDEIS, J.) and, therefore, timidity on the part of its officials in the fact of heretical or controversial ideas cannot be tolerated in a democratic society. When such timidity is embodied in an official regulation governing the use of school buildings, it must be struck down as violative of the First Amendment to our Federal Constitution.

The issue before me arises out of the refusal by the administrative committee of Hunter College—one of the municipal colleges established by the Board of Higher Education of the City of New York—to lease to petitioners, the editor and the publisher of the *National Review,* a journal of conservative opinion, the Hunter College auditorium for the purpose of conducting a series of forums. Since 1954, the *National Review* and *The Alliance,* a predecessor conservative organization, had sponsored an annual series of lectures or forums and leased the Hunter College auditorium for that purpose. In January, 1961, however, the *National Review* was advised by the dean of administration of Hunter College that the college would no longer lease its premises to the *Review.*

The circumstances under which the *Review's* long-standing lease arrangement was terminated are of some significance and they are set forth in the pleadings without dispute. On December 1, 1960, the *Review* had sponsored a lecture by Jacques Soustelle, one of the leaders of the French rightist movement aimed at keeping Algeria French. Evidently, the meeting had aroused great controversy and it had been picketed. The very next day, the dean of administration wrote the editor of the *Review* requesting a copy of his introductory remarks at the Soustelle meeting. It was after he had received a copy of the introductory remarks that the dean wrote the letter to the *Review* telling them that they could no longer lease the Hunter auditorium.

In this letter of January 12, 1961, the dean explained the basis of his action by saying that, as a result of reading the introductory remarks of the editor, he had formed the opinion that the *Review* was clearly "a political group presenting a distinct point of view of its own" and that the college was "enjoined from allowing the Assembly and the Playhouse to serve as a forum for such political groups." And he added, as if to indicate that this fact was plainly determinative of the matter, "picketing went on at the Soustelle meeting."

In April of 1961, after the matter had been brought to the attention of the president of Hunter College, he addressed a letter to the editor of the *Review* in which he said that "these halls are not available for political or other public movements or groups in presenting a distinct position or point of view opposed by substantial parts of the public." The president also added that the rationale of the policy was that "academic institutions of a public character must avoid giving the appearance or creating the suspicion that they favor particular movements or groups over other groups opposed to their positions or their points of view."

It should be noted that the statements of policy expressed by the administrative dean and the president did not refer to any preexisting regulations governing the use of Hunter College's facilities. They were more in the nature of expressions of personal views than implementations of existing regulations. In fact, it was not until June 1961, that the administrative committee of the college promulgated the set of "Policies Governing Use of Hunter College Facilities" which the college relies upon in this proceeding.

Turning now to this statement of policy, it provides that the college facilities are "primarily for academic use." It then goes on to specify permissible nonacademic uses. In the first category of nonacademic uses are student extracurricular activities; in the second, activities of professional or academic organizations; in the third, educational conferences; finally, the fourth and last category is set forth, as follows: "Other programs offered by outside organizations insofar as these are determined to be compatible with the aims of Hunter College as a public institution of higher learning. This criterion is not met, for example, by organizations whose meetings have caused disturbances; whose presence would tend to impair the good name or the academic prestige of the College; or whose character would give reasonable grounds for the assumption that the College favors particular groups or movements having a distinct point of view or position over other groups or movements opposed to their point of view or position."

In this article 78 proceeding, the editor and the publisher of the *National Review* challenge both the validity and the application of the regulations which have denied them the right to use Hunter College's auditorium. The petitioners contend that, although there is no duty to make public schools available for nonacademic uses, once having made them available, the regulations governing the use must meet constitutional standards, in particular, the standards of the First Amendment. To this the respondents answer by asserting that, as long as the regulations "do not discriminate against a prospective tenant by refusing him while renting to others in the same category for the same use," there is no constitutional infirmity and the regulations must be upheld.

It is plain, then, that both parties agree that the duly constituted school authorities may regulate the nonacademic use of school facilities. The only issue remaining, therefore, is whether the regulations concerned are reasonable and within the bounds of constitutional propriety. In my view, the Hunter College regulations are either so vague as to invite discriminatory and arbitrary regulations, or else must be taken to rest upon a classification of uses which has no place in a democratic society because it stifles rather than stimulates the free discussion of vital public issues.

Freedom of speech is "basic to a free and dynamic society." . . . [S]ome have even suggested that freedom of speech has a "preferred position" in the constellation of constitutional rights. . . . It is in the light of the paramount value of free expression that the courts have drawn the corollary rule that any limitations on such expression must be drawn with precision. . . . The reason for the requirement of clarity may be stated simply: we value speech so highly, that we will only enforce a restriction on speech which is not subject to expansion at the discretionary whim of one who applies it. We will not tolerate "dubious intrusions" . . . which arise out of vagueness in the standards which restrict this valued right.

* * *

Turning now to the standard by which Hunter College proposes to determine who shall use its facilities, I find that it partakes of that quality of indefiniteness which renders it offensive to First Amendment principles. As I have already indicated, the regulation concerned provides that "Other programs [using Hunter College's facilities may be] offered by outside organizations insofar as these are determined to be compatible with the aims of Hunter College as a public institution of higher learning." This is not a standard of such clarity that one who reads it can know whether a given use falls within it or without.

In the first place, the regulation bespeaks its own indefiniteness by reason of the fact that it expressly provides that in order to qualify, a program must be *"determined to be compatible* with the aims of Hunter College." Thus, a decision as to whether a program is permissible depends on a determination outside the scope and terms of the regulation. Who is empowered to make such a determination? And by what standards? In effect, whether a program is permissible or not rests on the untrammeled discretion of some official.

In the second place, even if we neglect this imperfection, and read the regulation as providing that "other programs" are permissible if they are "compatible with the aims of Hunter College as a public institution of higher learning," we are left to bare speculation and surmise in deciding whether a use is permissible or not. Search my mind as I will, I cannot state with any precision what the aims of Hunter College are. Furthermore, I have grave doubt that any two professors or administrators could agree on a precise definition of such aims.

I would have thought, for instance, that one of the aims of a college worthy of the name was to stimulate thought and to provoke intellectual controversy. The action of the dean of administration and the president of Hunter in this case bespeaks a contrary belief—they seem to regard intellectual quiescence and freedom from any conceivable identification with strongly expressed views as being necessary to their educational goals. I do not, of course, judicially deny them the right to determine the aims of their college. I do judicially hold, however, that consistency with the aims of the college is not a sufficiently clear standard by which to determine who shall use the college's facilities because reasonable men can and do differ as to what these aims are. As long as it is possible for reasonable men to differ as to what a given standard means, that standard cannot properly serve as a basis for a limitation on First Amendment rights.

The vice of vagueness in these matters is perfectly illustrated in the case at hand. For here, evidently, the college administration has found that a celebration of independence of new African nations and a commemoration of the political uprisings in Hungary, for example—which two programs were both sanctioned—were permissible uses because consistent with the aims of the college. But they found that a program in which Jacques Soustelle attacked French policy on Algeria fell outside the permissible uses and was inconsistent with the aims of the college. All three programs seem to have had a political content and all three seem to have taken a firm stand in favor of one or another political position. And yet two of them were found permissible, the third not.

What makes a distinction between one or another of these three programs at all plausible is the very vagueness of the applicable standard. The administrator, whether consciously or not, has substituted his own bias and predilection for the letter of the standard. And he has been able to do this because the standard itself does not supply him with sufficient criteria for decision; the administrator has filled a decisional vacuum, so to speak. Whatever the effect of the substitution of personal judgment and discretion for the letter of the law may be in other instances, it is intolerable when hallowed First Amendment rights are at stake.

The college authorities seem to argue, however, that there is a real distinction between Soustelle lecturing on a French Algeria and the celebration of Hungarian political uprisings. And they seem to believe that this distinction is embodied in the statement of "Policies Governing Use of Hunter College Facilities" and that it saves it from unconstitutional vagueness. The portion of the statement of policy referred to is that which provides that the criteria for use of the college's facilities are not met by organizations "whose character would give reasonable grounds for the assumption that the college favors particular groups or movements having a distinct point of view or position over other groups or movements opposed to their point of view or position."

Now, it is not at all clear to me exactly what this statement means and were I to have no other guide to what was intended to be prohibited than these words I would find them, like the positive criteria for use of the facilities discussed above, unconstitutionally vague. I am constrained to believe, however, that what is intended by this language is a thought expressed in one of the letters the president of Hunter wrote to the editor of the *Review*—a thought also expressed in the college's brief in this court. What is intended is that the college avoid scheduling unpopular or controversial lectures or forums. Thus, in the letter the president wrote to one of the petitioners in April, 1961, he said that "these halls are not available for political or other public movements or groups in presenting a distinct position or point of view opposed by substantial parts of the public." In respondents' brief is found the assertion that an organization "may not use these facilities for conducting controversial discussions." Similar expressions are found at other points in the correspondence between the parties and in other exhibits before me.

If I am correct in supposing that one of the criteria for the use of Hunter College's facilities is whether or not the proposed program presents a popular, noncontroversial point of view—one which is not "opposed by substantial parts of the public," to quote the president's words—it would follow that the standard for the use of the facilities is indeed clear. It would also follow, however, that this clear standard is itself unconstitutional because it discriminates against the expression of unpopular, minority opinion.

It should be stated at once that the college officials are not so crass as to reject minority viewpoints because of their content; they would prevent minorities of the right as well as of the left from expounding their views in the college halls. Their motives are rather to avoid identification with any minority position and to avoid picketing and other such "disturbances"—the quotation is from the college's statement of policy—which sometimes attend, as they did in the Soustelle meeting, the public meetings of dissident groups. To my mind, as well-intentioned as these aims are, they evidence a temper of mind alien to the spirit of liberty and incompatible with the philosophy of the First Amendment.

In his essay "On Liberty," John Stuart Mill stated in words which will ring true as long as democracy remains a vibrant form of government the value of the voice of dissent. He said: "the peculiar evil of silencing the expression of opinion is that it is robbing the human race; posterity as well as the existing generation; those who dissent from the opinion still more than those who hold it. If the opinion is right, they are deprived of the opportunity of exchanging error for truth; if wrong, they lose what is almost as great a benefit, the clearer perception and livelier impression of truth, produced by its collision with error." And he added, at a later point in the essay, the thought that: "if there are any persons who contest a received opinion, or will do so if law or opinion will let them, let us thank them for it, open our minds to listen to them, and rejoice that there is some one to do for us what we otherwise ought, if we have any regard for either the certainty or the vitality of our convictions, to do with much greater labor for ourselves."

Whosoever cherishes liberty and dissent as Mill did must be prepared to pay its price. And that price includes suffering the clamor and disturbance, the elevated emotions and postures of defiance, which are generated by giving the voice of dissent free rein. Whenever men disagree, and especially when they disagree about issues which are dear to them, there is the danger that the opposition may pass from the realm of ideas to the realm of action. Unless we are prepared to forswear the values attendant upon the free expression of ideas, we must sacrifice that sense of security and quietude which would attend unanimous belief.

Our dedication as a nation to this philosophy has, of course, been expressed with eloquence and force in courts of law as well as in many other forums of opinion. Nowhere, in my view, has it been more eloquently and forcefully expounded than in the concurring opinion of Justice Brandeis, in which Justice Holmes joined, in the case of *Whitney* v. *California* (274 U.S. 357, 375, supra) : "Those who won our independence believed that the final end of the State was to make men free to develop their faculties; and that in its government the deliberative forces should prevail over the arbitrary. They valued liberty both as an end and as a means. They believed liberty to be the secret of happiness and courage to be the secret of liberty. They believed that freedom to think as you will and to speak as you think are means indispensable to the discovery and spread of political truth; that without free speech and assembly discussion would be futile; that with them, discussion affords ordinarily adequate protection against the dissemination of noxious doctrine; that the greatest menace to freedom is an inert people; that public discussion is a political duty; and that this should be a fundamental principle of American government."

The Hunter College administration will answer, of course, that these pronouncements are misdirected when directed at them; that they have the same dedication to liberty that is here expressed; that they are not trying to stifle opinion but only to protect the good name of the college; that the use of school buildings is a privilege and not a right and that, therefore, it may be limited; and, finally, that they do not deny the *National Review* the opportunity to express its views, they only deny them the right to do so in a school building.

Let me make it clear immediately that I have no doubt that the Hunter College administration is motivated by good intentions and that they hold as steadfastly as any of us do to the fundamental principles of free speech. I am persuaded, however, that they are in error in their application of these principles to the facts of this case.

The overriding issue as to use of school facilities for nonacademic purposes is not raised. Thus, while there may be no duty to open the doors of the school houses for uses other than academic—and I have some doubt even as to this proposition—once they are opened they must be opened under conditions consistent with constitutional principle. . . . As the Supreme Court of California expressed it in the *Danskin* case, very similar to this: "The state is under no duty to make school buildings available for public meetings. . . . If it elects to do so, however, it cannot arbitrarily prevent any members of the public from holding such meetings [nor] . . . make the privilege of holding them dependent on conditions that would deprive any members of the public of their constitutional rights. A state is without power to impose an unconstitutional requirement as a condition for granting a privilege even though the privilege is the use of state property." . . .

The principle of these cases is the simple one that what the State cannot do directly it may not do indirectly. Since there is no power in the State to stifle minority opinion directly by forbidding its expression, it may not accomplish this same purpose by allowing its facilities to be used by proponents of majority opinion while denying them to dissenters. The Supreme Court declared . . . that the guarantee of the First Amendment "is not confined to the expression of ideas that are conventional or shared by a majority." This being so, Hunter College may not forbid its facilities—to quote again the words of its president— to "groups . . . presenting a distinct position or point of view opposed by substantial parts of the public."

To be sure, the Hunter College authorities are motivated by the desire to preserve the good name of their college, rather than by a desire to stifle minority opinion. But even if I were to suppose that they are correct in believing that to allow dissenting opinion to be expressed from their platforms has a tendency to besmirch the institution—and I, in fact, think they are wrong in this—this would not provide a sufficient reason to deny the expression of the opinion. To quote again from Justice Brandeis in the *Whitney* case (274 U.S. 357, 377, supra) —and it is a view, of course, which has been stated by the Supreme Court on so many occasions that it is superfluous to even cite them—"Only an emergency can justify repression."

The danger of our times is not that we as a people have become aroused to fever pitch by the excitement of ideas. It is rather the opposite, that we as a people have become inert and conformist, that we do not often enough hear the vital issues of our day mooted from public platforms. The danger is that our principles will lose—to quote Mill—"the clearer perception and livelier impression . . . produced by [their] collision with error" or that we will be "deprived of the opportunity of exchanging error for truth."

These being the dangers of our day a college should, to my mind, pursue a policy of fostering discussion and the exchange of opinion by providing an open forum for it to all who want to be heard. A college should generate intellectual excitement; it should attempt to awaken the public mind from the torpor and quiescence of accepted and conventional opinion.

This court cannot, of course, impose such a policy on officials who are themselves empowered under law to formulate the policy of their educational institution. This court can and must, however, forbid Hunter College from denying discussion of public issues from its halls on the ground that it is the voice of a minority or the voice of one not approved by an official acting under the present regulations. The current regulations governing the use of Hunter College's facilities are either unconstitutionally vague or else they embody unconstitutional principle of selection. In either case, they must be struck down and the administrative committee of the college must with all due speed enact a new set of regulations consistent with the foregoing, under which the petitioners may once again apply for a lease of Hunter College's facilities.

5
Loyalty Oaths—Fifth Amendment

Wieman v. *Updegraff*
344 U.S. 183
Dec. 15, 1952
MR. JUSTICE CLARK delivered the opinion of the Court.

This is an appeal from a decision of the Supreme Court of Oklahoma upholding the validity of a loyalty oath prescribed by Oklahoma statute for all state officers and employees. . . . Appellants, employed by the State as members of the faculty and staff of Oklahoma Agricultural and Mechanical College, failed, within the thirty days permitted, to take the oath required by the Act. Appellee Updegraff, as a citizen and taxpayer, thereupon brought this suit in the District Court of Oklahoma County to enjoin the necessary state officials from paying further compensation to employees who had not subscribed to the oath. The appellants, who were permitted to intervene, attacked the validity of the Act on the grounds, among others, that it was a bill of attainder; an *ex post facto* law; impaired the obligation of their contracts with the State and violated the Due Process Clause of the Fourteenth Amendment. They also sought a mandatory injunction directing the state officers to pay their salaries regardless of their failure to take the oath. Their objections centered largely on the following clauses of the oath:

> That I am not affiliated directly or indirectly . . . with any foreign political agency, party, organization or Government, or with any agency, party, organization, association, or group whatever which has been officially determined by the United States Attorney General or other authorized agency of the United States to be a communist front or subversive organization; . . . that I will take up arms in the defense of the United States in time of War, or National Emergency, if necessary; that within the five (5) years immediately preceding the taking of this oath (or affirmation) I have not been a member of . . .

any agency, party, organization, association, or group whatever which has been officially determined by the United States Attorney General or other authorized public agency of the United States to be a communist front or subversive organization.

The court upheld the Act and enjoined the state officers from making further salary payments to appellants. . . . We noted probable jurisdiction because of the public importance of this type of legislation and the recurring serious constitutional questions which it presents.

The District Court of Oklahoma County in holding the Act valid concluded that the appellants were compelled to take the oath as written; that the appellants "and each of them, did not take and subscribe to the oath as provided in section 2 of the Act and wilfully refused to take that oath and by reason thereof the Board of Regents is enjoined from paying them, and their employment is terminated." In affirming, the Supreme Court of Oklahoma held that the phrase of the oath "any foreign political agency, party, organization or Government, or with any agency, party, organization, association, or group whatever which has been officially determined by the United States Attorney General or other authorized agency of the United States to be a communist front or subversive organization" actually "refers to a list or lists of such organizations in existence at the time of the passage of the act which had been prepared by the Attorney General [of the United States] under governmental directive. Such list or lists are in effect made a part of the oath by reference." On this point the opinion continues: "There is no requirement in the act that an oath be taken of nonmembership in organizations not on the list of the Attorney General of the United States at the time of the passage of this act."

We read this part of the highest state court's decision as limiting the organizations proscribed by the Act to those designated on the list or lists of the Attorney General which had been issued prior to the effective date of the Act. Although this interpretation discarded clear language of the oath as surplusage, the court denied the appellants' petition for rehearing which included a plea that refusal of the court to permit appellants to take the oath as so interpreted was violative of due process.

The purpose of the Act, we are told, "was to make loyalty a qualification to hold public office or be employed by the State." . . . During periods of international stress, the extent of legislation with such objectives accentuates our traditional concern about the relation of government to the individual in a free society. The perennial problem of defining that relationship becomes acute when disloyalty is screened by ideological patterns and techniques of disguise that make it difficult to identify. Democratic government is not powerless to meet this threat, but it must do so without infringing the freedoms that are the ultimate values of all democratic living. In the adoption of such means as it believes effective, the legislature is therefore confronted with the problem of balancing its interest in national security with the often conflicting constitutional rights of the individual.

* * *

. . . We are thus brought to the question . . . whether the Due Process Clause permits a state, in attempting to bar disloyal individuals from its employ, to exclude persons solely on the basis of organizational membership, regardless of their knowledge concerning the organizations to which they had belonged. For, under the statute before us, the fact of membership alone disqualifies. If the rule be expressed as a presumption of disloyalty, it is a conclusive one.

But membership may be innocent. A state servant may have joined a proscribed organization unaware of its activities and purposes. In recent years, many completely loyal persons have severed organizational ties after learning for the first time of the character of groups to which they had belonged. "They had joined, [but] did not know what it was; they were good, fine young men and women, loyal Americans, but they had been trapped into it—because one of the great weaknesses of all Americans, whether adult or youth, is to join something." At the time of affiliation, a group itself may be innocent, only later coming under the influence of those who would turn it toward illegitimate ends. Conversely, an organization formerly subversive and therefore designated as such may have subsequently freed itself from the influences which originally led to its listing.

There can be no dispute about the consequences visited upon a person excluded from public employment on disloyalty grounds. In the view of the community, the stain is a deep one; indeed, it has become a badge of infamy. Especially is this so in time of cold war and hot emotions when "each man begins to eye his neighbor as a possible enemy."* Yet under the Oklahoma Act, the fact of association alone determines disloyalty and disqualification; it matters not whether association existed innocently or knowingly. To thus inhibit individual freedom of movement is to stifle the flow of democratic expression and controversy at one of its chief sources. . . . Indiscriminate classification of innocent with knowing activity must fall as an assertion of arbitrary power. The oath offends due process.

* * *

Reversed.

MR. JUSTICE JACKSON, not having heard the argument, took no part in the consideration or decision of this case.

MR. JUSTICE BURTON concurs in the result.

MR. JUSTICE BLACK, concurring

I concur in all the Court says in condemnation of Oklahoma's test

---

* Address by Judge Learned Hand at the 86th Convocation of the University of the State of New York, delivered October 24, 1952, at Albany, New York.

oath. I agree that the State Act prescribing that test oath is fatally offensive to the due process guarantee of the United States Constitution.

History indicates that individual liberty is intermittently subjected to extraordinary perils. Even countries dedicated to government by the people are not free from such cyclical dangers. The first years of our Republic marked such a period. Enforcement of the Alien and Sedition Laws by zealous patriots who feared ideas made it highly dangerous for people to think, speak, or write critically about government, its agents, or its policies, either foreign or domestic. Our constitutional liberties survived the ordeal of this regrettable period because there were influential men and powerful organized groups bold enough to champion the undiluted right of individuals to publish and argue for their beliefs however unorthodox or loathsome. Today, however, few individuals and organizations of power and influence argue that unpopular advocacy has this same wholly unqualified immunity from governmental interference. For this and other reasons the present period of fear seems more ominously dangerous to speech and press than was that of the Alien and Sedition Laws. Suppressive laws and practices are the fashion. The Oklahoma oath statute is but one manifestation of a national network of laws aimed at coercing and controlling the minds of men. Test oaths are notorious tools of tyranny. When used to shackle the mind they are, or at least they should be, unspeakably odious to a free people. Test oaths are made still more dangerous when combined with bills of attainder which, like this Oklahoma statute, impose pains and penalties for past lawful associations and utterances.

Governments need and have ample power to punish treasonable acts. But it does not follow that they must have a further power to punish thought and speech as distinguished from acts. Our own free society should never forget that laws which stigmatize and penalize thought and speech of the unorthodox have a way of reaching, ensnaring and silencing many more people than at first intended. We must have freedom of speech for all or we will in the long run have it for none but the cringing and the craven. And I cannot too often repeat my belief that the right to speak on matters of public concern must be wholly free or eventually be wholly lost.

It seems self-evident that all speech criticizing government rulers and challenging current beliefs may be dangerous to the status quo. With full knowledge of this danger the Framers rested our First Amendment on the premise that the slightest suppression of thought, speech, press, or public assembly is still more dangerous. This means that individuals are guaranteed an undiluted and unequivocal right to express themselves on questions of current public interest. It means that Americans discuss such questions as of right and not on sufferance of legislatures, courts or any other governmental agencies. It means that courts are without power to appraise and penalize utterances upon their notion that these utterances are dangerous. In my view this uncompromising interpretation of the Bill of Rights is the one that must prevail if its freedoms are to be saved. Tyrannical totalitarian governments cannot safely allow their people to speak with complete freedom. I believe with the Framers that our free Government can.

MR. JUSTICE DOUGLAS concurs in this opinion.

MR. JUSTICE FRANKFURTER, whom Mr. JUSTICE DOUGLAS joins, concurring.

The times being what they are, it is appropriate to add a word by way of emphasis to the Court's opinion, which I join.

* * *

That our democracy ultimately rests on public opinion is a platitude of speech but not a commonplace in action. Public opinion is the ultimate reliance of our society only if it be disciplined and responsible. It can be disciplined and responsible only if habits of open-mindedness and of critical inquiry are acquired in the formative years of our citizens. The process of education has naturally enough been the basis of hope for the perdurance of our democracy on the part of all our great leaders, from Thomas Jefferson onwards.

To regard teachers—in our entire educational system, from the primary grades to the university—as the priests of our democracy is therefore not to indulge in hyperbole. It is the special task of teachers to foster those habits of open-mindedness and critical inquiry which alone make for responsible citizens, who, in turn, make possible an enlightened and effective public opinion. Teachers must fulfill their function by precept and practice, by the very atmosphere which they generate; they must be exemplars of open-mindedness and free inquiry. They cannot carry out their noble task if the conditions for the practice of a responsible and critical mind are denied to them. They must have the freedom of responsible inquiry, by thought and action, into the meaning of social and economic ideas, into the checkered history of social and economic dogma. They must be free to sift evanescent doctrine, qualified by time and circumstance, from that restless, enduring process of extending the bounds of understanding and wisdom, to assure which the freedoms of thought, of speech, of inquiry, of worship are guaranteed by the Constitution of the United States against infraction by National or State government.

The functions of educational institutions in our national life and the conditions under which alone they can adequately perform them are at the basis of these limitations upon State and National power. These functions and the essential conditions for their effective discharge have been well described by a leading educator:

Now, a university is a place that is established and will function for the benefit of society, provided it is a center of independent thought.

It is a center of independent thought and criticism that is created in the interest of the progress of society, and the one reason that we know that every totalitarian government must fail is that no totalitarian government is prepared to face the consequences of creating free universities.

It is important for this purpose to attract into the institution men of the greatest capacity, and to encourage them to exercise their independent judgment.

Education is a kind of continuing dialogue, and a dialogue assumes, in the nature of the case, different points of view.

The civilization which I work, and which I am sure every American is working, toward, could be called a civilization of the dialogue, where instead of shooting one another when you differ, you reason things out together.

In this dialogue, then, you cannot assume that you are going to have everybody thinking the same way or feeling the same way. It would be unprogressive if that happened. The hope of eventual development would be gone. More than that, of course, it would be very boring.

A university, then is a kind of continuous Socratic conversation on the highest level for the very best people you can think of, you can bring together, about the most important questions, and the thing that you must do to uttermost possible limits is to guarantee those men the freedom to think and express themselves.

*   *   *

Baggett v. *Bullitt*
377 U.S. 360
June 1, 1964
MR. JUSTICE WHITE delivered the opinion of the Court.

Appellants, approximately 64 in number, are members of the faculty, staff and student body of the University of Washington, who brought this class action asking for a judgment declaring unconstitutional two Washington statutes requiring the execution of two different oaths by state employees and for an injunction against the enforcement of these statutes by appellees, the President of the University, members of the Washington State Board of Regents and the State Attorney General.

The statutes under attack are Chapter 377, Laws of 1955, and Chapter 103, Laws of 1931, both of which require employees of the State of Washington to take the oaths prescribed in the statutes as a condition of their employment. The 1931 legislation applies only to teachers, who, upon applying for a license to teach or renewing an existing contract, are required to subscribe to the following:

I solemnly swear (or affirm) that I will support the constitution and laws of the United States of America and of the State of Washington and will by precept and example promote respect for the flag and the institutions of the United States of America and the State of Washington, reverence for law and order and undivided allegiance to the government of the United States.

The oath requirements of the 1955 Act, Wash. Laws 1955, c. 377, applicable to all state employees, incorporate various provisions of the Washington Subversive Activities Act of 1951, which provides generally that "[n]o subversive person, as defined in this act, shall be eligible for employment in, or appointment to any office, or any position of trust or profit in the government, or in the administration of the business, of this state, or of any county, municipality, or other political subdivision of this state." . . . The term "subversive person" is defined as follows:

"Subversive person" means any person who commits, attempts to commit, or aids in the commission, or advocates, abets, advises or teaches by any means any person to commit, attempt to commit, or aid in the commission of any act intended to overthrow, destroy or alter, or to assist in the overthrow, destruction or alteration of, the constitutional form of the government of the United States, or of the state of Washington, or any political subdivision of either of them by revolution, force, or violence; or who with knowledge that the organization is an organization as described in subsections (2) and (3) hereof, becomes or remains a member of a subversive organization or a foreign subversive organization.

The Act goes on to define at similar length and in similar terms "subversive organization" and "foreign subversive organization" and to declare the Communist Party a subversive organization and membership therein a subversive activity.

* * *

I

Appellants contend in this Court that the oath requirements and the statutory provisions on which they are based are invalid on their face because their language is unduly vague, uncertain and broad. We agree with this contention and therefore, without treating the numerous other contentions pressed upon us, confine our considerations to that particular question.

In *Cramp* v. *Board of Public Instruction*, 368 U.S. 278, the Court invalidated an oath requiring teachers and other employees of the State to swear that they had never lent their "aid, support, advice, counsel or influence to the Communist Party" because the oath was lacking in "terms susceptible of objective measurement" and failed to inform as to what the State commanded or forbade. The statute therefore fell within the compass of those decisions of the Court holding that a law forbidding or requiring conduct in terms so vague that men of common intelligence must necessarily guess at its meaning and differ as to its application violates due process of law. . . .

The oath required by the 1955 statute suffers from similar infirmities. A teacher must swear that he is not a subversive person: that he is not one who commits an act or who advises, teaches, abets or advocates by any means another person to commit or aid in the commission of any act intended to overthrow or alter, or to assist the overthrow or alteration, of the constitutional form of government by revolution, force or violence. A subversive organization is defined as one which engages in or assists activities intended to alter or overthrow the Government by force or violence or which has as a purpose the commission of such acts. The Communist Party is declared in the statute to be a subversive organization, that is, it is presumed that the Party does and will engage in activities intended to overthrow the Government. Persons required to swear they understand this oath may quite reasonably conclude that any person who aids the Communist Party or teaches or advises known members of the Party is a subversive person because such teaching or advice may now or at some future date aid the activities of the Party. Teaching and advising are clearly acts, and one cannot confidently assert that his counsel, aid, influence or support which adds to the resources, rights and knowledge of the Communist Party or its members does not aid the Party in its activities, activities which the statute tells us are all in furtherance of the stated purpose of overthrowing the Government by revolution, force, or violence. The questions put by the Court in *Cramp* may with equal force be asked here. Does the statute reach endorsement or support for Communist candidates for office? Does it reach a lawyer who represents the Communist Party or its members or a journalist who defends constitutional rights of the Communist Party or its members or anyone who supports any cause which is likewise supported by Communists or the Communist Party? The susceptibility of the statutory language to require forswearing of an undefined variety of "guiltless knowing behavior" is what the Court condemned in *Cramp*. This statute, like the one at issue in *Cramp,* is unconstitutionally vague.

The Washington statute suffers from additional difficulties on vagueness grounds. A person is subversive not only if he himself commits the specified acts but if he abets or advises another in aiding a third person to commit an act which will assist yet a fourth person in the overthrow or alteration of constitutional government. The Washington Supreme Court has said that knowledge is to be read into every provision and we accept this construction. . . . But what is it that the Washington professor must "know"? Must he know that his aid or teaching will be used by another and that the person aided has the requisite guilty intent or is it sufficient that he know that his aid or teaching would or might be useful to others in the commission of acts intended to overthrow the Government? Is it subversive activity, for example, to attend and participate in international conventions of mathematicians and exchange views with scholars from Communist countries? What about the editor of a scholarly journal who analyzes and criticizes the manuscripts of Communist scholars submitted for publication? Is selecting outstanding scholars from Communist countries as visiting professors and advising, teaching, or consulting with them at the University of Washington a subversive activity if such scholars are known to be Communists, or, regardless of their affiliations, regularly teach students who are members of the Communist Party, which by statutory definition is subversive and dedicated to the overthrow of the Government?

The Washington oath goes beyond overthrow or alteration by force or violence. It extends to alteration by "revolution," which, unless wholly redundant and its ordinary meaning distorted, includes any rapid or fundamental change. Would, therefore, any organization or any person supporting, advocating or teaching peaceful but far-reaching constitutional amendments be engaged in subversive activity? Could one support the repeal of the Twenty-second Amendment or participation by this country in a world government?

II

We also conclude that the 1931 oath offends due process because of vagueness. The oath exacts a promise that the affiant will, by precept and example, promote respect for the flag and the institutions of the United States and the State of Washington. The range of activities which are or might be deemed inconsistent with the required promise is very wide indeed. The teacher who refused to salute the flag or advocated refusal because of religious beliefs might well be accused of breaching his promise. Cf. *West Virginia State Board of Education* v. *Barnette*, 319 U.S. 624. Even criticism of the design or color scheme of the state flag or unfavorable comparison of it with that of a sister State or foreign country could be deemed disrespectful and therefore violative of the oath. And what are "institutions" for the purposes of this oath? Is it every "practice, law, custom, etc., which is a material and persistent element in the life or culture of an organized social group" or every "established society or corporation," every "establishment, esp[ecially] one of a public character"? The oath may prevent a professor from criticizing his state judicial system or the Supreme Court or the institution of judicial review. Or it might be deemed to proscribe advocating the abolition, for example, of the Civil Rights Commission, the House Committee on Un-American Activities, or foreign aid.

It is likewise difficult to ascertain what might be done without transgressing the promise to "promote . . . undivided allegiance to the government of the United States." It would not be unreasonable for the serious-minded oath-taker to conclude that he should dispense with lectures voicing far-reaching criticism of any old or new policy followed by the Government of the United States. He could find it questionable under this language to ally himself with any interest group dedicated to opposing any current public policy or law of the Federal Government, for if he did, he might well be accused of placing loyalty to the group above allegiance to the United States.

Indulging every presumption of a narrow construction of the provisions of the 1931 oath, consistent, however, with a proper respect for the English language, we cannot say that this oath provides an ascertainable standard of conduct or that it does not require more than a State may command under the guarantees of the First and Fourteenth Amendments.

*   *   *

III

The State labels as wholly fanciful the suggested possible coverage of the two oaths. It may well be correct, but the contention only emphasizes the difficulties with the two statutes; for if the oaths do not reach some or any of the behavior suggested, what specific conduct do the oaths cover? Where does fanciful possibility end and intended coverage begin?

It will not do to say that a prosecutor's sense of fairness and the Constitution would prevent a successful perjury prosecution for some of the activities seemingly embraced within the sweeping statutory definitions. The hazard of being prosecuted for knowing but guiltless behavior nevertheless remains. "It would be blinking reality not to acknowledge that there are some among us always ready to affix a Communist label upon those whose ideas they violently oppose. And experience teaches us that prosecutors too are human." *Cramp*, supra, at 286–287. Well-intentioned prosecutors and judicial safeguards do not neutralize the vice of a vague law. Nor should we encourage the casual taking of oaths by upholding the discharge or exclusion from public employment of those with a conscientious and scrupulous regard for such undertakings.

It is further argued, however, that, notwithstanding the uncertainties of the 1931 oath and the statute on which it is based, the oath does not offend due process because the vagaries are contained in a promise of future conduct, the breach of which would not support a conviction for perjury. Without the criminal sanctions, it is said, one need not fear taking this oath, regardless of whether he understands it and can comply with its mandate, however understood. This contention ignores not only the effect of the oath on those who will not solemnly swear unless they can do so honestly and without prevarication and reservation, but also its effect on those who believe the written law means what it says. Oath Form A contains both oaths, and expressly requires that the signer "understand that this statement and oath are made subject to the penalties of perjury." Moreover, Wash. Rev. Code . . . provides that "[e]very person who, whether orally or in writing . . . shall knowingly swear falsely concerning any matter whatsoever" commits perjury in the second degree. Even if it can be said that a conviction for falsely taking this oath would not be sustained, the possibility of a prosecution cannot be gainsaid. The State may not require one to choose between subscribing to an unduly vague and broad oath, thereby incurring the likelihood of prosecution, and conscientiously refusing to take the oath with the consequent loss of employment, and perhaps profession, particularly where "the free dissemination of ideas may be the loser."

* * *

. . . . We do not question the power of a state to take proper measures safeguarding the public service from disloyal conduct. But measures which purpose to define disloyalty must allow public servants to know what is and is not disloyal. "The fact . . . that a person is not compelled to hold public office cannot possibly be an excuse for barring him from office by state-imposed criteria forbidden by the Constitution." *Torcaso* v. *Watkins*, 367 U.S. 488, 495–496.

Reversed.

MR. JUSTICE CLARK, whom MR. JUSTICE HARLAN joins, dissenting.

Slochower v. *Board of Education*
350 U.S. 551
April 9, 1956
MR. JUSTICE CLARK delivered the opinion of the Court.

This appeal brings into question the constitutionality of §903 of the Charter of the City of New York. That section provides that whenever an employee of the City utilizes the privilege against self-incrimination to avoid answering a question relating to his official conduct, "his term or tenure of office or employment shall terminate and such office or employment shall be vacant, and he shall not be eligible to election or appointment to any office or employment under the city or any agency."* Appellant Slochower invoked the privilege against self-incrimination under the Fifth Amendment before an investigating committee of the United States Senate, and was summarily discharged from his position as associate professor at Brooklyn College, an institution maintained by the City of New York. He now claims that the charter provision, as applied to him, violates both the Due Process and Privileges and Immunities Clauses of the Fourteenth Amendment.

On September 24, 1952, the Internal Security Subcommittee of the Committee on the Judiciary of the United States Senate held open hearings in New York City. The investigation, conducted on a national scale, related to subversive influences in the American educational system. At the beginning of the hearings the Chairman stated that education was primarily a state and local function, and therefore the inquiry would be limited to "considerations affecting national security, which are directly within the purview and authority of the subcommittee." Hearings Before the Subcommittee to Investigate the Administration of the Internal Security Act and Other Internal Security Laws of Senate Committee on the Judiciary, 82d Cong., 2d Sess. 1. Professor Slochower, when called to testify, stated that he was not a member of the Communist Party, and indicated complete willingness to answer all questions about his associations or political beliefs since 1941. But he refused to answer questions concerning his membership during 1940 and 1941 on the ground that his answers might tend to incriminate him. The Chairman of the Senate Subcommittee accepted Slochower's claim as a valid assertion of an admitted constitutional right.

It had been alleged that Slochower was a Communist in 1941 in the testimony of one Bernard Grebanier before the Rapp-Coudert Committee of the New York Legislature. See *Report of the Subcommittee of the Joint Legislative Committee to Investigate Procedures and Methods of Allocating State Moneys for Public School Purposes and Subversive Activities*, Legislative Document (1942), No. 49, State of New York, at 318. Slochower testified that he had appeared twice before the

---

* The full text of § 903 provides:

If any councilman or other officer or employee of the city shall, after lawful notice or process, wilfully refuse or fail to appear before any court or judge, any legislative committee, or any officer, board or body authorized to conduct any hearing or inquiry, or having appeared shall refuse to testify or to answer any question regarding the property, government or affairs of the city or of any county included within its territorial limits, or regarding the nomination, election, appointment or official conduct of any officer or employee of the city or of any such county, on the ground that his answer would tend to incriminate him, or shall refuse to waive immunity from prosecution on account of any such matter in relation to which he may be asked to testify upon any such hearing or inquiry, his term or tenure of office or employment shall terminate and such office or employment shall be vacant, and he shall not be eligible to election or appointment to any office or employment under the city or any agency.

Rapp-Coudert Committee, and had subsequently testified before the Board of Faculty relating to this charge. He also testified that he had answered questions at these hearings relating to his Communist affiliations in 1940 and 1941.

Shortly after testifying before the Internal Security Subcommittee, Slochower was notified that he was suspended from his position at the College; three days later his position was declared vacant "pursuant to the provisions of Section 903 of the New York City Charter."

Slochower had 27 years' experience as a college teacher and was entitled to tenure under state law. . . . Under this statute, appellant may be discharged only for cause, and after notice, hearing, and appeal. . . . The Court of Appeals of New York, however, has authoritatively interpreted §903 to mean that "the assertion of the privilege against self incrimination is equivalent to a resignation." . . . Dismissal under this provision is therefore automatic and there is no right to charges, notice, hearing, or opportunity to explain.

The Supreme Court of New York, County of Kings, concluded that appellant's behavior fell within the scope of §903, and upheld its application here. . . .

Slochower argues that §903 abridges a privilege or immunity of a citizen of the United States since it in effect imposes a penalty on the exercise of a federally guaranteed right in a federal proceeding. It also violates due process, he argues, because the mere claim of privilege under the Fifth Amendment does not provide a reasonable basis for the State to terminate his employment. Appellee insists that no question of "privileges or immunities" was raised or passed on below, and therefore directs its argument solely to the proposition that §903 does not operate in an arbitrary or capricious manner. We do not decide whether a claim under the "privileges or immunities" clause was considered below, since we conclude the summary dismissal of appellant in the circumstances of this case violates due process of law.

The problem of balancing the State's interest in the loyalty of those in its service with the traditional safeguards of individual rights is a continuing one. To state that a person does not have a constitutional right to government employment is only to say that he must comply with reasonable, lawful, and nondiscriminatory terms laid down by the proper authorities.

* * *

Here the Board, in support of its position, contends that only two possible inferences flow from appellant's claim of self-incrimination: (1) that the answering of the question would tend to prove him guilty of a crime in some way connected with his official conduct; or (2) that in order to avoid answering the question he falsely invoked the privilege by stating that the answer would tend to incriminate him, and thus committed perjury. Either inference, it insists, is sufficient to justify the termination of his employment. The Court of Appeals, however, accepted the Committee's determination that the privilege had been properly invoked and it further held that no inference of Communist Party membership could be drawn from such a refusal to testify. It found the statute to impose merely a condition on public employment and affirmed the summary action taken in the case. With this conclusion we cannot agree.

At the outset we must condemn the practice of imputing a sinister meaning to the exercise of a person's constitutional right under the Fifth Amendment. The right of an accused person to refuse to testify, which had been in England merely a rule of evidence, was so important to our forefathers that they raised it to the dignity of a constitutional enactment, and it has been recognized as "one of the most valuable prerogatives of the citizen." In *Ullmann* v. *United States,* decided last month, we scored the assumption that those who claim this privilege are either criminals or perjurers. The privilege against self-incrimination would be reduced to a hollow mockery if its exercise could be taken as equivalent either to a confession of guilt or a conclusive presumption of perjury. As we pointed out in *Ullmann,* a witness may have a reasonable fear of prosecution and yet be innocent of any wrongdoing. The privilege serves to protect the innocent who otherwise might be ensnared by ambiguous circumstances. . . .

With this in mind, we consider the application of §903. As interpreted and applied by the state courts, it operates to discharge every city employee who invokes the Fifth Amendment. In practical effect the questions asked are taken as confessed and made the basis of the discharge. No consideration is given to such factors as the subject matter of the questions, remoteness of the period to which they are directed, or justification for exercise of the privilege. It matters not whether the plea resulted from mistake, inadvertence or legal advice conscientiously given, whether wisely or unwisely. The heavy hand of the statute falls alike on all who exercise their constitutional privilege, the full enjoyment of which every person is entitled to receive. Such action falls squarely within the prohibition of *Wieman* v. *Updegraff,* supra.

It is one thing for the city authorities themselves to inquire into Slochower's fitness, but quite another for his discharge to be based entirely on events occurring before a federal committee whose inquiry was announced as not directed at "the property, affairs, or government of the city, or . . . official conduct of city employees." In this respect the present case differs materially from *Garner,* where the city was attempting to elicit information necessary to determine the qualifications of its employees. Here, the Board had possessed the pertinent information for 12 years, and the questions which Professor Slochower refused to answer were admittedly asked for a purpose wholly unrelated to his college functions. On such a record the Board cannot claim that its action was part of a bona fide attempt to gain needed and relevant information.

Without attacking Professor Slochower's qualification for his position in any manner, and apparently with full knowledge of the testimony he had given some 12 years before at the state committee hearing, the Board seized upon his claim of privilege before the federal committee and converted it through the use of §903 into a conclusive presumption of guilt. Since no inference of guilt was possible from the claim before the federal committee, the discharge falls of its own weight as wholly without support. There has not been the "protection of the individual against arbitrary action" which Mr. Justice Cardozo characterized as the very essence of due process. . . .

This is not to say that Slochower has a constitutional right to be an associate professor of German at Brooklyn College. The State has broad powers in the selection and discharge of its employees, and it may be that proper inquiry would show Slochower's continued employment to be inconsistent with a real interest of the State. But there has been no such inquiry here. We hold that the summary dismissal of appellant violates due process of law.

The judgment is reversed and the cause is remanded for further proceedings not inconsistent with this opinion.

Reversed and remanded.

MR. JUSTICE BLACK and MR. JUSTICE DOUGLAS join the Court's judgment and opinion. . . .

MR. JUSTICE REED, with whom MR. JUSTICE BURTON and MR. JUSTICE MINTON join, dissenting.

* * *

REED, J., dissenting.

* * *

The Court finds it a denial of due process to discharge an employee merely because he relied upon the Fifth Amendment plea of self-incrimination to avoid answering questions which he would be otherwise required to answer. We assert the contrary—the city does have reasonable ground to require its employees either to give evidence regarding facts of official conduct within their knowledge or to give up the positions they hold. . . . We disagree with the Court's assumption that §903 as a practical matter takes the questions asked as confessed. Cities, like other employers, may reasonably conclude that a refusal to furnish appropriate information is enough to justify discharge. Legally authorized bodies have a right to demand that citizens furnish facts pertinent to official inquiries. . . .

Barenblatt v. *United States*
360 U.S. 109
June 8, 1959
MR. JUSTICE HARLAN delivered the opinion of the Court.

. . . . In the present case congressional efforts to learn the extent of a nationwide, indeed worldwide, problem have brought one of its investigating committees into the field of education. Of course, broadly viewed, inquiries cannot be made into the teaching that is pursued in any of our educational institutions. When academic teaching-freedom and its corollary learning-freedom, so essential to the well-being of the Nation, are claimed, this Court will always be on the alert against intrusion by Congress into this constitutionally protected domain. But this does not mean that the Congress is precluded from interrogating a witness merely because he is a teacher. An educational institution is not a constitutional sanctuary from inquiry into matters that may otherwise be within the constitutional legislative domain merely for the reason that inquiry is made of someone within its walls.

* * *

Pursuant to a subpoena, and accompanied by counsel, petitioner on June 28, 1954, appeared as a witness before this Congressional Subcommittee. After answering a few preliminary questions and testifying that he had been a graduate student and teaching fellow at the University of Michigan from 1947 to 1950 and an instructor in psychology at Vassar College from 1950 to shortly before his appearance before the Subcommittee, petitioner objected generally to the right of the Subcommittee to inquire into his "political" and "religious" beliefs or any "other personal and private affairs" or "associational activities," upon grounds set forth in a previously prepared memorandum which he was allowed to file with the Subcommittee. Thereafter petitioner specifically declined to answer each of the following five questions:

Are you now a member of the Communist Party? (Count One.)
Have you ever been a member of the Communist Party? (Count Two.)
Now you have stated that you knew Francis Crowley. Did you know Francis Crowley as a member of the Communist Party? (Count Three.)
Were you ever a member of the Haldane Club of the Communist Party while at the University of Michigan? (Count Four.)
Were you a member while a student of the University of Michigan Council of Arts, Sciences, and Professions? (Count Five.)

In each instance the grounds of refusal were those set forth in the prepared statement. Petitioner expressly disclaimed reliance upon "the Fifth Amendment."

* * *

The Court's past cases establish sure guides to decision. Undeniably, the First Amendment in some circumstances protects an individual from being compelled to disclose his associational relationships. However, the protections of the First Amendment, unlike a proper claim of the privilege against self-incrimination under the Fifth Amendment, do not afford a witness the right to resist inquiry in all circumstances. Where First Amendment rights are asserted to bar governmental interrogation, resolution of the issue always involves a balancing by the courts of the competing private and public interests at stake in the particular circumstances shown. . . .

The first question is whether this investigation was related to a valid legislative purpose, for Congress may not constitutionally require an individual to disclose his political relationships or other private affairs except in relation to such a purpose. . . .

That Congress has wide power to legislate in the field of Communist activity in this Country, and to conduct appropriate investigations in aid thereof, is hardly debatable. The existence of such power has never been questioned by this Court, and it is sufficient to say, without particularization, that Congress has enacted or considered in this field a wide range of legislative measures, not a few of which have stemmed from recommendations of the very Committee whose actions have been drawn in question here. In the last analysis this power rests on the right of self-preservation, "the ultimate value of any society." . . . Justification for its exercise in turn rests on the long and widely accepted view that the tenets of the Communist Party include the ultimate overthrow of the Government of the United States by force and violence, a view which has been given formal expression by the Congress.

On these premises, this Court in its constitutional adjudications has consistently refused to view the Communist Party as an ordinary political party, and has upheld federal legislation aimed at the Communist problem which in a different context would certainly have raised constitutional issues of the gravest character. . . . On the same premises this Court has upheld under the Fourteenth Amendment state legislation requiring those occupying or seeking public office to disclaim knowing membership in any organization advocating overthrow of the Government by force and violence, which legislation none can avoid seeing was aimed at membership in the Communist Party. . . . Similarly, in other areas, this Court has recognized the close nexus between the Communist party and violent overthrow of government. . . . To suggest that because the Communist Party may also sponsor peaceable political reforms the constitutional issues before us should now be judged as if that Party were just an ordinary political party from the standpoint of national security, is to ask this Court to blind itself to world affairs which have determined the whole course of our national policy since the close of World War II.

We think that investigatory power in this domain is not to be denied Congress solely because the field of education is involved. Nothing in the prevailing opinions in *Sweezy* v. *State of New Hampshire* stands for a contrary view. The vice existing there was that the questioning of Sweezy, who had not been shown ever to have been connected with the Communist Party, as to the contents of a lecture he had given at the University of New Hampshire, and as to his connections with the Progressive Party, then on the ballot as a normal political party in some 26 States, was too far removed from the premises on which the constitutionality of the State's investigation had to depend to withstand attack under the Fourteenth Amendment. . . . This is a very different thing from inquiring into the extent to which the Communist Party has succeeded in infiltrating our universities or elsewhere, persons and troups committed to furthering the objective of overthrow. . . . Indeed we do not understand petitioner here to suggest that Congress in no circumstances may inquire into Communist activity in the field of education. Rather, his position is in effect that this particular investigation was aimed not at the revolutionary aspects but at the theoretical classroom discussion of communism.

In our opinion this position rests on a too-constricted view of the nature of the investigatory process, and is not supported by a fair assessment of the record before us. An investigation of advocacy of or preparation for overthrow certainly embraces the right to identify a witness as a member of the Communist Party . . . and to inquire into the various manifestations of the Party's tenets. The strict requirements of a prosecution under the Smith Act . . . are not the measure of the permissible scope of a congressional investigation into "overthrow," for of necessity the investigatory process must proceed step by step. Nor can it fairly be concluded that this investigation was directed at controlling what is being taught at our universities rather than at overthrow. The statement of the Subcommittee Chairman at the opening of the investigation evinces no such intention, and, so far as this record reveals, nothing thereafter transpired which would justify our holding that the thrust of the investigation later changed. The record discloses considerable testimony concerning the foreign domination and revolutionary purposes and efforts of the Communist Party. That there was also testimony on the abstract philosophical level does not detract from the dominant theme of this investigation—Communist infiltration furthering the alleged ultimate purpose of overthrow. And certainly the conclusion would not be justified that the questioning of petitioner would have exceeded permissible bounds had he not shut off the Subcommittee at the threshold.

Nor can we accept the further contention that this investigation should not be deemed to have been in furtherance of a legislative purpose because the true objective of the Committee and of the Congress was purely "exposure." So long as Congress acts in pursuance of its constitutional power, the Judiciary lacks authority to intervene on the basis of the motives which spurred the exercise of that power.

Affirmed.

MR. JUSTICE BLACK, with whom the Chief Justice and MR. JUSTICE DOUGLAS concur, dissenting.

The First Amendment says in no equivocal language that Congress shall pass no law abridging freedom of speech, press, assembly or petition. The activities of this Committee, authorized by Congress, do precisely that, through exposure, obloquy and public scorn. . . . The Court does not really deny this fact but relies on a combination of three reasons for permitting the infringement: (A) The notion that despite the First Amendment's command Congress can abridge speech and association if this Court decides that the governmental interest in abridging speech is greater than an individual's interest in exercising that freedom; (B) the Government's right to "preserve itself"; (C) the fact that the Committee is only after Communists or suspected Communists in this investigation.

(A) I do not agree that laws directly abridging First Amendment freedoms can be justified by a congressional or judicial balancing process. . . .

To apply the Court's balancing test under such circumstances is to read the First Amendment to say "Congress shall pass no law abridging freedom of speech, press, assembly and petition, unless Congress and the Supreme Court reach the joint conclusion that on balance the interest of the Government in stifling these freedoms is greater than the interest of the people in having them exercised." This is closely akin to the notion that neither the First Amendment nor any other provision of the Bill of Rights should be enforced unless the Court believes it is reasonable to do so. Not only does this violate the genius of our written Constitution, but it runs expressly counter to the injunction to Court and Congress made by Madison when he introduced the Bill of Rights. . . .

But even assuming what I cannot assume, that some balancing is proper in this case, I feel that the Court after stating the test ignores it completely. At most it balances the right of the Government to preserve itself, against Barenblatt's right to refrain from revealing Communist affiliations. Such a balance, however, mistakes the factors to be weighed. In the first place, it completely leaves out the real interest in Barenblatt's silence, the interest of the people as a whole in being able to join organizations, advocate causes and make political "mistakes" without later being subjected to governmental penalties for having dared to think for themselves. It is this right, the right to err politically, which keeps us strong as a Nation. For no number of laws against communism can have as much effect as the personal conviction which comes from having once accepted its tenets and later recognized their worthlessness. Instead, the obloquy which results from investigations such as this not only stifles "mistakes" but prevents all but the most courageous from hazarding any views which might at some later time become disfavored. This result, whose importance cannot be overestimated, is doubly crucial when it affects the universities, on which we must largely rely for the experimentation and development of new ideas essential to our country's welfare. It is these interests of society, rather than Barenblatt's own right to silence, which I think the Court should put on the balance against the demands of the Government, if any balancing process is to be tolerated. Instead, they are not mentioned, while on the other side the demands of the Government are vastly overstated and called "self preservation." It is admitted that this Committee can only seek information for the purpose of suggesting laws, and that Congress's power to make laws in the realm of speech and association is quite limited, even on the Court's test. Its interest in making such laws in the field of education, primarily a state function, is clearly narrower still. Yet the Court styles this attenuated interest self-preservation and allows it to overcome the need our country has to let us all think, speak, and associate politically as we like and without fear of reprisal. . . .

(B) Moreover, I cannot agree with the Court's notion that First Amendment freedoms must be abridged in order to "preserve" our country. That notion rests on the unarticulated premise that this Nation's security hangs upon its power to punish people because of what they think, speak or write about, or because of those with whom they associate for political purposes. The Government, in its brief, virtually admits this position when it speaks of the "communication of unlawful ideas." I challenge this premise and deny that ideas can be proscribed under our Constitution. I agree that despotic governments cannot exist without stifling the voice of opposition to their oppressive practices. The First Amendment means to me, however, that the only constitutional way our Government can preserve itself is to leave its people the fullest possible freedom to praise, criticize or discuss, as they see fit, all governmental policies and to suggest, if they desire, that even its most fundamental postulates are bad and should be changed. . . . On that premise this land was created, and on that premise it has grown to greatness. Our Constitution assumes that the common sense of the people and their attachment to our country will enable them, after free discussion, to withstand ideas that are wrong. To say that our patriotism must be protected against false ideas by means other than these is, I think, to make a baseless charge. . . .

(C) The Court implies, however, that the ordinary rules and requirements of the Constitution do not apply because the Committee is merely after Communists and they do not constitute a political party but only a criminal gang. . . .

No matter how often or how quickly we repeat the claim that the Communist Party is not a political party, we cannot outlaw it, as a group, without endangering the liberty of all of us. The reason is not hard to find, for mixed among those aims of communism which are illegal are perfectly normal political and social goals. And muddled with its revolutionary tenets is a drive to achieve power through the ballot, if it can be done. These things necessarily make it a political party, whatever other, illegal, aims it may have. . . .

The fact is that once we allow any group which has some political aims or ideas to be driven from the ballot and from the battle for men's minds because some of its members are bad and some of its tenets are illegal, no group is safe. . . .

MR. JUSTICE BRENNAN, dissenting.

I would reverse this conviction. It is sufficient that I state my complete agreement with my Brother Black that no purpose for the investigation of Barenblatt is revealed by the record except exposure purely for the sake of exposure. This is not a purpose to which Barenblatt's rights under the First Amendment can validly be subordinated. An investigation in which the processes of law-making and law-evaluating are submerged entirely in exposure of individual behavior—in adjudication, of a sort, through the exposure process—is outside the constitutional pale of congressional inquiry. . . .